Library of
Davidson College

JOHN POWELL CLAYTON

THE CONCEPT OF CORRELATION:
PAUL TILLICH
AND THE POSSIBILITY OF A MEDIATING THEOLOGY

THE CONCEPT OF CORRELATION:

PAUL TILLICH AND THE POSSIBILITY OF A MEDIATING THEOLOGY

BY

JOHN POWELL CLAYTON

WALTER DE GRUYTER · BERLIN · NEW YORK
1980

THEOLOGISCHE BIBLIOTHEK TÖPELMANN
HERAUSGEGEBEN VON
K. ALAND, C. H. RATSCHOW UND E. SCHLINK
37. BAND

Gedruckt mit Unterstützung der Alexander von Humboldt-Stiftung

Library of Congress Cataloging in Publication Data

Clayton, John Powell.
　　The concept of correlation.
　　(Theologische Bibliothek Töpelmann ; Bd. 37)
　　Bibliography: p.
　　Includes index.
　　1. Tillich, Paul, 1886—1965. 2. Theology — Methodology —
History. I. Title.
BX4827.T53C56　　　　　　230'.044　　　　　　80-11208
ISBN 3-11-007914-3

CIP-Kurztitelaufnahme der Deutschen Bibliothek

Clayton, John Powell:
The concept of correlation : Paul Tillich and the possibility of a mediating theology / by John Powell Clayton. — Berlin, New York : de Gruyter, 1980.
　　(Theologische Bibliothek Töpelmann ; Bd. 37)
　　ISBN 3-11-007914-3

© 1980 by Walter de Gruyter & Co., Berlin 30 (Printed in Germany)
Alle Rechte, insbesondere das der Übersetzung in fremde Sprachen, vorbehalten. Ohne ausdrückliche Genehmigung des Verlages ist es auch nicht gestattet, dieses Buch oder Teile daraus auf photomechanischem Wege (Photokopie, Mikrokopie) zu vervielfältigen.
Satz und Druck: Walter de Gruyter, 1 Berlin 30 · Einband: Fuhrmann, 1 Berlin 36

to
DOROTHY EMMET
with deep affection
on her 75th birthday
29 September 1979

FOREWORD

Paul Tillich's *method* of correlation is sufficiently well known not to require another exposition. Nor is this my intention. I have attempted instead to analyse Tillich's *concept* of correlation with a view toward assessing its adequacy as a principle of mediation. Exposition of Tillich's thought has been kept to a minimum. For instance, it seemed hardly necessary to give yet another summary of the whole of ST.I. 3–68. I have, nonetheless, given close attention to ST.I. 60–1, a section which in my view has been treated heretofore far too casually. As a corrective, I have stressed that different kinds of relationship are identified by Tillich as correlative relationships.

Two pieces by Tillich are being published here for the first time. I am grateful to Carl Heinz Ratschow, director of the German Tillich-Archiv, for permission to publish *Systematische Theologie* (1913) and *Die Gestalt der religiösen Erkenntnis* (1927–1928). In order to aid scholars who might not have access to the originals, the two pieces appear in German. All quotations from them, however, have been translated into English.

Some sections of the book are adapted from previously published articles. I should like to acknowledge permission of the editors and publishers concerned for the use made of the following articles: 'Dialektik und Apologetik in der theologischen Entwicklung Paul Tillichs', *ZThKirche*, LXXV (1978); 'Is Jesus Necessary for Christology?: An Antinomy in Tillich's Theological Method', *Christ, Faith and History: Cambridge Studies in Christology*, eds. S.W. Sykes and J. P. Clayton (Cambridge University Press, 1972[1], 1978[2]); 'Questioning, Answering and Tillich's Concept of Correlation', *Kairos and Logos*, ed. J. J. Carey (North American Paul Tillich Society, 1978); 'Was heißt "Korrelation" bei Paul Tillich?', *NeueZSysTh*, XX (1978); and 'Was ist falsch in der Korrelationstheologie?', *NeueZSysTh*, XVI (1974). In chapter two, I have also drawn on parts of a forthcoming article entitled 'Can Theology be both Cultural and Christian?: Ernst Troeltsch and the Possibility of a Mediating Theology' which will appear in the *Festschrift* for Eric Rust, *Science, Faith and Revelation*, ed. B. E. Patterson.

Acknowledgements of a more personal sort also want making. I have benefited enormously from being able to try out some of the arguments advanced here on students and colleagues at Lancaster and Marburg. Especially helpful were the students in the course at Lancaster on 'Religion and Culture in Modern Christian Theology' and those who took part in the seminar at Marburg on 'Paul Tillichs Kulturtheologie'. As a result of their questions and comments, some arguments are clearer than they might have been. Regular discussion with Lancaster colleagues in modern religious thought stands behind much of this book. One is indeed fortunate to have had as regular *Gesprächspartner* such colleagues as Sarah Coakley, Adrian Cunningham, James Richmond, Patrick Sherry, and Ninian Smart. Two former colleagues – Robert Morgan, now of Oxford University, and Steven Katz of Dartmouth College – will recognise those points in the argument which stem from our *Zwiegespräch* at Lancaster. To this list must be added my friend and former student at Marburg, Christoph Schwöbel, from whom I have learned more than he from me. For their warm hospitality and many kindnesses toward my wife and me, I should also like to thank the members of the theological faculty at Marburg, especially the successive deans during our time here: Otto Kaiser and Theodor Mahlmann.

Three people in particular have influenced the direction of my interests and the shape of my research: C. W. Christian, who introduced me to Tillich's thought at Baylor; Dorothy Emmet, who supervised my doctoral dissertation at Cambridge; and Carl Heinz Ratschow, under whose tutelage at Marburg the manuscript for this volume was completed. I am deeply grateful to each. The book is dedicated to Dorothy Emmet, who by the time it is published will be about to celebrate her seventy-fifth birthday.

Finally, I express my appreciation to the Alexander-von-Humboldt-Stiftung for having awarded me a research fellowship tenable at the University of Marburg, and also to the Vice Chancellor of the University of Lancaster, Sir Charles Carter, for having allowed me sabbatical leave during 1977–1978. It is no understatement to say that, without their generosity, writing this book would not have been possible.

Marburg an der Lahn
September, 1978

J. P. C.

CONTENTS

Foreword VII
Abbreviations XI

I. A Dilemma in Modern Theology

1. Introduction: The Legacy of Paul Tillich and the Concept of Correlation 3
2. The Dilemma and the Concept of Correlation 34

II. Religion and Culture

3. Religion and the Concept of Correlation 87
    Tillich's 'Two' Senses of Religion 87
    The Place of Religion in Geistesleben 101
    Religion, Theology and Correlation 112
4. Culture and the Concept of Correlation 117
    Culture as Cultivation 123
    Culture as Geistesleben 129
    Culture as 'Complex Whole' 140

III. Two Models of a Correlative Relation

5. Questioning, Answering and the Concept of Correlation 155
    The Role of Questioning and Answering in the Development of Tillich's Thought 160
    Questioning and Answering as a Model of Correlation 177
6. Form, Content and the Concept of Correlation 191
    The Role of 'Form' and 'Content' in the Development of Tillich's Thought 191
    Form and Content as a Model of Correlation 222
    Conclusion: The Dilemma Resolved? 248

Appendices 251
(1) Paul Tillich: *Systematische Theologie* (1913) 253
(2) Paul Tillich: *Die Gestalt der religiösen Erkenntnis* (1927–1928) . . 269
Bibliography 309
Index of Names 325

ABBREVIATIONS

Titles of periodicals have been abbreviated throughout in accordance with the schemes used in the *Index to Religious Periodical Literature* and *The Philosopher's Index*.
Wherever possible, references to Tillich's works or works to which he contributed have been incorporated into the text and enclosed within round brackets. The following abbreviations have been used throughout:

BR	*Biblical Religion and the Search for Ultimate Reality* (Chicago, 1955).
CA	*The Christian Answer*, ed. H. P. van Dusen (London, 1946).
CB	*The Courage to Be* (New Haven, 1952).
CE	*Christianity and the Encounter of the World Religions* (New York, 1963).
DF	*Dynamics of Faith* (New York, 1957).
EN	*Ergänzungs- und Nachlaßbände zu den Gesammelten Werken*, 3 vols. (Stuttgart, 1971–3).
FR	*The Future of Religions* (New York, 1966).
GW	*Gesammelte Werke*, ed. Renate Albrecht, 14 vols. (Stuttgart, 1959–1975).
HCT	*A History of Christian Thought*, ed. Carl E. Braaten (London, 1968).
IH	*The Interpretation of History* (New York, 1936).
K&B	*The Theology of Paul Tillich*, ed. C. W. Kegley and R. W. Bretall (New York, 1952).
LPJ	*Love, Power and Justice* (Oxford, 1954).
MB	*Morality and Beyond* (London, 1969).
OB	*On the Boundary* (London, 1967).
PE	*The Protestant Era*, ed. James Luther Adams (Chicago, 1957^2).
PNT	*Perspectives on 19th and 20th Century Protestant Theology*, ed. Carl E. Braaten (New York, 1967).
RGG	*Die Religion in Geschichte und Gegenwart*, 5 vols. (2nd ed.; Tübingen, 1927–32).
R&R	*Philosophical Interrogations*, ed. S. Rome and B. Rome (New York, 1964).
RS	*The Religious Situation* (Cleveland, 1956).
RV	*Religiöse Verwirklichung* (Berlin, 1930).
ST	*Systematic Theology*, 3 vols. (Chicago, 1951–63).

STd	*Systematische Theologie*, 3 vols. (Stuttgart, 1957²−66).
TC	*Theology of Culture* (Oxford, 1964).
WW	*Werk und Wirken Paul Tillichs*, T. W. Adorno *et al.* (Stuttgart, 1967).

PART ONE
A DILEMMA IN MODERN THEOLOGY

CHAPTER ONE

INTRODUCTION:
THE LEGACY OF PAUL TILLICH
AND THE CONCEPT OF CORRELATION

It is no doubt still too soon to assess with confidence what, if anything, Paul Tillich contributed of lasting significance to the history of christian thought. His influence in Great Britain has always been marginal, despite the efforts of a number of individual scholars to win for him a hearing. Tillich emigrated from Germany at a time when his call for a new 'cultural theology' seemed singularly irrelevant to the new situation faced by the christian churches there. And, indeed, the history of German religious thought after 1933 can be traced without significant reference to Tillich until his 'rediscovery' well after the war.[1] As his thought had been popularised in Great Britain largely through J. A. T. Robinson's *Honest to God*, it was similarly popularised – if somewhat less sensationally received! – in Germany through *Die Sache mit Gott* by Heinz Zahrnt, who presented Tillich's theology of correlation as a way out of the Barth-Bultmann impasse in German theology. In addition, it might be plausibly suggested that Dorothee Sölle's tracing the roots of 'political theology' to Tillich's early religious socialist writings has been a significant factor in the increased interest in his thought among the current generation of German students.[2]

---

[1] It is perhaps not insignificant that nothing by Paul Tillich was published in Germany between 1935 and 1946. His major, post-emigration writings began being translated into German from about 1950. Throughout the war, however, Tillich regularly broadcast 'an meine deutsche Freunde' on the Voice of America. For a recent collection of those broadcasts, edited and introduced by Karin Schäfer-Kretzler, see EN. III. Concerning Tillich's being 'rediscovered' in Germany, see Wilhelm and Marion Pauck, *Paul Tillich: Life and Work*, vol. I (New York, 1976), pp. 265ff.

[2] Cf. Dorothee Sölle, *Politische Theologie: Auseinandersetzung mit Rudolf Bultmann* (Stuttgart and Berlin, 1971), p. 7. For a competent and helpful survey of Tillich's political theology, see Eric Schwerdtfeger, *Die politische Theorie in der Theologie Paul Tillichs* (Marburg, 1969). See also Jean-Claude Petit, 'Tillichs Religionsphilosophie und der Anspruch der neuen Politischen Theologie', *NeueZSysTh*, XIX (1977), 150–71.

Whatever the reasons, Tillich's thought has within the past several years become a frequent topic for research and teaching within German universities.³ But, whether the rediscovery of Tillich by students and younger theologians is, as Zahrnt maintained, one of the most significant developments in recent German theology must for the moment remain an open question. It was in the United States, however, that Tilllich enjoyed the greatest, though sometimes the least critical, influence. Nor was this influence restricted to the faculties of religion and theology. As befits one who endeavoured to execute his theology 'on the boundary', Tillich enjoyed considerable influence within the American republic of letters. His standing in the American intellectual community by 1960 is perhaps suggested by his having been among the artists and intellectuals specifically invited to be guests of the President at the inauguration of John F. Kennedy.⁴

Even though it is too early to specify with certainty Tillich's contribution to the theological enterprise, it is perhaps not out of order to make three tentative predictions as to his likely significance. First, and most surely, his work will be seen to have a 'period piece' quality. His writings are very much part and parcel of the times. This holds both for those published during the Weimar Republic and for those produced after his emigration. And this, surely, is as Tillich himself intended. Speaking 'out of the *kairos*' meant for him that 'not everything is possible at every time; not everything is appropriate [*wahr*] to every time; not everything is required in every moment.' (GW. VI. 10) Tillich's work as a whole records a serious and sustained attempt to respond theologically to the uncertainties and the questions implied in the cultural situation of the first half of the present century. In doing so, he sought to do for his own time what Schleiermacher had done earlier for his. Interestingly, not only has his *Systematic Theology*

---

3   Between 1974 and 1977, the same number of seminars were offered in German theological faculties on Tillich as on Luther! This information comes from statistics prepared by Heinrich Leipold for the Fachgruppe Systematische Theologie of the Wissenschaftliche Gesellschaft für Theologie. In the same period, the theologians who were most frequently topics for lectures, seminars, colloquia, etc., were Luther, Schleiermacher, Barth and Tillich.

4   See A. J. Schlesinger, Jr., *A Thousand Days: John F. Kennedy in the White House* (New York, 1965), p. 631. For a sociological account of Tillich's influence in the nontheological community, see S. P. Mews, 'Paul Tillich and the Religious Situation of American Intellectuals', *Religion*, II (1972), 122–40. See also Pauck and Pauck, *Paul Tillich*, vol. I, pp. 246ff.

been compared with *Der christliche Glaube* as regards scope and intent,[5] but his lectures on *The Courage to Be* have been compared with Schleiermacher's *Reden*.[6] Whether or not these particular comparisons should be regarded as appropriate, it remains the case that Tillich – like Schleiermacher – not only interpreted the time in which he lived, but to some extent contributed to its formation through his persistent attempt to lead 'the cultured among the despisers' to rediscover what he sometimes called 'the lost dimension' of cultural life, that is to say, its religious dimension. (GW. V. 43–50; but cf. ST. III. 113)

By incorporating the present cultural situation into his methodology, Tillich gave to his theology a planned obsolescence which precludes his system's having direct relevance for any but the cultural context in which and for which it was constructed. Tillich made no claim to speak 'for all times'. He spoke, rather, out of his own time and to his own time. This holds not only for Tillich's work as a whole, but also for the individual phases of his theological development. Speaking 'out of the kairos' meant for Tillich something different in 1919 than in 1926 or 1934 or 1956.[7] The demands of the present were in each case understood differently. In each case, Tillich rethought not only the nature of the present moment but also what would count as a kairos. It would be a mistake, therefore, to impose a single meaning on the use made of many key terms in the different phases of his development. The *concept* of kairos, as well as the *content* of any specific kairos, remained subject to revision throughout his writings. Tillich's tendency constantly to rethink his basic concepts causes no small difficulty for anyone who would comprehend his thought. But it is a tendency wholly consistent with Tillich's avowed intention to do theology *in* 'the present situation'. Therein lies one aspect of his strength and his limitation for the future of theology.

By responding so systematically to the 'questions' of a single generation, Tillich achieved a certain timeliness for his work. He also thereby insured

---

[5] Schubert M. Ogden, *Christ without Myth* (New York, 1961), p. 131. See also G. H. Tavard's review of ST. II in *Commonweal* (7 February 1964), repr. *JRel*, XLVI (1966), 233. For a more thorough comparison of Schleiermacher and Tillich, see F. T. White, *Systematic Theological Principles of Schleiermacher and Tillich* (Ph. D. diss., Columbia, 1966), and M. Michel, *De Schleiermacher a Tillich* (Diss. Strasbourg, 1975).

[6] I. Henel, *Religion des konkreten Geistes* (Stuttgart, 1968), p. 44f.

[7] See below, Part III.

that as the time for which he was writing recedes into the past, so diminishes also the contemporary significance of his particular 'correlations'. Tillich's obsolescence, in this sense, is a frank feature of his methodology. Such obsolescence is said to be the fate of every theological system, for 'every concrete system is transitory and . . . none can be final.' (ST. III. 4)

> New organizing principles appear, neglected elements acquire central significance, the method may become more refined or completely different, with the result that a new conception of the structure of the whole emerges. This is the fate of every system. But this is also the rhythm in which the history of Christian thought has moved through the centuries. The systems were points of crystallization toward which the discussion of particular problems moved and from which new discussions and fresh problems arose. It is my hope that, in however limited a way, the present system may perform the same function. (Ibid.)

And it might be reasonably asserted that the period for which Tillich was writing was already past or at least nearly so by the time he completed his *Systematic Theology*.[8] There was perhaps a certain inevitability in this. Philosophical reflection of the sort in which Tillich engaged tends to come, as Hegel was keenly aware, at the end rather than at the beginning or the zenith of an age.[9] But, in the case of Tillich's generation in particular, there was a deep consciousness of having been hurled into history 'between the times'.[10] The first world war gave them an unmistakeably objective point of reference for the dissolution of nineteenth-century thought and values, a dissolution which had been proclaimed already, though to little effect, by such writers as Kierkegaard and Nietzsche. But, Tillich's generation had only the thought forms and the philosophical tools of the nineteenth century with which to shape the philosophy of the 'new age'. And taking

---

[8] This would seem also to have been Tillich's own fear. See Pauck and Pauck, *op. cit.*, p. 244.

[9] See Hegel's preface to the *Grundlinien der Philosophie des Rechts*: ‚Wenn die Philosophie ihr Grau in Grau mahlt, dann ist eine Gestalt des Lebens alt geworden, und mit Grau in Grau läßt sie sich nicht verjüngen, sondern nur erkennen; die Eule der Minerva beginnt erst mit der einbrechenden Dämmerung ihren Flug.'

[10] Cf. GW. X. 108–20, esp. p. 120: ‚Und so stehen wir in einer Zeit, die zwischen den Zeiten liegt . . .'

Kierkegaard as his model, this is precisely what Tillich at least set out to do: to use idealism to transcend idealism. Such early works as *Das System der Wissenschaften* record Tillich's early attack upon idealism from within.[11]

Secondly, Tillich kept alive discussion of many of the central issues of nineteenth-century theology even during what has been termed 'the Barthian captivity of the history of modern Christian thought'.[12] Among those issues which Tillich kept alive is the question of the possibility of a 'theology of mediation' or, as it is called in Germany, *Vermittlungstheologie*. Claude Welch has reminded us that 'the epithet "mediating theology" has its proper origins in the programme announced for the theological journal *Theologische Studien und Kritiken*, namely, to serve the "true mediation" (*wahre Vermittlung*) between the idea of Christianity and the modern scientific consciousness, that is, to effect the valid reconciliation of historical Christianity and contemporary culture.'[13] In the discussion which follows, however, Welch seems to conflate different senses of 'theology of mediation'. For, even if we ignore the not inconsiderable difference between the senses in which Hegel and Schleiermacher were each of them mediating theologians, the word *Vermittlungstheologie* has had two distinct uses in nineteenth-century theology and in studies of nineteenth-century theology. Only the second of these senses is relevant to our analysis of Tillich's concept of correlation. First, Ferdinand Kattenbusch used the term in reference to those theologians who sought to mediate between the 'liberal' and the 'confessional' or 'conservative' wings of the German protestant churches in the nineteenth century.[14] Secondly, the more usual

---

[11] Göttingen, 1923; repr. GW. I. On the significance of this formidable work for Tillich's intellectual development, see Robert Scharlemann, 'Der Begriff der Systematik bei Paul Tillich', *NeueZSysTh*, VIII (1966), 242–54, and *Reflection and Doubt in the Thought of Paul Tillich* (New Haven, 1969). See also James Luther Adams, *Paul Tillich's Philosophy of Culture, Science and Religion* (New York, 1965).

[12] Richard R. Niebuhr, *Schleiermacher on Christ and Religion* (New York, 1964), p. 11.

[13] *Protestant Thought in the Nineteenth Century* (New Haven, 1972), vol. I, p. 269. See also Horst Stephan and Martin Schmidt, *Geschichte der evangelischen Theologie in Deutschland seit dem Idealismus* (3rd. ed.; Berlin, 1973), pp. 228ff.

[14] *Die deutsche evangelische Theologie seit Schleiermacher* (4th. ed.; Gießen, 1924), vol. I, pp. 36, 45ff.

meaning is that given by Martin Kähler — himself a student of one of the leading theologians of mediation, Richard Rothe — and by Emanuel Hirsch, both of whom used the term to designate those theologians who in their diverse ways sought to mediate between historical christianity and contemporary culture.[15]

There are those who argue that the word *Vermittlungstheologie* should be used only in its narrowly historical sense to cover a specific group of theologians, which included such people as Lücke, Ullmann and Nitzsch.[16] The term can, of course, be used in this historical sense. But, the word *Vermittlungstheologie* is also capable of being extended in such a way as to include all those theologians whose understanding of the theological task has been shaped by Schleiermacher's call for a 'perpetual alliance' between learning and faith, to include all those theologians for whom 'the split between a faith unacceptable to culture and a culture unacceptable to faith' is intolerable. (See ST. III. 4—5) It is in this second and more extended sense that the phrases 'mediating theology' and 'theology of mediation' will be used in this volume. The object of the book is to analyse Tillich's principle of mediation between historical christianity and contemporary culture, namely, his concept of correlation.[17]

The history of christian theology since the second world war has surely vindicated Tillich's argument that issues which centrally occupied the theologians of meditation are indeed inescapable. For in the two and one-half decades since Gerhard Ebeling's essay on the significance of the historical-critical method for theology,[18] there has been an ever-increasing renewal of interest in the problems, if not also the solutions, which occupied the major

[15] M. Kähler, *Geschichte der protestantischen Dogmatik im 19. Jahrhundert* (Munich, 1962) and E. Hirsch, *Geschichte der neuern evangelischen Theologie* (Gütersloh, vol. IV, 1949; vol. V, 1968⁴).

[16] E.g., J. Wirsching, *Christologische Texte aus der Vermittlungstheologie des 19. Jahrhunderts* (Gütersloh, 1968), p. 5.

[17] Jochen Buchter also stresses that the method of correlation is a method of mediation and that Tillich is first and foremost a theologian of mediation. *Die Kriterien der Theologie im Werke Paul Tillichs* (Bonn, 1975), pp. 83—145. A similar emphasis is made by P. Schwanz in 'Das für Tillich „Methode der Korrelation" grundlegende Problem der Vermittlung', *NeueZSysTh*, XV (1973), 254—71.

[18] 'Die Bedeutung der historisch-kritischen Methode für die protestantische Theologie und Kirche', *ZThKirche*, XLVII (1950), 1—46.

theologians of the nineteenth century. Among those problems must be included the issue addressed in this book, namely, the proper structure of relations between religion and culture within christian theology.[19]

In view of the *Kirchenkampf* and the disastrous attempt by the *deutsche Christen* to forge a new synthesis between christianity and the prevailing unity of cultural values, this question was thought by many to have been settled by Barth's emphatic 'Nein!'[20] But Ebeling was among the first following the war to argue that the question was not to be dispensed with so quickly: theology is essentially a mediation between what he terms 'tradition' and the present times. 'Thus theology, in so far as it remains true to its task, of its very nature moves with the times, i. e. it accepts the language, thought-forms and approach of the present.'[21] Even if, as Barth more than once complained, the history of theology from Schleiermacher to Troeltsch were to be judged a mistake, the question addressed by the 'modern protestants' would be both legitimate and unavoidable, so that 'the question as to the rightness and limits of theology's conforming to the times is really the basic problem of the theological situation today'. This judgment, implying as it does the contemporary significance of the nineteenth-century tradition, was widely regarded as eccentric in 1950. It is no longer generally thought to be so. For there is a widely held opinion today in Germany and the United States especially, but to an increasing extent in

---

[19] This, however, cannot be regarded as a *single* problem. It is rather a rarely differientiated cluster of more or less connected issues. The question of the relationship between religion and culture could be asked, for example, as a sociological or an anthropological question ('What is the role or function of religion in social structures?'), as an historical question ('How have religion and culture been related in, say, the formation of modern European history?'), as a political or constitutional question regarding the relationship between church and state, as a properly theological question ('To what extent is God knowable in and through human culture?'), as an apologetic question ('How does one communicate religion persuasively to its "despisers" in modern culture?'), as a hermeneutical question ('How does one interpret traditional religion in the light of contemporary cultural experience?'), as an ethical question ('How can religion take culture up into itself and give it a special direction?'). Most of these different ways of asking the question of the relationship between religion and culture can be seen as dimensions of Tillich's conception of the problem, though some forms of the question are more congenial to him than are others.

[20] ‚Nein!: Antwort an Emil Brunner', *Theologische Existenz Heute*, nr. 14 (1934).

[21] Cited from *Word and Faith* (Philadelphia, 1963), p. 26.

Great Britain as well, that the constructive task of theology will be advanced only after a reassessment of the theological contribution of the nineteenth century.

Though the reasons for this renewed interest are manifold, in some instances it owes not a little to the persistence with which Paul Tillich — moving as he did in this case 'against the stream' — kept alive the discussion of such central issues as the problem of the relationship between religion and culture. As we shall see, however, he persisted not only in the problems of the nineteenth-century theologians, but in their methods of solution as well. One must in the end agree with John Heywood Thomas's judgment that Tillich is a 'nineteenth-century thinker in twentieth-century dress', even if one cannot agree that this is wholly to be deplored.[22] Yet, it must be granted that Tillich's failure clearly to differentiate the sorts of *problems* which occupied the nineteenth-century theologians and philosophers of religion from the philosophical *tools* which they used in dealing with those issues signals one of the most severe limitations on his lasting influence within the Anglo-American world, where the standards of philosophical discussion are more nearly set by the analytical tradition of philosophy. That tradition provides methods and techniques which might be usefully employed even by the theologian who busies himself with some of the issues set by nineteenth-century philosophical theology.

Not all analytical philosophers have clearly differentiated the content of their philosophy from the techniques of philosophical analysis. For Russell and those who called themselves 'logical atomists', analysis entailed a particular sort of metaphysical theory about the world, facts, propositions and their relationships; for the 'logical positivists', on the other hand, analysis was thought to entail the rejection of all metaphysical theories; and Moore employed analysis more or less in defence of what he termed 'common sense'. 'Philosophical analysis' can be used in reference to just these sorts of philosophical position. But 'philosophical analysis' can be used in a less stringent way. In its weaker and broader sense, philosophical analysis could be understood simply as a useful group of techni-

---

[22] *Paul Tillich: An Appraisal* (London, 1963), p. 176. Tillich's own nostalgia for the nineteenth century is openly acknowledged by him: 'I am one of those in my generation who, in spite of the radicalism with which they have criticized the nineteenth century, often feel a longing for its stability, its liberalism, its unbroken cultural traditions.' (K&B, 3)

ques for disentangling different strands of arguments, different kinds of issues, and various sorts of confusions which sometimes arise in many kinds of linguistic activities. Analysis in this sense would simply be a way of clarifying what issues are at stake in apparent disputes. It might on occasion show that no substantial issue is at stake, or at least not the issue which the protagonists take to be at stake, and this despite the heat of the discussion. As simply a technique, analysis would commit one to no particular philosophical stand-point. One could in principle be an idealist or a materialist, an essentialist or an existentialist, and still usefully apply the techniques of philosophical analysis. Indeed, it would be a category mistake to regard 'analytic philosophy' as a type of philosophy alongside of and in a series with such philosophies as 'idealism', 'materialism', 'empiricism', etc. Rather than speaking of 'analytic philosophy' as a particular school of philosophy, it might be more appropriate to speak of analysis as a 'style' of philosophy, as a particular way of going about the business of philosophy. On this weaker understanding of 'philosophical analysis', one would also not be obliged to apply analytic techniques only to those sorts of issues which have typically been the concern of British analytic philosophers. Such techniques could be applied equally helpfully to issues which have more typically been the concern of recent German philosophers and theologians.

Had these sorts of distinctions been made more clearly by analytic philosophers themselves, it is possible that Tillich might not have formed such a jaundiced view of philosophical analysis. Even so, there are rare occasions when Tillich managed one or two kind words for this, the dominant tradition in modern English philosophy. (cf., e.g., TC, 171–2) And there is some indication that he gradually came to have at least some respect for analytic philosophy. Some of his later writings especially show a growing appreciation of at least the intentions of modern Anglo-American philosophers. Tillich once went so far as to suggest that analytic philosophy could potentially serve the present age as a sort of 'conceptual clearing house' in the way that scholastic philosophy served the mediaeval period. Yet, even here, he is less than enthusiastic about the possibility: in contrast to the middle ages, 'we have no such clearing house, and this is one point at which we might be in sympathy with the present day so-called logical positivists or symbolic logicians or logicians generally. They at least try to produce such a clearing house. The only criticism is that this clearing house is a very small room, perhaps only a corner of a house, and not a real house. It excludes most of life. But it could become useful if it increased in reach and acceptance of realities beyond the mere logical calculus.'[23]

On the whole, the opportunity for encounter with analytic philosophers in North America was for Tillich a wasted opportunity. For, as I hope to show at various points in the present volume, Tillich could have avoided certain serious but unnecessary difficulties in his philosophical theology had he been more open to this style of philosophy. Nor were his rare attempts to move toward analytic philosophy very successful. One thinks particularly of his so-called 'principle of semantic rationality' and his disastrous effort to relate his concept of 'correlation' to ordinary language.[24]

Not all the blame must be allowed to fall on Tillich. Analytic philosophers sometimes seemed to take great pleasure in not being able to comprehend anything said by Tillich. There is, for instance, that occasion when the doyen of the older generation of English philosophers, G. E. Moore, rose to his feet after having heard Tillich read a paper to say, 'Now really, Mr. Tillich, I don't think I have been able to understand a single sentence of your paper. Won't you please try to state one sentence, or even one word, that I can understand?' (K&B, 133) Fortunately, the mood of philosophy has mellowed somewhat since then. This is evidenced in a number of ways, including the recovery of the sense of philosophy as 'conversation' or 'dialectic', a notion perceptively and persuasively devel-

---

[23] TC, 53. A similar stress is made in his unpublished (and undated) paper entitled 'The Rationality of Faith': 'Whoever, like myself, has had the occasion to discuss theological and philosophical problems in different places of the Western world is first astonished by, then reconciled with, the fact that most discussions, after a few minutes, take on the character of a semantic controversy . . . But it may well be that the powerful rise of semantics as a substitute for philosophy is, at least partly, due to the incredible confusion about most of those concepts which are relevant for the description of existence generally and human existence especially. And further, it may be that the longing of many thoughtful people for a conceptual clearing house such as scholasticism was for the Middle Ages must be explained in this way. But', he adds, 'there is no such clearing house today, and with this handicap we must start our inquiry.'

[24] Tillich's abortive attempt to derive his own usage of the term 'correlation' from its ordinary uses is to be considered below in chapter two. The view that the 'principle of semantic rationality' was intended as a sort of concession to analytic philosophy is in effect supported in STd. I. 67, n. 1. For a critique of that 'principle', see J. H. Thomas, *Paul Tillich: An Appraisal*, pp. 26 ff.

oped by Renford Bambrough in his article on twentieth-century philosophy in *The New Cambridge Modern History*.[25]

The conversational character of philosophy shows itself in many ways, not least being the 'conversation' through *time* between, for instance, modern philosophy and ancient philosophy or even nineteenth-century philosophy (!) and the 'conversation' through *space* between, for instance, Anglo-Saxon philosophy and continental European philosophy. Regarding the latter sort of conversation, Bambrough notes that the differences between the two traditions 'are exaggerated both by critics of contemporary British philosophy who hold up Sartre and Camus and Heidegger and Jaspers as models to imitate, and also by neo-positivist and linguistic philosophers who hold up the same Continental philosophers as warnings of the snares that threaten those who are not vigilant in the preservation of their emancipation from ancient metaphysics.'[26] Then, in a mood of diplomacy foreign to Anglo-American philosophers of not so long ago, Bambrough adds

> Since most philosophers at all times and in all places are bad philosophers, and since even the best philosophers are occasionally guilty of folly and absurdity, it is easy for both parties in this wrangle to compile *sottisiers* from the works of their opponents' heroes. But the idea that either side has a monopoly of serious concern with the central problems of philosophy is one that will not survive the examination that it is at last receiving. German-, French- and English-speaking philosophers have read the same philosophical classics and inherited from them substantially the same preoccupations. There are differences of idiom between one place and another, but they are no more important than the differences of idiom between one time and another, or between different philosophers who share the same time and place.[27]

Nor does this renewed conversation show signs of abating in the years since Bambrough wrote his account, though it must be conceded that whether in philosophy or in theology we are still far from achieving a 'common market'.[28]

---

[25] Vol. XII (Cambridge, 1968).
[26] *Ibid.*, p. 655.   [27] *Ibid.*, pp. 655–6.
[28] See, e.g., G. J. Warnock, 'Modern European Philosophy', *Common Factor*, I (October, 1964), 30, cited in James Richmond, *Faith and Philosophy* (London,

On the whole, analytic philosophy has moved beyond the tight perimeters set up by the 'logical positivists' mentioned by Tillich, and beyond the cheerful reduction of all metaphysical puzzles to merely linguistic problems. Nor is it only 'descriptive metaphysics' which is being discussed seriously. On occasion one hears raised the question as to the possible shape of a new revisionary metaphysic.[29] The atmosphere is perhaps now more congenial for a useful — even 'therapeutic' — interchange than it was when in the 1940's and the 1950's Tillich was regularly and sometimes mercilessly confronted with his 'mistakes' and 'confusions' by zealous supporters of the then recent 'revolution in philosophy'.

Each of these two senses in which Tillich is likely to be seen to have made a contribution to the history of christian thought points to the importance of his methodology. Indeed Tillich's greatest contribution to the constructive work of the theologian is for reasons already stated more likely to lie in his methodology than in his dogmatics proper.[30] This follows from the other two and constitutes a third sense in which Tillich is likely to be regarded by history as a significant theologian. It also helps account for the considerable attention which methodological issues have received in the existing literature on Tillich's thought.

The method of correlation in particular has been intensively examined from virtually every perspective imaginable. It might be thought, and not entirely without warrant, that nothing further remains to be learned from or even about this aspect of Tillich's thought. I shall attempt to show that this assumption is in fact ill founded. Though there have been several studies of the *method* of correlation and its implications for various aspects of theological and ecclesiastical work, there has been no proper analysis of the *concept* of correlation. The present volume is intended to fill that gap.

The present work is both more restricted and more comprehensive in scope than existing studies of Tillich's theological method. It is more restricted in the sense that I do not propose a complete analysis of Tillich's entire methodology or 'fundamental theology', nor even of that aspect of

---

1966), pp. 221–2. See also S. W. Sykes, 'Deutschland und England', *ZThKirche*, LXIX (1972), 439–65, and my own 'Sprache, Sinn und Verifizierungsverfahren: Aspekte moderner Religionsphilosophie in Großbritannien', *PhilJahr*, LXXXV (1978), 144–62.

[29] See, e.g., D. M. MacKinnon, *The Problem of Metaphysics* (Cambridge, 1974).

[30] A similar judgment has been made by Carl Heinz Ratschow in his foreword to the final volume of Tillich's collected works. (GW. XIV. 10–1)

his methodology known as the 'method of correlation'.[31] Rather, attention is focused on the concept of correlation presupposed by and exemplified in his methodology. *What sort of a relation is a correlative relation? What are the component elements of Tillich's concept of correlation?* These are the kinds of questions which shall occupy us in this volume, rather than such questions as the following: Does Tillich consistently follow the method of correlation in the construction of his theological system?; What is the relèvance of that method for systematics, dogmatics, apologetics, preaching, religious education? These are all questions of a different sort. They may be valid, even important, questions; but they are not the questions with which we shall be concerned.[32]

The present study is more comprehensive than existing studies of Tillich's theological methodology in the sense that I propose to place Tillich's concept of correlation in the context of the development of his theological programme, from its earliest sketch in a little-known and, until recently, unpublished work entitled *Kirchliche Apologetik* to its final exposition in the much-discussed *Systematic Theology*.

By common consent, Tillich never developed sufficiently his notion of correlation.[33] Consequently, an analysis of that concept must be slightly indirect. Four routes are available. First, one can analyse the actual usage of the term 'correlation' in Tillich's writings, with some attention to its usage

---

[31] In agreement this time with Kenneth Hamilton and Robert Scharlemann, I would say that Tillich's theological methodology cannot be reduced to his 'method of correlation'. See K. M. Hamilton, *The System and the Gospel* (London, 1963), pp. 27, 116ff, and R. P. Scharlemann, *Reflection and Doubt in the Theology of Paul Tillich*, pp. 45ff. And Joachim Track is surely right to speak of the *methods* used by Tillich in the ST. Cf. *Der theologische Ansatz Paul Tillichs* (Göttingen, 1975), pp. 242ff.

[32] These latter questions have in fact been widely discussed already in the literature. For instance, see H. D. Bastian, *Theologie der Frage: Ideen zur Grundlegung einer theologischen Didaktik und zur Kommunikation der Kirchen der Gegenwart* (Munich, 1969); Egon Brinkschmidt, *Paul Tillich und die pädagogische Normproblematik* (Bielefeld, 1977); V. Brügmann, *Die Durchführung der Methode der Korrelation in der religiösen Reden Paul Tillichs* (Hamburg, 1969); M. von Kriegstein, *Die Methode der Korrelation und der Symbolbegriff Paul Tillichs* (Hamburg, 1972); Andreas Rößler, *Die Predigttheorie Paul Tillichs* (Tübingen, 1971); J. Schmitz, *Die apologetische Theologie Paul Tillichs* (Mainz, 1966), etc. See bibliography below.

[33] A point made most recently by Joachim Track, *op. cit.*, p. 276.

in ordinary language and in certain forms of technical discourse. This can be usefully and easily done, though no one to my knowledge has bothered to do it before. Such an analysis is undertaken in chapter two. Showing the main senses in which the term is used leads both to some clarification and to a new round of questions regarding the sense of 'correlation'. Though necessary, this route is not sufficient for a proper understanding of Tillich's concept of correlation.

Second, one can analyse terms thought by Tillich to be correlates, such as *religion* and *culture*. In his *Systematic Theology* Tillich tends to speak mainly of the correlation of *theology* and *philosophy*. Not surprisingly, therefore, most previous studies of correlationship in Tillich's thought have concentrated almost exclusively upon the alleged correlation of theology and philosophy. A careful analysis of the development of Tillich's concept of correlation, however, would make clear that, though not wholly mistaken, this is a somewhat restricted view of correlation. As a corrective to such studies, I have stressed instead the inclusive character of correlation as a relationship between culture and religion generally, and not merely philosophy and theology.[34] In chapters three and four a study is made of those aspects of Tillich's concepts of religion and culture which bear directly upon his understanding of correlation.

Third, one can analyse the relatively more developed aspects of Tillich's thought which, when taken together, provide the main component elements for his concept of correlation. Such a task would be quite involved and demanding, requiring as it would, a perspective on the whole range of Tillich's thought, its development and the way it hangs together. Even so, it is perhaps the most important — and generally most neglected — route towards an adequate understanding of Tillich's notion of correlation. For that concept, though itself a relatively late addition to Tillich's methodology, is in the main constituted by long-standing elements within his thought, many of which are present in his earliest writings. A thorough analysis of all the various elements within Tillich's thought which in some way feed into his concept of correlation clearly cannot be undertaken within a single volume.[35] Nor is such an analysis necessary for our

---

[34] M. von Kriegstein is among the few to have seen something of this inclusive character of correlation. *Op. cit.*, pp. 34—5.

[35] Some of the component elements which could not be treated in this volume are discussed in relation to the method of correlation by Robert Scharlemann in his *Reflection and Doubt in the Theology of Paul Tillich*.

restricted purposes. Not all such elements are equally important for an analysis of Tillich's concept of correlation; in addition, some are built upon and presuppose others. One must be selective, with a view toward choosing those components which seem to determine the way Tillich conceives what would count as a correlative relation. With this end in view, two sets of component elements are to be analysed in detail: questioning and answering, form and content.

When Tillich set out to explain the sort of relation between religion and culture which is to be regarded as a correlative relation, he characteristically resorted to one of two metaphors. He would say that such a relation is like the relationship between 'questioning' and 'answering', as in a conversation. Or he would say it is like the relationship between 'form' and 'content' or 'substance', as in his dictum 'the form of religion is culture and the substance of culture is religion'. Sometimes, as in the account of the method of correlation in the *Systematic Theology*, he would combine the two sets of metaphors:

> The Christian message provides the answers to the philosophical questions implied in human existence . . . Their content [*Inhalt* — STd. I. 78] cannot be derived from the questions, that is, from an analysis of human existence. They are 'spoken' *to* human existence from beyond it . . . But the relation is more involved than this, since it is correlation. There is a mutual dependence between question and answer. In respect to content the Christian answers are dependent on the revelatory events in which they appear; in respect to form they are dependent on the structure of the questions which they answer. (ST. I. 64).

But Tillich nowhere in that work adequately explains the 'cash value' of such metaphors. Almost everyone who has ever written anything about Tillich complains at some point either about his use of the metaphors 'questions' and 'answers' or about his distinction between 'form' and 'content', but no one to my knowledge has adequately analysed Tillich's use of those terms or set them properly within the context of his general system of thought. In chapters five and six I shall undertake to examine in turn these two sets of metaphors in order to determine their role in the formation and extension of Tillich's theory of correlation, their relationship to one another and their adequacy as 'models' of correlationship. The unfortunately fashionable term 'model' is currently used in a large number of different senses. When I use the term 'model', I shall be using it in the sense of what Max Black calls a 'submerged model' or a 'conceptual archetype'.[36]

The fourth route available to one who would analyse Tillich's notion of correlation is perhaps the most travelled. One can study the way the method of correlation actually works in the *Systematic Theology* and elsewhere. There is much sense in such an approach. Not a little misunderstanding of Tillich's conception of correlation has arisen in the past because of the tendency of some to concentrate on what Tillich *says about* correlation and to ignore what he *does with* it. Tillich himself had emphasised that 'method and system belong together', not only in the sense that his method determined the shape of his system, but also in the sense that the method itself took shape in the construction of his system (cf. ST. I. 34, 60). A similar point had also been made in the article 'The Problem of Theological Method' which appeared in 1947: 'No method can be found in separation from its actual exercise; methodological considerations are abstractions from methods actually used. . . . The methodological remarks made in this paper describe the method actually used in my attempts to elaborate a theology of "self-transcending Realism" (*gläubiger Realismus*), which is supposed to overcome supra-naturalism as well as its naturalistic counterpart.'[37] This no doubt accurately represents the way the method of correlation actually came about in Tillich's intellectual development. It does not follow from this of course that putative defects in Tillich's system *necessarily* reflect defects in his methodology. They may as a matter of fact, but this would have to be shown to be the case. For it may be that Tillich did not use effectively his own method. Nor would it follow that the absence of defects in the system would entail absence of defects in methodology. It might be the case that theologians tend to be better in practice than they are when they set out to describe what they do, and it might also be the case that the account given by Tillich of his methodology is a distorted and inferior account of his actual work as a theologian. It follows from these two types of possible incongruity between method and system,

---

[36] See *Models and Metaphors* (Ithaca, New York, 1962). Some helpful distinction are also made by Mary Hesse in her *Models and Analogies in Science* (2nd. ed.; Notre Dame, 1966). See below, chapter five, pp. 155–9.

[37] *Journal of Religion*, XXVII (1947), 16.

that some sorts of judgments about the one can be formed more or less independently of judgments about the other. It does not follow, however, that the two cannot be profitably compared in order to learn whether Tillich in fact follows his own avowed methodology in the construction of his theological system. Much valuable research has already been done along such lines. These existing studies make an additional analysis of a similar sort generally unnecessary here, except at specific places to correct misunderstandings or to extend points made in these previous studies arising largely from their failure to attend to the actual usage of 'correlation' in Tillich's writings or to its place in his developing thought.

Most existing studies of Tillich's method of correlation are in at least one of two additional respects limited. Almost all were undertaken before the *Systematic Theology* was completed or before the bulk of Tillich's early papers were readily accessible. The importance of these two limitations will become clearer as the line of argument is developed in subsequent chapters. To anticipate, however, the following points can be made: (1) Tillich's notion of correlation is constructed on foundations laid in his early writings, some of which remain unpublished; (2) Tillich returns in the final volume of the *Systematic Theology* to problems which he originally worked through before formulating his method of correlation and to which he subsequently attempted to apply the new method, with sometimes unsatisfactory results. These two points raise two further problems of interpretation: the one has to do with the text of volume three of the *Systematic Theology* and the other has to do with the proper use of Tillich's early and sometimes unpublished writings.

The final volume of the *Systematic Theology* is especially important for an assessment of Tillich's concept of correlation and its connexion with other aspects of Tillich's thought. This volume, concerning as it does the problems of a *Lebensphilosophie* and a philosophy of history and culture, is arguably the heart of Tillich's philosophical theology. Volume three is also the least well written of the whole work. It was generally regarded by critics as the least satisfactory volume. Nor was Tillich satisfied with it. He at times despaired of ever finishing his 'system' and completed the volume under intense pressure from himself and from his publisher, who shared with him – though not necessarily for the same reasons – his fear of the obvious, that he might not live to complete his system. At one point during its preparation, he desperately wrote a friend, 'I am worried more than ever. The system crumbles. What shall I do? Shall I collect fragments? Declare that the attempt failed?'[38] Proving that he was not wholly in despair, he immediately added that he should probably 'try it again'. And, he was contemplating its further revision not long before his death. It is not clear whether he would have been content simply to revise the existing text. For at the same time he was coming increasingly to feel that the whole work should be recast to take more account than it did of the history of religions. (FR, 80–94; cf. pp. 31f) That is a task which Tillich was not allowed even to begin.

Yet, we are not entirely without a revised text of the final volume of the *Systematic Theology*. For the German edition of that volume is more than a translation in the usual sense; it is in fact a sort of 'second edition'. The new translation afforded Tillich the opportunity to make corrections and additions to the text in order to clarify ambiguities – whether theological or grammatical – and inconsistencies which had so characterised the third volume in particular. For instance, to name but two, 'inorganic' in ST. III. 25 is corrected to 'organic' in STd. III. 36 and the mistaken reference to 'spirit' in ST. III. 255 is altered to 'Spirit' or *göttlicher Geist* in STd. III. 292. The section on the ambiguities of expressionism, which had been inadvertently omitted (whether by Tillich or by the printers) from the English-language editions, could be restored to the text. (STd. III. 90–1; cf. ST. III. 72) Ironically, there are passages in the German edition which are more straightforward and less 'Teutonic' in the pejorative sense than the parallel passages in the English-language editions. (cf., e.g. STd. III. 237 and ST. III. 236) As a result the third volume of the *Systematische Theologie* is in general more readable than the English-language 'original'. One must be careful not to claim too much for the German edition, which has its own limitations.

The fact that the German edition is more readable does not imply that Tillich's theology becomes 'simple' in German. Nor does it imply that it ceases to be problematic. What it does mean, however, is that the complexity of his theology is to less an extent further complicated by the grammatical and stylistic obscurities of the English-language editions. In some cases this leads to a clarification of the nature of certain problems in Tillich's thought. For instance, to anticipate something discussed in chapter

---

[38] Cited in R. May, *Paulus: A Personal Portrait of Paul Tillich* (New York, 1973), p. 71.

five, one reason for Tillich's failure to distinguish in English between 'asking for' and 'asking about' or between undertaking a quest and asking a question becomes clearer when the German text is consulted. In this case the ambiguity remains, though one reason for the ambiguity is discovered.

There are exceptions. In the elaboration of the meaning of 'the Spiritual Presence' in the final volume of the *Systematic Theology,* Tillich very carefully distinguishes 'spirit' and 'Spirit', the former referring to the human spirit and the latter to the divine spirit. Obviously, another device for distinguishing the two would have to be employed in a German translation. The most natural perhaps would be simply to translate 'spirit' as *menschlicher Geist* and 'Spirit' as *göttlicher Geist.* Although this device was frequently used, there are occasions in the *Systematische Theologie* when 'spirit' and 'Spirit' are both rendered simply as *Geist,* with no adjectival qualification, even in cases when the context does not clarify the sense in which the term is used. (cf. STd. III. 134; ST. III. 111)

What has been claimed for volume three does not hold equally for the other volumes of the *Systematische Theologie.* Tillich would seem to have played hardly any part in the translation of some parts and to have taken only a minor interest in others. For instance, the translation of the first volume, which appeared in 1955, was plagued with so many mistakes that the publishers felt obliged to bring out a revised edition the following year. Although Tillich seems to have contributed little to the translation of the first edition of that volume, he did play a somewhat more active role in the reworking of that translation for the second edition. (STd. I^2.8)

The second problem regarding the interpretation of Tillich requires more extensive attention than did the first. The relationship between ideas expressed in an author's earliest works and those expressed in his 'mature' writings is a problem by no means restricted to Tillich's thought. The publication of the early works of such figures as Hegel and Marx provoked a large outpour of articles and books on the significance of the newly available material. Not uncommonly the claims made for these early fragmentary writings were disproportionate to their actual significance. Even so, it would be as much a mistake simply to ignore those early manuscripts as it would be to give them disproportionate weight. Our contemporary understanding of both those writers has been much enhanced by a judicious reading of their early writings. The situation is not altogether dissimilar as regards Tillich, whose life as a productive theologian spanned more than five decades. With the now complete edition of his *Gesammelte Werke,* most of his writings — some of which had not been previously published — are now readily accessible. There is in addition a considerable amount of unpublished material in the Tillich archives. (GW. XIV. 283 ff) Two such pieces are being published for the first time here: Tillich's earliest known outline of a systematic theology (1913) and the propositions from his lectures on 'the structure of religious knowledge' which he delivered at Dresden in 1927–8. The word 'correlation' occurs in neither. Even so, I shall hope to show in subsequent chapters that each contributes measurably to our understanding of Tillich's concept of correlation. Caution is clearly in order. One must be careful not to read too much into these early pieces, which in any case were probably not intended for publication. Tillich's thought took many turns between 1913, the year in which he wrote the first sketch, and 1951, the year in which the first volume of his *Systematic Theology* appeared.

It might be the case that these early pieces should be given no weight whatever in an analysis of a concept, such as correlation, which is a later addition. One can find some support from Tillich's own reflexions on the development of his thought for a radical discontinuity between his 'earlier' and his 'later' works, whether the turning-point be regarded as World War I, the year spent at Marburg (1924–5), or his emigration to the United States in 1933. For instance, Tillich states on occasion that idealism ceased being an option for him as a result of his experiences in the trenches during the Great War. Or, again, he mentions that from Heidegger he learned a *new* way of relating philosophy and theology (GW. XII. 36), the clear implication being that as a result he abandoned an *old* way. Such appeals are of only limited value. For few would contend that none of Tillich's works after 1914–1918 exhibits the lasting influence of 'German classical philosophy' on his thought. Nor, in the light of certain unpublished pieces from the period, can it be claimed that Tillich had been uninfluenced by Kierkegaard's existentialism prior to that War. And, whereas Tillich may have learned a new way of relating philosophy and theology — a way which eventually came to be called 'the method of correlation' — he did not ever abandon entirely the old way, the way implied in the notion of *theonome Metaphysik*. Indeed, the continued presence of 'correlation' and 'theonomy' side-by-side, especially in the final volume of the *Systematic Theology*, raises questions regarding the integrity of his system which must be considered later in this volume. Nor, as we shall see, was 'correlation' unprepared for in Tillich's pre-Marburger thought.

Tillich sometimes explicitly called attention to elements of continuity in his thought. There is, for instance, a remarkable persistence throughout Tillich's writings as to the problems with which he dealt. This is illustrated in his comments in the foreword to his collection of essays entitled *Theology of Culture*: 'The title is an abbreviation of the title of my first published speech . . . *Über die Idee einer Theologie der Kulture* [sic] . . . It is a source of great satisfaction to me that after the passing of forty years I can take the title for this volume from my first important public speech.' (TC, v) He goes on to remark that the problem of religion and culture 'has always been in the centre of my interest' and that in most of his writings – including the *Systematic Theology* – he had sought to define that relationship. He did not mention it specifically, but he could have called attention to the interest in that same problem expressed as early as 1911 in his recently published manual on 'church apologetics'. (GW. XIII. 34–63) There he defined the task of 'theoretical apologetics' to be that of determining the place of theology within the 'system of the sciences' in terms of method and content. (GW. XIII. 34) But this is precisely the object of his *Das System der Wissenschaften,* the subtitle of which is 'nach Gegenständen und Methoden'. Consequently Tillich's two published systems are more closely linked as regards motive and intent than one might otherwise have thought. For Tillich nowhere in *Das System der Wissenschaften* openly confesses the apologetic intention of that work.

Nor is continuity in Tillich's intellectual development limited to the persistance of the issues addressed. For example, the dialectic of separation and participation, which is arguably the controlling material dialectic of the *Systematic Theology,* was the central problem with which Tillich wrestled in his *Mystik und Schuldbewußtsein.* (1912; repr. GW. I) Likewise, the main outlines of his solution to the problem of the relationship between christianity and historical research – as well as the formulation of the problem itself – are clearly adumbrated in his still unpublished paper entitled 'Die christliche Gewißheit und der historischer Jesus' (1911). It has already been mentioned that volume three of the *Systematic Theology* recapitulates many of the dominant motifs found in Tillich's pre-emigration writings. Finally, Tillich's own comments about his 'Religionsphilosophie' (1925) in the foreword to the first volume of the *Gesammelte Werke,* in which that essay was reprinted, should dissuade any who might still maintain that Tillich's mature work should not be interpreted in the context of his earlier writings: 'It is for me a particular satisfaction that my first sketch of a philosophy of religion has through this reprint been raised from the grave in which it had been concealed unnoticed since its publication.' He then added, 'It includes ideas which I have never disavowed, but which I have in many ways developed further.' As we shall see, the nature of that development is far from simple. There are important mediating steps; nor would all seem to be in the same direction! Attention to this complex development modifies one's perception of the 'fabric' of Tillich's thought. Indeed, quite a different pattern emerges in respect to the role of questioning and answering in particular. This obviously has considerable importance for any estimate of Tillich's theological method. Contrary to the view proffered by Alistair Macleod, there are indeed some aspects of the *Systematic Theology* which can be understood properly only when seen against the background of their development.[39] I shall attempt to show that 'correlation' is among them. It is not, I think, widely known that Tillich had used that term in respect to the relationship between religion and culture as early as 1924! (cf. GW. IX. 32) That is not to say that 'correlation' there had precisely the meaning which it had acquired by the time Tillich published the first volume of his *Systematic Theology*.

If it is a mistake to disregard Tillich's pre-emigration writings when considering his mature thought, it is an even greater mistake to disregard the sometimes considerable differences between those early pieces and his *Systematic Theology*. This is the greater danger. For the possibility of misunderstanding Tillich's theology would be less if the earlier writings were ignored altogether than if they were to be regarded as presenting 'essentially the same' ideas as are to be found in the *Systematic Theology*. Even in the cases where terminology remains fairly constant throughout Tillich's writings, the meaning of those words may vary considerably. For instance, the meaning of the term 'theonomy' in the 1919 article 'Über die Idee einer Theologie der Kultur' and the 1922 article on 'Kairos' is very considerably different from its meaning in the third volume of the *Systematic Theology*. Its relationship to other concepts within Tillich's theology is also variable. One aim of chapter six is to sort out some of the main lines of its relation-

---

[39] *Tillich: An Essay on the Role of Ontology in his Philosophical Theology* (London, 1973). A similar criticism of Macleod has been made by Adrian Thatcher in *The Ontology of Paul Tillich* (Oxford, 1978), a book which appeared just as this volume was going to press. I regret that I was not able to make use of it in my own study. It seems a significant work.

ship to the concept of correlation. Much hangs on the relationship between theonomy and correlation for our assessment of Tillich's success in resolving what will be defined in the next chapter as 'Schleiermacher's Dilemma'.[40]

Introducing at this point the two previously unpublished documents appended to this volume can also serve to illustrate something of the nature of the continuities and discontinuities within Tillich's thought. The earlier of the two pieces is apparently Tillich's first attempt to sketch out for himself a systematic theology. It is not known what value, if any, Tillich himself attached to the seventy-two theses which were drawn up in late 1913. It is known, however, that he did not regard them as standing directly behind his published systematic theology, which appeared in three volumes between 1951 and 1963. In the third of those volumes, Tillich explicitly states, 'I consider my lectures on "systematic theology" in Marburg, Germany, in 1924, as the beginning of my work on this system.' (ST. III. 7) Nor can it be denied that there is considerable contrast both in structure and in substance between the 1913 theses and the *Systematic Theology*. Even so, there are some similarities. Woven into the fabric of both systems in the dialectical interplay between identity and separation. Estrangement and reunion is clearly a central motif, if not the controlling material dialectic, in the *Systematic Theology*.[41] The 1913 systematic theology is also dominated to some extent by the argument begun in the first section to the effect that the necessary conflict or contradiction (*Widerspruch*) which is said to arise between what is there termed 'the absolute standpoint' or *intuition* (§§ 1–15) and 'the relative standpoint' or *reflection* (§§ 16–21) is resolved only within 'the theological standpoint', based as it is in the *paradox* (§§ 22–8). Stress in both works is placed upon the specifically christological character of the paradox. (§ 37; ST. I. 57, 150–2) Nonetheless, it would be a mistake not to look for possible differences between the two works even at those points where they seem to be similar: for it is not altogether clear in the seventy-two theses, as it tends to be in the *Systematic Theology*, that 'the absolute standpoint' is *ideal* and describes what Tillich later calls the *essential* relationship between man and God, finite and infinite, whereas 'the relative standpoint' is *actual* and describes rather the *existential* disruption of that relationship.

---

[40] See below, pp. 39–46, esp. p. 42.
[41] See Guy Hammond, *Man in Estrangement* (Nashville, 1965).

There is an important structural difference as well, and not only that which can be accounted for by Tillich's having adopted the question-answer schema with which his concept of correlation is most generally associated. In the *Systematic Theology*, Tillich denies that apologetics is a separate section of theology, a sort of 'prolegomena' to theology proper: it is rather a dimension of constructive theology and is itself an expression of theological (confessional) principles. He further denies that there should be a separate section for 'ethics'; there is an ethical dimension to the whole of theology. (ST. I. 30−2) Yet this three-fold series − apologetics, dogmatics, ethics − constitutes the structure of the seventy-two theses. In part one, which is termed *fundamental theology*, Tillich seeks to ground 'the theological principle in the scientific principle in general' (§§ 1−28). In the second part, called *dogmatics,* he treats 'the development of the theological principle into a system of religious knowledge' (§§ 29−49). And in the final part, which is called *theological ethics,* Tillich turns to 'the application of the theological principle to the cultural life of mankind' (§§ 50−72). In repudiating the three-fold division of theology into apologetics, dogmatics and ethics, he was rejecting not only the schema used by many nineteenth-century protestant theologians,[42] but also the schema he too had employed in his initial attempt to outline a system of theology. The contrast between the two works is significant and raises serious questions for any claim that the development of Tillich's thought is fundamentally continuous from before the first world war.[43] There *are* important continuities and there are *also* equally important discontinuities. But, in any case, the system of 1913 is a very important resource for insight into the early direction of Tillich's constructive thought from before the first world war. Most of the other works from that period are rather more analyses of other people's ideas than sustained expressions of Tillich's own. These are rightly treated by Kenneth Schedler and others as having only marginal significance.[44] The main importance of the 1913 system, therefore, is that it − together with the short paper on the historical Jesus and the now published *Kirchliche Apologetik* − is a pre-war document in which Tillich is

---

[42] Tillich's own mentor, Martin Kähler, had made use of such a schema in his *Die Wissenschaft der christlichen Lehre* (3rd. ed.; Leipzig, 1905).
[43] E.g., David Hopper, *Paul Tillich: A Theological Portrait* (Philadelphia, 1968).
[44] See *Natur und Gnade* (Stuttgart, 1970), p. 190, n. 1.

presenting his own views.⁴⁵ Consequently, I have relied rather more on those writings than upon the dissertations on Schelling and on 'supranaturalism'. Hopper's claims notwithstanding, the experience of the carnage of war *did* make a considerable difference in the way Tillich went about his work as a theologian,⁴⁶ as it did in the case of virtually every other major theologian of Tillich's generation, with the possible exception of Rudolf Bultmann.⁴⁷

It simply is not the case that Tillich's mature thought merely unfolded or 'evolved' out of his earlier thought.⁴⁸ There are breaks, some more radical than others. Nor should this have been unexpected. For one must remember that (even if nothing else) the Third Reich — and the shattering of Tillich's political hopes for Germany — stands between, for example, the concepts theonomy and kairos in the early works and the use of the same terms in the *Systematic Theology*. Furthermore, his important contact with Heidegger's thought at Marburg — and Tillich's subsequently modified understanding of the relation which obtains between philosophy and theology — stands between his early definition of *theonome Metaphysik* and his mature formulation of the correlation-concept in the *Systematic Theology*. Thus, the complexity of the relation between the early Tillich and his later writings is particularly acute in regard to his theological method inasmuch as a keen methodological consciousness has characterised every phase of Tillich's intellectual development from almost the first.

Tillich traced the origins of his *Systematic Theology* back to the lectures which he gave at Marburg during the winter semester of 1924–5. His lecture-notes for that course seem unfortunately not to be extant. It is not possible therefore, to measure the extent to which their structure and

---

45 Among other primary sources from the period 1909–18 which should not go unmentioned, however, are Tillich's numerous sermons which have been catalogued and analysed by Andreas Rößler, *op. cit.*

46 See, e.g., the evidence from Tillich's early sermons in *ibid.*, pp. 132–63. See also the illuminating chapter on the War in Pauck and Pauck, pp. 40–56. One can support their judgment that 1914–18 was a turning point for Tillich, even if one demurs from their over-bold claim that 'these years represent *the* turning point in Paul Tillich's life — the first, last, and only one.' *Op. cit.*, vol. I, p. 41.

47 In this regard, see Bultmann's letter to Erich Förster which is cited in W. Schmithals, *An Introduction to the Theology of Rudolf Bultmann* (London, 1968), p. 9f.

48 Cf. Hopper, *Op. cit.*, p. 49.

content contributed to the published version of the *Systematic Theology*. Some clues may be found, however, in Tillich's lectures on epistemology which were delivered in 1927–8 at the Technische Hochschule in Dresden, where Tillich had become professor in 1925, immediately after his short and evidently unhappy year as associate professor at Marburg.[49] The importance of those lectures for our understanding of the development of Tillich's thought generally, and his concept of correlation particularly, is discussed below in chapter four. I do not want to anticipate here what is to be argued there. However, I do want to suggest the possibility that, the title of those lectures notwithstanding, they could be regarded as Tillich's outline of a new systematic theology. Were that the case, they would be the first lectures in systematic theology delivered by Tillich after the course at Marburg which he came to regard as the 'beginning of my work on this system'. Would we not then be obliged to regard the Dresden lectures as a continuation of that work begun first in Marburg? I think we probably are obliged to do so, though I do not want to make too extravagant a claim for 'Die Gestalt der religiösen Erkenntnis'. Nor would it be extravagant to regard that document as the outline of a systematic theology. The claim would rest on Tillich's own words: 'The traditional names for work on the formation of religious knowledge, especially "dogmatics" and "Glaubenslehre", are for the moment unusable in virtue of their canonical taint. The name "structure of religious knowledge" is an attempt to re-express the subject matter [of theology] in a way that has symbolic power for our situation.' (§ 14) Deviation from traditional ecclesiastical language is not unknown in Tillich's later theological writings! 'Without such deviation, I would not have deemed it worthwhile to develop a theological system for our period.' (ST. II. viii) 'A special characteristic of these three volumes', wrote Tillich in the *Systematic Theology*, 'is the kind of language used in them and the way in which it is used. It deviates from the ordinary use of biblical language in systematic theology. . . . Instead, philosophical and psychological concepts are preferred, and references to sociological and scientific theories often appear. . . . Since the split between a faith unacceptable to culture and a culture unacceptable to faith was not possible for

---

[49] See K&B, 14. Additional details of the impression which Marburg made on the Tillichs during their time there may be found in Hannah Tillich, *From Time to Time* (London, 1974), pp. 115ff. See also GW. XIII. 556–7, as well as Pauck and Pauck, *op. cit.*, pp. 94ff.

me, the only alternative was to attempt to interpret the symbols of faith through expressions of our own culture.' (ST. III. 4–5) Tillich speaks there as well of having tried 'during the larger part of my life to penetrate the meaning of the Christian symbols, which have become increasingly problematic within the cultural context of our time.' 'Die Gestalt der religiösen Erkenntnis' must surely be seen as part of that attempt. Its structure is even recognisably theological, despite the non-traditional language employed. The second and more constructive half of the lectures is fragmentarily trinitarian, Tillich having failed to move beyond the second person of the trinity, owing one supposes to the semester having come to a close.[50] Within each half many of the traditional problems of dogmatic theology are tackled, albeit in fairly untraditional language. That, however, seems an integral part of Tillich's way of doing theology in the *Systematic Theology*, no less than in 'Die Gestalt der religiösen Erkenntnis'.

Granting that the intention of the two works is not wholly dissimilar, one becomes aware that there are more substantial connexions between them. In volume one of the *Systematic Theology*, Tillich specifies two formal criteria of any possible theology: (i) 'The object of theology is what concerns us ultimately. Only those propositions are theological which deal with their object in so far as it can become a matter of ultimate concern for us'; (ii) 'Our ultimate concern is that which determines our being or not-being. Only those statements are theological which deal with their object in so far as it can become a matter of being or not-being for us.' (ST. I. 12, 14) Similar criteria occur in the Dresden lectures. In the section entitled 'Theologische Axiomatik', Tillich states that the general character of religious knowledge determines the relationship between the knowing subject and the object of knowledge. Propositions expressing that relationship have an axiomatic character. Tillich specifies four theological axioms, the first two of which very nearly anticipate what he would later call the two formal criteria of theology: (i) 'Religious knowledge is knowledge which concerns us unconditionally. No statement contains religious knowledge which does not deal with an object in so far as it concerns us unconditionally'; (ii) 'That concerns us unconditionally which determines our being. No statement contains religious knowledge which does not deal with an object in so far as it determines our being.' (§§ 26–7)

---

[50] Tillich in fact indicates on the manuscript that the semester ended with § 170.

Nor is the similarity between the two works, separated though they are by a quarter of a century, restricted to Tillich's specification of the formal criteria of theology. The object of religious knowledge is also closely similar. Tillich stresses in the Dresden lectures, no less than in the *Systematic Theology*, that the object of religious knowledge is not an object. 'It is the character of the religious object not to be an object.' (§ 42) God is neither an object alongside other objects nor the sum of all existing things: God is the power of being in all things and beyond all things. (cf. §§ 43–5) Other similarities and dissimilarities will be discussed as specific points in later chapters. What has been presented, however, is perhaps sufficient to show that the Dresden lectures are not wholly unrelated to what would later become one of the impressive products of sustained theological reflection in the twentieth century, Tillich's *Systematic Theology*. Indeed, instead of speaking just of Tillich's 'two systems',[51] we must I think grow accustomed to speaking of at least *four* systems, each of which is apologetic in intent: the systematic theology of 1913, the *System der Wissenschaften* of 1923, the 'Gestalt der religiösen Erkenntnis' of 1927–8 and, of course, the *Systematic Theology* of 1951–63.

We must also grow accustomed *not* to speak of an 'early Tillich' and a 'late Tillich'. The evidence will not support neat divisions of Tillich's theological development into, say, 'Tillich I' and 'Tillich II'. As will be shown in the chapters which follow, there are rather numerous strands which are roughly interwoven in the process of his theological and philosophical development. Some strands are extremely persistent, running all the way through from the earliest to his most mature writings, though there are sometimes slight and at other times great changes in colour and texture; some strands begin abruptly and others begin almost imperceptably; some end as abruptly and others simply fade out, perhaps to be revived later and perhaps to be abandoned altogether. The resulting 'fabric' is far from consistent, either in pattern or in texture. Tillich himself was more aware of this than are many of his admirers: 'Even at its best this system is fragmentary and often inadequate and questionable. Nevertheless, it shows the stage at which my theological thought has arrived.' (ST. III. foreword) 'There is even in a well organized work such as my *Systematic Theology* a certain inconsistency and indefiniteness of terminology; there is

---

[51] See Robert Scharlemann, 'The Scope of Systematics: An Analysis of Tillich's Two Systems', *JRel*, XLVIII (1968), 136–49.

the influence of different, sometimes competitive motives of thought . . .' (K&B, 15) We shall have occasion more than once in the chapters which follow to recall these words!

In the next chapter an attempt is made to place the concept of correlation within the context of the dilemma it was intended by Tillich to resolve. Schleiermacher is sometimes credited with having set a methodological dilemma for modern theology when he spoke of the need to establish between christian faith and modern knowledge an 'alliance' in which there is a thorough-going reciprocity (*Wechselwirkung*) and yet in which the autonomy (*Selbständigkeit*) of neither is threatened. Determined efforts were made to resolve this dilemma by the 'theologians of mediation' in particular, including Ernst Troeltsch, who was regarded by the younger 'dialectical theologians' as the epitome of the *Kulturprotestantismus* they had disavowed. The attempted synthesis of christianity and race nationalism by Emanuel Hirsch and others gave new impetus and plausibility to Karl Barth's earlier and independent rejection of cultural protestantism and its theologies of mediation. Tillich's theology of correlation is an attempt to revitalise the tradition of mediation in such a way that due account is taken of the two-fold challenge to that tradition represented by Hirsch and Barth. As 'alliance' had been Schleiermacher's formal principle of mediation and 'compromise' had been Troeltsch's, 'correlation' became Tillich's mediating principle between religion and culture. It is widely held that Tillich failed sufficiently to clarify and carefully to disentangle the multiple senses in which he used the term 'correlation'. Indeed, at times in his writings it seems almost as if every sort of relationship were regarded as a correlative relationship! For the purposes of the present study, however, a correlative relationship must satisfy two conditions: namely, what I shall later define as the *reciprocity condition* and the *autonomy condition*.[52]

Before determining whether Tillich's concept of correlation satisfies both these conditions, it is necessary first to get a clearer view of the terms correlated. 'Correlation' is, in one of its main senses, the sort of relation which Tillich believes ought to obtain between religion and culture. The object of chapters three and four is to determine the sense of 'religion' which is thought to stand in a correlative relation to culture and the sense of 'culture' which is thought to stand in a correlative relation to religion. It is shown that the two main senses in which Tillich uses the word 'religion' —

---

[52] See below, pp. 42–6, 82–3.

religion as a dimension of all man's cultural life and religion as a special sphere within culture — correspond closely with another distinction drawn in his earlier writings but subsequently abandoned: the distinction between *cultural theology* and *church theology*. It is argued that 'correlation' is a function principally of what Tillich would earlier have called a species of church theology and that it has to do principally with religion in the second and narrower sense, though there is considerable ambiguity in Tillich's writings in this regard. Despite the extensive attention given to Tillich's theology of culture in the literature, no one to my knowledge has succeeded in sorting out the various strands of his concept of culture. This task is undertaken in chapter four. There are three main strands in Tillich's use of 'culture', each of which corresponds to a strand in the modern German usage of *Kultur*: culture as 'formation' or human perfection; culture as *Geistesleben*; culture as a patterned whole or a structured totality. Each of these strands is shown to play a part in Tillich's understanding of the correlationship of religion and culture, but attention is focused particularly upon the third sense of the term. Extensive comment is made regarding his claim that *style* is the key to interpreting cultures. Certain criticisms are offered toward the end of the fourth chapter concerning Tillich's understanding of what it is to relate religion and culture. Especial stress is placed upon the highly complex character of the phenomena of religion and culture, a complexity which precludes the structure of their relationship being reduced without serious loss to a single sort of relation.

In the third and final part of the volume, I undertake first to show the role of 'questioning and answering' and 'form and content' in the development of Tillich's theory of correlation; secondly, to show that each of these metaphors satisfies one but not both conditions of a correlative relation; and, thirdly, to suggest a way in which both conditions might be met. Although it can be construed in such a way that it satisfies the reciprocity condition, 'questioning and answering' is on its own too shapeless to be an adequate model of correlationship. And, although it can be construed in such a way that it satisfies the autonomy condition, the dialectic of 'form and content' as developed by Tillich cannot be regarded as sufficiently reciprocal since cultural 'form' is immune from influence by religious 'content' and since religious 'content' is made immune from influence by cultural 'form'. Tillich's frequent claims notwithstanding, the particular way these two sets of metaphors are combined in the 'method of correlation' tends greatly to restrict if not exclude altogether any genuine reciprocity in relations between religion and culture. This is in the main a consequence of his increased concern after 1933 with the need to preserve what he then called 'the catholic substance' of christianity, by which he seems to have meant that which makes christianity christian. But, the question arises, can justice be done to that undeniably legitimate concern in such a way that a thorough-going reciprocity between religion and the rest of culture is nonetheless allowed? In chapter six, I suggest one way this question might be answered affirmatively. My comments there must of necessity be brief and suggestive. Some readers may feel that the programme indicated in the final chapter owes more to Troeltsch than to Tillich. They might be right.

CHAPTER TWO
THE DILEMMA AND THE CONCEPT OF CORRELATION

Determining the proper structure of relations between christianity and culture has been throughout the history of theology a persistent problem, to which there has been no one solution which could be prudently acclaimed '*the* christian solution'. Variety in approach to this issue is no less a feature of primitive christianity than of theology in the modern period. Rather than a single, normative model, one finds within christian thought from the outset a family of loosely related attempts to resolve the problem of the church's existence within the world.[1]

Although a persistent issue, the theological problem of religion and culture has been significantly reshaped in modern times. Reasons for this are no doubt numerous, but among the most important of them must be reckoned the changing status of the christian religion in the formation and preservation of the beliefs and values of modern western societies. In part symptom and in part cause of such change was the widespread demand during the enlightenment for an emancipation of the several spheres of social and cultural life from religious tutelage. In his 1784 essay in answer to the question 'Was ist Aufklärung?', Kant went so far as to define *enlightenment* as man's release from his self-imposed status as a minor, unable to make decisions without direction from those guardians who, in Kant's ironic turn of phrase, 'have so kindly assumed superintendence over him.'[2] To be enlightened, man must be free rationally to generate rules of belief and action; but, in order for this to be possible, he must be free from the fetters of heteronomously imposed authority. Whether in morality or in

---

[1] That this is the case is amply supported by such general studies as Ernst Troeltsch's analysis of *Die Soziallehren der christlichen Kirchen und Gruppen* (Tübingen, 1912) and H. Richard Niebuhr's briefer, though more wide-ranging study of *Christ and Culture* (New York, 1956), a volume which was said by its author 'to do no more than to supplement and in part to correct' Troeltsch's earlier study. (p. x) But, see also Werner Elert, *Der Kampf um das Christentum* (Munich, 1921).

[2] *Kants Gesammelte Schriften* (Berlin, 1910ff), vol. VIII, pp. 35ff.

religion, the basis for belief and action must be found within man himself, and not be imposed from the outside in the form of external authority. True religion, as well as true morality, must find its basis 'within the limits of reason alone', that is, within human autonomy.[3]

The modern refocusing of the problem of christianity and culture occurs against the backdrop of this new sense of self-confidence, this 'recovery of nerve',[4] of which Kant is one example. Indeed, according to one of its most significant interpreters, the end of what he termed 'church culture' and the emancipation of the several spheres of culture from religious direction forced upon christian theology, however unwillingly, a refocusing of the problem.[5] The history of christian theology since the eighteenth century can be written from one point of view as a history of different responses to this new situation. For the question is not simply whether that recovery of nerve occurred. No one denies this — not even the dialectical theologians! The question is, rather, its significance for the way theology is to be done.[6] And theologians since the enlightenment divide according to their relative acceptance or relative rejection of this new sense of autonomy as a proper starting-point for theology.

Within limits which will become clear, Tillich is to be classed among those who affirmed it and who conducted themselves theologically within its terms. In his early and generally fruitless debate with Barth on 'paradox', he at one stage asserted to the bemusement of Barth and Gogarten

---

[3] The following year (1785), Kant developed this argument further as regards morality in his *Grundlegung zur Metaphysik der Sitten,* which appears in the *Gesammelte Schriften* in vol. IV, pp. 387–463. Cf. esp. the second and third chapters, pp. 406 ff, 446 ff. Cf also the *Opus postumum* in *Gesammelte Schriften,* vol. XXI, pp. 103, 106. It is perhaps not irrelevant that the concept 'autonomy', which had been a central political category for the Greeks in ancient times, seems to have dropped out of usage entirely during the middle ages and to have made its reappearance only in modern times, most importantly in the seventeenth and eighteenth centuries. See. R. Pohlmann, 'Autonomie', *Historisches Wörterbuch der Philosophie,* ed. by Joachim Ritter and Karlfried Gründer (Darmstadt, 1971), vol. I, cols. 701–19.

[4] The phrase is from Peter Gay, *The Enlightenment: An Interpretation* (2 vols; New York, 1966 and 1969).

[5] I mean, of course, Troeltsch.

[6] A similar point is made as regards historicism by Friedrich Gogarten in 'Historismus', *Zwischen den Zeiten,* VIII (1924), 7–25.

alike that the contemporary cultural situation forces one as theologian, not to be theologian, but to become philosopher of culture. (GW. VII. 242)[7] The divine Logos for Tillich, as for the Greek apologists whom he in so many respects followed (cf. HCT, 24 ff), is not restricted to the christian scripture and cultus. And Tillich held that in a 'secular culture', made free from the domination of heteronomous religion, this Logos may be more unambiguously discerned in autonomous cultural spheres, such as art and philosophy, than in the more specifically 'religious' sphere. (GW. VIII. 241 f) The theologian's task in such circumstances is to show that even in those cases when open hostility is shown toward religion in the institutional sense, the spirit of truth is present as unconditional demand. But, since religion in its widest sense is understood by Tillich as 'directedness toward the unconditioned' (cf. GW. I. 320),[8] this means that in his view there is a religious element in autonomy wherever the spirit of truth is present as unconditional demand. This sort of autonomy, possessing as it does 'depth and seriousness', Tillich terms *theonomy*. True religion is for the early Tillich a function of human autonomy: far from being opposed to autonomy, therefore, theonomy is for him from the start a particular sort of autonomy, which he would later call 'self-transcending autonomy'. (PE, xii)

It is perhaps not wholly insignificant that the concept of theonomy was first introduced by Tillich in an address to the Kant-Gesellschaft. (cf. GW. IX. 13 ff) For there are some points of similarity between Tillich's conception of the relationship between heteronomy, autonomy and theonomy and Kant's own use of heteronomy and autonomy in his moral philosophy, especially as it is developed in the *Grundlegung zur Metaphysik der Sitten* (1785). Kant does not, of course, there use the term 'theonomy'. But, autonomy is for Kant – as for Tillich – double-sided. Negatively stated, autonomy signifies freedom from every heteronomy, a freedom which is necessary for man to be a free moral agent. Negative autonomy is not itself productive of new values; it implies merely the rejection of externally imposed values. In his autonomy, however, man is aware of a sense of

---

[7] For Gogarten's bemused response to this assertion, see GW. VII. 244–6.
[8] Tillich had earlier spoken of religion more mystically as 'the experience of the unconditioned' (cf. GW. IX. 18), which the phrase 'directedness toward the unconditioned' replaced. This phrase was, in turn, replaced by 'was uns unbedingt angeht' and then by 'ultimate concern'.

oughtness which is neither imposed from the outside nor a product of his own desires. This 'oughtness' is nonetheless present as unconditional demand, as categorical imperative. Rather than a threat to human autonomy, the moral imperative is said by Kant to give seriousness and depth to that autonomy, making it a positive principle. What Kant called 'negative autonomy' appears in Tillich's thought merely as 'autonomy'; what Kant called 'positive autonomy' is referred to by Tillich as 'theonomy', the central concept of his theology of culture. Kant himself had rigidly restricted his argument to ethics, although the neo-Kantians later extended it to cover epistemology and aesthetics as well.[9] A similar extension was required by Tillich, too, in order to replace 'theological ethics' with a 'theology of culture' (GW. IX. 16), one task of which is to analyse the unconditioned moment in the various spheres of human culture.

By arguing as he did in his earlier writings especially that the 'unconditioned' breaks through from within autonomous cultural activity (GW. IX. 18, 19ff), Tillich from the beginning rejected the view held by many that religious awareness is in some way antithetical to the hard-won autonomy of the enlightenment period. Tillich wrote enthusiastically throughout the early 1920's of the breakthrough of the unconditioned in all realms of autonomous cultural life. This signalled for him and his colleagues in the 'religious socialist movement'[10] the imminent formation of a new theonomous unity of cultural beliefs and values. Military metaphors abound in the following passage written not long after Tillich had returned to civilian life:

> For almost two hundred years, theology has been in the unfortunate but unavoidable position of a defender who holds an ultimately untenable emplacement and who has been forced to abandon position after position. After giving up the final vestiges of its untenable,

---

[9] Cf. Hermann Cohen, *Ethik des reinen Willens* (Berlin, 1907), pp. 327ff, and Heinrich Rickert, *Allgemeine Grundlegung der Philosophie* (Tübingen, 1921), p. 310.

[10] Regarding Tillich and the 'religious socialist movement', see E. Amelung, *Religious Socialism as an Ideology* (Th. D. diss.; Harvard, 1962); R. Breipohl, *Religiöser Sozialismus und bürgerliches Geschichtsbewußtsein zur Zeit der Weimarer Republik* (Zürich, 1971); A. Pfeiffer (ed.), *Religiöse Sozialisten* (Olten and Freiburg, 1976); J. R. Stumme, *Socialism in Theological Perspective*, 'AAR Dissertation Series' (Missoula, 1978); and T. Ulrich, *Ontologie, Theologie, gesellschaftliche Praxis* (Zürich, 1971).

culturally heteronomous position, theology must again return to the offensive. It must fight under the banner of theonomy. Under this banner it will conquer, not the autonomy of culture, but the profanation, emptiness and fissure of culture in recent years. Theology will conquer, because religion is — as Hegel says — the beginning and the end of all things, just as it is the centre, which gives to all things life and soul and spirit. (GW. IX. 31)

There is evidence to suggest that Tillich thought this conquest would be soon coming. The enthusiasm and rhetorical excess of this quotation, typical though it may be of his earlier writings, no longer tends to characterise his works from the later 1920's onwards. The mood is quite different, for instance, in the opening essay of his collection *Religiöse Verwirklichung*, an essay which appeared later as well in *The Protestant Era* under the title 'The Protestant Message and the Man of Today'. Tillich by then no longer laid stress as earlier upon the sort of self-confident autonomy associated with the enlightenment period: having lost the surety of a firm world-view, the 'decisive spiritual type' of man in the twentieth century is now seen as 'the autonomous man who has become insecure in his autonomy'. (PE, 192) 'He still stands in the autonomous tradition of recent centuries. But his situation is different from that of former generations in that he no longer possesses an autonomy in which he is self-assured and creative; rather he possesses one that leaves him disturbed, frustrated, and often in despair.' (PE, 193) He may be tempted from time to time to seek release through an escape into some kind of heteronomy (PE, 193 ff) or by a flight into what Tillich had earlier termed 'anomie'.[11] But, neither sort of self-surrender can in the end satisfy this sort of man, who — despite the 'brokenness of his autonomy' — cannot let go that autonomy which he still possesses, 'however feeble and empty it may be'. (PE, 195) Consequently, Roman catholicism, being in Tillich's view 'consistently heteronomous' (PE, 194), can offer no final refuge. Only protestantism, speaking as it does from the 'boundary-situation' in the power of the 'protestant principle', has a healing message for this 'modern man' who differs in so many respects from that self-sufficient and self-assured 'modern man' of whom theologians spoke in the nineteenth century (and not only then!). According to Tillich, only protestantism has the power to speak to him in such a way

---

[11] See 'Kairos', *Die Tat*, XIV (1922), 344.

that his autonomy is not denied, in such a way that 'culture is not subjected to religion, nor is religion dissolved into culture'. (PE, 205)

Almost exactly one hundred years earlier, Friedrich Schleiermacher had also written regarding the peculiar power of the protestant message for that earlier, more self-assured 'modern man'. Concerned about the largely negative stance adopted by many protestant theologians, not least the notorious Steudel of Tübingen,[12] toward the 'new learning' in general and the natural and historical sciences in particular, Schleiermacher expressed to his friend Lücke an obvious sense of unease for the future of a christian theology, which he envisaged entrenched behind walls of defence and blockaded in by modern knowledge. 'The occasional bombardment of mockery and ridicule is a small matter. . . . But, the blockade! The mass starvation from all learning which is forced upon you precisely because you are so entrenched, with the additional consequence that modern knowledge has no choice but to hoist the flag of unbelief!'[13] There then follows the worried and much-quoted question, 'Shall the knot of history unravel in such a way that christianity is identified with barbarism and modern knowledge with unbelief?'[14] A little later in the same letter to Lücke he spoke of the need to establish between christian faith and modern knowledge a 'perpetual alliance' or 'pact'[15] in which the autonomy of neither party to the treaty would be threatened:

---

[12] Regarding this, the earlier 'Tübingen School', see Emanuel Hirsch, *Geschichte der neuern evangelischen Theologie* (4th. ed.; Gütersloh, 1968), vol. V, pp. 70ff. Tillich's own habilitation dissertation at Halle was an analysis of the 'supranaturalism' perpetrated by Steudel, Storr, Süskind and the two Flatts. Part one was published as *Der Begriff des Übernatürlichen, sein dialektischer Charakter und das Prinzip der Identität, dargestellt an der supranaturalistischen Theologie vor Schleiermacher* (Königsberg, 1915). A typescript of part two, which was never published, is in the Tillich-Archiv.

[13] *Schleiermacher-Auswahl*, ed. H. Bolli (Munich & Hamburg, 1968), p. 146.

[14] ‚Soll der Knoten der Geschichte so auseinander gehn; das Christentum mit der Barbarei, und die Wissenschaft mit dem Unglauben?' *Ibid*. Elsewhere Schleiermacher would, however, contrast 'culture' (*Bildung*) with 'barbarism'. Cf. *Kleine Schriften und Predigten*, ed. by Hayo Gerdes and Emanuel Hirsch (Berlin, 1970), vol. I, p. 51. We shall see later that Troeltsch interestingly, and significantly, misquotes Schleiermacher's question cited above. See below, note 35.

[15] *Vertrag*. It is at best misleading to translate this as 'covenant', as Gerhard Spiegler does in *The Eternal Covenant: Schleiermacher's Experiment in Cultural Theology*

> If the reformation in which our church has its origins has not the objective to establish a perpetual alliance between the living christian faith and that scientific research which is in every respect free to explore and to pursue its own ends independently, so that faith does not hinder learning, nor learning exclude faith, then that reformation is not adequate for the needs of our time and we require yet another one, regardless of the extent of struggle required to bring it about. But it is my firm conviction that the basis for this alliance was already established earlier in that first reformation. . . .[16]

Unfortunately, Schleiermacher does not there nor, to my knowledge, anywhere else specify in precisely what respects that foundation was thought to have been laid in the sixteenth-century reformation. But, be that as it may, to establish such an alliance — and on protestant foundations — was a principal objective of all Schleiermacher's work, including his own systematic theology, *Der christliche Glaube* (1821–22^1, 1830^2). He found intolerable the sort of partition between, say, philosophy and religion implied in Jacobi's quip that he was a pagan with his intellect and a christian with his heart.[17] Schleiermacher had written to Jacobi in 1818, chiding him for his remarks and in the process clarifying his own position on the relationship between intellect and feeling, which may be taken in this case as signifying speculative philosophy and religion generally:

> I am a philosopher with my intellect, because that is the original and underived activity of the intellect. But with my feeling I am wholly devout and moreover as such a christian. . . . As we all know, you

---

(New York, 1967). Had he meant to say 'covenant', Schleiermacher — a theologian of the Reformed tradition — would surely have used the word *Bund*. An 'ewiger Vertrag' is simply a pact unlimited by time, as opposed to a temporary alliance. In German law, an 'ewiger Vertrag' is binding for ninety-nine years!

16 *Schleiermacher-Auswahl*, p. 149. 'Learning' translates *Wissenschaft*.

17 In a letter to Karl Leonhard Reinhold cited in the *Schleiermacher-Auswahl*, p. 116. For Schleiermacher's reply, dated 30 March 1818, see pp. 116–9. Regarding Schleiermacher's own early studies of Jacobi's philosophy, studies which in some ways illuminate the background of the exchange, see Eilert Herms, *Herkunft, Entfaltung und erste Gestalt des Systems der Wissenschaften bei Schleiermacher* (Gütersloh, 1974), pp. 121ff, as well as Erwin H. U. Quapp, *Christus im Leben Schleiermachers: Vom Herrnhuter zum Spinozisten* (Göttingen, 1972), pp. 263–74, 375–89.

are a philosopher with your intellect . . . and therein we are already united because I, too, refuse to allow anyone to prevent my continuing to philosophise so long as I may live. . . . [No more than yours] does my [intellect] want to go beyond [nature]. But, because I do not wish to be caught in a contradiction, I have taken a firm stand that no one else shall be allowed to ascertain for me the limits of nature. If then my christian feeling is itself aware of a divine spirit within me and this is contrary to my intellect, then I will not cease to search this out in the deepest depth of nature. . . . This is my way of giving equal weight to both: it is nothing other than an alternating between them, so that as the one ascends, the other descends. But, dear [friend], why do we not content ourselves with this state of affairs? This oscillation is clearly the general pattern of all finite existence and there is surely an immediate awareness that this is merely an expression of the two foci of my own ellipse out of which this suspension arises and I have in this suspension the whole fulness of my mortal life. Consequently, my philosophy and my dogmatics are rigidly determined so that neither contradicts the other. But for that reason neither will ever be finished. As long as I can recall, they have always stood in a kind of correspondence with one another and have ever moved increasingly toward one another.[18]

Yet Schleiermacher did not envisage a point at which the two would intersect or merge. The two remain for him ever distinct: there is for Schleiermacher no final synthesis between intellect and feeling, philosophy and theology, culture and religion.[19] He is in this respect most clearly to be distinguished from his colleague Hegel. The letter to Jacobi ends with the following words: 'I do not want to unify the two. . . . Intellect and feeling remain also for me distinct from one another, but they form together a galvanic couple. The innermost life of the spirit occurs for me only in this galvanic operation, in which feeling affects intellect and intellect feeling, but in such a way that both poles remain always distinct from one another.'[20] Here, as in the letter to Lücke, the two components — in the one case

---

[18] *Schleiermacher-Auswahl*, pp. 117–8.
[19] These three pairs of terms are not, of course, strictly parallel. The extrapolation is based, however, on Schleiermacher's letter to Jacobi and his two letters to Lücke reprinted in *ibid.*, pp. 120–75.
[20] *Ibid.*, p. 119.

learning and faith; in the other, intellect and feeling — affect one another and yet they are said to remain distinct and ever 'nebeneinander'. Their relationship is said by Schleiermacher in the one place to be similar to that between partners in an alliance, and in the other between the two poles in a galvanic reaction. In both cases, however, the relationship between the two must in Schleiermacher's view satisfy two conditions: there must be a mutual dependence and interaction in which neither is reduced to the other, indeed, in which the two remain in some sense independent. The dilemma for a theology of mediation along Schleiermachrian lines lies precisely in this two-fold requirement: is it possible to conceive, let alone establish, a relationship between christianity and culture in which there is a genuine and thorough-going reciprocity that threatens the autonomy neither of religion nor of culture?

Consequently, two conditions must be met if Schleiermacher's problem is to be resolved successfully: I shall call them *the autonomy condition* and *the reciprocity condition*. The requirement that both conditions be satisfied, I shall call *Schleiermacher's dilemma*.

But, the question might arise, are not the demands of these two conditions mutually exclusive, such that x and y cannot be at the same time both autonomous and reciprocally related? No such paradox is intended. Some reasons why it need not be understood as a paradox can be explained by attending briefly to selected features of 'autonomy'. The word *autonomy* is subject to a wide variety of uses, some of which are not always distinguished from one another as carefully as one might have hoped.[21] 'Autonomy' is also among those words in our language which are constantly in danger of being priced out of the market place of linguistic usage. 'Knowledge' and 'altruism' are other examples.[22] For we are tempted to think of such terms only in an absolute sense, so that any claim to autonomy which does not entail absolute independence from any sort of external influence is disallowed; or, so that any claim to empirical knowledge which does not entail apodictic certainty is disallowed. The effect in each of these cases would be to disallow every claim to have autonomy or to have empirical

---

[21] For a brief history of some of the various uses of the word 'autonomy', see Pohlmann, 'Autonomie', *loc. cit.* For an attempt philosophically to disentangle some of the different senses of the term in ethical contexts, see R. S. Downie and E. Telfer, 'Autonomy', *Phil.* XLVI (1971), 293–301.

[22] I owe this last example to my Lancaster colleague John Benson.

knowledge. One could, of course, make the conditions under which one would allow such claims so astringent that the terms would have no applicability. But it would hardly be desirable. For it would, at the very least, deprive us of a number of words which have enjoyed common usage and, at the same time, artificially create the need for new words to use in those contexts where we might like to have used 'autonomy' or 'knowledge' or 'altruism'. There are obviously degrees of autonomy, so that things may be autonomous to a greater or to a lesser extent. But, we do not in fact ordinarily use the word 'autonomy' in an absolute sense. We might say that an academic discipline is autonomous when at least some of the main propositions which it generates are irreducible to propositions of another type. But this would not preclude there being areas of overlap between that discipline and other disciplines. Or we might say that an emotionally healthy person is autonomous in the sense of being an integrated and self-directed personality, but this would not in any way imply that that person is wholly immune from all influence by all other persons. These two examples are perhaps sufficient to show that the two conditions laid down above as necessary for the resolution of Schleiermacher's dilemma are not necessarily and irreconcilably contradictory. They are, nonetheless, problematic and the precise character of their relationship does constitute a major problem in modern theology since Schleiermacher.

'Autonomy' will be used principally in the sense of self-direction: x has autonomy when the basic rules governing its behaviour are internally generated, rather than externally imposed; that is to say, no x can be said to have autonomy when the rules governing its activity are either reducible to or deducible from some sphere outside x. This is, of course, a purely formal definition, the ramifications of which will become clearer as the argument is developed.

When Schleiermacher speaks of 'autonomy', he characteristically uses either the term *Selbständigkeit* or the term *Unabhängigkeit*, both of which can also mean 'self-sufficiencey' or 'independence'. He seems to have held that religion must in some sense have entirely independent origins and even be entirely free of external influence as regards content (*Inhalt*) in order for it to be judged autonomous in the sense that I have given that term. He was particularly keen in his letter to Lücke and indeed elsewhere to refute the charge made by some that his theology was deduced from speculative philosophy, 'that I make the christian faith dependent upon speculation or, what is perhaps essentially the same thing, that I wish to reintroduce paganism into christianity. . . .'[23] Against Steudel in particular Schleiermacher protests that this is a gross misunderstanding of his intention and procedure, which is to explicate the specifically christian self-consciousness from no other ground than itself.[24] In the sometimes fierce battle between orthodoxy and rationalism, the orthodox – of whom Storr and Steudel may be fairly regarded as representative – defended the autonomy of religion or, more particularly, christianity on the basis of its putatively supranatural origins in miracle and revelation. As part of his effort to negotiate a peaceful settlement to that by then sterile struggle, Schleiermacher sought to ground the autonomy of religion in its independent origins within the structure of the human personality or spirit. In doing so, he sought both to show that religion is autonomous in the sense of not being a function of, say, speculative philosophy or moral philosophy and also to show that it is a constituent aspect of man qua man. His particular conception of religion, and its relationship to Tillich's conception, will be discussed in greater detail in the next chapter. It is nonetheless necessary here to draw a distinction which Schleiermacher himself did not clearly or consistently draw: namely, autonomy in the sense of self-direction and autonomy in the sense of immunity from external influence. But these are clearly different senses of autonomy. For instance, from the fact that Jones is autonomous in the sense of being a self-integrated and self-directed personality, it does not follow that he is in every case immune from the influence of others. Nor does it follow from the fact that Jones is in every case immune from the influence of others that he is autonomous in the sense of being a self-integrated and self-directed personality![25] Schleiermacher's failure clearly to make a similar distinction in respect to the autonomy of religion creates problems for his approach to the matter, some aspects of which are taken up afresh by later mediating theologians, including Troeltsch and Tillich. The nature of the difficulty becomes clearer

---

[23] *Schleiermacher-Auswahl*, p. 122.
[24] Nor was it only members of the earlier Tübingen school who misunderstood Schleiermacher: he did not fare much better at the hands of Baur. See C. E. Hester, *Schleiermacher in Tübingen: A Study in Reaction* (Ph. D. diss., Columbia, 1970) and H. Liebing, 'F. C. Baurs Kritik an Schleiermacher', *ZThKirche*, LIV (1957), 225–43.
[25] Indeed, social psychologists sometimes stress that the capacity to be influenced by others is a necessary moment in the healthy personality! See, e.g., Karen Horney, *Our Inner Conflicts* (New York, 1945).

in relation to Schleiermacher's attempt to determine the limits of the reciprocity to be allowed in relations between learning and faith.

The word *reciprocity* is likewise subject to a wide variety of uses, especially within the social sciences where it has over the past several years enjoyed something of a vogue. I shall be using the term primarily in the sense of mutual influence or mutual dependence, which is termed in German *Wechselwirkung* or *gegenseitige Abhängigkeit*. Though her main object is to distinguish different sorts of moral relativism, Dorothy Emmet's distinction between what she terms 'functional dependence' and 'reciprocal dependence' is not irrelevant to the present context. According to her account, x is functionally dependent upon y when x varies systematically in accordance with variations in y. But, if y is also shown to vary systematically with changes in x, then the dependence is no longer one-directional or 'functional', but two-directional and 'reciprocal'.[26] There are a number of ways in which this distinction could be further refined, some of which are suggested in the literature in social and cultural anthropology regarding the sorts of possible reciprocal relations.[27]

When Schleiermacher speaks of the reciprocity between religion and culture, he is not always clear regarding the actual extent each is to be allowed appropriately to influence the other. At times, he writes with exuberance of the benefits to each which are derived from their interaction, implying that in isolation there is a necessary impoverishment of each.[28] And yet, he is less than explicit about the precise nature of the contribution each is supposed to make to the other. For instance, he states almost in passing at one point in his second letter to Lücke that speculative philosophy cannot be allowed in any respect to influence the content of christian faith.[29] Defining the nature and extent of the reciprocity between culture and faith is one of the unresolved difficulties bequeathed by Schleiermacher to his successors. This particular difficulty just about defeated Troeltsch, as

---

[26] Dorothy Emmet, *Rules, Roles and Relations* (London, 1966), pp. 90−1.
[27] Cf., e.g., M. D. Sahlins, 'On the Sociology of Primitive Exchange', *The Relevance of Models for Social Anthropology*, ed. M. Banton (London, 1965), pp. 139−225. As in the case of 'autonomy', there are obviously also degrees of reciprocity, such that things are to a greater or lesser extent reciprocally related to one another.
[28] Cf., e.g., *Schleiermacher-Auswahl*, p. 146.
[29] See *ibid.*, p. 172.

we shall see. We shall be particularly interested in determining the degree of Tillich's success in resolving this issue.

There is widespread agreement that Schleiermacher's 'experiment in cultural theology', as it has been called, ultimately failed. There is no such agreement, however, as to the reasons why it did not finally succeed. Some have argued in effect that what I have termed the autonomy condition is not satisfied and others that the reciprocity condition is not met.[30] Nor were such criticisms unknown already in the nineteenth century, this having been a major factor in Schleiermacher's decision to publish a second edition of his *Der christliche Glaube*.[31] Even so, there were theologians who persisted throughout that century and into the next in the attempt to establish or explicate an appropriate mediation between historical christianity and modern culture and to do so along lines which had been suggested by Schleiermacher.[32] Foremost among these must be included Ernst Troeltsch.[33]

Troeltsch's posthumously published *Glaubenslehre*, delivered originally as lectures at Heidelberg, demonstrates clearly that he firmly supported 'the reorganisation of modern theology' with which he credited Schleiermacher.[34] And he did so, not only in the obvious sense that the religious self-consciousness is regarded by Troeltsch as the proper starting-point for theology, but moreover in the sense that he shared Schleiermacher's

---

[30] Typical of those who would argue the former are Karl Barth and his one-time student, F. Flückiger. See *Philosophie und Theologie bei Schleiermacher* (Zürich, 1947). Though his thesis is slightly eccentric, Gerhard Spiegler (*op. cit.*) would be typical of those who would argue the latter.

[31] *Schleiermacher-Auswahl*, pp. 120ff.

[32] These included, of course, Tillich's own teacher, Martin Kähler, through whom he was introduced to the idea that mediation is of the essence of theological activity. Cf. PE, ix–x; GW. XII. 31–2; XIII. 23f.

[33] For some perceptive, though highly compressed, remarks suggesting comparisons between Schleiermacher and Troeltsch, see Ferdinand Kattenbusch, *Die deutsche Theologie seit Schleiermacher* (Gießen, 1926⁵), pp. 91ff, where he treats Troeltsch as a proponent of 'die neue Schleiermacherianismus'! See also B. A. Gerrish, 'Ernst Troeltsch and the Possibility of a Historical Theology' in *Ernst Troeltsch and the Future of Theology*, edited by J. P. Clayton (Cambridge, 1976), pp. 100–35.

[34] Ernst Troeltsch, *Glaubenslehre*, edited by Gertrud von le Fort (Munich and Leipzig, 1925), p. 1.

concern that history not show christianity finally allied with barbarism and unbelief with culture.[35] In those lectures, Troeltsch – as Schleiermacher, albeit ambiguously and problematically, had done before him – defended the view that theology could be substantially influenced by extra-christian sources[36] and yet remain in some sense 'relatively independent'.[37] Troeltsch shared also Schleiermacher's concern that society not be simply abandoned to the entirely secular forces. This is made clear in the *Soziallehren*, where Troeltsch identified a central concern of his theological work when he asked how the church can co-operate with the main, non-religious forces of society so that together they establish a unification of culture.[38] Given the shape of the new situation after the collapse of 'church culture', Troeltsch

---

[35] On one occasion Troeltsch curiously misquotes Schleiermacher's question cited above in note 14: '. . . von den akademischen Lehrern ist Milde und Toleranz zu fordern, damit nicht, um mit Schleiermacher zu reden, der Knoten schließlich so auseinandergeht, daß es das Christentum mit der Barbarei, der Unglaube aber mit der Kultur hält.' *Glaubenslehre*, p. 18. The use of *Kultur* here reflects developments in German usage of that term since the time of Schleiermacher.

[36] See, e.g., *Die wissenschaftliche Lage und ihre Anforderungen an die Theologie* (Tübingen: J. C. B. Mohr, 1900), pp. 52ff; 'Die Bedeutung der Geschichtlichkeit Jesu für den Glauben' (1911), repr. in the Siebenstern edition of *Die Absolutheit des Christentums und die Religionsgeschichte*, edited by Trutz Rendtorff (Munich and Hamburg, 1969), p. 152f; *Glaubenslehre*, pp. 22ff.

[37] *Glaubenslehre*, pp. 56ff.

[38] *Gesammelte Schriften* (4 vols.; Tübingen, 1912–25), vol. I, p. 12. Thus, Troeltsch defines the problem in terms of *Ethik*, in Schleiermacher's sense, namely, philosophy of history and culture. See Schleiermacher's *Grundriß der philosophischen Ethik*, edited by August Tweston (Berlin, 1841), p. 251, § 50. Troeltsch regarded the philosophical *Ethik* as Schleiermacher's greatest and most original achievement. See 'Die Bedeutung der Geschichtlichkeit Jesu für den Glauben', Rendtorff collection, p. 140. Like Schleiermacher, Troeltsch too wanted to ground his theology in *Ethik*, understood as 'Geschichts- und Geistesphilosophie'. 'Geschichte und Metaphysik', *ZThKirche*, VIII (1898), 27f. Even so, Troeltsch judged that the actual details of Schleiermacher's *Ethik* 'no longer have anything to do with the vital problems of the present'. *Gesammelte Schriften*, II, 568f. On Schleiermacher's *Ethik*, see P. H. Jørgensen, *Die Ethik Schleiermachers* (Munich, 1959), H.-J. Birkner, *Schleiermachers christliche Sittenlehre* (Berlin, 1964), and the very carefully worked out article by Eilert Herms on 'Die Ethik des Wissens beim späten Schleiermacher' which appeared in the *ZThKirche*, LXXIII (1976), 471–523. The best study of Troeltsch's ethics remains W. F. Kasch, *Die Sozialphilosophie Ernst Troeltschs* (Tübingen, 1963).

perceived two imminent dangers: *either* christianty would withdraw into itself and become increasingly irrelevant as a cultural force *or* it would become increasingly assimilated and lose its distinctiveness as a force in society. Troeltsch intended to construct a christian theology which avoided both these dangers. 'Religion becomes a power in ordinary life only by taking up civilization into itself and giving it a special direction.' He immediately added the important but frequently forgotten disclaimer, 'But it always remains distinct from this civilization.'[39] In undertaking to construct a theology along such lines, Troeltsch had clearly accepted the challenge given by Schleiermacher to develop a theology of mediation between religion and culture.

Not only did Troeltsch accept Schleiermacher's challenge, but he also came through the years to broaden the terms in which that problem was conceived. This he did in two ways. First, he considerably broadened the concept of *culture* so that it came in his writings to include not only 'the cultured' elite *(die Gebildeten)*, nor even just the intellectual and imaginative activities and products of a society (its *Geistesleben*), but the social and economic 'infrastructure' as well. This trend in Troeltsch's developing thought runs roughly parallel to the emergence in Germany of modern, descriptive conceptions of culture out of earlier, evaluative conceptions.[40] For Schleiermacher, on the other hand, 'culture' was conceived principally as the process of cultivating human capacities, in analogy with the way that plants and animals are cultivated. Schleiermacher cannot, therefore, within the terms of his culture-concept speak of '*a* culture'. Troeltsch *can*. And that has important consequences for his understanding of what it is to mediate between religion and culture. Schleiermacher speaks typically of the problem of mediating between religion and its 'cultured despisers'. Troeltsch, too, sometimes speaks in similar terms.[41] But, he also and perhaps more characteristically speaks of the problem of mediating between the christian religious tradition and a culture or a cultural epoch.[42] Schleier-

---

[39] Cited from *Protestantism and Progress*, trans. by W. Montgomery (1912; Boston, 1958), p. 176. Cf. *Die Bedeutung des Protestantismus* (Munich und Berlin, 1928), p. 87f.

[40] Cf. A. L. Kroeber and C. Kluckhohn, *Culture: A Critical Review of Concepts and Definitions* (1952; New York, n. d.).

[41] Cf. esp. *Die wissenschaftliche Lage und ihre Anforderungen an die Theologie*.

[42] This is the way that he typically uses the term throughout *Die Soziallehren der christlichen Kirchen und Gruppen* (= *Gesammelte Schriften*, I) and the two

macher lacked the conceptual apparatus to discuss the problem of mediation in just these terms.

Not surprisingly, the broadened conception of culture contributed, secondly, to a wider conception of the nature of *religion* and (as just suggested) the problem of the relationship between religion and culture. Schleiermacher had arguably reduced essential religion to 'piety'. Though he emphasised, both in the *Reden* and in *Der christliche Glaube*, that the religious self-consciousness necessarily finds expression at some stage of its development both in doctrine and community, Schleiermacher nonetheless treated as secondary and derived dogma and doctrine, sacrament and cultus. A not entirely dissimilar line is to be found in Troeltsch's earlier writings, though it is noticeably less the case in his writings after the appearance of the *Soziallehren*. Despite his strong emphasis there upon the 'mystical' and 'personal' aspects of religion,[43] there is in that and subsequent works a growing appreciation for what might be termed the 'multi-dimensional' character of religion,[44] with particular emphasis upon its social and ethical, rather than − as in some of Troeltsch's earlier writings − its psychological dimension.[45]

Troeltsch reserves his greatest scorn, as had Schleiermacher before him,[46] for those who would reduce religion, however tacitly, to its intellectual dimension. He frequently complained that the academic theology of his day tended to view dogma and doctrine in isolation from the total religious context of which it formed only one part and in terms of which it gained its own significance.[47] A purely ideological or doctrinal approach to relations between christianity and culture was for him a

---

volumes on historicism: *Der Historismus und seine Probleme* (= *Gesammelte Schriften*, III) and *Der Historismus und seine Überwindung*, edited by Friedrich von Hügel (Berlin, 1924).

[43] Cf. *Gesammelte Schriften*, I, 977ff, et passim.

[44] Cf. Ninian Smart *The Religious Experience of Mankind* (New York, 1976²) and *The Phenomenon of Religion* (New York, 1973).

[45] Cf. 'Geschichte und Metaphysik', p. 28. Even so, one must express reservation about Lessing's judgment, supported also by Pannenberg, that psychology is the fundamental element in Troeltsch's system. Eckhard Lessing, *Die Geschichtsphilosophie Ernst Troeltschs* (Hamburg, 1965), pp. 51−6. Cf. Wolfhart Pannenberg, *Wissenschaftstheorie und Theologie* (Frankfurt/Main, 1973), p. 106.

[46] *Über die Religion*, ed. R. Otto (Göttingen, 1967⁶), pp. 23ff, 38ff.

[47] Cf., e.g., *Gesammelte Schriften*, II, 12.

distortion of the actual state of affairs.[48] Consequently, Troeltsch came to regard as a serious mistake any attempt to produce a purely dogmatic history of christianity: his *Soziallehren* is intended largely as a corrective to this overly ideological approach to the history of christianity, as typified especially in the work of Harnack and Seeberg.[49] In the brief autobiographical essay entitled 'Meine Bücher', Troeltsch mentioned that his *Soziallehren* is to be understood as a parallel account to Harnack's history of dogma in the sense that he, unlike Harnack, emphasised the primacy of the socio-ethical over the doctrinal or theological aspects of christianity.[50] This new perspective is evidenced in much of Troeltsch's 'middle' and 'later' work besides the study of the *Soziallehren der christlichen Kirchen und Gruppen*. In a short article on religion, economics and society which appeared originally in 1913,[51] Troeltsch argued that no theoretical advance regarding the relationship between religion and, say, economics would be possible so long as religion were interpreted in a purely ideological way as a body of dogma or doctrine or as a system of metaphysics. Protestants are accused of having been much more guilty of this distortion than have been Roman catholics, who are said at least to have had a deeper appreciation for the cultic and the institutional, the mythic and the irrational aspects of religion. Yet, in Troeltsch's view, neither protestants nor catholics have appreciated fully the significance for religion of the wider socio-economic sphere of culture. It may very well be the case that Troeltsch himself was not entirely successful in incorporating this socio-economic infrastructure into his theory of culture,[52] but it must be conceded that the structure of relations between religion and culture came through the years to be conceived by Troeltsch in much broader terms than it had been by any theologian before him, including Schleiermacher.

---

[48] For his sometimes controversial remarks on the social role of the doctrine of Christ in the history of the christian cultus, see 'Die Bedeutung der Geschichtlichkeit Jesu für den Glauben', Rendtorff collection, pp. 147ff. See also B. A. Gerrish, 'Jesus, Myth, and History: Troeltsch's Stand in the "Christ-Myth" Debate', *JRel* LV (1975), 13–35.

[49] Cf. *Gesammelte Schriften*, IV, 739ff, for his criticisms of Seeberg's tendency to intellectualise the history of christianity.

[50] *Gesammelte Schriften*, IV, 11f, 99.

[51] *Ibid.*, pp. 21–33.

[52] As Hans Bosse has argued in *Marx, Weber, Troeltsch: Religionssoziologie und marxistische Ideologiekritik* (Munich, 1971²).

By asking how the church can co-operate with the main secular forces of society so that together they form a unified culture, Troeltsch specified the terms in which he would tackle the dilemma set by Schleiermacher. In order to clarify somewhat the extent to which Troeltsch may have contributed to the resolution of that dilemma, I propose to look briefly at his notions of reciprocity and autonomy, and then to turn to his conception(s!) of 'compromise', which I shall treat as his principle of mediation between christianity and culture. The decisive question is whether, within the framework allowed by Troeltsch, it would be possible to satisfy the conditions required for the successful resolution of Schleiermacher's dilemma. To what extent would it be possible within the limits of Troeltsch's methodology to effect between historical christianity and contemporary culture a relationship of mutual influence in which the independence of neither were undermined?

Part of Troeltsch's case against the representatives of both the older orthodoxy and also some forms of the newer 'liberalism'[53] is built on their allegedly having failed to grasp that the relationship between the christian religion and the rest of culture is reciprocal without remainder. There is in Troeltsch's view no aspect of christianity – not its dogma,[54] nor its ethic,[55] nor its founder[56] – which stands outside the nexus of causal relations which together constitute cultural history. The theologians of the older orthodoxy are said to have evaded the relativising effects of historical consciousness by means of their 'dogmatic method' with its inherent appeal to supranatural authority – whether bible or tradition or miracle – which was held not to be continuous with ordinary history, even if it happened 'within' history.[57] Proponents of some sorts of idealism are said by Troeltsch to have contrived to evade the relativising effects of the historical consciousness by asserting that christianity is the absolute realisation of a universal religious principle.[58] And advocates of some forms of protestant

---

[53] One is made cautious in the use of this term by Hans-Joachim Birkner's 'Liberale Theologie' in *Kirchen und Liberalismus im 19. Jahrhundert*, edited by Martin Schmidt and Georg Schwaiger (Göttingen, 1976), pp. 33–42.
[54] ‚Was heißt „Wesen des Christentums"?', repr. *Gesammelte Schriften*, II, 386 ff.
[55] *Gesammelte Schriften*, I, 986, et passim.
[56] ‚Die Bedeutung der Geschichtlichkeit Jesu für den Glauben', inter alia.
[57] *Gesammelte Schriften*, II, 739 ff.
[58] *Die Absolutheit des Christentums und die Religionsgeschichte*, repr. Rendtorff collection, pp. 32 ff. For an analysis of this aspect of Troeltsch's thought, see

liberalism are judged to have sought security vainly either in the 'Jesus of history'[59] or in a persisting 'essence' of christianity which was thought to provide a point of identity in all authentic manifestations of christianity.[60]

Troeltsch attacked each and every one of the these attempts to evade the full consequences of historical relativism. He argued in effect that the historical consciousness which arose in and after the European enlightenment[61] calls into question not merely this or that 'fact', but one's view of the past and present and even the future. The historical method cannot be adopted piecemeal or applied *ad hoc*. It must be applied consistently and dispassionately in every field of learning, including christian theology.[62] Nor did Troeltsch restrict its significance for theology merely to the way ancient texts are to be studied. Rather, the historical method is said to act as a leaven which permeates the whole of theology and which in the end 'bursts the confines' of all earlier methods.[63]

Few would claim that he quite succeeded, and many would hold that he was somewhat overimpressed by the putatively skeptical consequences of this historical relativism.[64] It must be granted nonetheless by all that more than most theologians of his own generation – not to mention those of the next![65] – Troeltsch did make a serious and determined effort to apply historical method to theology with utter consistency in the sense of his having attempted to construct a christian theology based on a methodology orientated toward general cultural and religious history.[66] This being the

---

Gunnar von Schlippe, *Die Absolutheit des Christentums bei Ernst Troeltsch auf dem Hintergrund der Denkfelder des 19. Jahrhunderts* (Neustadt/Aisch, 1966).

[59] *Gesammelte Schriften*, II, 213–4. Troeltsch refers there approvingly to Schweitzer's *Von Reimarus bis Wrede* (= *The Quest of the Historical Jesus*).

[60] *Gesammelte Schriften*, II, 386 ff. For one view of the difference between the way Troeltsch handled the questions of the essence of *christianity* and of the essence of *religion*, see Michael Pye, 'Ernst Troeltsch and the End of the Problem about "Other" Religions' in *Ernst Troeltsch and the Future of Theology*, pp. 171–95.

[61] Cf., *inter alia*, *Gesammelte Schriften*, II, 744–5; IV, 353.

[62] Cf. *Gesammelte Schriften*, II, 734.

[63] *Ibid.*, p. 730.

[64] For one such assessment, see P. F. Carnley, 'The Poverty of Historical Scepticism' in *Christ, Faith and History: Cambridge Studies in Christology*, edited by S. W. Sykes and J. P. Clayton (Cambridge, 1972), pp. 165–89.

[65] Cf. Van A. Harvey, *The Historian and the Believer* (London, 1967).

[66] *Gesammelte Schriften*, I, viii; II, 738.

case, the problem arises as to how Troeltsch can hope to hold together his claim that religion is an independent factor within social history and his apparently contrary claim that religion stands in a radically reciprocal relationship to the rest of society. What then are we to make of this apparent tension in his methodology?

Troeltsch laid out the main lines of his methodology in a number of scattered articles, including his essay 'Über historische und dogmatische Methode in der Theologie', which was his 'final word' in the controversy with Julius Kaftan and his pupil Friedrich Niebergall regarding the autonomy or *Selbständigkeit* of christianity within the history of religion and culture.[67] Of the three principles of historical explanation outlined there, only the principle of reciprocity is of direct concern here.[68] Reciprocity or the mutual interaction of all historical phenomena implies for Troeltsch that there 'can be no change at one point without some preceding and consequent change elsewhere, so that all historical happening is knit together in a permanent relationship of correlation, inevitably forming a current in which everything is interconnected and each single event is related to all others.'[69] There is no point in history exempt from this

---

[67] *Gesammelte Schriften*, II, 729f. The basic texts of that controversy appeared mainly in the *ZThKirche*: Troeltsch, ‚Die Selbständigkeit der Religion', V (1895), 361–436; VI (1896), 71–110, 167–218; J. Kaftan, ‚Die Selbständigkeit des Christentums', VI (1896), 373–94; Troeltsch, ‚Geschichte und Metaphysik', VIII (1898), 1–69; Kaftan, ‚Erwiederung', VIII (1898), 70–96. Friedrich Niebergall published 'Über die Absolutheit des Christentums' in *Theologische Arbeiten aus dem Rheinischen wissenschaftlichen Predigerverein*, IV (1900), 46–86, in which Troeltsch's 'final word' (!) 'Über historische und dogmatische Methode in der Theologie' also appeared.

[68] Even so, it must be remarked that this principle is not entirely unrelated to the other two, namely, criticism and analogy. For an interpretation of the latter two, see Lessing, *Die Geschichtsphilosophie Ernst Troeltschs*, pp. 20–3.

[69] *Gesammelte Schriften*, II, 733. Bosse has pointed out, and I think rightly, that when in this particular article Troeltsch spoke of the reciprocity between religion and the other spheres of culture, he had in mind principally the 'superstructure' of societies and had not at this point become alert to their socio-economic 'infrastructure'. Only after his contact with Max Weber was the notion of reciprocity broadened so as to take account of the marxian problem of relations between superstructure and infrastructure. *Marx, Weber, Troeltsch*, p. 76. But, see Hans-Georg Drescher, 'Troeltsch's Intellectual Development', in *Ernst Troeltsch and the Future of Theology*, pp. 25–7.

correlative involvement or reciprocal influence. Everything is relativised – 'Alles und Jedes' – in the sense that there can be no absolute points in history: 'Every historical configuration and moment can be understood only in relationship with others and ultimately with the total context.'[70]

The main difficulties, both philosophical and theological, inherent in Troeltsch's methodology are easy enough to catalogue. Nor has there been hitherto any shortage of those willing to add new charges to the bill of indictment. For our present purposes, it is perhaps sufficient to note that Troeltsch's conception of reciprocity raises at least two questions for any attempt to do theology within the framework which it allows. First, would not this understanding of reciprocity inevitably lead to the reduction of christianity to 'no more than' a sphere of culture and result in its total assimilation?[71] Second, if christianity is completely relativised in the manner proposed by Troeltsch, how can it maintain its identity through history and across cultures?[72] The two questions raise in different ways the issue forced first by Kaftan and Niebergall as to whether the autonomy or Selbständigkeit of christianity is not largely sacrificed in Troeltsch's account of the thoroughly reciprocal character of the relationship between christianity and the rest of culture. If either charge can be sustained, and until recently there has been widespread agreement that both must be allowed to stand, then Troeltsch's approach to the matter offers no solution to Schleiermacher's dilemma.

Schleiermacher had employed several metaphors in order to elucidate his conception of the proper relationship between faith and culture. They

---

[70] *Gesammelte Schriften*, II, 737; cf. 747.

[71] Discussion of this question was reopened by Walter Bodenstein in his still influential book *Neige des Historismus* (Gütersloh, 1959) where he asserted that Troeltsch treated christianity 'in the final analysis as no more than a phenomenon of cultural life, perhaps its highest and noblest, but nonetheless fixed in the frame of human historical life in the same way as any other cultural value.' (p. 67)

[72] The answer to this question hinges largely upon how one is to explain Troeltsch's occasional diffidence in describing his own thought as 'christian' (cf., e.g., 'Ein Apfel vom Baume Kierkegaards', *Die christliche Welt*, XXXV, 17 March 1921, col. 189) and upon how literally one is to interpret his claim that the future development of christianity is entirely open-ended. For a spirited critique of Troeltsch's concept of the essence of christianity, see S. W. Sykes, 'Ernst Troeltsch and Christianity's Essence' in *Ernst Troeltsch and the Future of Theology*, pp. 139–71.

included 'alliance' or 'pact'. Troeltsch also favoured contractual terms when discussing the relationship between christianity and culture. In the *Soziallehren*, for instance, he found occasion to use for such purposes all of the following images: 'accommodation', 'agreement', 'alliance', 'amalgam', 'coalition', 'merger', 'negotiated settlement'. The metaphor with which his thought is most typically associated, however, is *compromise*.

Troeltsch's election to favour that metaphor was not an altogether happy choice, for its primary associations have to do largely with the mutual concession of *Realpolitik*. His defenders frequently warn that this is not at all what he meant, that his use of the word 'compromise' has none of the derogatory overtones which usually accompany that term. This claim cannot be sustained. Troeltsch used the word 'Kompromiß' in a number of different senses, some of which are clearly negative.[73] And Troeltsch allows that there are some situations in which compromise would be undesirable,[74] even immoral[75] or dishonourable.[76] More often than not, however, he employed the term in a double-sided way: compromise is necessary, but in each particular compromise something is lost as well as gained. Needless to say, Troeltsch himself thought that the gains outweighed the losses.[77] In at least this stress, he stands quite near to Harnack. For, according to the latter, the so-called 'hellenisation of the gospel' was both necessary for the survival of the young christian sect and a very high price to pay for its continued existence.[78] But, in any case, there was in his view no practical alternative if the new religion were not to pass away with the age that had produced it. This double-sided emphasis is sometimes missed by Harnack's

---

[73] Cf. *Vernunft und Offenbarung bei Johann Gerhard und Melanchthon* (Göttingen, 1891), p. 10; 'Protestantisches Christentum und Kirche in der Neuzeit', *Die Kultur der Gegenwart*, edited by Paul Hinneberg, vol. I/IV (Leipzig and Berlin, 1906), 427; 'Die Selbständigkeit der Religion', p. 366; *Gesammelte Schriften*, I, 2f, 23, 79, 227, 393, 551, etc.; II, 410, 412, etc.; IV, 802; *Deutscher Geist und Westeuropa*, edited by Hans Baron (Tübingen, 1925), p. 7.

[74] *Christian Thought: Its History and Application*, edited by Friedrich von Hügel (London, 1923), p. 166f, which does not appear in the German edition, *Historismus und seine Überwindung*.

[75] *Der Historismus und seine Überwindung*, p. 19.

[76] *Das historische in Kants Religionsphilosophie* (Berlin, 1904), p. 41.

[77] *Gesammelte Schriften*, I, 980; *Historismus und seine Überwindung*, p. 43f.

[78] This double-sided argument is found, not only in the *Dogmengeschichte*, but in the popular lectures on *Das Wesen des Christentums* as well!

critics;[79] and a similarly double-sided emphasis is sometimes frequently overlooked by Troeltsch's more uncritical interpreters.

What then does Troeltsch mean by *Kompromiß*? Nowhere to my knowledge does he offer an adequate definition of what in his view would count as a compromise; nor does he anywhere give an adequate account of the logic of compromise. In order to learn what Troeltsch means by 'compromise', one must therefore look at the way he actually used the term, with a view toward determining from its usage its basic features as a principle of mediation. Leaving aside some of his more obviously casual uses of the term, Troeltsch tends to apply the word 'compromise' in four distinct senses: first, and perhaps most literally, in a legal or political sense; secondly, in an intellectual sense in reference to the mediation between different beliefs, ideas and ideologies; thirdly, in an inclusive sense in reference to accommodations between culture and christianity; and, finally, in an ethical or moral sense.[80] Owing to its thematic role in the *Soziallehren*, the ethical compromise is the sense most frequently employed by Troeltsch, although this requires a qualification. Inclusive compromises are frequently negotiated on an ethical base, according to Troeltsch, such that the all-embracing compromise between christianity and culture is regularly treated by him as a problem for ethics. This is the meaning of 'compromise' with which we shall be principally concerned.

Discounting its occasional and clearly casual use in earlier writings, 'compromise' begins to be used as a *terminus technicus* for mediation in Troeltsch's writings from about 1900. In his study of *Die wissenschaftliche Lage und ihre Anforderungen an die Theologie*, the word is introduced without explanation in special reference to the intellectual rapprochement in ancient times between the christians and the 'cultured' of the Roman Empire, in which society the new sect had gradually gained a firm standing.[81] The term is restricted there to the various aspects of just this alliance between christianity and antiquity,[82] an alliance in which 'culture

---

[79] Including Paul Tillich! See, e.g., EN. II. 183 and ST. II. 140−2.
[80] These four uses are discussed in detail in my essay 'Can Theology be both Cultural and Christian?: Ernst Troeltsch and the Possibility of a Mediating Theology' which is due to appear soon in *Science, Faith and Revelation: Essays in Honor of Eric C. Rust*, ed. B. E. Patterson.
[81] *Die wissenschaftliche Lage*, pp. 15−6.
[82] *Ibid.*, pp. 23, 26, 28, 40, 44f, 46f.

was christianised and morality was secularised.'[83] Elsewhere, Troeltsch speaks also of compromises having been struck between 'natural ethics' and 'supranatural ethics',[84] or between 'natural law' and 'divine law',[85] or between the ancient 'secular ethic' and the 'christian ethic'.[86] This is in fact Troeltsch's paradigm case, it being the compromise which eventually made possible the mediaeval catholic synthesis.[87] Troeltsch's detailing of the various steps which finally led to this compromise provides the surest source for determining the contours of his conception of an inclusive compromise between christianity and culture.

In the *Soziallehren*, Troeltsch traces with sensitivity the gradual modifications both within the social context and within christian thought which eventually made possible the multi-sided mediaeval synthesis, the major theological expression of which was thomism.[88] That synthesis, which was the sole product neither of a single theologian nor of a single generation of theologians, was in good measure the product of a gradual and largely unconscious[89] reinterpretation of traditions which had for centuries shaped western thought.[90] All the main elements, save one, which went to make up that synthesis had according to Troeltsch's analysis been available for some time.[91] These resources from christian moral traditions and secular *lex naturae* traditions were combined in such a way that the radical character of the christian ethic was largely preserved through the

---

[83] *Ibid.*, p. 25. This process is not, however, restricted by Troeltsch just to morality: it includes the whole of christianity and all the dimensions of culture, especially learning (*Wissenschaft*).
[84] *Gesammelte Schriften*, I, 481.
[85] *Ibid.*, p. 393; 'Protestantisches Christentum', p. 372.
[86] *Die Bedeutung des Protestantismus*, p. 39.
[87] *Gesammelte Schriften*, I, 144 ff, 171 ff, 252 ff, *et passim*.
[88] For a highly compressed survey of that process, see *Gesammelte Schriften*, I, 330 ff.
[89] *Gesammelte Schriften*, I, 198 ff, cf. 203. *Der Historismus und seine Überwindung*, p. 37.
[90] Here, as elsewhere in Troeltsch's writings, the focus is less on matters of passing fancy and more on long-term historical developments. See, e.g., also *Glaubenslehre*, pp. 18–9.
[91] Even so, they could not in Troeltsch's view have been combined earlier in such a compromise, because the social conditions were not right. *Gesammelte Schriften*, I, 178 ff.

introduction of the novel concept of degrees or gradations.[92] This 'creative compromise' is said by Troeltsch to have seemed to the mediaeval church entirely natural and quite unremarkable,[93] even though its basis was in fact *non*-christian.[94] This was due to long-standing modifications within both secular and religious ethical traditions which made the distance between them seem not all that great. The notion of degrees simply completed a process which had been developing over a long period.

While it lasted, this inclusive compromise on an ethical foundation gave meaning and structure to social life. It did not go unchallenged, as the remainder of the *Soziallehren* amply records! Nor, in Troeltsch's view, could that same compromise hope to serve its previous unifying role for our time,[95] owing in part to the greater diversity and complexity of contemporary social life.[96] There are also other differences. Thomism, for instance, held it to be an endemically christian idea that there should be a 'christian society' or unity of culture effected on a christian foundation.[97] This is an assumption which Troeltsch found impossible to share, so that he rejected any suggestion either simply to repristinate the thomistic synthesis[98] or even to attempt to renegotiate terms for a 'christian society' on some other basis.[99] This resistance on Troeltsch's part owes less to possible doubts about the importance of the concept of *lex naturae*[100] than to increasing skepticism about any attempt to re-establish in the modern

---

[92] Cf. *Ibid.*, pp. 274 ff.

[93] It was seen by the church as being 'von selbst'. *Ibid.*, p. 202 f. It was for this reason all the more powerful in its hold. *Die Bedeutung des Protestantismus*, p. 9.

[94] *Gesammelte Schriften*, I, 272 ff.

[95] In addition to the conclusion of the *Soziallehren*, see 'Protestantisches Christentum und Kirche in der Neuzeit', p. 451, and *Der Historismus und seine Überwindung*, pp. 41–61, esp. 56 f.

[96] He warns elsewhere, however, against exaggerating the difference in this respect between the middle ages and modern society. *Der Historismus und seine Überwindung*, pp. 50–1.

[97] Cf. *Gesammelte Schriften*, I, 290. The notion of a 'christian society' is itself judged by Troeltsch to have been the product of a long and complicated historical process, in which a number of extra-religious factors were assimilated into christianity. For a brief summary of that process, see *ibid.*, pp. 286 ff.

[98] *Ibid.*, pp. 965–6, 979 ff, 983 ff.

[99] *Historismus und seine Überwindung*, pp. 41–61, esp. 52 ff.

[100] See, e.g., 'The Ideas of Natural Law and Humanity in World Politics', in Otto Gierke, *Natural Law and the Theory of Society, 1500–1800* (Cambridge, 1923).

world a 'church-culture', and to increasing respect for the independence and integrity of the various spheres of culture and institutions of society.[101] But, it must be stressed, he did not abandon the ideal of an ethically based compromise. Precisely because an inclusive compromise in the thomistic sense is no longer possible, the need for a new ethical compromise was in Troeltsch's view all the more pressing.[102] And that compromise, while more limited in scope and more complicated in structure,[103] would be arrived at in much the same way that the earlier one had been effected: namely, through a reshaping and reinterpretation of the traditions, both secular and religious, in terms of which modern western society has been formed and by which it continues to be influenced.[104] Troeltsch, however, seems not to have been fully aware of a major difference between his account of the earlier synthesis and his call for a new 'creative compromise' between christianity and modern society.

As regards the thomistic synthesis, compromise was said by Troeltsch to have been merely an unintended by-product, and not the principal goal of theological construction.[105] But, in the *Soziallehren*, Troeltsch also commends to his readers the notion of compromise as a legitimate goal of theology. Just as it had done in various ways in the past, albeit unconsciously, christianity is now urged firmly to seek a new basis for accommodation or 'Anpassung' with the modern world.[106] This same

---

[101] This is especially evident in the *Soziallehren* (pp. 983 ff) and in *Der Historismus und seine Überwindung*. In earlier writings, however, Troeltsch had stressed the necessity for a religious foundation for culture. (See *Die Bedeutung des Protestantismus*, p. 92) Later, religion was treated increasingly as one element among others, all of which make unique but interlocking contributions to culture.
[102] *Gesammelte Schriften*, I, 982.
[103] As suggested, e.g., in *Historismus und seine Überwindung*, pp. 52 ff.
[104] This is in fact the goal of the 'cultural synthesis' advocated by Troeltsch in *Der Historismus und seine Probleme*, pp. 71 ff, 164 ff. This synthesis, too, would have only temporary validity, but it would — if effective — give structure to meaning and values while it lasted. Cf. *Gesammelte Schriften*, IV, 297 ff, as well as *Der Historismus und seine Überwindung*, p. 60.
[105] *Gesammelte Schriften*, I, 203; cf. *Das historische in Kants Religionsphilosophie*, p. 59, and *Die Absolutheit des Christentums und die Religionsgeschichte*, Rendtorff collection, p. 131.
[106] *Gesammelte Schriften*, I, 986. Cf. also 'Protestantisches Christentum und Kirche in der Neuzeit', p. 372.

recommendation even more urgently dominates his major post-war works, *Der Historismus und seine Probleme* and *Der Historismus und seine Überwindung*, in both of which synthesis and compromise are more often than not held up as proper objectives, rather than merely tolerated as unfortunate by-products of some more serious undertaking. It seems to have been his view then that it was a time too important for theology in the narrow sense: it must become *Ethik* in Schleiermacher's sense — that is, philosophy of culture — and play its part in laying foundations for a new 'conscious and constructive' European synthesis which would overcome the threatened anarchy of values and beliefs. And that is how Troeltsch saw the situation shortly before his death in 1923. Whilst perhaps more urgently touted in his post-war writings, similar recommendations are made in some of his earlier writings, including *Die Bedeutung des Protestantismus für die Entstehung der modernen Welt*. Having distinguished between 'old' and 'new' protestantism, Troeltsch there underscores the importance of the developments in recent times whereby protestantism had become a religion of culture, a 'Bildungsreligion'.[107]

Troeltsch was above all a proponent of what we ordinarily call *Kulturprotestantismus*, which came under assault from all sorts of directions in the years immediately following the first world war.[108] Important though some of those assaults may have been, it was later events which would effect the heaviest damage upon this position. In an emotional sense, if no other, the greatest single challenge in this century to the *kulturprotestantisch* tradition was the attempted synthesis of christianity and the then-prevailing 'unity of cultural values' by the *deutsche Christen* and related groups within German protestantism.[109] Perhaps the most coherent and intelligent apologia for the stand taken by such groups after 1933 is to be found in Emanuel Hirsch's *Die gegenwärtige, geistige Lage*, a slim volume which was originally delivered as lectures at the University of Göttingen.[110]

---

[107] *Die Bedeutung des Protestantismus*, p. xx.

[108] Despite several minor historical errors, George Rupp's short monograph on *Culture Protestantism: German Liberal Theology at the Turn of the Twentieth-Century* (Missoula, Montana, 1977) is a helpful attempt to reassess this movement.

[109] For a competent analysis of the so-called 'German Christians', see K. Meier, *Die deutschen Christen* (3rd. ed.; Halle and Göttingen, 1967).

[110] Göttingen, 1934. In order to understand how Hirsch came to the position which he propounded in 1934, it is necessary to read as well his earlier volume entitled

However firmly its author may have repudiated the programmes of theological mediation proffered by the 'white-haired theologians', *Die gegenwärtige, geistige Lage* can itself be interpreted only as first and foremost an essay in mediating theology.[111] In the final chapter especially,

---

Deutschlands Schicksal (Göttingen, 1921). Hirsch himself stressed the connexion between those two books both in *Die gegenwärtige, geistige Lage* and in his letter to Stapel which was printed in *Christliche Freiheit und politische Bindung* (Hamburg, 1934). For Hirsch's later reflections on the place of *Deutschlands Schicksal* in his own intellectual development, see 'Meine Wendejahre (1916–21)', *Freies Christentum*, nr. 12 (1 December 1951), pp. 5–6. On Hirsch's 'political theology', see Klaus Scholder, *Die Kirchen und das Dritte Reich*, vol. I: *Vorgeschichte und Zeit der Illusionen, 1918–1934* (Frankfurt, 1977), pp. 127–33, 531 ff *et passim*, and G. Schneider-Flume, *Die politische Theologie Emanuel Hirschs* (Bern and Frankfurt, 1971). There is unfortunately no full-scale analysis of Hirsch's general contribution to modern theology, though a helpful sketch is available in Ulrich Neuenschwander, *Denker des Glaubens*, vol. II (Gütersloh, 1974), pp. 9–36.

[111] It might be wondered if Hirsch can in any proper sense be counted among the 'mediating theologians'. Obviously he could not be so regarded if we were to follow Johannes Wirsching and rigidly restrict the term to a narrow historical period in the nineteenth century. But, even if the phrase be used in the broader sense which was introduced above in chapter one – so that Tillich and Troeltsch are also to be classed as mediation theologians – doubts may still arise as to the appropriateness of including Hirsch within the bounds of *Vermittlungstheologen*. It must be admitted that even as a student at Berlin, Hirsch could not fully accept the then-prevailing 'liberal theology'. [See 'Meine theologische Anfänge', *Freies Christentum*, nr. 10 (1 October 1951), pp. 2–4]. And, later he explicitly rejected the ideal of 'Bildungsreligion' which he associated with 'bürgerliche Religiosität'. [See, e.g., Der *Weg der Theologie* (Stuttgart, 1937), p. 12, *Die gegenwärtige, geistige Lage*, pp. 112, 134, and *Christliche Freiheit und politische Bindung*, p. 15] Even so, there are three reasons which would seem to justify his inclusion within the broader sense of 'mediating theology'. First, his understanding of the theological task is taken over from Schleiermacher. At one point, he even seems to support what the *Kulturprotestanten* made of Schleiermacher. (See *Geschichte der neuern evangelischen Theologie*, V, 156!) Second, a prominent place in his theological writings is given over to *Ethik* and, more specifically, to what today is popularly called 'political theology'. As a result of the first world war, Hirsch later recollected, he vowed not merely to do theology 'in the narrow sense', but to do theology in conscious relation to the historical crisis of the German people. (See, 'Meine Wendejahre') Third, there is in all of Hirsch's

Hirsch reiterates over and over again that 'protestant theology and church and the present moment in the life of the people and of the nation belong together'. What is meant by this *zusammengehören*?

Sometimes Hirsch seems to be saying only that the present moment is ambiguous, that a number of possibilities are latent within it and that it is the responsibility of christians to confront the age with the gospel of Christ so that it is not allowed to fall into secularism and unbelief. Hirsch becomes almost homiletical in warning his students and readers that 'one day God will ask us what we did with the possibilities of this moment'.[112] But, more is claimed for 'this moment' when he asserts that God is at work in the reawakening, in 'the new beginning and the new hope', of the German people, and that the task of theology in the present is to join in and to support this new work which the Lord of history is now doing. He admits that such a decision is a matter of risk and of daring, without any guarantees, but adds that the failure to take the risk, the failure to affirm the new movement, would make one guilty of having failed to respond to the Lord of history and to what he is doing in and through the German people.

There is yet one other sense in which protestant christianity and 'the present moment' are said to belong together. The fate of protestantism and the fate of Germany are said to be bound up together in such a way that the health of the one is necessary for the health of the other, the demise of the one entails the demise of the other. 'Unlike the Catholic church', Hirsch asserts, 'our protestant christianity has no possibility of life independent of the destiny of the German people'.[113] Consequently, the 'death-struggle' in which Germany has become involved is also 'death-struggle' for protestant

---

theological work – historical as well as systematic – the persistent attempt to mediate between history and the present, between 'christianity' and 'humanity', between autonomous reason and faith. This moment in Hirsch's work is rightly stressed by Neuenschwander in *Denker des Glaubens*. But, a final word of caution: in saying that *Die gegenwärtige, geistige Lage* is classifiable as a piece of mediating theology, I do not intend – as Barth might have intended – thereby to condemn the whole mediating theological tradition 'from Schleiermacher to Troeltsch'. Nor, in classifying Hirsch's thought as 'political theology' do I intend – as Scholder might intend – thereby to condemn all varieties of political theology, past and present. See *Die Kirchen und das Dritte Reich*, I, 133, *et passim*.

[112] *Die gegenwärtige, geistige Lage*, p. 135.
[113] *Ibid.*, p. 134.

christianity. The emancipation and bursting-forth of the new age, he continues, will also mean the emancipation and bursting-forth of protestant christianity. But, compare this with Troeltsch's earlier claim that, since christianity has become the religion of Europe, the future of christianity stands or falls with the future of European culture.[114]

Such emphases as these allowed the dialectical theologians who took the side of the so-called Confessing Church to identify the programme projected by Troeltsch and the cultural protestants with that projected by Hirsch and the *deutsche Christen*, thereby giving new impetus and plausibility to Barth's earlier and independent rejection of *Kulturprotestantismus* and its theologies of mediation.

Troeltsch was for Barth the epitome of cultural protestantism and the theology of 'the circle of friends of *Die christliche Welt*'. He symbolised for Barth the end (in both senses) of that *cul-de-sac* in which he regarded christian theology as having been travelling at least since Schleiermacher. In his well-known review of Overbeck's posthumously published collection *Christentum und Kultur*,[115] Barth recalled having heard Troeltsch read a paper in the Aarau in 1911[116] 'with the dark foreboding that it had become impossible to advance any farther in the dead-end street where we were strolling in relative comfort.'[117]

Whilst he may have had misgivings in 1911, his decisive break with the theological tradition of the nineteenth century is said by Barth to have occurred a few years later.[118] In one account of that break, two precipitating factors are cited by Barth: Ernst Troeltsch gave up his chair in systematic theology at Heidelberg to become professor of philosophy and culture at Berlin[119] and, secondly, 'almost all' Barth's former professors are said to

---

[114] *Christian Thought*, p. 24; *Historismus und seine Überwindung*, pp. 76–7.
[115] (Basel, 1919). Regarding Barth's interpretation of Overbeck, see A. Pfeiffer, *Franz Overbecks Kritik des Christentums* (Göttingen, 1975), pp. 70–97.
[116] Correcting Barth's text, which reads '1910' – this, however, is clearly a mistake. See W. Groll, *Ernst Troeltsch und Karl Barth – Kontinuität im Widerspruch* (Munich, 1976).
[117] Cited from *Theology and Church* (New York, 1962), pp. 60–1.
[118] A point confirmed by his recently published sermons from 1913 and 1914 in the *Gesamtausgabe* (Zürich, 1976, 1974).
[119] On Troeltsch's appointment to the chair in Berlin, see U. Pretzel, 'Ernst Troeltschs Berufung an die Berliner Universität', *Studium Berolinense* (Berlin, 1960), pp. 507–14.

have signed the so-called 'Manifesto of the German Intellectuals' in support of the war policy.[120] 'In despair over what this indicated about the signs of the time', Barth continued in what seems something of a *non sequitur*, 'I suddenly realised that I could not any longer follow either their ethics and dogmatics or their understanding of the Bible and of history'.[120a] And most of Barth's writings during the Weimar Republic, from the *Römerbrief* onwards, can be regarded as a frontal attack against 'their' theology and 'their' ethics. Though the so-called 'dialectical theology' gained almost steadily in influence during the early- and mid-1920's, serious differences among its various representatives soon fragmented the movement.[121] Barth himself came to the view that their early co-operation had been in some cases a mistake from the beginning. Although the definitive history of those days remains to be written, many would perhaps agree with the judgment that Barth's lasting influence was enormously strengthened ba the new challenge faced by German christianity after 1933.[122] Among other things, the new situation gave new persuasiveness to Barth's earlier attack upon all sorts of 'natural theology', which for him included 'Kulturtheologie'.

Barth's renewed attack upon cultural protestantism after 1933 comes, not only in the debate with Brunner or in the various issues of *Theologische Existenz Heute*, but also in the *Kirchliche Dogmatik*, especially the section on the knowability of God. There Barth gives a most interesting commentary on the first article of the Barmen Confession. His attack there upon cultural protestantism comes in the form of a tongue-in-cheek 'defence' of such theologians as Hirsch. In effect, Barth argues — however unfairly — that there is no basis for disallowing the new combination by such theologians as Hirsch of christianity with a nationalism of race[123] since there were clear precedents throughout the history of theology for

---

[120] But, see W. Härle, „Der Aufruf der 93 Intellektuellen und Karl Barths Bruch mit der liberalen Theologie', *ZThKirche*, LXXII (1975), 207–24.

[120a] Cited from *The Humanity of God* (Richmond, 1960), p. 14.

[121] Concerning this fragmentation, see C. Gestrich, *Neuzeitliches Denken und die Spaltung der dialektischen Theologie* (Tübingen, 1977).

[122] But, see H. Prolingheuer, *Der Fall Karl Barth, 1934–1935* (Neukirchen, 1977)! Cf. K. G. Steck, „Der Einfluß Karl Barths in der Bekennenden Kirche Deutschlands seit 1935', *EvTheol*, XXXVIII (1978), 252–68.

[123] Hirsch in fact claims to take 'Rasse und Blut' metaphorically to mean 'Volk und Staat'. *Die gegenwärtige, geistige Lage*, pp. 34–5. But, see pp. 22 ff.

synthesising christianity with prevailing cultural beliefs and values. And, he continues, within the context of German cultural history there were good reasons for this particular synthesis.

> If it was [sic] admissible and right and perhaps even orthodox to combine the knowability of God in Jesus Christ with His knowability in nature, reason and history, the proclamation of the Gospel with all kinds of other proclamations – and this had been the case, not only in Germany, but in the Church in all lands for a long time – it is hard to see why the German Church should not be allowed to make its own particular use of the procedure. And the fact that it did so with customary German thoroughness is not really a ground of reproach. What the 'German Christians' wanted and did was obviously along a line which had for long enough been acknowledged and trodden by the Church of the whole world: the line of the Enlightenment and Pietism, of Schleiermacher, Richard Rothe and Ritschl.[124]

It was perhaps sheer oversight that Troeltsch was not mentioned here as well, for he was typically included by Barth in such listings.[125] But, in any case, the framers of the Barmen Confession came to oppose not only this particular combination, this particular 'cultural synthesis', but they came to oppose every combination, every 'cultural synthesis' in which christianity might be asked to serve as a partner. In the light of its context and of subsequent developments, this radical negation of the tradition of mediating theology cannot be dismissed flippantly as no more than an instance of one-sided dogmatism. Nor can Ernst Fuchs's admittedly ironical question in 1944, 'But how do things stand today.... with the European cultural synthesis demanded by Troeltsch?', be dismissed as no more than cynical rhetoric.[126]

Every contemporary suggestion, whether merely implicit or fully explicit, simply to revive the *Kulturtheologie* of the protestant theologians

---

[124] Cited from *Church Dogmatics*, II/1 (Edinburgh, 1957), p. 174.
[125] Cf., e.g., *Protestant Theology in the Nineteenth Century* (London, 1972), pp. 307, 308, 361, *et passim*. For an assessment of Troeltsch's fate at the hands of these theologians, see Robert Morgan, 'Ernst Troeltsch and the Dialectical Theology', in *Ernst Troeltsch and the Future of Theology*, pp. 33–77.
[126] Cited from James M. Robinson, *A New Quest of the Historical Jesus* (London, 1959), p. 82.

of mediation stands condemned by such questions. One cannot simply resuscitate the theological programmes of Schleiermacher and Troeltsch (nor of Hegel, Rothe and Ritschl!) as if none of this had happened, as if there had been no Emanuel Hirsch, no Karl Barth. A 'theology of mediation' is a live option today if and only if Barth can be answered and the ghost of Emanuel Hirsch exorcised. Can Schleiermacher's dilemma be resolved in such a way that these conditions are met? This is precisely what Paul Tillich set out to do, in part, by means of his concept of the correlation of 'the present situation' and 'the christian message'. (Cf. ST. I. 3–8)

What Barth had earlier regarded as a *cul-de-sac*, Tillich regarded as the *Hauptstraße*, not only of modern protestant theology, but of all theology worthy of its name. According to Tillich, the object of theology has always been mediation: 'The term "theology of mediation" is almost a tautology, for a theology that does not mediate the tradition is no theology. In this sense I would defend every theologian who is accused of being a theologian of mediation, and I myself would cease being a theologian altogether if I had to abandon the work of mediation'. (PNT, 209) But, more specifically, Tillich's method of correlation is an effort to revitalise the tradition of the mediating theologians in such a way that due account is taken of the serious questions forced on that tradition by Barth's attempted diastasis of religion and culture on the one side and Hirsch's abortive attempt at mediation on the other. As we shall see in chapter six especially, this two-fold challenge had a significant impact upon the development of Tillich's theological methodology. Yet, that challenge did not dissuade Tillich from attempting to construct a theology of mediation. Rather, it intensified his effort to resolve the dilemma implied in Schleiermacher's call for a new alliance between christianity and culture. In the wake of 1933, Hirsch accused Tillich of having sided with Barth, to which Tillich replied that he sided neither with Barth nor with Hirsch, but sought instead to show 'a third way' between the two of them.[127] *Correlation* is fundamental to that third way, and to Tillich's attempt to revitalise the theology of mediation.

As 'alliance' had been Schleiermacher's formal principle of mediation and 'compromise' Troeltsch's, 'correlation' became Tillich's mediating

---

[127] 'Um was es Geht: Antwort an Emanuel Hirsch', *Theologische Blätter*, XIV (1935), col. 118.

principle between theology and culture. 'Philosophy and theology are not separated, and they are not identical, but they are correlated, and their correlation is the methodological problem of a Protestant theology.' (PE, xxiii; HCT, 293) Although in this particular instance Tillich refers explicitly to the correlation only of *philosophy* and theology, it is clear from his work as a whole that 'correlation' is more inclusive than this would seem to suggest, that in fact it is intended to apply to the relationship between theology and the whole of culture. (cf. ST. I. 62f; TC, 68–75, 112–26) *The Courage to Be*, for instance, should be regarded as Tillich's attempt concretely to make correlations between psychoanalysis and theology. Yet, for reasons which will be considered in the next two chapters, philosophy has a certain primacy in Tillich's concept of culture: philosophy is regarded – on one account at least – as the expression of the self-understanding of an age or of a people. And it is that self-understanding which is placed in correlation by Tillich with the christian gospel.

Tillich sometimes defines the object of theology as the mediation between 'the christian message' and the present cultural 'situation': '. . . the task of theology is mediation, mediation between the eternal criterion of truth as it is manifest in the picture of Jesus as the Christ and the changing expressions of individuals and groups, their varying questions and their categories of perceiving reality.' (PE, ix) Elsewhere he speaks of theology's 'moving back and forth between two poles', i.e. the christian message and the cultural context, 'the eternal truth of Christianity's foundation and the temporal situation in which the eternal truth must be received.' (ST. I. 3; cf. ST. III. 185ff) Both poles are said to be necessary to the theological task so that the theologian is regarded by Tillich as having done his job properly if and only if 'message and situation are related in such a way that neither of them is obliterated.' (ST. I. 8)

Though we must consider the terms in greater detail in subsequent chapters, it is nonetheless necessary here to offer a preliminary indication as to the meaning of 'message' and 'situation'. By *situation* Tillich means what he called the 'totality of man's creative self-interpretation in a special period'. (ST. I. 4) This self-interpretation is to be found in the various spheres of cultural life, including the scientific and artistic, the ethical and the social, the economic and the political. These are the 'forms' or the 'structures' in which the self-understanding of an age is expressed. Tillich is somewhat less specific as to what he means by the *eternal message* of christianity. It would not be unfair to describe it as systematically elusive.[128] Though he makes various suggestions at one time or another, it would seem that the 'message' — which on the whole he tends to prefer to Kerygma — is identifiable in some sense with the confession 'Jesus is the Christ'. This would seem to hold, for example, for the quotations in the previous paragraph. And Tillich would seem to have more than Hegel in mind when he noted that 'the universal synthesis between Christianity and the modern mind stands and falls with the christological question.' (PNT, 134) Nor is it mere rhetoric when in the *Systematic Theology* he indicates that christology constitutes 'the heart of every Christian theology' (ST. II. vii) or when he claims that the confession Jesus is the Christ 'contains in some way the whole theological system'. (ST. III. 201) If the confession 'Jesus is the Christ' is not itself the christian 'message', it is certainly regarded by Tillich as both a necessary and a sufficient condition for the affirmation of that message. (cf. ST. II. 97) From these entirely preliminary remarks about Tillich's conception of 'situation' and 'message', it is clear that more systematic attention is required both of his culture theory and of his christology before we shall be in a position to assess the adequacy of Tillich's notion of correlation as a possible key to solving the methodological dilemma. The concept of culture will be dealt with at length in chapter four and Tillich's christology will receive attention in chapter six.[129]

---

[128] J. Buchter offers two reasons why the character of the 'message' is less clearly defined than the 'situation': first, that Tillich — over against the purely 'kerygmatic theology' — is at great pains to justifiy the role of the 'situation' in theology, the role of the 'kerygma' not being controversial nor requiring justification; secondly, that the character of the christian message is such that it is more elusive and less capable of clear definition than is the 'situation'. ‚Daher ist die Botschaft nicht direkt faßbar, vielmehr gibt es so viele nur in einer konkreten Situation gültige Antworten der Botschaft, wie es jeweils konkrete Fragen des Menschen gibt. Deshalb kann Tillich auch hier nicht den Begriff der Botschaft allgemeingültig definieren ... Botschaft gibt es also nur jeweils als konkrete Botschaft in Beantwortung einer konkreten Frage, aber nicht irgendwie „an sich".' *Die Kriterien der Theologie im Werke Paul Tillichs* (Bonn, 1975), pp. 90, 91. Compare this with Tillich's own claim that ‚unsere Antworten müssen so viele Formen haben, wie es Fragen und Situationen gibt.' GW. VIII. 270.

[129] See also my article 'Is Jesus Necessary for Christology: An Antinomy in Tillich's Theological Method', in *Christ, Faith and History: Cambridge Essays in Christology*, eds. S. W. Sykes and J. P. Clayton (Cambridge, 1972), pp. 147–63.

Tillich frames one of the questions addressed by him in his method of correlation in the following terms: 'Can the Christian message be adapted to the modern mind without losing its essential and unique character?' (ST. I. 7) But, this is merely another way of defining the dilemma set by Schleiermacher and addressed by the theologians of mediation. And it is this problem which Tillich persisted in attacking – despite Hirsch, despite Barth – in all his work after as well as before 1933. This holds especially for his *Systematic Theology*. As Schleiermacher had done before him, Tillich attempted to construct 'an honest theology of cultural high standing'. (ST. I. 7) And he sought to do so by means of his much-discussed 'method of correlation'.

Not only have theologians failed to agree regarding the significance of Tillich's method of correlation, they have furthermore failed to agree as to what is meant by 'correlation' in that method. Nor is this state of affairs entirely the fault of Tillich's would-be interpreters: for Tillich himself failed to clarify sufficiently and to disentangle carefully the multiple senses in which he used the term.

When setting out to define meanings of words in his writings, Paul Tillich would typically offer an etymological analysis from which he would then attempt to derive the contemporary meaning of the term in question. Or he would set out to define the 'essential' meaning of a word and then subsume all of its instances under that essence. Sometimes, as in *Love, Power and Justice*, he combined both approaches, thereby attempting to derive the 'essential' meaning of a word from its 'root meaning'. (GW. XI. 143 ff) But he followed neither of these procedures when he came to delineate the meanings of the word 'correlation'. In that, and only in that case,[130] he set out instead to link his special usage of 'correlation' as a technical term of relation with its usage in ordinary language. (ST. I. 60–1) This departure from normal practice was possibly intended as a gesture toward linguistic philosophy, the dominant philosophical tradition within the anglo-saxon world in which Tillich had done his theologising since 1933. The result, however, might not be found entirely satisfactory by an analytic philosopher. I shall try to show why.

In the first volume of the *Systematic Theology*, Tillich distinguishes three ordinary senses of the term 'correlation': the 'statistical' correspon-

---

[130] But, see ST. III. 21–5, 67.

dence of different series of data, as in statistical charts; the 'logical' interdependence of notions, 'as in polar concepts': the 'real' or 'factual' interconnexions between entities or events in 'structural wholes'. (ST. I. 60)

It is worth noting that, not only does Tillich not tell us the etymology of 'correlation', neither does he set out to define the 'essence' of a correlative relation. Rather, he offers a simple list of different sorts of correlative relationships, a variety of different uses of the word 'correlation'. And Tillich is surely right to distinguish these three uses as *different* uses in the sense of being instances of different kinds and not merely different instances of the same kind. For 'correlation' is clearly not being used in the same sense when one speaks of the correlation of wages and prices, the correlation of 'up' and 'down' and the correlation of factors and events and personalities which led to the resignation of Richard Nixon. Although one might want to add to Tillich's list of possible sorts of correlative relations, taking into account other ways we ordinarily use the word 'correlation' and its cognates, one must grant that Tillich was right to have made at least those distinctions which he did make.

Tillich then claims that each of these three sorts of correlative relations has 'important applications' when the word 'correlation' is used in theology: 'There is correlation in the sense of correspondence between religious symbols and that which is symbolized by them. There is a correlation in the logical sense between concepts denoting the human and those denoting the divine. There is a correlation in the factual sense between man's ultimate concern and that about which he is ultimately concerned.' (ST. I. 60) In the German edition of the *Systematische Theologie*, 'concern' is replaced by the more obviously passive concept of 'being grasped'. Otherwise, however, the English-language text is faithfully followed: 'Es gibt Korrelation in dem Sinne der Entsprechung zwischen religiösen Symbolen und dem, was durch sie symbolisiert wird. Es gibt Korrelation im logischen Sinne zwischen Begriffen, sie sich auf menschliche Bereiche und solche, die sich auf Göttliches beziehen. Und es besteht eine reale Korrelation zwischen dem Zustand des religiösen Ergriffenseins des Menschen und dem, was ihn ergreift.' (STd. I. 74f)

Tillich's attempted translation of 'correlation' from its ordinary usage to its usage as a special theological term is perplexing. For it is not altogether clear that the two series of uses correspond with one another in the way that Tillich seems to claim. We shall look briefly at each in turn in order to clarify the nature of the perplexity.

Tillich's concept(s?) of symbol is many sided and has been the object of much critical attention, especially within anglo-american philosophy of religion.[131] When discussing relations between symbols and that which they symbolise, Tillich makes no clear distinction between the different kinds of relations which obtain between a word and its object, a work of art and that which it represents or expresses, a symbolic object or gesture (such as a flag or a salute) and what it represents, a natural object or process or occurrence (such as a tree or a flood) and what it signifies to a particular group of people. But, these are very different kinds of relationship, each of which presents different sorts of philosophical problems. For our present purposes, however, it is sufficient to limit our comments about 'symbols and that which they symbolise' to selected features of the relationship between words and objects.

One might very well want to speak, as Tillich sometimes does speak, of the correlation between a word and an object, but that would hardly be the very same sort of correlation as between 'different series of data, as in statistical charts'. Statistical correlation analysis, which later came to be called 'multi-variant analysis', was an attempt rigorously to measure the degree of association between one variable factor and one or more other variables.[132] It was first used in genetics, and later used in economics and the other social sciences. Practitioners of such techniques sometimes shy away from making claims of causal connexion between the variables, preferring instead to speak of degrees of statistical regularity. This is the weaker sense of correlation analysis. Tillich specifically states elsewhere that this is not a sense in which he uses the word 'correlation'. (ST. II. 13) We must assume, therefore, that he refers to 'statistical correspondence' in the stronger sense of causal connexion. This, however, makes his attempted 'theological application' of *correlation* in this particular sense highly problematical.

The attempt to correlate, for instance, wage increases and rising prices is thought to be important because there is imagined to be a causal connexion between wages and prices, though the precise character and degree of that

---

[131] See, e.g., W. L. Rowe, *Religious Symbols and God: A Philosophical Study of Tillich's Theology* (Chicago, 1968), and the symposium edited by S. Hook, *Religious Experience and Truth* (London, 1962).

[132] See M. Ezekiel, 'Correlation', *Encyclopedia of the Social Sciences*, ed. E. R. A. Seligman and A. Johnson (New York, 1931), vol. IV, pp. 438–44.

connexion might be in dispute among the experts. But, would one want to claim that there is also a causal connexion of an analogous sort between a word and its object? One might go so far as to say that the existence of an object occasions the need for it to be named. There is here a kind of correlation between object and word, but it is hardly the sort of connexion as exists between two series of data in statistical charts. Generally speaking, the correlation of words and objects is more nearly habitual than causal in nature: we habitually use just this word as a name for that object, so that one might want to say that this particular name is habitually correlated with that particular object. Not all words, moreover, are even capable of being correlated with objects. For not all words are names of objects. We do all kinds of things with words — also within specifically religious contexts! — besides name things. It is, therefore, a mistake to think that the meaning of every word is an object. Consequently, some philosophers have suggested that it is better to correlate a word with its context, than with an object. This recommendation has direct and immediate consequences for the analysis of religious uses of language.[133] Granting that not all words are names, one might still be tempted to argue that all substantives, at least, are always correlated with an object. Yet, this, too, would be a mistake; the temptation must be resisted. Just why it is a mistake can be illustrated simply, if also slightly flippantly, by reference to Lewis Carroll's book *Through the Looking Glass*. Alice is there asked by the White King whether someone were coming along the street. '"I see nobody on the road", said Alice. "I only wish *I* had such eyes", the King remarked in a fretful tone. "To be able to see Nobody! And at that distance too! Why, it's as much as *I* can do to see real people, by this light!"'[134] The existence of a substantitive, such as 'nobody' or 'nothing', sometimes misleads us into thinking that there must be a substance or an object correlated with the substantive. But, 'nobody' is not just a very elusive or hard to get to know 'somebody'. Nor is 'non-being' the name of a very deeply profound sort of 'being'.[135] And this example shows that there need be no connexion,

---

[133] See, e.g., my survey article 'Sprache, Sinn und Verifizierungsverfahren', *Philosophisches Jahrbuch*, LXXXV (1978), 144–62.

[134] *Through the Looking Glass* (Harmondsworth, 1962), p. 286.

[135] Remarking on the persistence of the doctrine of 'non-being' within the history of western philosophy, Quine has named that doctrine 'Plato's beard', in that 'it has proved tough, frequently dulling the edge of Occam's razor'. See *From a Logical Point of View* (2nd. ed.; New York, 1963), p. 2.

correlative or otherwise, between every substantive and an object, since not every substantive refers to an object, whether material or mental. Consequently, Tillich's first theological application of the word 'correlation' is problematic on two grounds: not every word has an object and even those which do are not correlated with their object in a way similar to two series of data in statistical charts. This is no less true of religious than of other uses of language.

Matters are almost equally problematic when we turn to the second usage of 'correlation' isolated by Tillich: namely, 'the logical interdependence of concepts, as in polar relations'. It is not altogether clear from the context precisely what is meant by 'logical interdependence'. Even so, by that phrase I shall here understand Tillich to mean *mutual implication*, such that one cannot speak of *a* without implying *b* and vice versa without making *a* (or *b*) logically self-contradictory or incoherent. There are a number of such pairs of terms which we ordinarily use, including over/under, up/down, in/out. Polarity, as is well known, plays an important role in Tillich's philosophical theology. Anyone with a basic knowledge of his *Systematic Theology* might have expected Tillich to cite as examples of this particular purported 'theological application' of the word 'correlation' some of the basic polar concepts of his ontology. One might have expected mention, for instance, of the subject-object structure of knowledge (ST. I. 75ff), the elements which constitute the basic structure of being (ST. I. 174ff), or the dialectic of essential and existential being. (ST. I. 202ff) Each of these examples would have been in its own way problematic and each would have required to have been dealt with individually as possible instances of just this sense of 'correlation'. Even so, it would not have been wholly incomprehensible to list them as examples of correlation in the sense of logical interdependence or of mutual implication. As an example of the theological application of this particular sense of correlation, however, Tillich cited something quite different. He adduced, namely, 'concepts denoting the human and those denoting the divine'. Tillich adds that this particular sense is utilised in his treatment of statements about the relations between God and world, as for instance in 'the correlation of the finite and the infinite'. (ST. I. 61) The problem of God-world relations and the problem of the relationship between finite and infinite cannot in Tillich's particular case be simply identified with one another, as he himself elsewhere acknowledged. (ST. I. 189ff) The two problems would, therefore, require separate analysis before coming to a decision about the appropriateness of this particular sense of correlation. Yet, this much can be said with reasonable confidence: whatever the precise relationship between 'God' and 'world' according to Tillich, it cannot be a relationship of mutual implication in the way that 'up' and 'down' mutually imply one another. For 'up' and 'down' are *reversible correlates* in the sense that 'up' is related to 'down' in just the same way that 'down' is related to 'up'. This cannot be the case as regards the relationship between 'God' and 'world'. For it belongs to the concept of God that God cannot be related to the world in just the same way that the world is related to God: God cannot be dependent upon the world in just the same way that the world is dependent upon God. Not all 'logical correlates', however, are reversible in the way that 'up' and 'down' are reversible. There are also *non-reversible correlates* like parent/son or daughter or like action/reaction in physics. It might be that the correlation of 'God' and 'world' is more akin to these examples. Yet there is a problem here as well. It would be nonsense to speak of a parent without a son/daughter or, within the framework of Newtonian physics, of a reaction without an action. In the case of both examples it belongs to the meaning of the words that each implies the other. But it would not be nonsense, even within the particular framework of Tillich's concept of God, to speak of God's having existed before the world existed or of his continuing to exist after the world's having possibly ceased to exist. It may be that God is precisely the God he is because the world exists, because he stands in relation to the world. (cf. ST. I. 271 ff; III. 283 ff, 420−3) Even so, it does not belong to the meaning of the words 'God' and 'world' that each without the other is logically incoherent or self-contradictory; but, this *is* the case as regards 'parent' and 'son' or 'daughter'. That Tillich may have important and persuasive things to say about the relationship between God and world is not being brought into question. Nor is it being denied that, in Tillich's theological system, the concepts of God and world stand in a correlative relationship with one another. However, they are not correlated with one another in the strict sense of mutual implication. The only point being advanced here is that Tillich inappropriately linked his specifically theological usage of the word 'correlation' to the ordinary usage of that word in the sense of 'the logical interdependence of concepts'.

Tillich also speaks of *correlation* in the sense of 'the real interdependence of things or events in structural wholes'. At first reading, this is highly reminiscent of Ernst Troeltsch's use of the word 'correlation' as a principle of historiography.[136] That, however, is not borne out by Tillich's theological application of 'correlation' in this third sense: namely, the relationship between 'man's ultimate concern and that about which he is ultimately concerned'. This particular 'application' causes some puzzlement. It may very well be the case that the relationship between 'ultimate concern' and its object is, as Tillich on at least one other occasion claims (ST. I. 12),[137] a correlative relation. But, one must wonder, can it be a correlative relation in the sense of 'real interdependence ... in a structural whole'? For instance, the constellation of forces and factors in a historical event is *contingent*, both in the sense that the same forces and factors could have combined in a slightly or even dramatically different way to produce results of a different sort and also in the sense that different forces and factors could have come into play. Anyone who followed the investigations during America's so-called 'Watergate' crisis will be well aware of the decisive role that contingent factors and sheer accident played in those investigations and in the eventual downfall of Richard Nixon. Yet, when Tillich attempts to elucidate his dark concept of 'ultimate concern', a quite different sort of connexion emerges between one's concern and the object of one's concern. Tillich seems to come very near to saying in more than once place that 'concern about the ultimate' and 'one's ultimate concern' mutually imply one another, so that ultimate concern is always concern about the ultimate. (cf. ST. I. 11–5; BR, 59) Now this is an aspect of Tillich's theology which is highly problematic, in and of itself, based as it is on the ambiguity of the term 'ultimate' and, more especially, the phrase 'ultimate concern'.[138] But, whatever sense can be given that phrase, on Tillich's account, the relationship between the concern and the 'object' of that concern in this case at least is more nearly a relationship of mutual implication than a relationship of contingent fact.

These then are some of the reasons why an analytic philosopher might not have found entirely satisfactory the particular way in which Tillich tried to relate his special use of 'correlation' as a technical term of relation to its variegated usage in ordinary language. He would not want to object to Tillich's having distinguished the three 'ordinary' uses as different senses of correlative relations, though he would probably want to add further

---

[136] See *Gesammelte Schriften*, vol. II, pp. 733, 737.
[137] The word 'correlation' does not occur in the corresponding passage in the German edition. See STd. I. 19.
[138] See below, chapter three, pp. 108–12.

distinctions to cover other sorts of 'ordinary' uses not mentioned by Tillich. Nor would he necessarily want to object to Tillich's having distinguished the three special senses in which he committed himself to using the term theologically, though an analytic philosopher might want to express doubts about this or that detail and though he would want to look at the way Tillich actually used the word in practice before taking a final decision as to the sufficiency of just those three distinctions.[139] In no circumstances, however, could he grant that the three 'ordinary' uses listed by Tillich correspond to his three 'special' uses in precisely the ways that Tillich claimed. He would, at the very least, press for further clarification about the meaning of 'correlation'.

An analytic philosopher could therefore only welcome Tillich's announced attempt in the introduction to the second volume of the *Systematic Theology* to 'restate' more clearly his conception of 'correlation' with a view toward defining more precisely what is to count as a correlative relationship. By the time he came to write that introduction, however, Tillich had changed tactics altogether by reverting to one of his more usual techniques of delineating the meaning of a term. Rather than attempting yet again to relate his usage of the word 'correlation' to the range of its uses in ordinary language, he there offered instead an account of its essential features. Rather than *particular cases* of correlative relations, we are now presented a *general theory* of what it is for any *a* to be correlated with any *b*. 'Correlation' is now to be understood in every case as 'the independence of two independent factors': 'It is not understood in the logical sense of quantitative or qualitative co-ordination of elements without causal relation, but it is understood as a unity of the dependence and the independence of two factors.' (ST. II. 13) It is not clear from the context whether this definition is intended to cover all the senses in which the term is to be used by Tillich or only some of those senses. Regardless of Tillich's intention, we shall soon see that this characterisation of the essential features of a correlative relation cannot cover all of the various senses in which Tillich customarily used 'correlation' in his writings. Nor would this seem to have been Tillich's intention when he 'restated' his concept of correlation in a single definition. For in the German translation of the *Systematische Theologie* the meaning of 'correlation' as the interdependence

---

[139] He would probably suspect from the outset that Tillich would use the word 'correlation' in more than just those three senses!

of two independent factors is even more narrowly restricted to the 'Einheit von Abhängigkeit und Unabhängigkeit zwischen existentiellen Fragen und theologischen Antworten.' (STd. II. 19) But this is only *one* of the various senses in which Tillich uses 'correlation' in his *Systematic Theology*. If the meaning of 'correlation' is to be restricted to the relationship between existential questions and theological answers, then what are we to make of Tillich's having, not just occasionally, but regularly used 'correlation' in other and sometimes very different sorts of contexts? Indeed, what are we to make of the three main senses of 'correlation' which Tillich himself distinguished, and in my view rightly so, in volume one of his *Systematic Theology*?

It may be that what Tillich *says about* the meaning of 'correlation' is a less reliable guide to its meaning in his thought than what Tillich *does with* that word in his writings.[140] Ironically, Tillich's attempt to clarify the meaning which he attached to the word 'correlation' may have been a major factor in many of his critics not having seen that Tillich's concept of correlation is far richer and far more subtle than the popularly conceived correlation of philosophical questions and theological answers. For it may have had the effect of discouraging some critics from attending to those other senses of 'correlation' which are not so easily assimilable into the correlation of philosophical questions and theological answers. But, that is only one of the several senses in which Tillich used 'correlation'.

Indeed, anyone who looks at the ways in which 'correlation' is used by Tillich must surely at first be thoroughly baffled by the quite casual and seemingly unreflective manner of much of its usage in his writings. For instance, at one point or another, each of the following is explicitly identified as a correlative relationship:

a) the correspondence between a word in one language with the word which would be used in a similar context in another language: '*Fatum* ("that which is foreseen") or *Schicksal* ("that which is sent"), and their English correlate "fate", designate a simple contradiction to freedom . . .' (ST. I. 185);

---

[140] It is perhaps not accidental that in his recent attempt to delineate Tillich's theological method, Schrader did not find very helpful Tillich's own account of his methodology. See *The Nature of Theological Argument*, 'Harvard Dissertations in Religion' (Missoula, Montana, 1975), p. xi.

b) the balance of the categories of space and time in a particular dimension of life: 'Under the dimension of self-awareness, spatiality is correlative with temporality' (ST. III. 316f; but cf. STd. III. 363);

c) the bondage between the two epistemic functions of reason: 'The term "shaping" in correlation to "receiving" points to what is usually called "practical" in the sense of Kant's "practical reason"' (K&B, 333);

d) the correspondence between 'self-affirmation of being' and 'the power of being': 'Every being affirms its own being. Its life is its self-affirmation — even if its self-affirmation has the form of self-surrender. Every being resists the negation against itself. The self-affirmation of a being is correlate to the power of being it embodies' (LPJ, 39–40);

e) the interdependence of the concepts of holiness and divinity: 'The holy and the divine must be interpreted correlatively. A doctrine of God which does not include a category of holiness . . . transforms the gods into secular objects whose existence is rightly denied by naturalism. On the other hand, a doctrine of the holy which does not interpret it as the sphere of the divine transforms the holy into something aesthetic-emotional . . .' (ST. I. 215);

f) the continuum between the history of revelation and the final revelation: '"The history of revelation" is a necessary correlate of final revelation. It should neither be leveled down to a history of religion nor be eliminated by a destructive supranaturalism' (ST. I. 138);

g) the parallelism between *agapē*-love among men with God's love for man: '*Agapē* between men and the *agapē* of God toward men correspond with each other, since the one is the ground of the other. But the *agapē* of man toward God falls outside this strict correlation' (ST. I. 281);

h) the interconnexions between certain overlapping concepts: '. . . the metaphor "level" (and such similar metaphors as "stratus" or "layer") must be excluded from any description of life processes . . . and be replaced by the metaphor "dimension", together with correlative concepts such as "realm" and "grade".' (ST. III. 15; but cf. STd. III. 25)

These and other such examples all occur in the *Systematic Theology* or in writings published after the first volume of that work had appeared. The word 'correlation' is clearly being used in a great variety of ways in these examples, such that it would be impossible to give a single definition of 'correlation' which could encompass them all: the pairs of elements involved are simply not all correlative in the same way. Nor are they all correlative in just the ways that questions and answers are correlative.

An even greater variety is evidenced in Tillich's earlier works, where the following are mentioned explicitly as correlative relations: the relationship between the divine and the demonic (GW. X. 23) or between the holy and the profane, (GW. VIII. 50) the bond between grace and revelation, (GW. I. 359) the interaction between self and world, (GW. IX. 156 *et passim*) the mutual implication of myth and cult, (GW. V. 189) as well as the historical coincidence of skepticism and appeals to revelation or the collapse of rationalism and a return to supranaturalism. (GW. VIII. 32,40) Confronted with this virtual rag-bag of different kinds of relations, one may be forgiven for having been tempted to conclude that Tillich would describe every relation as a correlative relation. This conclusion, however, cannot be supported.

If it is not the case that all the senses in which Tillich uses the word 'correlation' are capable of being reduced to a single meaning, it is also not the case that the main senses in which he regularly uses the term in his *Systematic Theology* are wholly unrelated to one another. They overlap in various kinds of ways and collectively considered form a fairly coherent family of uses.

The first main use which Tillich makes of 'correlation' is the *ontological* and this use has two quite different senses: the correlation of *God and world* and the correlation of *self and world*. These two must be distinguished as different senses because, as Tillich constantly stresses, God is not related to the world in the way that things within the world are related to one another. (ST. I. 235 ff, 168 ff) But this means that God cannot be correlated with the world in just the way that things within the world, including persons, are correlated with one another. 'The holiness of God makes it impossible to draw him into the context of the ego-world and the subject-object correlation. He himself is the ground and meaning of this correlation, not an element within it.' (ST. I. 272; cf. 248) Nor is the correlative relationship between God and world their 'essential' relationship; it is a consequence of the disruption of their essential relationship. 'Correlation' here implies the distance between God and man which is a consequence of what Tillich called 'existential estrangement': 'In the human spirit's essential relation to the divine Spirit, there is no correlation, but rather, mutual immanence.' (ST. III. 114 *et passim*; I. 170f *et passim*; cf. GW. IX. 32, 156ff)

That this first main use of 'correlation' has different meanings has implications for the second, and closely related, use of that term in Tillich's theological system. Indeed, the *epistemological* use of correlation is said by him to be a function of the ontological. (ST. I. 168ff) Like the ontological use, the epistemological must also be similarly divided into the epistemic correlation of *subject and object* and the revelatory correlation of *revelation and its reception*. Both these senses have to do with the correlation between the human mind and reality external to that mind. Yet, they must nonetheless be distinguished as different senses of correlation because mind and reality are not in each case correlated in the same way. Since God is not an object among other objects in the world, he cannot be known in the way that objects are known. (ST. I. 204ff; cf. 171ff) And the correlation in which God manifests himself is not in Tillich's view reducible to the ordinary correlation between a knowing subject and the object of knowledge, even though revelation is said to contain a subjective element (ecstasy) and an objective element (miracle) in strict interdependence. (ST. I. 106ff, esp. 111–8) 'Correlation' in the epistemological sense is also a function of that existential disruption of the essential unity of God and world, self and world. That this is the case is emphasised by Tillich both in the way he handles the correlation between 'human questions' and 'divine answers', including his discussion of the traditional arguments for God's existence (ST. I. 204ff), and in the way he develops his theory of 'distance' and 'immediacy' in cognitive relations generally (ST. I. 94ff; cf. GW. IV. 107–17).

This *revelatory correlation* plays such a central role in Tillich's theology that it must be counted as the third main use of that term. A further distinction is required. Tillich writes about a *general* presence of revelatory correlations in the history of religions[141] and also the *specifically christian* revelatory correlation of Jesus as the christ and the reception of him as the christ. (ST. I. 127; cf. II. 97ff) These are not, however, different senses of correlation, only different instances of the revelatory correlation. The issues raised in each of the two cases are essentially the same. Yet, within both the general history of revelation and the christian revelation, which is treated as 'final revelation', (ST. I. 132–7) Tillich distinguishes two different senses of revelatory correlation: the one *original* and the other *dependent*.

---

[141] Instead of 'history of religion', Tillich preferred to speak of 'history of revelation'. See ST. I. 137ff.

The history of revelation indicates that there is a difference between original and dependent revelations. This is a consequence of the correlative character of revelation. An original revelation is a revelation which occurs in a constellation that did not exist before. This miracle and this ecstasy are joined for the first time. Both sides are original. In a dependent revelation the miracle and its original reception together form the giving side, while the receiving side changes as new individuals and groups enter the same correlation of revelation. (ST. I. 126)

These *are* different senses of correlation: for the two elements which in the first case are correlated with one another become in the second case the one component in every subsequent correlation based on that original revelatory correlation. Even so, these two senses of correlation have an important similarity in Tillich's view: 'Revelation, whether it is original or dependent, has revelatory power only for those who participate in it, who enter into the revelatory correlation.' (ST. I. 127)

Within a specifically christian context, this dependent revelatory correlation is very closely connected with the correlation between *message and situation*, which is the fourth main use of 'correlation' within Tillich's theology. This particular use of the term is perhaps most familiar in its association with the so-called 'method of correlation', a method which is also said by Tillich to allow philosophy and theology to be brought into proper relation. (cf. ST. I. vii, 62 *et passim*) But the relationship between theology and philosophy cannot be simply equated with the relationship between revelation and its reception or between the christian message and the human/cultural situation. Contrary to his own better judgment, Tillich did sometimes write as if each of these pairs of terms were the equivalent of the other. This lack of precision led to no little lack of clarity in much of the *Systematic Theology*, a lack of clarity about which many have complained.[142] Once a distinction is drawn between the alleged correlationship of philosophy and theology and that between situation and message, it becomes clearer that some of the standard objections most frequently leveled against 'the method of correlation' do not apply equally to

---

[142] For one attempt to bring order to the relations between Tillich's concepts of culture/religion, situation/message, philosophy/theology, see S. Wittschier, *Paul Tillich: Seine Pneuma-Theologie* (Nürnberg, 1975), p. 210, n. 14.

the purported correlation of philosophy and theology and to that between the cultural situation and the christian message.] For instance, a large number of people protested against what they took to be Tillich's attempt to limit the philosopher's task to raising questions which it was the theologian's job to answer. Leaving aside the issue of whether these protesters rightly understood Tillich's views, one could imagine that some of these same people would not want to protest with equal force against the thought that the christian message should in principle at least answer some of the perennial questions of human existence or some of the most urgent questions of a given cultural situation. It must be allowed that the problems of the relationship of philosophy and theology and of the relationship of culture and christianity impinge upon one another. Nor can it be denied that Tillich intended his method of correlation to have competency in both sorts of relationship. For various reasons, some of which will be given in chapters three and four, we will be principally concerned with the alleged correlation of the christian message and the cultural situation. Without denying that there are other aspects, this is at least one central aspect of the concept of correlation implied in Tillich's method of correlation.

This fourth main use of 'correlation' is the one which most nearly parallels Schleiermacher's notion of a 'perpetual alliance' and Troeltsch's idea of a 'creative compromise' between historical christianity and contemporary culture. That correlation is to be understood as Tillich's principle of mediation is made clear in the introduction to the *Systematic Theology*. Tillich writes there of the necessity of formulating a theological method 'in which message and situation are related in such a way that neither of them is obliterated. If such a method is found, the two centuries old question of "Christianity and the modern mind" can be attacked more successfully. The following system is an attempt to use the "method of correlation" as a way of uniting message and situation.' (ST. I. 8) Although each of the four main senses of 'correlation' is brought to bear upon aspects of the problem of the relationship between christianity and culture, this fourth sense is most explicitly associated with the methodological dilemma in modern theology. Consequently, it will be our principal object of interest. We shall want to determine whether Tillich's concept of correlation, considered in just this sense, constitutes in any way a resolution of Schleiermacher's dilemma. Given that just this sense of 'correlation' was defined by Tillich as 'an interdependence of two independent factors', we shall feel free in the remaining chapters to speak of the reciprocity condition and the autonomy condition as *the two conditions of a correlative relation*.

Before determining whether Tillich's concept of correlation satisfies both these conditions, however, a prior issue must be addressed. Since there are no relationships which do not relate, it is necessary to get a sharper view of that which Tillich seeks to bring into correlationship.

PART TWO
RELIGION AND CULTURE

CHAPTER THREE
RELIGION AND THE CONCEPT OF CORRELATION

'Correlation' in all of its main senses is brought to bear upon the problem of the relationship between religion and culture. But Tillich uses both 'religion' and 'culture' in various senses. The object of this and the following chapter is to determine in what ways these several senses of 'religion' and of 'culture' contribute to his concept of correlation. These two aspects of Tillich's thought are both problematic, but not for the same reasons.

'Religion' is treated at length by Tillich in his various writings and in the main the sorts of difficulties it presents are not the sort which might have been eradicated had Tillich only spelt out his theory in greater detail. Many of the most serious difficulties are inherent within the theory itself.

Although 'culture' is in some ways as central as 'religion' in Tillich's writings, he never worked out a theory of culture with the same thoroughness that he had worked out a theory of religion. Consequently, our task is in part to tease out this aspect of Tillich's thought in the hope of determining from the available fragments what shape his theory would take. One way to achieve this end is to determine where possible ways his remarks on culture relate to established uses of *Kultur* in those modern German philosophies of history and culture which largely influenced the formation of Tillich's own conception of culture.

Tillich's 'Two' Senses of Religion

Shortly after taking up his post as *Privatdozent* at the University of Berlin and not long after the appearance of the first edition of Barth's *Römerbrief*,[1] Tillich addressed the Berlin chapter of the Kant-Gesellschaft on the notion of a 'theology of culture'.[2] His lecture can hardly be said to

---
[1] Bern, 1919. Even so, the book appeared in December 1918.
[2] The address was held on 16 April 1919 and was published along with an essay by Gustav Radbruch in *Religionsphilosophie der Kultur*, 'Philosophische Vorträge

have had either the immediate or the long-term impact of Barth's commentary.³ Even so, 'Über die Idee einer Theologie der Kultur' can be seen in retrospect to have charted the direction Tillich's work would take him, even if not perhaps protestant theology as well, in the years ahead. The formative importance of that piece for his subsequent work was not missed by Tillich himself when in the preface to *Theology of Culture* he remarked how pleased he was to be able to adapt as the title for his new collection that of his 1919 address, adding that the problem of religion and culture had been central in most of his subsequent writings, including the *Systematic Theology*. (TC, v)

That early address was in fact and not merely in name a programmatic essay. Themes are introduced there which were to become in more developed and sometimes considerably modified form *Leitmotive* of Tillich's theological method. We shall be required to return to that address time and again throughout this and the remaining chapters. In this chapter, however, we are principally concerned with the distinction drawn there, and followed in most of Tillich's subsequent works, between at least two senses of 'religion'. He characteristically used the term 'religion' in a broad sense (religion$_1$) to designate a particular dimension – which he would later term 'the depth dimension' of every aspect of man's mental and cultural life, whether in the theoretical or the practical sphere. Religion$_1$ is the sense in which Tillich in that early address spoke of 'religion' as *experience of the unconditioned*⁴ as well as the sense in which he would later speak of

---

der Kant-Gesellschaft' (Berlin, 1919). It is reprinted in GW. IX. 13–31, from which all citations are to be made.

3   It did, nonetheless, attract some critical attention, most notably perhaps from Hans von Soden, who would later become one of Tillich's closest associates at Marburg. See von Soden's 'Kirchentheologie und Kulturtheologie', *ZThKirche*, II (1921), 468–77. According to one person who heard the lecture, it 'brought him instant recognition'. Hannah Tillich, *From Time to Time* (London, 1974), p. 102.

4   GW. IX. 18. By the mid-twenties, however, Tillich spoke no longer of 'experience of the unconditioned'. By then he preferred instead the phrase *directedness toward the unconditioned:* 'Religion ist Richtung auf das Unbedingte, Kultur ist Richtung auf die bedingten Formen und ihre Einheit.' (GW. I. 320) Leaving aside possible differences between *the experience of* the unconditioned and *directedness toward* the unconditioned, Tillich's concept of the 'Unconditioned' is itself notoriously obscure. Even so sympathetic an interpreter as J. L. Adams was forced to admit that Tillich used it as 'a universal solvent' which

'religion' as *ultimate concern*. He also used 'religion' in a second and narrower sense (religion$_2$) to specify that sphere of socio-cultural life which exists alongside the other spheres and is called 'the religious sphere'. It was in the sense of religion$_2$ that he would speak of 'a religion'. We shall come to see, however, that this is hardly more than a rough and ready distinction, that each of these 'two' senses is actually more various than Tillich would lead us to believe.

We shall also be concerned in this chapter with a second distinction made in 'Über die Idee einer Theologie der Kultur' which was at that time thought by Tillich to follow from his having differentiated two senses of religion, namely the distinction between 'cultural theology' and 'church theology'. (GW. IX. 27ff) Although at first regarded as a consequence of the distinction between religion$_1$ and religion$_2$, this second distinction was subsequently abandoned by Tillich first in favour of a distinction between 'philosophical theology' and 'kerygmatic theology' (PE, 83ff) and eventually in preference for that between 'apologetic theology' and 'kerygmatic theology'. (ST. I. 6ff) Even so, I shall hope to show in part three of this volume that the tension highlighted in that original distinction helps to illuminate a persistent tension within Tillich's theological programme.

'Correlation' is to be understood broadly as the sort of relationship which Tillich envisaged between religion and culture. Yet, he used the word 'religion' in more than one sense. It is imperative, therefore, to determine how these different senses of 'religion' figure in connexion with the notion of correlation. Does Tillich hold that religion in 'both' senses of the term stands in a correlative relationship to culture? Is it perhaps religion in only one of its senses which is thought to be correlatively related to the rest of culture? A further problem remains. Given that the distinction between the two sorts of theology mentioned in the 1919 address was put forward there as a consequence of the distinction between these senses of 'religion', we must also establish whether correlation is supposed to play a role in both sorts or only in one sort of theology. Is the method of correlation equally

---

is in fact wholly inadequate for the jobs it is forced to do. *Paul Tillich's Philosophy of Culture, Science and Religion* (New York, 1965), pp. 261, 263, *et passim*. But, see F. Wagner, 'Absolute Positivität: Das Grundthema der Theologie Paul Tillichs', *NeueZSysTh*, XV (1973), 173ff.

applicable to what in that address are referred to as 'cultural theology' and as 'church theology'?

It is not my intention to offer a full analysis of Tillich's concept of religion, a concept which has in any case attracted considerable attention elsewhere in the literature.[5] What is required, however, is that we attend specifically to those aspects of Tillich's concept of religion which have a significant bearing upon an analysis of his concept of correlation.

In the essay on the notion of a theology of culture Tillich distinguishes between 'the religious principle', which is said to be absolute but potential, and the 'specifically religious sphere of culture', which is said to be relative but actual. (GW. IX. 28f) It is not at all clear precisely what is meant there by 'the religious principle'.[6] Tillich could mean at least two things. First, he could be speaking simply of man's *capacity for revelation* which may or may not be actualised. He is clearly willing enough elsewhere to speak of a sort or religious apriori[7] or, as he tends to prefer in the *Systematic*

---

[5] See, e.g., Benkt-Erik Benktson, *Christus und die Religion: Der Religionsbegriff bei Barth, Bonhoeffer und Tillich* (Stuttgart, 1967); R. E. Groves, *The Concept of Religion in the Writings of Dietrich Bonhoeffer and Paul Tillich* (Ph.D. diss., Baylor, 1974); M. Satrom, *Der Begriff der Religion im Werk Paul Tillichs* (Marburg, 1973); as well as numerous articles and chapters within more general studies of Tillich's thought.

[6] Nor, as we shall see in the next section of this chapter, is this the only ambiguity in that essay!

[7] Troeltsch, according to Tillich, 'dealt with the meaning of religion in the context of the human spirit or man's mental structure. Here Troeltsch followed Kant by accepting his three critiques, but he said that there is not only the theoretical *a priori* . . ., not only the moral . . ., and not only the aesthetic . . ., but there is also a religious *a priori*. This means that there is something which belongs to the structure of the human mind itself from which religion arises. It is essentially present, although always only potentially as with the other three structures. Whether it becomes actualized in time and space is another question, but if it is actualized it has its own kind of certainty as the others have . . . If somebody has the character of man, if he has a human mind and human rational structure, then these categories develop under the impact of experience. This is what Troeltsch tried to show in regard to the religious *a priori*. I would say that on this point he stands in the great tradition of the Franciscan-Augustinian school of the Middle Ages. It is impossible for me to understand how we could ever come to a philosophical understanding of religion without finding a point in the structure of man as man in which the finite and the infinite meet or are within each other.' PNT, 231.

Theology, a mystical apriori.[8] Man has this capacity, just as he has certain other capacities which may or may not be actualised. This interpretation of 'the religious principle' is further strengthened by his references elsewhere to man's capacities, including the religious capacity. (GW. IX. 236ff) This is not the only sense which can be given the phrase 'the religious principle' in the essay on the notion of a theology of culture. Tillich seems also to have in mind something rather more than a mere *capacity* for religion. He seems to have in mind something more substantial and vital, something which shatters all 'forms' which seek to constrain it. He calls it *Gehalt*, which he contrasts sharply with *Inhalt* as well as with *Form*. (GW. IX. 20) For the moment, let us call it the *meaning-giving substance* which is thought by Tillich to be the life-force not only of all 'concrete religions' but every cultural act as well.

These two quite different understandings of what is to count as 'the religious principle' which is said to be absolute but potential are intertwined throughout Tillich's address. Although he does not himself distinguish between the two, they clearly do want distinguishing and must be looked at separately. The first sense of 'the religious principle' is treated in the next section of this chapter, together with certain closely related difficulties surrounding Tillich's talk of religion as a dimension of *Geistesleben* (a term which, for the moment, can remain untranslated). The second sense of 'the religious principle' can be treated in part here and in part in chapter six, where we turn more specifically to the role of *Form* and *Gehalt* in the development of Tillich's concept of correlation.

Although the term *Gehalt* does not appear there, 'the religious principle is first used by Tillich in this second sense in his seventy-two theses on systematic theology (1913). In the thirteenth of those theses, Tillich differentiated between 'the religious principle' and 'the concrete religious function': 'From the combination of the religious principle with a definite stage of cultural development [*Kulturstufe*], concrete religion attains to a specifically religious culture'. He then immediately attempted to illuminate this thesis by adding that 'it is concrete insofar as it conceives God in concrete forms and acts, that is, it develops a definite mythology and

---

[8] ST. I. 9. For a helpful and competent study of this aspect of Tillich's thought, see L. D. Streiker, *The Mystical A Priori* (Ph.D. diss., Princeton, 1968). But, any discussion of a mystical a priori must take cognizance of the questions raised by Steven Katz in *Mysticism and Philosophical Analysis* (London and New York, 1978).

experiences the presence of God in concrete natural objects and in concrete historical events, that is, it sets apart [*erklärt*] definite objects for the holy. — The affirmation of a concrete mythology and the acknowledgement of certain objects as holy is what is meant by "faith" or "the concrete religious function".'[9] This attempted elucidation perhaps raises for some more questions than it answers.[10] The question of the nature and standing of what is called 'the religious principle' is among those issues which are left outstanding. There are clues, however.

Elsewhere in this early manuscript Tillich refers interestingly and, in the light of subsequent comments made by him, surprisingly to 'the absolute religion' as the end of the history of religions: 'As at the end of the natural process man stands as the perfection of nature [*als vollendetes Naturwesen*], so at the end of the historical process stands the perfect order, the ideal kingdom. In the ideal kingdom, the history of religions has accordingly attained its end [*Ziel*]: absolute religion is actualised [*verwirklicht*].' (§ 14) Although the influence of Schelling is strongly present in many ways throughout this piece, which was written not that long after Tillich's having completed his dissertations on Schelling, the language of this particular proposition betrays rather stronger affinities to that of Hegel instead.[11]

---

[9] Allowing for certain different emphases and forms of expression, this very closely parallels the position adopted by Tillich in his 1919 address: 'Durch die Verbindung von religiösem Prinzip und Kulturfunktionen kann nun eine spezifisch religiöse Kultursphäre entstehen, ein religiöses Erkennen: Mythos oder Dogma; ein Gebiet religiöser Ästhetik: Kultus; eine religiöse Formung der Person: Heiligung; eine religiöse Gesellschaftsform: Kirche, mit ihrem besonderen Kirchenrecht und ihrer besonderen Gemeinschaftsethik.' (GW. IX. 17)

[10] Nor is this wholly surprising in view of the character of the document. It is, after all, only an outline consisting entirely of propositions.

[11] Though not to be ignored, the role of Schelling in Tillich's thought is frequently exaggerated, both by Tillich and by his commentators. Nor is this a fault only of weaker studies. It is a feature even of more competent studies, such as G. F. Sommer, *The Significance of the Late Philosophy of Schelling for the Formation and Interpretation of the Thought of Paul Tillich* (Ph.D. diss. Duke, 1961). A more balanced account of Tillich's philosophical mentors is available in J. L. Adams, *Paul Tillich's Philosophy of Culture, Science and Religion*, as well as in S. T. Crary, *Idealistic Elements in Tillich's Thought* (Ph.D. diss., Yale, 1955). For an interesting, and at times penetrating, analysis of the influence of Schelling

This fourteenth proposition, which comes immediately after that one in which is introduced the distinction between 'the religious principle' and 'concrete religion', suggests that a key to understanding that distinction may perhaps be found in Hegel's philosophy.[12] In his posthumously published lectures on the philosophy of religion, Hegel made a distinction between 'the concept of religion as such' and 'the specific, existing religions', the latter being the historical expression and progressive manifestation of the former. He clearly wants to stress, whether or not convincingly, that the abstract concept of religion is not to be regarded as something separate and apart from the concrete religions: rather, the concept 'is the content itself, the absolute subject matter [*Sache*], the substance; it is the germ from which the entire tree grows'.[13] Appealing to a favorite metaphor which was also commonly used in ancient philosphy, Hegel remarks that a mature tree is but the unfolding or the development according to its own principles of properties which, whilst invisible, were present at the outset. Then he draws the analogy that 'in a similar fashion, the concept the whole character of the content [*die ganze Natur des Gegenstandes*], and knowledge itself is nothing other than the development of the concept, of that which is implicitly contained in the concept and which has not come into existence, been made explicit, or been displayed'.[14] When applied to religion, this analogy would seem to suggest that in Hegel's view the history of religions is potentially present in the abstract concept of religion, so that the entire history of religions can be viewed as the progressive unfolding and development of the concept of religion as such. Each particular religion in history, whilst in itself defective or 'imperfect', is regarded as a moment in the life of 'religion in general or perfected religion'.[15] The self-actualisation

---

on Tillich in respect to the relationship between metaphysics and ethics, see R. Mokrosch, *Theologische Freiheitsphilosophie* (Frankfurt, 1976).

[12] Of the numerous recent studies of Hegel's philosophy of religion, I have found most helpful Erik Schmidt, *Hegels System der Theologie* (Berlin, 1974). I have also benefitted from Charles Taylor's massive study *Hegel* (Cambridge, 1975), even though philosophy of religion is not a major emphasis in that volume. See also B. M. G. Reardon, *Hegel's Philosophy of Religion* (London, 1977), and Chr. Frey, *Reflexion und Zeit* (Gütersloh, 1973).

[13] *Hegels Werke in 20. Bänden* (Frankfurt, 1969–71), vol. XVI, p. 66.

[14] *Ibid.*

[15] *Ibid.*, p. 80. Hegel's views of the non-christian religions are detailed in R. Leuze, *Die außerchristlichen Religionen bei Hegel* (Göttingen, 1975).

of the abstract concept of religion is predetermined in the sense that ultimately it finds full and complete or 'perfect' expression in the highest religion, that religion which is anticipated by the preceeding developments in the history of religions and which cannot be surpassed by a further development. For Hegel that religion is christianity.[16] The history of religions is the history of the appearance of increasingly suitable forms in which the religious principle is actualised until, as in christianity, 'form' and 'principle' or 'content' are perfectly matched in a one to one correspondence.[17]

Needless to say, this account is highly problematic as an explanation of the history of religions and one which was forcefully criticised by Ernst Troeltsch.[18] It is, however, an account which held no small attraction for Tillich, and not merely the so-called 'early Tillich', but the Tillich of the *Systematic Theology* as well. Tillich no longer speaks there, as he had done in 1913, of 'the absolute religion' as the goal of the history of religions. Even so, he did there and elsewhere continue to speak of the event upon which the christian religion was founded as being absolute. Christianity has 'a foundation which transcends the foundation of any other [non-christian] theology and which itself cannot be transcended', so that christian theology can rightly claim to be '*the* theology'. (ST, I. 16; cf. CE, 77ff)

Even laying aside issues which arise from Tillich's willingness to speak of an absolute *theology* but not of an absolute *religion*, his separation of 'the foundation' of the christian religion from the christian religion as such wants examining. Just as Hegel had regarded christianity as the end or goal of the history of religions, so Tillich claimed that 'the trends which are immanent in all religions and cultures move toward [and are fulfilled in] the Christian answer'. (ST. I. 15; cf. ST. III. 131) On what basis can Tillich make such an apparently audacious claim? He characteristically grounds his claim in christology: in the incarnation the idea has become concrete, the word has become flesh, 'the *principle* of the divine self-manifestation has become *manifest* in the event "Jesus is the Christ".' (ST. I. 16) I have italicised two key words to emphasise one connection between this claim

---

[16] *Werke*, vol. XVII, pp. 187ff.
[17] On the matching of 'form' and 'content', see also Hegel's lectures on art. *Werke*, vols. XIII–XV.
[18] See *Die Absolutheit des Christentums und die Religionsgeschichte* (1902; 1912²; repr. Munich, 1969).

and the distinction earlier drawn by Tillich, following Hegel and others, between the religious principle and its concrete manifestation. It is this manifestation of the religious principle which gives christianity a foundation which transcends all preceding foundations and which cannot itself be transcended. It is said not to be capable of being surpassed since the event on which christianity is founded is at one and the same time absolutely universal and absolutely concrete. (ST. I. 15ff; 135−44, *et passim*) It is 'final' revelation in a metaphysical rather than in an historical sense:[19]

> Christianity claims to be based on the revelation in Jesus as the Christ as the final revelation. . . . The word "final" in the phrase "final revelation" means more than *last*. Christianity often has affirmed, and certainly should affirm, that there is continuous revelation in the history of the church. In this sense the final revelation is not the last. Only if *last* means the last *genuine* revelation can final revelation be interpreted as the last revelation. There can be no revelation in the history of the church whose point of reference is not Jesus as the Christ. If another point of reference is sought or accepted, the Christian church has lost its foundation. But final revelation means more than the last genuine revelation. It means the decisive, fulfilling, unsurpassable revelation, that which is the criterion of all the others. This is the Christian claim, and this is the basis of a Christian theology. (ST. I. 132−3)[20]

But christianity as a *religion$_2$* is said not to enjoy the same finality as its foundation. (cf. TC, 41) Even qualities traditionally ascribed to the church − such as holiness, unity and catholicity − are said by Tillich to apply properly only to its 'foundation'. (ST. III. 167ff) The only superiority the christian religion$_2$ enjoys over other religious$_2$ groups is the superiority of its 'foundation'. (ST. III. 381)

In Tillich's view, no religion$_2$ can be 'final' in an absolute sense. (ST. III. 337) In an early piece on the concept of religion he even described the notion of an absolute religion as a logical impossibility, as *hölzernes Eisen*. (GW. I. 370; but cf. 382) Yet the logic of Tillich's argument would seem to demand that if some new religion$_2$ were to surpass the christian religion it

---

[19] Or, as he puts it in vol. III, 'final' in a *vertical*, rather than in a *horizontal* sense. (ST. III. 338).
[20] Cf. also ST. III. 147ff, 336−8, 364ff.

would have to be established on the same 'event' on which the christian religion$_2$ is founded since no new foundation could in principle surpass that foundation, the event 'Jesus is the christ'. (Cf. ST. III. 141–59) This is a curious state of affairs and it would seem to imply that the only religion$_2$ which could surpass the christian religion$_2$ would be a higher form of christian religion$_2$! But this puzzle need not be solved here. Nor need it be established whether similar claims are made by apologists for some other religions regarding their own peculiar 'focus', as it has been called.[21] For our immediate interest lies not so much in the essentially apologetic claim that the 'foundation' upon which christianity is said to be built is 'final' and 'absolute' as in the distinction which Tillich attempts to draw between the christian religion$_2$ and its 'foundation' or, as he sometimes describes it, its 'basic content' or its 'substance and criterion'. In the first volume of the *Systematic Theology*, Tillich warns that christian theology 'loses itself if it is not based on the kerygma as the substance and criterion of each of its statements'. (ST. I. 7) And in the final volume he reminds his readers, 'There is one answer which underlies all parts of the present system and which is the basic content [*Inhalt* – STd. III. 104] of the Christian faith, and that is that Jesus is the Christ, the bringer of the New Being. There are many possible ways of expressing this assertion, but in a [christian] church there is no way of avoiding it. Every [christian] church is based upon it'. (ST. III. 174) This confession is elsewhere in the *Systematic Theology* described by Tillich as the 'permanent point of reference' for any christian theology, the unchanging content which makes christianity christian through history and across cultures. (ST. I. 126–8)

Whilst he does not do so himself, I should like to suggest nonetheless that 'the christian message', regarded as the foundation of the christian religion, is the principle by which Tillich interprets the christian tradition, or rather the several traditions which when taken together we term 'christianity'. Although this issue is taken up in chapter six, a few preliminary remarks are required here. When Tillich speaks of mediating between the christian tradition and the modern mind, it is not the whole of that tradition in a theologically neutral sense that is mediated; it is rather a theologically charged reading of those traditions interpreted from the standpoint of the confession 'Jesus is the christ'.[22]

---

[21] See R. N. Smart, *The Phenomenon of Religion* (New York, 1973).
[22] For a different interpretation of what Tillich means by the christian tradition and

Tillich would seem to be speaking for himself and not merely for the so-called kerygmatic theologians when he states that the christian message 'is contained in the Bible, but it is not identical with the Bible. It is expressed in the classical tradition of Christian theology, but it is not identical with any special form of that tradition'. (ST. I. 4) The *kerygma*, a word which is not given sufficient clarity in Tillich's writings,[23] is said to be – as in volume one of the *Systematic Theology* – 'the substance and criterion' of every genuinely christian theological statement. And, whilst it is the case that the actual word *kerygma* appears relatively rarely in the second and third volumes of that work, one must surely be aware that such phrases as 'the christian message', 'the catholic substance' and 'the unchanging content' of christianity continue to appear regularly and to serve a similar function in the remaining volumes of the *Systematic Theology*. Whichever word is used, it points to the christological confession which is the foundation of the christian religion:

> Christianity is what it is through the affirmation that Jesus of Nazareth, who has been called "the Christ", is actually the Christ, namely, he who brings the new state of things, the New Being. Wherever the assertion that Jesus is the Christ is maintained, there is the Christian message; wherever this assertion is denied, the Christian message is not affirmed. Christianity was born ... in the moment in which one of his followers was driven to say to him, "Thou art the Christ". And Christianity will live as long as there are people who repeat this assertion. (ST. II. 97)

It would appear that in Tillich's view this confession is both a *sufficient* ('Wherever the assertion ... is maintained, there is the Christian message') and a *necessary* ('wherever this assertion is denied, the Christian message is not affirmed') expression of the 'essence' or the 'unchanging content' of christianity: it makes christianity 'what it is' rather than something else. (Cf. ST. I. 132–3)

It is also the criterion by which christianity judges itself. Being 'beyond our grasp and never at our disposal' (ST. I. 52) this *kerygma* or 'message' is

---

'the christian message', see R. W. Schrader, *The Nature of Theological Argument*, 'Havard Dissertations in Religion' (Missoula, Montana, 1975).

[23] But, see J. Buchter, *Die Kriterien der Theologie im Werke Paul Tillichs* (Bonn, 1975), p. 90f. On the use of the word *kerygma* in recent theology, see G. Ebeling, *Theology and Proclamation* (London, 1966), pp. 113ff, *et passim*.

the specifically christian 'religious principle', as he would earlier have termed it. Only this 'message' is final and absolute and not the 'actual' christian religion as such, including any particular theological formulation of that 'message' (ST. III. 176f): it is, rather, the original revelation upon which the christian religion is based. (ST. I. 126–8)

Tillich writes sometimes as if it were that 'foundation' as such which is mediated in the method of correlation. Yet, at other times, he suggests that what is correlated is the interpretation of that foundation in the proclamation and the traditions of the christian religion. 'Systematic theology is not the message itself'; it is rather the 'interpretation' of that message made from within the christian church. (ST. I. 52) The theologian who uses the method of correlation 'makes an analysis of the human situation out of which the existential questions arise, and . . . demonstrates that the symbols used in the Christian message are the answers to these questions'. (ST. I. 62) His object is in part to achieve 'an interpretation of the traditional symbols of Christianity . . . which preserves the power of these symbols . . .' (ST. I. 64)[24] Even so, those symbols, too, stand ultimately under the criterion of the 'foundation'. Thus an element of radical self-criticism and a principle of reform is incorporated into Tillich's conception of religion. This is in keeping with what he characteristically termed 'the protestant principle', which is in no case to be identified simply with the protestant tradition. That critical principle is not on its own sufficient. It must be used in conjunction with a formative principle.[25] In Tillich's later writings especially, he speaks of the complementary character of 'the protestant principle' and 'the catholic substance' (cf. ST. III. 245),[26] by which he seems to have meant 'the basic content' of the christian message, namely, the confession 'Jesus is the Christ'. This confession is, in fact, treated by Tillich as embodying in some sense 'the essence of christianity'.[27]

---

[24] See also *Die Gestalt der religiösen Erkenntnis*, § 14.

[25] Tillich dealt with certain aspects of this problem earlier in his essays 'Der Protestantismus als kritisches und gestaltendes Prinzip' (1929; repr. GW. VII. 29–53) and 'Protestantische Gestaltung' (1930; repr. GW. VII. 54–69). See also U. Reetz, *Das Sakramentale in der Theologie Paul Tillichs* (Stuttgart, 1974), pp. 50ff, and K. Schedler, *Natur und Gnade* (Stuttgart, 1970), pp. 106ff.

[26] See also 'The Permanent Significance of the Catholic Church for Protestantism', *Protestant Digest*, III (1941), 23–31.

[27] See below, chapter six.

Throughout his writings it is always and only 'the religious principle' as such or 'the foundation' of the christian religion$_2$ which is regarded by Tillich as absolute. Even so, in his post-emigration writings, he increasingly came to emphasise the permanent necessity of the religious sphere. Religion$_2$ is necessary for 'the religious principle' so as to protect it from being distorted and put to wholly demonic uses. For, as Tillich would come to express himself, 'the spiritual community in its latency is open to profanization and demonization without an ultimate principle of resistance, whereas the Spiritual Community organized as a church has the principle of resistance in itself and is able to apply it self-critically . . .' (ST. III. 154) Whether it will do so on all occasions, of course, is another matter, and one about which Tillich harboured no illusions.

In his last public address on 'The Significance of the History of Religions for the Systematic Theologian' Tillich posed for himself the question whether religion as 'a realm of symbols, rites, and institutions' is necessary for the theologian. Contrary to the position attributed by him to the so-called 'death-of-god' theologians of that day, Tillich insisted firmly that the christian theologian 'must assume that religion as a structure of symbols of intuition and action — that means myths and rites within a social group — has lasting necessity for any, even the most secularized culture and the most demythologized theology'. (FR, 82) Tillich then added, in phrases reminiscent of his earliest writings and once again reminding one of his indebtedness to the idealist tradition, 'I derive this necessity, the lasting necessity of religion$_{[2]}$, from the fact that spirit requires embodiment in order to become real and effective'. He further reinforced his point at a less metaphysical level by an illustration from church history: 'The reformers were right when they said that every day is the Lord's Day and, therefore, they devaluated the sacredness of the seventh day. But in order to do this, there must have been a Lord's Day, and that not only once upon a time but continuously in counterbalance against the overwhelming weight of the secular'. (FR. 83; cf. ST. III. 379–80) Whilst not entirely unknown in his early writings (cf. GW. VI. 37), this is an increasingly characteristic emphasis in Tillich's post-emigration writings. In them he argued that there must be a sort of focal point of the holy in order for it not to be demonised by the destructive forces of history. As earlier, however, this focal point remains paradoxical or, as he later preferred, ambiguous. (ST. III. 162 ff) Even though the grounds on which this claim stands are no doubt to be found in Tillich's early writings on philosophy of religion,[28] the particular way he applies those earlier foundations reflects in part his reaction to the attempt by Hirsch and others to combine christianity with the race nationalism of National Socialism. I shall show in chapter six especially that these experiences help to a certain extent to explain why religion as a separate sphere within culture came to be seen increasingly clearly by Tillich as having a 'lasting significance'. It would be too simple, however, to suggest that 1933 was the only consideration. As we shall see, there are other and even earlier factors to be taken into account.

Religion as a separate sphere is not within time *aufgehoben*. 'The abolition of religion' becomes increasingly for Tillich an eschatological concept of which there are in history only anticipations. Theonomy, which had been such a central notion in Tillich's religious socialist writings, comes to be regarded more nearly as an eschatological 'symbol' than as an empirical condition, even though there are in history still said to be 'fragmentary' anticipations of theonomy. (ST. III. 249ff) Religion is 'abolished' in what Tillich terms 'the Spiritual Community', but that too is an eschatological symbol:

> There is no religion as a special function in the Spiritual Community. Of the two concepts of religion, the narrower and the broader, the narrower does not apply to the Spiritual Community, for all acts of man's spiritual life [*des geistigen Lebens* – STd. III. 185] are grasped by the Spiritual Presence. In biblical terms: There is no temple in the fulfilled Kingdom of God, for "now at last God has his dwelling among men! He will dwell among them and they shall be his people, and God himself will be with them". The Spiritual Presence which creates the Spiritual Community does not create a separate entity in terms of which it must be received and expressed; rather, it grasps all reality, every function, every situation. It is the "depth" of all cultural creations and places them in a vertical relation to their ultimate ground and aim. There are no religious symbols in the Spiritual Community because the encountered reality is in its totality symbolic of the Spiritual Presence, and there are no religious

---

[28] See especially the 1922 address to the Kant-Gesellschaft: 'Die Überwindung des Religionsbegriffs in der Religionsphilosophie', *Kant-Studien*, XXVII (1922), 446–69; repr. GW. I. 367–88. See J.-C. Petit, *La philosophie de la religion de Paul Tillich* (Montréal, 1974), pp. 71ff.

acts because every act is an act of self-transcendence. Thus, the essential relation between religion and culture — that "culture is the form of religion and religion the substance of culture" — is realized in the Spiritual Community. (ST. III. 157−8; cf. also p. 403)

There may be no temple in the heavenly Jerusalem, but that is not where men in history live. Whilst there may be 'fragmentary anticipations' of such religionless$_2$ theonomy, Tillich characteristically stresses that in space and time there are and even must be temples and religions$_2$ in the sense of 'myths and rites within a social group' in order for the religious principle to be 'real and effective' in human culture and history. The overall direction of Tillich's development shows an increasing emphasis of this sort. This tendency, as we shall see in part three, corresponds in the main with the development of his method of correlation.

I am well aware this brief account does justice neither to the intricacy of Tillich's theory of 'the religious principle' (in the second of its senses) nor to the serious difficulties which beset his attempts to explain the relations between religion$_1$ and religion$_2$. Some of these difficulties can best be discussed in connexion with his conception of 'ultimate concern'; others are considered below in part three. In both cases, however, I have had to restrict myself only to some of the main difficulties in Tillich's conception of religion which pertain directly to his notion of correlation. There are, of course, other difficulties, many of which are treated in the literature.[29] We must turn now to the other sense in which Tillich spoke of 'the religious principle', namely man's capacity for religion.

The Place of Religion in Geistesleben

As noted in chapter two, Schleiermacher sought to define the nature of christianity in association with the nature of religion as such and to demonstrate the role of religion in the structure of the human personality. In the

---

[29] In addition to the studies listed above in footnote 5, the reader is also referred to E. Amelung, *Die Gestalt der Liebe* (Gütersloh, 1972), where much is made of the difficulty as to the relations between Tillich's 'two' main senses of the word 'religion'. J. L. Adams's book on *Paul Tillich's Philosophy of Culture, Science and Religion* is in this respect also a helpful resource regarding Tillich's mainly pre-emigration thought on religion$_1$.

struggle between orthodoxy and rationalism, the othodox defended the autonomy of religion, and more particularly, the christian religion on the basis of its putatively supranatural origins. As part of his attempt to redraw the lines of that largely futile debate, Schleiermacher sought to establish the autonomy of religion through establishing its independent status within the structure of the mind. In doing so, he sought both to show that religion is autonomous and to show that it is a constituent aspect of man qua man.

Schleiermacher expressed his theory within the then accepted framework of the so-called 'faculty psychology', according to which there are three and only three irreducible 'faculties' or 'functions' or 'processes' of mind: the intellect, the will and the affect.[30] Whilst certainly held to be distinct, those three classes of mental processes were not regarded as unconnected, since the integrity of the personality depended upon their unity. For any attempt within such a framework to find a place for religion in the structure of personality the main issue was to determine how religion is connected with the three established 'faculties'. Is it, for instance, a function principally of one faculty rather than another or is it perhaps in some way a function of all three? Or, again, does religion in some sense stand over against and along side the three traditional faculties as a separate mental process?

Stated in such terms as these, the questions sound quite dated and outmoded. Today one would be more inclined to approach such issues, not through an analysis of mental processes, but through an analysis of the different sorts of relations which obtain between religious statements and other kinds of statements, stressing as well that not even all properly religious statements have the same logical standing. Our immediate purposes, however, do not require us here to assess the adequacy of this now generally abandoned framework or to determine, for instance, whether this way of even conceiving mental processes is 'entirely false, and

---

[30] In saying this, I am not unaware of the recent tendency to dissociate Schleiermacher from 'faculty psychology'. Clearly he must not be interpreted too crudely in his views of the three *Fähigkeiten*. It may be, as Claude Welch stresses, that 'feeling' is not for Schleiermacher 'a "faculty" parallel to the faculties of thinking and willing'. *Gefühl* remains, however, a faculty for Schleiermacher – albeit one whose status is unique in the structure of mental processes. See Welch, *Protestant Thought in the 19th Century* (New Haven, 1972), p. 66. Cf. also R. R. Niebuhr, *Schleiermacher on Christ and Religion* (New York, 1964). For a careful consideration of this problem in the *Reden*, see F. W. Graf, 'Ursprüngliches Gefühl unmittelbarer Koinzidenz des Differenten', *ZThKirche*, LXXV (1978), 147–86.

false not in detail but in principle'.[31] For our immediate purposes it is sufficient to note that it was mainly in such terms that Tillich too from the start conceived the problem of the place of religion within the structure of *Geistesleben*, a term which in German is not without considerable ambiguity. As we shall soon see, the structure of *Geistesleben* meant for Tillich both the structure of mind and also the structure of culture. (cf. GW. IX. 24)

This way of conceiving the problem in terms of 'faculty psychology' is especially prevalent in Tillich's earlier writings. It is also to be found in the *Systematic Theology*, despite his comments there about the 'psychological crudeness' of the traditional distinctions within the so-called 'faculty psychology' between the intellect, the will and the affect. (ST. III. 131) Yet on the pages which follow this very comment, Tillich proceeds without even apparent embarrassment to chart the place of 'faith' in relation to each of those three mental functions, reaching the conclusion that

> The preceding discussion of faith and the mental function [sic; *Geistesfunktionen* – STd. III. 158] has shown two things: first, that faith can neither be identified with nor derived from any of the mental functions. Faith cannot be created by the procedures of the intellect, or by endeavors of the will, or by emotional movements. But, second, faith comprehends all this within itself, uniting and subjecting it to the Spiritual Presence's transforming power. This implies and confirms the basic theological truth that in relation to God everything is by God. Man's spirit cannot reach the ultimate, that toward which it transcends itelf, through any of its functions. But the ultimate can grasp all these functions and raise them beyond themselves by the creation of faith. (ST. III. 133)

This is said by Tillich, however, not to be a heteronomous imposition from without, but a theonomous self-transcendence from within human *Geistesleben*.

As Schleiermacher and Troeltsch before him, not to mention Kant and Hegel, Tillich sought to show that religion is not an alien intruder in the life of man. No less than science, morals and art, it is an expression of an apriori possibility within the structure of the human personality. In Tillich's terms religion is a function of autonomy, not heteronomy. Religion is, as Tillich called it in an essay included in *Theology of Culture*, 'a dimension of

---

[31] The allusion is to Gilbert Ryle, *The Concept of Mind* (New York, 1949).

man's spiritual life' (TC, 3–9), or even 'the all-embracing function of man's spiritual life', as he had written in the first volume of his *Systematic Theology*. (ST. I. 15)

Later, however, Tillich would abandon almost altogether the word 'spiritual', preferring to speak instead of religion as a dimension of 'the human spirit'. (PNT, 120) By the time he published the final volume of the *Systematic Theology* he had come round to the view that 'while it may be possible to rescue the term "spirit", the adjective "spiritual" is lost beyond hope' when applied to human life. Tillich added that he would 'not even attempt to re-establish it in its original meaning'. (ST. III. 22; cf. 108 *et passim*) Even so, he seems not to have had such misgivings about the use of 'Spiritual'as regards the divine life. For the notion of 'the Spiritual Presence' is a central motif in part four of the *Systematic Theology*. Such variations as these reflect Tillich's almost perpetual attempt to come to grips with English usage, so that he could express more or less adequately in his adopted language ideas which had been formed originally in his *Muttersprache*. That this is the case in this particular instance is perhaps borne out by the omission of the passage cited above from the German edition of the *Systematic Theology*. (cf. STd. III. 33) The arguments which follow in this section of the chapter are not affected materially by whether one speaks of religion as 'a dimension of man's spiritual life' or as 'a dimension of the human spirit'. In either case, similar problems and ambiguities plague Tillich's conception of the place of religion in *Geistesleben*.

In his first address to the Kant-Gesellschaft (1919), Tillich argued that religion – and it would seem only religion – has the peculiarity of not being identifiable as a function of a mental faculty. Religion is said to be 'an attitude of the mind', *ein Verhalten des Geistes*. (GW. IX. 17; cf. ST. III. 131–3) Yet in that address and indeed elsewhere when Tillich speaks of religion as a dimension of *Geistesleben* he sometimes means that religion is a constituent element of mind and at other times that religion is a dimension of the various spheres of culture without itself being a separate sphere.

Both these meanings are perfectly possible within acceptable senses of *Geist*. However, Tillich creates considerable problems when, as he frequently does, he conflates the two senses of 'spiritual' and slides in his writings from the one sense to the other.[32] For instance, in the address from

---

[32] Not that Tillich alone was guilty of such mistakes! See, e.g., R. Bultmann, *Glauben und Verstehen*, vol. I (Tübingen, 1933), pp. 87f.

which the above citation is taken Tillich argues that the religious principle can actualise itself in the mind only in and through the three mental functions since religion does not itself constitute such a faculty or function. But this putative connexion between the religious principle and the mental faculties is thought by Tillich without additional argument to warrant his further claim that 'only in connexion with cultural functions outside religion has the religious principle existence'. (GW. IX. 17) Nor does he seem to be aware that he has made a very different sort of judgment from that regarding the place of religion in the structure of mind. The distinction is further blurred in his additional comment, 'The religious [principle] forms no principle alongside others in *Geistesleben*; rather the religious [principle] is actual in all provinces of the *Geistigen*'. I have left two terms untranslated because in German they can refer either to the mind or to culture. And it is clear that Tillich used the term to refer to both. (cf. ST. III. 275) This double meaning (not that *Geist* has only two meanings) may help account for Tillich's ability to slide so easily between the place of religion within the mind to its role in culture.

Even though one would certainly not want to deny that some judgments regarding the structure of mind and some judgments regarding the shape of culture are in some way related, one would not I think want to claim that the two sorts of judgments are always and simply interchangeable. For some judgements can be formed regarding the mind which are not applicable to culture, and vice versa. For instance, from the judgment that there is no religious 'faculty' it does not follow that there is no specifically religious 'sphere' of culture, any more than from the judgment that there is no economic 'faculty' in the mind does it follow that there is no economic sphere of culture.[33]

Tillich's claim about the peculiarity of religion is problematic in yet another way. From the beginning he characteristically argued that man cannot be 'also' religious. It is a mistake, we are told by Tillich on numerous occasions, to regard religion as one sphere of culture alongside others since that would be tantamount to holding that man is 'ethical, scientific, artistic, political and also religious'. (GW. I. 370) In truth religion is said to be a dimension of everything that man does, so that one should

---

[33] Nor is this ambiguity restricted to Tillich's early writings. As we shall soon see, one can find a similar tendency to conflate the two sorts of judgments in the 1954 essay on 'Religion as a Dimension in Man's Spiritual Life'.

speak instead of the religious dimension of morality or science or art or politics. Whilst such an emphasis no doubt gives valid expression to a legitimate pastoral or even theological concern that religion not be partitioned off from the rest of life and made into 'merely' an isolated sphere separate and distinct from other spheres, such an emphasis is in serious danger of having another and perhaps unwelcome effect. For this no doubt valid emphasis regarding religion looks as if it is being made at the expense of all the other spheres of man's cultural life. One might with similar justification want to emphasise that politics is not merely one sphere of life alongside other spheres, that there is rather a political dimension within all human cultural activity, including man's religious activity. Or, again similar claims could be made with equal justification regarding the aesthetic dimension. Tillich might be right in affirming as he does that religion is a 'dimension' of all spheres and not merely one sphere alongside others, but he would be wrong to infer from this that religion is in this respect peculiar or that no other sphere of cultural life can be regarded similarly as a dimension of all other spheres.[34]

Some of the defects of Tillich's conception of religion$_1$ as 'ultimate concern' can be illustrated by comparing it with Schleiermacher's conception of religion. Tillich more than once remarked in his later writings especially that his own account of religion as 'ultimate concern' varies only slightly from Schleiermacher's account of religion as 'the feeling of utter dependence'. (Cf. ST. I. 41–2; PNT, 105) Yet, in his early writings he tended to contrast his own theory of religion as what he then termed 'directedness toward the Unconditioned' with Schleiermacher's theory, even though those writings betray a certain lack of perceptiveness as to the true contours of Schleiermacher's attempt to determine the role of religion in the structure of personality.

In his article 'Über die Idee einer Theologie der Kultur', for instance, Tillich asserted that Schleiermacher 'assigned' religion to 'the emotional

---

[34] Tillich may in fact have anticipated this sort of criticism in ST. III. 94 ff. According to this account of religion in relation to morality and culture, religion remains unique, but not in the sense that it alone is a dimension of the other spheres. Morality and culture are treated not only as dimensions of one another, but also as dimensions of religion as well. The stance adopted by Tillich here is not wholly unrelated to the standpoint of his earlier writings, but the emphasis is certainly placed elsewhere.

sphere'. Having claimed, as noted already, that religion cannot be attached exclusively to one particular mental function, Tillich asserted emphatically if somewhat easily that every attempt to allocate religion to a single function had been untenable, 'whether the Hegelian attempt to assign it to the theoretical function; or the Kantian, to the practical or the Schleiermachrian, to the emotional'. (GW. IX. 16) Even there, however, Tillich remarked that of the three Schleiermacher came closest to the truth 'to the extent that [he] brings to expression the neutrality [*Indifferenz*] of the specifically religious as regards its cultural manifestation'. By 'neutrality' here Tillich would seem to have intended to stress that any 'cultural form' could in principle at least be filled with and manifest 'religious import', that there are in principle no uniquely consecrated 'cultural forms' – indeed, that there are no religious forms at all, only religious 'import' in autonomous cultural 'form'. This stress, which persists in Tillich's writings right through to the final volume of his *Systematic Theology*, creates difficulties some of which are considered below in chapter six. Despite his at least limited recognition of such 'neutrality', Schleiermacher is nonetheless faulted for putatively having identified religion with feeling or *Gefühl*. For if by 'feeling' Schleiermacher meant feeling as such, then it would be arbitrary to label it as religious, reasons Tillich, since feeling accompanies every cultural experience. But, if by 'feeling' he meant a definite sort of feeling, then with its specification there would already be given a theoretical or practical aspect. (GW. IX. 16–17) So, Tillich concludes, 'Religion is not a feeling, but an attitude of the mind [*ein Verhalten des Geistes*] in which the practical, theoretical and emotional aspects are bound up together into a complex unity'. (GW. IX. 17)

This is a curious line of argument in that it begins with an explicit criticism of Schleiermacher's theory of the place of religion in the personality and concludes by stating a view very similar to that actually held by Schleiermacher, even though it is put forward as an alternative. It varies mainly in being less precise. For Schleiermacher, unlike Tillich but like Kant, goes on to delineate the nature of that 'complex unity' to which Tillich appeals. And Schleiermacher additionally defines more precisely than does Tillich the relationship of specifically *religious* thought and *religious* action to *religious* feeling.[35]

---

[35] This is no less true of the *Reden* than of the *Glaubenslehre*. See speeches three, four and five.

As Tillich's own teacher Martin Kähler had realised,[36] Schleiermacher denied both that religion is a mental function alongside other functions and that religion is assigned to one of the three mental 'faculties'. Tillich misunderstands in part the status of 'feeling' or 'immediate self-consciousness' in Schleiermacher's picture of the structure of mental processes, a misunderstanding which he shared with Rudolf Otto, amongst others. 'Feeling' for Schleiermacher is neither mere emotion nor unconscious urges, as Tillich sometimes implies especially in his early writings. 'Feeling' is rather the total sense of self-hood which underlies and unifies every aspect of personality.[37] Contrary to what Tillich seems early to have held, 'feeling' is not itself simply a faculty alongside the other mental faculties;[38] it is rather that integrating force in the human personality. Nor is the sense of *immediate* self-consciousness to be confused – as Tillich mistakenly does – with what Schleiermacher calls *reflective* self-consciousness in which 'I' become an object of consciousness. When 'I' am conscious of and reflect upon 'me' the self is divided into knowing subject ('I') and known object ('me') and self-consciousness is no longer immediate. But since knowledge requires a knowing subject and a known object, Schleiermacher reasons, the immediate self-consciousness does not in and of itself entail a 'knowing' in the reflective sense nor a 'doing' in the active sense. When self-consciousness is reflected and acted upon – as, in Schleiermacher's view, it must be – it necessarily is as a 'knowing' and as a 'doing' Consequently, Tillich's objections in his 1919 address, objections which betray the extent of his continued dependence at that time upon research carried out before the war,[39] cannot be sustained. Nor is his misunderstanding of Schleiermacher confined to that address. (Cf., e.g., GW. I. 369f; V. 132)

In later writings Tillich quietly recanted. (cf. ST. I. 15) He allied Schleiermacher increasingly with himself until Schleiermacher's 'feeling of utter dependence' had been virtually identified with his own notion of

---

[36] *Geschichte der protestantischen Dogmatik im 19.Jahrhundert* (Munich, 1962), pp. 64ff.

[37] D. F. E. Schleiermacher, *Der christliche Glaube*, vol. I (repr. Berlin, 1960), pp. 14ff. Niebuhr, Welch and others are right to stress this.

[38] It is nonetheless a faculty according to Schleiermacher.

[39] See his 1910 dissertation on *Die religionsgeschichtliche Konstruktion in Schellings positiver Philosophie* (Breslau, 1910), pp. 94f. See also G. F. Sommer, *The Significance of the Late Philosophy of Schelling for the Formation and Interpretation of the Thought of Paul Tillich*, pp. 93ff.

'ulitmate concern'. (PNT, 105; ST. I. 41–2; but cf. ST. III. 285) But this too is problematic. There is a superficial similarity between the two conceptions of religion, a similarity which has been seized upon by friendly and hostile critics alike. Even so, it is their much less frequently detected dissimilarity which is upon closer examination more striking.

Leaving aside the obvious fact that 'ultimate concern' is active and 'feeling of utter dependence' entirely passive, the two conceptions of religion have very different roles in the theological methods of Tillich and Schleiermacher. For the 'feeling of utter dependence' is regarded by Schleiermacher as uniquely a relation between man and God; 'ultimate concern' is regarded by Tillich as the sort of relation which obtains between man and whatever is for him of greatest value, whether or not it is God. One can be utterly dependent in Schleiermacher's sense only upon God, but in a certain sense one can be ultimately concerned in Tillich's view about many sorts of things, only one of which is God. (cf. ST. I. 24f) There are, however, serious difficulties which his conception of 'ultimate concern' creates, some of which we must consider in this section.

Schleiermacher argues that all man's relations with objects in the world are characterised by reciprocity [*Wechselwirkung*] and that, owing to his relative dependence upon things other than himself man cannot ever be – as Hegel perhaps implies – utterly free.[40] Yet, man is according to Schleiermacher utterly dependent upon something other than himself and, indeed, other than the world, something upon which he can exercise no influence whatever.[41] The 'whence' or *Woher* of this awareness is God. And by 'God' Schleiermacher would seem to mean *God* and not merely a particular idea of God or an object or ideal which is called 'God' or which functions as 'God for me'.

Tillich, on the other hand, tells us that 'ultimate concern' is a phenomenological description of religious commitment in the sense that it describes the sort of commitment which the religious person exhibits toward the object of his commitment. It is a *phenomenological* description in the sense that 'ulitmate concern' is purely formal and tells us nothing about the content or the object of the concern. (DF. 1–4, *et passim*; cf. ST. I. 12ff, esp. 14) This point is worth emphasising in view of the apparently widespread misunderstanding that 'ultimate concern' is always

---

[40] *Der christliche Glaube*, vol. I, p. 27.
[41] *Ibid.*, pp. 28–9.

regarded by Tillich 'in the last analysis' as concern about that which is 'really' ultimate.[42] Whilst a misunderstanding, this is not *merely* a misunderstanding. Tillich occasionally writes as if ultimate concern is necessarily concern about the ultimate. (cf. BR, 59) In addition, he frequently fails to keep separate in practice that which he explicitly distinguishes in his account of the notion of ultimate concern.

This 'misunderstanding' arises in part from a *slide* and a *jump* in Tillich's argument about 'ultimate concern'. From the use of 'ultimate concern' as a phenomenological description of the sort of relation which exists between the religiously committed person[43] and that to which he is religiously committed,[44] Tillich *slides* into a more general use of 'ultimate concern' as a phenomenological description of the sort of relation which obtains between every person and that which he values most, whether it be his career, money, the state, etc. Since everyone is committed to something[45] Tillich *jumps* to the conclusion that everyone is religious. And he gives this conclusion the status of a theological judgment in the sense that this conclusion enables him to make correlations between apparently 'secular' judgments and more specifically 'theological' judgments: the religious character of man's commitments provides a point of contact between 'the human situation' and 'the christian message'.

What is to be made of this? I should like to call attention in particular to three features of Tillich's ploy. First, Tillich uses 'ultimate' in different senses in the first two steps above. 'Ultimate' is used differently not only in the sense that the content of the term is changed from, e.g., 'the gods' or 'Nirvana' or 'JHWH' or 'career' or 'money' or 'the State'. That would be possible in a phenomenological account of the character of religious belief. But the term 'ultimate' actually has a different status in the two cases. In the first case 'ultimate' specifies some object or entity which stands outside the space-time continuum. The 'ultimate' is not merely the highest member in a series, but is not even a member of that series. The 'ultimate' is the power and meaning of the whole series, rather than its highest member. In the second case, however, the 'ultimate' is that which is valued most within the

---

[42] The misunderstanding is typified by Kenneth Hamilton, *The System and the Gospel* (London, 1963), p. 99.
[43] In the straightforward sense of religious$_2$.
[44] That is, that which he regards as 'the holy' in Otto's sense.
[45] Absolute nihilism is not for Tillich even a possibility in theory – see ST. III. 227f.

series. It is the highest member of the series. Although clearly an illicit procedure, sliding from one sense of 'ultimate' to another is necessary for Tillich's argument to proceed at all.[46]

But 'ultimate' is not the only term used here in different senses. 'Religion' is used both in the straightforward sense of commitment to specific myths and membership in a specific cultus, and also in the broader, perhaps metaphorical sense, of any sort of commitment. Sliding from one sense of 'religion' to the other is also necessary for Tillich's argument to advance to its conclusion that everyone is religious.

Each of these ambiguities is present in the following passage pertaining to 'ultimate concern' and taken from the article on 'Religion as a Dimension of Man's Spiritual Life':

> Religion, in the largest and most basic sense of the word, is ultimate concern. An ultimate concern is manifest in all creative functions of the human spirit. It is manifest in the moral sphere as the unconditional seriousness of the moral demand. Therefore, if someone rejects religion in the name of the moral function of the human spirit, he rejects religion in the name of religion. Ultimate concern is manifest in the realm of knowledge as the passionate longing for ultimate reality. Therefore, if anyone rejects religion in the name of the cognitive function of the human spirit, he rejects religion in the name of religion. Ultimate concern is manifest in the aesthetic function of the human spirit as the infinite desire to express ultimate meaning. Therefore, if anyone rejects religion in the name of the aesthetic function of the human spirit, he rejects religion in the name of religion. You cannot reject religion with ultimate seriousness, because ultimate seriousness, or the state of being ultimately concerned, is itself religion. (TC, 7–8; cf. 27)

---

[46] Something of the confusion which is created can be simply illustrated. The non-religious$_2$ man has an 'ultimate concern', according to Tillich, in that he must value one finite thing more than he values all other finite things. Tillich seems to exclude the possibility that he might value all/several finite things equally. The religious$_2$ man has an 'ultimate concern' which transcends all finite things. But, insofar as finite things have *some* value even for the religious$_2$ man, he must (it would seem) also value some finite thing more than all other finite things. Does Tillich's religious$_2$ man then not have two 'ultimate concerns', one which belongs to the series of finite things and one which transcends that series infinitely? This would seem to be the logic of his position, even though it is most certainly not what he intended.

It is perhaps such passages as this one, liberally sprinkled as it is with *infinite*'s and *unconditional*'s and *ultimate*'s and *religion*'s (all used in more than one sense), which have led some philosophers to assert that Tillich attempts covertly to 'convert by definition' and unashamedly to exploit linguistic ambiguity to apologetic ends.

Under the circumstances one would be hard pressed to discover reasons why this charge should not in some cases be allowed to stand.

Nor is one bound to think otherwise when one sees the lengths to which Tillich is prepared to push this sort of 'argument'. Just as no one is without religion, Tillich further asserts, no one is an atheist. Atheism is regarded as logically impossible on the grounds that '. . . whatever concerns a man ultimately becomes god for him, and conversely . . . a man can be concerned ultimately only about that which is god for him'. (ST. I. 211) It is possible for Tillich to stipulate that he is going to use the word 'god' in this metaphorical way. And, indeed, we do sometimes ordinarily use both 'religion' and 'god' metaphorically: 'He attends the test matches religiously'; 'Art is my religion': 'She worships money as her god'. But it is not permissible to conflate the senses of such terms and to confuse such metaphorical uses of 'God' and 'religion' with strictly phenomenological uses of the terms. Nor is it permissible without additional argument to draw, as Tillich does draw, theological conclusions from putatively phenomenological statements of that sort. From the statement 'Jones attends the test matches religiously' it does not follow that 'Jones is religious', much less that 'Jones is not an atheist'! Jones may in fact be religious and he may in addition not be an atheist, but one could infer neither from his 'infinite passion' for and 'ulimate concern' about cricket, virtuous though such 'passion' and 'concern' may be thought by some to be.

We must conclude, therefore, that there are in Tillich's conception of 'ultimate concern' serious difficulties which raise questions about its usefulness in any earnest attempt to resolve the dilemma set by Schleiermacher.

Religion, Theology and Correlation

We are now in a position to form judgments about some of the ways in which 'religion' in its various senses contributes to Tillich's concept of correlation. As regards the structure of relations between culture and religion, the concept of correlation has to do principally with the relationship between the cultural 'situation' and 'the christian message' as expressed in the symbols and traditions of christianity. That 'message' expresses the christological foundation of the christian religion and is to that extent identifiable with the religious principle which is thought to be at one and the same time absolutely universal and absolutely concrete. The christian message is summarised in the ancient baptismal formula 'Jesus is the Christ'. But this 'foundation', whilst held to be in some sense absolute, is the 'unchanging content' of the christian religion$_2$. As such it is part of the 'concrete mythology' of a particular religion and it is preserved only in the symbols of that religion$_2$.

This specifically christian mythology or *kerygma* is for systematic theology 'the substance and criterion of each of its statements'. (ST. I. 7) The substance of theological statements should not merely be private opinion, nor should the norm be the product of the individual theologian: 'its appearance is not the work of theological reflection but of the Spiritual life of the church . . .'; it arises 'in and through the encounter of the church with the Christian message'. (ST. I. 48) The theologian can seek to discover the norm in the collective experience of the church and seek to express it for his generation, but he should not seek intentionally to produce or create the norm. Here the theologian is servant and not virtuoso.[47]

Tillich offers 'with reservations' what he takes to be the norm operative in the christian community at the present time. But he emphasises, following in this respect Troeltsch, that its adequacy can only be judged in retrospection. That norm is now well-known, even if its adequacy is still contested: 'the new being in Jesus as the christ'. This is the material norm of Tillich's theology. It is the norm by which he sought to reinterpret the christian message in the present situation in such a way that the substance of that message is preserved. (ST. I. 49f) We shall have occasion to return in a later chapter to some issues raised by Tillich's christological norm.[48] At the moment, however, it is necessary only to point out, first, that there is such a norm and, second, that it is purported to express the collective experience of the christian church rather than the mind of a single theologian. For it is relevant to the matter at hand to establish firmly that the christian theologian's room for intellectual maneuver is in Tillich's view circum-

---

[47] The allusion is, of course, to Barth's characterisation of Schleiermacher.
[48] See below, chapter six, pp. 205 ff, 228–36.

scribed by the particular community to which he belongs; he is *not* a free agent. (cf. GW. IX. 29) The christian theologian has not merely *an* ultimate concern of a private, individual sort. He has a *particular* ultimate concern, namely, 'the christian message'. (cf. ST. III. 24) He remains a christian theologian if and only if that particular concern remains his ultimate concern (cf. ST. I. 10–11), if and only if he continues to stand within what Tillich calls 'the [christian] theological circle'. (ST. I. 8ff; cf. GW. IX. 30)

But religion in the 'wider' sense of 'ultimate concern' is not without its role in Tillich's attempt to correlate culture and religion. Indeed, it can be said that the universal 'ultimate concern' which is thought to be exhibited throughout culture, and not merely within the specifically religious$_2$ sphere, is in Tillich's view necessary for there to be in principle any such correlations. In the account of the 'method of correlation' in the first volume of the *Systematic Theology*, Tillich argues that, despite their differences, some sorts of 'philosophical questions' can be correlated with some sorts of 'theological answers' in part because there is said to be a 'religious' element in both. From the presence in 'all' philosophy of an 'ultimate concern', he infers that 'every creative philosopher is a hidden theologian'. (ST. I. 24–5 q.v.) Tillich's account there of relations between philosophy and theology has been much criticised in the literature. And my arguments in the previous section regarding certain slides and jumps in Tillich's 'argument' regarding 'ultimate concern' would seem to apply equally here. That being the case, a certain amount of difficulty is created for Tillich's concept of correlation to the extent that, according to his own account, correlation is possible only when there is on both sides of the relationship a 'religious' dimension. This, as we have seen, is problematical.

It is not, however, the only sort of problem which arises from Tillich's attempt to define the relationship between philosophical questions and theological answers. For Tillich also insists that, despite the allegedly religious dimension in both, philosophy and theology remain somehow on 'different levels', so that neither conflict nor synthesis is possible in principle since 'there is no common basis between theology and philosophy'. (ST. I. 26) Tillich's ability, without falling into contradiction, to hold both this claim and the claim that any one theological statement can answer any one philosophical question has been challenged by several, including Douglass Lewis: 'If philosophy and theology really operate in different realms of discourse (as Tillich has been telling us they do), then one cannot raise questions in one realm of discourse and answer them from another, but this is precisely what Tillich tells us we must do'.[49] The notion of there being a 'religious' dimension to both philosophy and theology might have contributed slightly to a solution to this difficulty. Yet that notion is rendered virtually useless by its own difficulties. We must, therefore, ask whether it is incoherent to think of correlating questions of one sort with answers of a different sort? I shall endeavour to answer this question below in chapter five.[50]

These difficulties arise principally from regarding the concept of correlation implied in the method of correlation as a function of what Tillich early called 'church theology'. And it cannot be denied that he insists at the outset of his *Systematic Theology* that theology must be church theology in that it is said to be 'a function of the Christian church' and 'must serve the needs of the church'. (ST. I. 3) The church is the theologian's 'place of work'. (ST. I. 48) Or, as he also put it, '. . . the theologian exercises a function of the church within the church and for the church.' (ST. I. 32)

But there is another side to Tillich's conception of the theological task which is difficult to reconcile with these high aims, a fact which Kenneth Hamilton and others have been quick to seize upon.[51] In the final volume of the *Systematic Theology* we are told that 'Spirit-created symbols'[52] are 'not bound to a particular revelatory event, Christian or non-Christian'. Nor are they bound 'to religion in the narrower sense'. (ST. III. 254) In the German edition this claim is extended even further, so that Spirit-created symbols are bound neither to religion in the narrower sense nor to religion in the broader sense! (STd. III. 291) Additionally we are told they are not even 'tied up with a definite content or a definite form'. (STd. III. 291; cf. ST. III. 254) Such symbols exist in moments of 'linguistic self-transcendence' and express the theonomous unity of subject and object, spirit and Spirit. Whilst in itself perhaps problematical, such a view might form part of a cultural theology in which the theologian is regarded as one who

---

[49] 'The Conceptual Structure of Tillich's Method of Correlation', *Encounter*, XXVII (1967), p. 269.
[50] See below, pp. 177–90, esp. 184ff.
[51] Most lucidly perhaps in his largely negative critique of *The System and the Gospel*, but see also 'Tillich's Method of Correlation', *CanJTh*, V (1959), 87ff.
[52] As opposed to what he there calls 'ordinary symbols' – though this distinction creates difficulties for Tillich's general theory of symbols. ST. III. 254.

'stands free [from concrete commitments to a specific religious tradition] in the living cultural movement, open not only to every other form, but also to every new Spirit'. (GW. IX. 29) It is somewhat more difficult to conceive it as the foundation for a dogmatic theology in which the theologian is seen as working 'in the church, for the church' and speaking, as David Kelsey would have him, as a confessional theologian.[53]

This may create a serious problem for Tillich. His programme of a cultural theology, the symbol of which is the *theonomous unity* of faith and value, and his programme of a church theology, the symbol of which is the *correlation* of existential questions and theological answers, would seem to have different aims and serve different ends. Whether they are also competitive aims and competitive ends cannot be determined with certainty at this point. This is one of the principal tasks of part three. Is the 'vision of Paul Tillich' unified, as Armbruster suggests,[54] or does Tillich perhaps see double? We shall want to determine whether and, if so, how he achieves that 'personal synthesis' of cultural theology and dogmatic theology called for in his early address to the Kant-Gesellschaft. But, first, we must determine in what ways Tillich's understanding of *culture* contributes to his concept of correlation.

---

[53] See *The Fabric of Paul Tillich's Theology* (New Haven, 1967). On the relationship between Tillich's concept of symbol and his method of correlation, see M. von Kriegstein, *Die Methode der Korrelation und der Symbolbegriff Paul Tillichs* (Hamburg, 1972).

[54] C. J. Armbruster, *The Vision of Paul Tillich* (New York, 1967).

CHAPTER FOUR
CULTURE AND THE CONCEPT OF CORRELATION

'Culture' has been described as one of the two or three most complicated words in the English language.[1] It cannot be denied that we use that word in an enormous variety of ways which, at least at first glance, seem to bear little or no relation to one another. Confronted with the exacting task of trowelling through the various strata of our modern usage of the term 'culture' — whether in ordinary speech or in the technical literature of the social sciences, not to mention the humanities — one may perhaps be forgiven having been tempted to concur with the assertion by E. H. Gombrich that no analysis of the term is required since we all know what it means anyway. Nor is he entirely without justification when he subsequently claims that 'at least everybody knows this who has ever travelled from one country to another, or even moved from one social circle to another, and has experienced what it means to be confronted by different ways of life, different systems of reference, different scales of value — in short, different cultures.'[2]

Perhaps this sort of vague, commonsense understanding of 'culture' is sufficient for some purposes.[3] Yet it will not suffice for our purposes here. For the term 'culture' occupies such an important place in Tillich's theological programme that closer scrutiny of its usage there is required.

Despite the not inconsiderable attention paid to Tillich's 'theology of culture', no one to my knowledge has succeeded satisfactorily in sorting out

---

[1] Raymond Williams, *Keywords: A Vocabulary of Culture and Society* (London, 1976), p. 76.
John Bowker, Paul Heelas and Stuart Mews — all colleagues in the department of religious studies at Lancaster — read and commented on an earlier draft of this chapter, as did Suzette Heald of the department of sociology. I am very grateful for their criticisms and suggestions.
[2] *In Search of Cultural History* (Oxford, 1968), p. 2.
[3] Nor do I wish to offer a judgment here as to whether such an intuitive or impressionistic conception will bear the weight required by Gombrich as an adequate foundation for the construction of a discipline called 'cultural history'.

118   Religion and Culture

his concept of culture and the various layers of influence which are at work in it.[4] Nor has sufficient curiosity been shown about the relative novelty of the very idea of a 'theology of culture'. Even if the relationship between religion and what we now call 'culture' were a persistent problem throughout the history of christian thought, an explicit 'theology of culture' would remain a decidedly recent innovation. For such an enterprise presupposes a conception of 'culture' which was virtually unknown before the nineteenth century. The development of a *Kulturtheologie* follows on the emergence in Germany during the nineteenth century and early twentieth century of such new fields of enquiry as 'cultural history' (Burckhardt, Lamprecht), 'cultural science' (Rickert, extending Dilthey's notion of *Geisteswissenschaft*), 'philosophy of culture' (Schweitzer, Kroner), 'sociology of culture' (Alfred Weber), and 'psychology of culture' (Wundt). Such new enterprises as these reflect the gradual development of a descriptive, non-honorific conception of 'culture'.[5]

---

[4] Some helpful, though over-brief, comments are made by C. J. Armbruster in *The Vision of Paul Tillich* (New York, 1967). He seems content, however, to say that Tillich uses culture in a broad sense to mean 'the spiritual creativity manifest in every area of human life and institutions'. (p. 83) Not even J. L. Adams takes sufficient care in analysing what precisely is meant by 'culture', despite the title of his book: *Paul Tillich's Philosophy of Culture, Science and Religion* (New York, 1965). The problem of what Tillich means by 'culture' is relegated to a single footnote in E. Amelung, *Die Gestalt der Liebe: Paul Tillichs Theologie der Kultur* (Gütersloh, 1972), p. 43. But, one looks in vain for even a footnote on the issue in W. B. Green's dissertation entitled *The Concept of Culture in the Theology of Paul Tillich* (Edinburgh, 1955).

[5] One should be warned, however, not to assume that recent uses of 'culture' are wholly descriptive or entirely non-honorific. 'Culture', after all, was C. L. Stevenson's prime example of those words which 'have both a vague conceptual meaning and a rich emotive meaning. The conceptual meaning of them all is subject to constant redefinition. The words are prizes which each man seeks to bestow on the qualities of his own choice'. 'Persuasive Definitions', *Mind*, XLVII (1938), 333. For a history of the mainly conceptual meaning of 'culture', see the massive anthology edited by A. L. Kroeber and K. J. Kluckhohn, *Culture: A Critical Review of Concepts and Definitions* (New York, 1952), as well as the more recent study by M. Harris of *The Rise of Anthropological Theory: A History of Theories of Culture* (London, 1968). In this chapter I make no mention of the putative difference between the German concepts of *Kultur* and *Civilisierung* or *Zivilisation*. There are two reasons for this: (1) the difference is

The term 'culture' is of course by no means a neologism. Even so, it has had a varied history of usage and began to acquire its modern associations only gradually from about the eighteenth century. This seems to hold equally for English and German uses of the term. Raymond Williams, for example, has traced the development of uses of 'culture' in modern English, concentrating almost exclusively on literary sources. In his study of *Culture and Society*, Williams differentiates four phases in the use of the word 'culture' since the late eighteenth century. Before the modern period, 'culture' had been used primarily in the sense of the process of cultivation by training or education. 'But this latter use', he observes,

> which had usually been a culture *of* something, was changed, to *culture* as such, a thing in itself. It came to mean, first, 'a general state or habit of the mind', having close relations with the idea of human perfection. Second, it came to mean 'the general state of intellectual development, in a society as a whole'. Third, it came to mean 'the general body of the arts'. Fourth, later in the [19th] century, it came to mean 'a whole way of life, material, intellectual, and spiritual'.[6]

Thus, by small but significant shifts of meaning, the modern usage of 'culture' is said by Williams to have developed from earlier uses. Williams, who deals ony with the literary tradition, does not in his study take into account the uses of 'culture' within English and American anthropology.[7]

The classic definition of 'culture' from which virtually every anthropological definition developed is to be found in E. B. Tylor's study of *Primitive Culture*.[8] There 'culture' is defined as '. . . that complex whole which includes knowledge, belief, art, morals, law, custom, and any other capabilities and habits acquired by man as a member of society'.[9] This is a common source to which both social anthropologists and cultural anthropologists have appealed, despite the deep differences which until very recently have separated not only those two anthropological traditions,

---

actually not all that clear during the modern period, i.e., eighteenth century onwards; (2) the difference plays no role in Tillich's concept of culture.
[6] *Culture and Society, 1780–1950* (Harmondsworth, 1963), p. 16. See also *Keywords*, pp. 76–82.
[7] But, see *Keywords*, pp. 80ff.
[8] London, 1871; repr. New York, 1924.
[9] *Ibid.*, p. 1.

but cultural anthropology and sociology as well. These differences at one time generated heated and bitter arguments which, in the view of two leading protagonists, had 'impeded theoretical advance'. The controversy reached such proportions in the United States that in the late 1950's those two protagonists — A. L. Kroeber and Talcott Parsons — publicly proclaimed a truce 'to quarreling over whether culture is best understood from the perspective of society or society from that of culture'.[10]

The situation in Britain has been quite different, owing partly to the clear domination of social anthropology over cultural anthropology. After the split between the two traditions, most social anthropologists have seemed to share Radcliffe-Brown's hardly secret suspicion that cultural anthropology is inherently wooly-minded and unscientific.[11] Despite the current revival of interest in a particular kind of 'cultural anthropology' (conceived as the study of symbol systems), there remain British social anthropologists who without hesitation would place even the word 'culture' under a general ban, as if it were a danger to the purity of their science.[12] This counts against the hopeful view expressed by some — on both sides of the Atlantic — that the traditional cleavage between cultural anthropologists and social anthropologists is a thing of the past.[13]

Cultural anthropology is in large measure a product of the same intellectual tradition within which Tillich's concept of culture is to be interpreted. But, the immediate background of his usage of the word 'culture' lies not so much in scientific anthropology as in the work of certain speculative philosophers of history and culture who have been largely responsible for shaping the modern German (and American?) conceptions of *Kultur*. Rooted though it may be in mediaeval mysticism and in the classical tradition,[14] the German conception of culture gained its specifically modern shape only gradually from about the eighteenth century.

---

[10] 'The Concepts of Culture and of Social System', *American Sociological Review*, XXIII (1958), 582—3.

[11] See esp. *Structure and Function in Primitive Society* (London, 1952) and *A Natural Science of Culture* (Glencoe, Ill., 1957).

[12] See, e.g., Mary Douglas's review in the *Times Literary Supplement* (8 August 1975, pp. 886f) of Clifford Geertz, *The Interpretation of Cultures* (London, 1975).

[13] Cf., e.g., Z. Barbu, *Society, Culture and Personality* (Oxford, 1971).

[14] See Ernst Lichtenstein, *Zur Entwicklung des Bildungsbegriffs von Meister Eckhardt bis Hegel*, "Pädagogische Forschungen" (Heidelberg, 1966).

Broadly speaking, three strands can be said to constitute this modern conception of culture: (1) 'culture' as the cultivation of natural capacities; (2) 'culture' as *Geistesleben*; (3) 'culture' as a complex whole. The last of the three is the most extended sense of the term and is associated with the rise of scientific anthropology in America, as well as in Germany. There is a certain sense in which these three senses could be called phases or stages in the development of our modern usage of the word 'culture': the first sense tends to dominate in the literature of the late-18th and early-19th centuries; the second one in the early- and mid-19th century; whilst the final one plays an increasingly important role from about the latter third of the 19th century. It is tempting to think, therefore, that we have to do with phases of development. Some people who have attempted to trace the history of conceptions of culture have in fact yielded all to readily to this temptation.[15] There are, however, three reasons why it should be resisted. First, examples of all three senses can be found already in the late-18th century.[16] Even when the word 'culture' does not itself appear, each of the three concepts is already present, sometimes developed in relationship to one another.[17] Secondly, within both English and German the word 'culture'/'Kultur' continues to be used commonly in all three senses, so that it would be misleading to describe the three strands merely as stages or phases. Thirdly, not only do we continue to use the word 'culture' in each of these relatively distinct senses, but those earlier and less extended uses of 'culture' continue in many cases to inform and influence even its modern anthropological meaning, which is generally supposed to be purely descriptive (whether 'thin' or 'thick') and non-honorific.

The first of the three senses — culture as cultivation — seems to be the 'root meaning' both in the sense that it is the earliest and in the sense that the other two are extensions/modifications of it. I do not want to make too much of this idea of a 'root meaning', since the importance of etymology and word-history is sometimes overstressed to the point of grotesqueness in the work of some philosophers who have enjoyed widespread influence in

---

[15] E.g., Kroeber and Kluckhohn, *Culture*.
[16] We shall see shortly that all three strands are present in J. G. Herder, *Ideen zur Philosophie der Geschichte der Menschheit* (1784–91; repr. Darmstadt, 1966).
[17] See, e.g., J. G. Fichte, *Grundlage des Naturrechts nach Principien der Wissenschaftslehre* (1796) in *Sämmtliche Werke*, ed. J. H. Fichte (Berlin, 1854–6), vol. III.

our time. Etymology is sometimes more misleading than it is illuminating as to a word's current usage, which may in fact be the direct opposite of its 'root meaning'. One does not have to be a Heideggerian, however, to acknowledge that in some cases the history of a word's usage can help clarify aspects of the way it is currently used. It was after all the Oxford analytic philosopher, J. L. Austin, who once said that a word never entirely escapes from its own past.[18] Whether this holds for all words, it seems to hold for the word 'culture' so that some of the difficulties which continue to beset cultural historians and cultural anthropologists seem to stem in part from the peculiar history of the word 'culture'.[19] For all that is specifically modern in his attempt to give an account of the interrelationship between biological, psychological, sociological and cultural factors in the evolution of man, Clifford Geertz's claim that 'we are . . . incomplete or unfinished animals who complete or finish ourselves through culture'[20] has a quaintly 18th-century ring to it, if of a romanticist rather than rationalist tone. Likewise, his attempt to redefine culture as 'an historically transmitted pattern of meanings embodied in symbols'[21] is a conception of culture which would not have been entirely foreign to many writers in the early-19th century — even if the way Geertz operationalises that conception would have been quite alien to those more speculatively inclined philosophers of *Geist*.

These, then, are three reasons why it would be more appropriate to refer to the three main senses of 'culture' as strands or dimensions, rather than as temporary stages on the way to our modern conception of culture. Even if this were not true of the ordinary usage of the word 'culture', it would still be true of Tillich's particular usage of 'Kultur'/'culture'. Tillich says surprisingly little about what he means by 'culture', though he uses the term frequently in all periods of his intellectual development. An analysis of how the word functions in his writings, however, shows that each of the three strands is present. By separating out the strands for individual consideration,

---

[18] J. L. Austin, *Philosophical Papers* (Oxford, 1961), p. 149: '. . . a word never — well, hardly ever — shakes off its etymology and its formation. In spite of all changes in and extensions of and additions to its meanings, and indeed rather pervading and governing these, there will still persist the old idea.'

[19] On some of the ways the use of 'culture' within cultural history has been dogged by its own past, see Gombrich, *In Search of Cultural History*.

[20] *The Interpretation of Cultures*, p. 49.

[21] *Ibid*, p. 89.

it is hoped that a clearer understanding will be gained as to the various dimensions of Tillich's attempt to mediate between religion and culture.[22]

1. Culture as Cultivation

Although the word 'culture' began to acquire its modern associations during the latter part of the 18th century, it had already a long history of usage. It was used in Roman times principally in the sense of tending and cultivating the land — a meaning preserved in our words 'agriculture' and 'horticulture'. It was also sometimes used in the sense of domesticating or training animals. In either case, something which is found wild in nature — whether plants or animals — is trained and tended. This meaning was extended by Cicero when he spoke of cultivating the mind or the spirit, that is, *cultura animi*.[23] The image is clear and forceful. Through culture or cultivation man's natural capacities are trained and developed or perfected.[24] Culture is here to be understood as the process whereby this 'perfection' is accomplished, rather than as the result of that process, though the word later came to be used for the result as well. Just as one could be educated or have education, one could be cultured or have culture. In either case, the human mind must be cultivated and tended, just as plants and animals are cultivated and tended. This analogy proved persuasive and is one of the main roots of our modern conception of culture. It is associated with the emphasis during the enlightenment upon education and improvement, whether of individuals, of nations or of mankind as a whole. In general, this use of 'culture' was highly evaluative, honorific and, ultimately, self-

---

[22] As in the case of 'religion' in the previous chapter, our analysis here must be selective and partial.

[23] *Tusculanae disputationes*, Book III, ch. 5: 'Cultura autem animi philosophia est. . . .' Cf. also Immanuel Kant, who described *metaphysics* as 'die Vollendung aller Kultur der menschlichen Vernunft.' *Kritik der reinen Vernunft*, A, 850/B, 878.

[24] This explains in part why 'culture' and 'education' are such closely related notions — a kinship preserved more clearly in the German words *Bildung* and *Ausbildung*. However, it should not be thought that human cultivation was always thought of just as *mental* training. Kant spoke of the culture of the body, as well as the culture of the mind, in his lectures on education theory. See the Academy edition of the *Gesammelte Schriften* (Berlin, 1910ff), vol. IX, p. 469.

congratulatory: the end of culture is perfection and enlightenment! In the universal histories of the period, the history of mankind from the origins of the race to modern times was quite commonly treated in fairly strict analogy with the development of the individual from birth to complete physical and mental maturity.[25] The German philosopher Fichte distinguished three states or conditions of mankind: the state of innocence or man's natural condition; the state of culture, in which man is on the way to the realisation of his natural capacities; and, finally, the state of perfection, which is also called 'the age of philosophy'.[26] Perfection is the end of culture; culture is the means of human perfection.

What was true of mankind as a whole was also true of individual men. Self-cultivation (*Bildung*) is the means of individual perfection; perfection is the end of self-cultivation. This more individualistic understanding of *cultura animi* is the primary meaning of the word as used by those humanistically trained writers and philosophers of the late-18th century who made 'culture' and associated terms some of the most fashionable words of the period, at least among those who frequented the most fashionable salons — that is, among those whose social positions and personal fortunes allowed the luxury of self-cultivation! Having rejected for the most part traditional christianity under the impact of its critique during the enlightenment, 'culture' became for many intellectuals a kind of ersatz-religion. And, like the pietism which they had shed, culture was conceived in an intensely personal, internal and individual way. Culture was a means for the salvation of the soul, to borrow a phrase used by Wilhelm von Humboldt. 'The true aim of earthly existence', he wrote, 'is the development of all the germs that lie in the individual's personal endowment.'[27] In

---

[25] In his *Versuch einer Geschichte der Kultur des Menschlichen*, published anonymously in Leipzig in 1782, Johan Christoph Adelung traced the history of the progressive ennobling of mankind from the origins of the race to modern times in more or less strict analogy with the development of the individual from an embryo to complete physical and mental maturity. This analogy proved popular and was used later, though to different ends, by such writers as Hegel and Spengler.

[26] Vorlesung der Logik und Metaphysik, summer semester 1797, in *Gesamtausgabe*, IV/1, p. 193. Cf. *System der Sittenlehre nach den Principien der Wissenschaftslehre* (1798) in *Sämmtliche Werke*, vol. IV.

[27] *Briefe an eine Freundin* (Berlin, 1909), vol. II, p. 244, adapted from W. H. Bruford, *The German Tradition of Self-Cultivation* (Cambridge, 1975), p. 26.

the achievement of this aim, religion is both unessential and also a hindrance for the free spirit: 'The idea of spiritual perfection in itself is great and satisfying and inspiring enough not to be in any need of a veil or personal form', that is theistic religion.[28] One's spirit is free through self-sufficiency in the consciousness of its own inner strength. It would seem that culture has itself taken on religious qualities. Culture is conceived as a secularised substitute for religion in the traditional sense.[29] It would not of course become so for everyone. It was allowed that the masses would in the nature of things remain tied to the mythological and anthropomorphic trappings of religion; only the intellectual elite, the sensitive few whose spirits had been freed from such veils through a higher degree of culture could rid themselves entirely of religion.

These are just the people adressed by Friedrich Schleiermacher in the *Speeches on Religion*, a volume directed at those who 'have raised themselves above the vulgar and are saturated by the wisdom of the centuries'.[30] Schleiermacher took their understanding of culture, as the cultivation of all natural capacities, and built his defense of religion around it. He argued in effect that their rejection of religion stood in flat contradiction to their quest for perfection through self-cultivation, through culture. Since the germ of religion is in every man, whether or not it is allowed to grow, it must be among his natural capacities or *Fähigkeiten*. Since one cannot be fully 'cultured' unless one has developed each of one's innate capacities, one cannot ignore or suppress the religious impulse and be completely 'cultured'. Consequently, according to Schleiermacher's largely ad hominem but widely effective argument, not only *can* the 'cultured' also be religious, one *must* be religious in order to be cultured. It may be observed that Schleiermacher addresses the cultured not as a member of the

---

For much that is contained in this paragraph, I am dependent on Bruford. Cf. E. Spranger, *Wilhelm von Humboldt und die Humanitätsidee* (Berlin, 1909) and *Wilhelm von Humboldt und die Reform des Bildungswesens* (Berlin, 1910). See also E. L. Stahl, *Die religiöse und die humanitätsphilosophische Bildungsidee* (Bern, 1934).

[28] *Gesammelte Schriften*, Academy edition (Berlin, 1918), vol. I, p. 151, cited in Bruford, *op. cit.*, p. 18.

[29] Cf., e.g., Franz Rauhut, 'Die Herkunft der Worte und Begriffe „Kultur", „Civilisation" und „Bildung"', *Germanisch-Romanische Monatsschrift*, n.s. III (1953), 81.

[30] New York, 1958, p. 1.

vulgar crowd which they despised, but as one of their own — a point not missed by Barth![31] He spoke as one of the cultured in whom the germ of religion has taken root and grown, in whom the religious capacity has been actualised. It need hardly be mentioned that there is in this view of culture an implicit elitism, even if Schleiermacher is in other respects anti-elitist.[32]

In view of this elitism and the frankly *bürgerlich* character of *Bildung*, one might suppose that Tillich's own usage of 'culture' is considerably removed from this first strand. For, as a member of the religious socialist movement during the Weimar Republic, he had attacked the way the capitalist classes, through their control of the education system, had used education as the means both of their own self-fulfillment and also of suppression of the working masses. (e.g., GW. II. 116f; X. 16, 43f, 58ff) In so doing, Tillich had moved far from not only Schleiermacher but also from the *bürgerlich* form of 'christian socialism' advocated by his ethics teacher at Halle, Wilhelm Lütgert, who had argued that workers must rest content with their particular station in society since society must be organised according to functions in order to work efficiently and effectively to the good of the whole nation (*Volksganzen*).[33] For the Tillich of the 1920s, the 'social situation' was defined by the struggle of the proletariat against the capitalist society in its decadent phase. Nor was this struggle thought to be restricted to the economic and political spheres. It was thought to be seen in every sphere of cultural life in the revolt against the spirit of capitalism. (GW. X. 19f *et passim*) It follows from this that in at least one situation the proletariat — not the intellectual elite — was regarded by Tillich as the agent of social and, ultimately, cultural change.

These views, developed by Tillich in a number of places, would seem to give substance to a claim that his use of *Kultur* has little to do with *die Gebildeten*. It would seem that his view of culture could hardly be elitist in

---

[31] Cf. *Protestant Theology in the Nineteenth Century* (London, 1972), pp. 433ff.

[32] On Schleiermacher's 'elitism', see Y. Spiegel, *Theologie der bürgerlichen Gesellschaft: Sozialphilosophie und Glaubenslehre bei Friedrich Schleiermacher* (Munich, 1968). Even though the ideal of self-cultivation was essentially for the few, rather than the masses, it was sometimes held that the cultured few would eventually lead the masses to freedom and enlightenment as well. This would seem to be the view expressed, for instance, in Kant's essay 'Was ist Aufklärung?' and in Fichte's *Grundlage des Naturrechts* (1796).

[33] See especially his collection *Natur und Geist Gottes* (Leipzig, 1910), pp. 102ff.

the sense that Schleiermacher's transparently was. Nor would such a judgment be simply mistaken. But it must be qualified in two ways.

First, and most obviously, the role of the proletariat in social change is in Tillich's view contingent, not necessary. That is to say, from Tillich's claim that the proletarian class was the principal agent of social change in the years following the first world war it does not follow that Tillich also held that the proletariat is in all situations the principal agent of social change. The notion of the individual social class as the carrier and transmitter (*Träger*) of beliefs and values appears first in Tillich's elaborately argued pamphlet on 'Masse und Geist' which appeared in 1922 (repr. GW. II. 35—90) and is developed further in his subsequent writings on religious socialism. (GW. II. 159—174, 175—192) It also underlies the argument of *Die religiöse Lage*. In each case, however, it is obvious that the class which serves as carrier varies from situation to situation. (cf., e.g., GW. II. 193—208)

Secondly, there is in Tillich's mainly unpublished writings from before the first world war evidence of an elitism not unlike that ascribed already to Schleiermacher. Tillich's interest then was not with the proletariat or with the 'masses'. His interest was 'the cultured', the *Gebildeten*, among whom many had rejected christianity outright. It was *their* alienation from historical christianity, rather than the alienation (in the marxian sense) of the proletariat in society which occupied the centre of Tillich's concern then. When in 1912 he was examined for his *Licentiat* in theology, Tillich defended ten theses, the last of which concerns the church's apologetic mission to the cultured ('. . . ihrer apologetischen Aufgabe an die Gebildeten . . .').[34] And the *Kirchliche Apologetik* in particular substantiates the view that before the first war Tillich was primarily concerned to mediate between the christian message and the cultured who were estranged from christianity. (GW. XII. 38—9) At that time he regarded *their* estrangement, and not the self-alienation of the proletariat, as defining the social situation and dictating the tasks of theology. There is even the near-explicit claim that the cultured are the transmitters of culture, so that the formation and preservation of social beliefs and values is committed to their care. There is in that work no interest in 'mass culture' or in 'the proletarian situation' which was to play such a vital role in Tillich's writings

---

[34] See below, p. 165f.

after the first world war. Nor is this quasi-elitism restricted to Tillich's writings before 1914–1918.

A continued preoccupation with the 'cultured' is evidenced in the *Systematic Theology*. One thinks not least of Tillich's desire to produce 'an honest theology of cultural high standing'. (ST. I. 7) This is even more explicit in the introduction to the final volume of that work where, seeking to justify his departure from traditional theological language in preference for 'philosophical and psychological concepts', Tillich states, 'This procedure seems more suitable for a systematic theology which tries to speak understandably [intelligibly?] to the large group of educated people . . . for whom traditional language has become irrelevant.' (ST. III. 4) In his earlier writings he might have spoken of the working masses for whom traditional language has become irrelevant. (e.g. RV, 38; cf. GW. XII. 37–42) The shift in the *Systematic Theology* is not insignificant. He would seem to have come full circle, back to the position of the *Kirchliche Apologetik*. That the circle is in the respect round is made even more obvious by the wording chosen in the German edition: '. . . eine Theologie . . ., welche versucht . . . zu einer breiten Gruppe Gebildeter . . . zu sprechen . . .' (STd. III. 14)

The continued presence of this particular dimension of *Kultur* is evident as well in the procedure used by Tillich to determine the character of the present 'cultural situation'. From the way he went about analysing the situation, one learns a great deal about his conception of culture and its effect upon his understanding of the problem of religion and culture. Though he is hardly blatantly elitist in the way the early Schleiermacher may have been, Tillich is consistently selective in his choice of sources for interpreting 'the present situation'. It is fairly clear from the sorts of sources chosen he does *not* want to determine how most people at a given time understand themselves and the times in which they live. For, had he wanted to know that, he would have turned to the 'popular culture' or 'mass culture' of the day: the mass media (including radio and the cinema and, later on, television), the tabloid newspapers, the pulp magazines, the paperbacks which sell well at railway stations and airports. But this is not where Tillich turned and one suspects it is because that is not what Tillich wanted to know about 'the present cultural situation'. That this is the case is perhaps confirmed when we are told that 'the proletarian situation' is not to be confused with the situation of the proletariat! (GW. VII. 87) When Tillich describes the present cultural situation, he turns not to those sources

I have just listed, but to those writers whose appeal is mainly to the intellectuals, to those painters whose works had little popular appeal, to the leading philosophers of the day and to those mythologies (such as psychoanalysis) which appeal again mainly to a relatively small and educated segment of society. It is to the 'cultured' that Tillich's apologia is addressed and it is their self-understanding which determines for him the self-understanding of the age. (cf. TC, 46f) Tillich's definition of culture as the *totality* of man's self-interpretation has a rather more restricted meaning that one might have assumed.[35]

This view of the cultural situation both contributes to and follows from the tendency in the *Systematic Theology* in particular to reduce the problem of the relations between religion and culture to the problem of the correlation of theology and philosophy. Despite his oft-repeated emphasis in the latter 1920's that *Kultur* cannot be reduced to 'Geistesleben', but must include the socio-economic dimension as well (GW. X. 95, 108f), it is arguable that not only later but even in those works the infrastructure of society is never successfully incorporated into Tillich's theory of culture.[36] For he persisted even in those writings to speak primarily of relations of religion to *Geistesleben* and the *Geisteslage*. This raises issues some of which can best be treated in relation to the second dimension of the concept of *Kultur*.

2. Culture as Geistesleben

The second strand of our modern conception of culture is also traceable to the speculatively spun universal histories of the enlightenment, with their stress upon the gradual education of the human race from its rude beginnings to its virtually complete perfection during the enlightenment. The stress here, however, is not as in the first strand. There the emphasis was on the *process* of cultivation, whereas here the emphasis is more on the *individual stages* of that process. In the universal histories of the eighteenth century it

---

[35] I do not quarrel with Tillich's judgment that the sources selected are intrinsically interesting and culturally important; I quarrel with his assumtion that they constitute the culture of the present, in the sense of 'the entire way of life of a society'. There is a wide gap between his cultural 'data' and what he claims for them.
[36] For a contrary view, see E. Amelung, *Die Gestalt der Liebe*, pp. 133ff.

was common to speak of each successive civilisation – whether Chinese, Indian, Greek or modern European – as representing a higher stage in the progress of human culture. The notion of culture-stages allowed one to draw contrasts between 'our culture' and 'their culture'.[37] It also seems to have encouraged one to talk increasingly of the individual 'stages' as distinct 'cultures'. Herder, for instance, spoke not only of different *degrees* of culture, but also of different *sorts* of culture.[38] This would have been unthinkable within the confines of the first strand. In many ways Herder signifies a transition between these first two strands. He is for that reason crucial for any account of the emergence of modern conceptions of culture.

Herder's thought is not without a certain amount of tension. On the one hand, he held that each society and each historical period is unique and, in some sense, incomparable. Each may be judged only according to its own criteria, and not according to the standards appropriate to another society or to another time. This is a function of his concept of *Individualität*. Every human perfection is 'individual' in the sense of national: 'Each [nation] carries within itself the symmetry of its own perfection wholly independent of and incomparable with other [nations].'[39] It follows, according to Herder, that each people and each period is equally worthy of respect. No group or age can be dismissed as simply 'unenlightened'.[40] Nor can any group or age be regarded merely as a lower stage on the way to some higher level of culture, especially not stages on the way to European culture. 'Those who have perished through the ages', he writes, 'have not lived merely to fertilise the earth with their ashes so that at the end of time their posterity should be made happy by European culture. Would not the very thought of a superior European culture be an insult to the majesty of Nature?'[41] This line of thinking allowed a new valuation not only of primitive cultures or even of mediaeval culture, but also of contemporary, non-European cultures – something which had not been possible within

---

[37] Herder, *Ideen*, p. 199 *et passim*.
[38] *Ibid.*, pp. 207ff. He also speaks, e.g., of 'asiatic culture' (p. 205) and 'european culture' (p. 227).
[39] *Ibid.*, p. 407. The spirit of the people (*Volksgeist*) is regarded as the driving force of culture and the expression of the group's individuality.
[40] The difference between 'enlightened' and 'unenlightened' is for Herder only a difference of degree. No people is wholly without culture. *Ibid.*, pp. 227, 39.
[41] *Ibid.*, p. 224.

the framework of the enlightenment histories of the progressive cultivation of mankind. But this is only one side of Herder's philosophy of culture. For Herder, too, held to the notion of a universal, progressive and purposeful history of mankind.[42] This is a function of his concept of *Humanität*, and of his belief in divine providence. 'A wise goodness governs the destiny of mankind.'[43] The powers (*Kräfte*) inherent in nature and history drive toward order through conflict.[44] This is accomplished through 'the chain of culture',[45] each link of which is unique. Each *Volksgeist* is both unique and a stage in the culture of humanity, though it must be acknowledged that these two moments in Herder's philosophy are not completely reconciled with each other.

Some of the tension in Herder's philosophy of culture is resolved by Hegel through the introduction of the notion that each individual culture or historical period is a moment in the life of the 'world spirit'. The notion of the dialectical manifestation of spirit in increasingly suitable structures provides Hegel both with a historical principle which allows him to explain the history of cultures and also with an integrative principle which allows him to explain the uniqueness of each individual culture. Each aspect can be easily illustrated from his writings. On the one hand, in his lectures on the fine arts, the history of art is traced from symbolic art through classicism to romanticism. This history is said to record the dialectical evolution of the 'idea' coming to be expressed in increasingly appropriate forms until, as in romanticism, 'form' and 'content' are perfectly matched.[46] Religion is similarly presented in the lectures on the philopshy of religion. On the other hand, in the briefer but nonetheless wider-ranging lectures on the philosophy of history, the individual stages of the development of art forms are correlated with the other spheres of the culture in question. Classicism in art, for instance, is correlated with Greek philosophy and political structure. Though there are two main aspects of Hegel's philosophy of culture, the notion of *Geist* as the driving force of human creativity supports both. Individual cultures grow out of and are moments in the life of the spirit; every aspect of a given culture — its science, its art, its

---

[42] *Ibid.*, pp. 395—420.
[43] *Ibid.*, p. 416.
[44] *Ibid.*, pp. 400 ff.
[45] *ibid.*, p. 406.
[46] *Werke*, XIII, pp. 111 ff.

religion, its philosophy — reflects the stage to which the spirit has attained in that culture or at that time. Each culture and each phase in culture history is to be interpreted in the light of its mental products, but most especially its philosophy. For philosophy, according to Hegel, is 'its own time expressed in thought'.

For Hegel and Herder alike, culture is the self-expression of spirit in the speech, institutions, activities and artifacts of a group or of a period. In fine, culture is *Geistesleben*. But Hegel's philosophy of spirit and Herder's philosophy of spirit would seem to have less in common than at first appears. There is something earthy about Herder's conception of 'the spirit of the people', but in Hegel's thought it seems — perhaps wrongly — to be increasingly abstracted from the actual life of the people, until it is peculiarly the province of the few. Indeed, it would seem that only the philosopher is competent to determine its true character, everyone else having only a partially clear vision of it contours. The philosopher alone comprehends the determinate spirit of the particular people or the specific time as expressed in its mental products. Thus, the spirit of a time or of a group is most immediately grasped in its philosophy.

The extent to which Tillich was indebted to this second strand in the German conception of culture is clearly evidenced by the central role of *Geist* in all his writings on culture from his preliminary sketch of the modern intellectual situation (*Geisteskultur*) in the *Kirchliche Apologetik* to his systematic treatment of culture in the fourth part of his dogmatics entitled 'Life and the Spirit'. (ST. III. 11–294) Tillich — like Hegel — viewed culture as belonging to the realm of objective spirit, to man's 'second nature' which he himself has created and in which he becomes conscious of himself as 'spirit'. (GW. IX. 13–4) 'Culture is that which the human spirit creates out of the given — from the level of mere technology, from the most primitive tool to the highest forms of artistic and intellectual life . . .' (GW. IX. 94) Although it would be misleading to label him simply an 'hegelian', Tillich held that each particular time or group has its own character or spirit and that this character is most directly grasped in its philosophy. He defined a cultural period or, as he sometimes preferred, 'situation' as 'the totality of man's creative self-interpretation in a specific period', (ST. I. 4) the analysis of which is said to be a peculiarly philosophical task, even if it is undertaken by a theologian. (ST. I. 63) But, the hegelian connexion is made even clearer elsewhere in Tillich's writings. For, according to one account at least, Tillich regarded philosophy as 'the immediate expression of the age in the theoretical sphere' (GW. X. 27) Philosophy has a certain primacy over science and art, though science is said to be more important for the formation of the cultural situation and art for its apprehension, albeit symbolically. (GW. X. 33) Implied here is a characteristically hegelian move: metaphysics expresses conceptually what art apprehends symbolically and art apprehends symbolically what science knows objectively. That is to say, art serves dialectically as a bridge between nature (science) and spirit (philosophy). But, Tillich shrinks back from the hegelian conclusion, and — rejecting what he terms bourgeois notions of progress — opts instead for a 'belief-full realism'.[47]

Tillich was not strictly speaking an hegelian in his philosophy of culture. He had drunk deep at the wells of the sort of historicism which has as one of its sources Herder and as one of its last proponents Tillich's esteemed colleague at Berlin, Ernst Troeltsch.[48] Like Herder and Troeltsch before him, Tillich stressed the uniqueness and individuality of cultural totalities and, in the main, rejected the notion of history's moving through progressive stages of development from one culture to the next. Even so, Tillich never rejected entirely the notion of progress. (FR. 64ff; cf. ST. III. 333ff, 352—4) Each age stands directly and equally near the ultimate and unconditioned ground of history, so that there is no simple progress from 'primitive' to 'cultured' societies. (but, cf. ST. III. 365) Though, like Herder, Tillich held that history is ultimately directed by and fulfilled in God, one misses in his writings the confidence with which Hegel traced the progressive manifestation of the *Weltgeist* in increasingly appropriate forms. There is, for instance, in Tillich's aesthetic theory no continuous history of art forms. The individual 'styles' are said to have a history, but there is no 'development' (*Entwicklung*) from one style to another, as there is for Hegel. Each style carries within itself its own perfections, as for Herder.[49] Nor is there for Tillich any historical necessity in the evolution either within or between societies: moments of 'theonomy', for instance, are always in danger of degenerating into self-sufficient autonomy on the one hand or into heteronomy on the other. Tillich characterised the confidence with which Hegel read history as Hegel's hubris. (PNT, 119f; cf. ST. III. 373)

---

[47] The concept of 'belief-full realism' will be considered briefly below in chapter six.
[48] For a helpful 'history of historicism', see G. Iggers, *The German Conception of History* (Middleton, Conn., 1968).
[49] Compare ST. III. 334 with Herder, *Ideen*, pp. 407—8.

There is one decisive point at which Tillich follows Hegel in seeing the emergence of progressively suitable 'forms' of expression until 'form' and 'content' are perfectly and insuperably suited to one another: namely, in the history of religions, which is said to lead to and find fulfillment in the incarnation.[50] This alone would suggest that Tillich refused to follow a 'historicist' line consistently. He held back from the consequences drawn by Troeltsch's putatively excessive relativism, especially as regards the relationship between christianity and western culture. Even though Tillich conceded that christianity as a religion is totally relative, its foundation is regarded as absolute and the criterion by which all religions are to be judged, including christianity. Tillich attempts to escape from the threatened 'anarchy of beliefs and values' by distinguishing the 'eternal content' of the 'christian message' from its 'temporal forms of expression'. The question forces itself on us, however, whether this distinction can be sustained.[51] The adequacy of Tillich's solution to Schleiermacher's dilemma depends in part on the answer to that question.

Not everything, of course, hangs on the answer to a single question. One could also mention a second way Tillich attempts to break out of the 'western' corner into which Troeltsch had with great consistency painted himself. Tillich does not characteristically speak of a 'universal history of humanity' in the way the enlightenment philosophers of history were inclined. Instead, he joined Troeltsch in rejecting such a notion outright. (See ST. III. 311, 340f, 382ff) In addition, Tillich held that even if it were possible to speak of a universal history, in the sense of a 'world situation', no one person would be able to comprehend it in its entirety. (CA, 69) He did nonetheless speak of a *universal human nature* and of a *universal human condition*. Whenever and wherever man lives, he must come to terms with certain basic questions having to do with the meaning of human existence. (cf. ST. III. 5) The asking of such questions is universal and culture-independent, though the particular way they are asked, of course, remains culture-dependent. This helps account both for the comparability and also for the distinctness of religions and cultures. He does not deny that the religions of disparate culture systems are in large measure comparable, owing to the universality of the human condition and of the function which religions serve. Even so, he also holds that, since

---

[50] See above, pp. 92ff.
[51] This issue is treated below in chapter six.

'existential knowledge presupposes participation', one's ability to 'know' other religious traditions is limited, first, by one's intimate knowledge of the culture of which they form an integral part and, second, by one's ability to construct analogies between religious traditions and cultural systems. (ST. III. 141; cf. STd. III. 167)

Even though Tillich's theory of culture is not simply hegelian, he was nonetheless much influenced by the tradition in which culture was treated as principally *Geistesleben*. One might feel justified in holding that Tillich's theory of culture remained fundamentally an idealist theory of culture, and this despite the undeniable influence of Marx and some marxists on Tillich's thought.[52] Even when he criticised the idealist tradition, Tillich remained to some extent entangled in its web. That this is the case can be shown by reference to Tillich's assessment of Marx's theory of culture/society.

Whereas Hegel had held that cultural creativity is an expression of spirit, Marx sometimes countered that the real basis of society is material, not spiritual. Concentrating initially upon Hegel's philosophy of law, Marx argued that culture in the sense of *Geistesleben* is a kind of 'superstructure' (*Überbau*) erected upon the real foundation, the economic 'substructure' (*Unterbau*) which determines the structure of relationships within society. The function of the *Überbau* is to rationalise and to legitimate the economic conditions of existence. This is the view Marx came eventually to hold, though it is well known that the picture which is presented in his earlier, more speculative philosophical writings is more subtle and intricate and, in the view of some, for that reason more interesting. Adumbrated to some extent in his article 'Toward the Critique of the Hegelian Philosophy of Law' (1844), the later view begins to take shape in the only posthumously published *German Ideology* (written in 1845–6) and more explicity in the "Preface" (1859) to the never completed work to have been entitled *Toward the Critique of the Political Economy*. Having formed the main outlines of his position, Marx subsequently attempted to substantiate its detail by analysing particular historical situations, as when he argued in *The Eighteenth Brumaire of Louis Bonaparte* (1885) that the rivalry between the two royalist parties, the Bourbons and the Orleans, is to be explained in terms of the differences in the 'material conditions of their existence', the

---

[52] One thinks, e.g., of the members of the 'Frankfurt School' with whom Tillich had contact, both in Germany and in New York. See T. W. Adorno, et al., WW, 11ff, 123ff. See also M. Jay, *The Dialectical Imagination* (London, 1973).

Bourbons representing the interests of holders of property and the Orleans the interests of capital. The various arguments put forward by each party in favour of its respective candidate for the crown were, according to Marx, merely ideological rationalisations of the real basis of their competitiveness, namely the conflict of the vested interests of capital and land: 'Upon the different forms of property, upon the social conditions of existence, rises an entire superstructure of distinct and peculiarly formed sentiments, illusions, modes of thought and views of life. The entire class creates and forms them out of its material foundations and out of the corresponding social relations.'[53] What obtains for the relation of economic conditions and ideology in this particular instance is held by Marx to obtain for all times and in all places: the real basis of any society, its beliefs and values and institutions, is to be found in the material conditions of existence. In the earlier preface (1859) to his projected critique of political economy, Marx asserted not only that consciousness is an expression of the material conditions of existence, but also that any change in the economic basis of society is followed 'more or less rapidly' by a transformation of the whole *Überbau*. 'In considering such transformations', he insists, 'a distinction should always be made between the material transformation of the economic conditions of production ... and the legal, political, religious, aesthetic or philosophic — in short, ideological [−] forms in which men become conscious of this conflict and fight it out'.[54]

This distinction between the economic structure of society and its ideological superstructure has proved fruitful in subsequent studies of religious phenomena, even in instances when Marx's account of their interaction is being specifically attacked.[55] It is also a distinction which plays no small role in Tillich's cultural analyses of modern society. One thinks, for instance, of *Die religiöse Lage der Gegenwart* (1926: repr. GW. X), in which Tillich attempted to delineate the cultural transformations which indicate and contribute to the collapse of bourgeois society. The character of bourgeois society, insists Tillich, is not exclusively the character of a particular economic class. It is, rather, an over-all *attitude* toward life and society (GW. X. 9—10), which may be defined in terms of three related

---

[53] *Selected Works* (Moskow and London,1968), p. 117.
[54] *Ibid.*, p. 182.
[55] As, for example, in Max Weber's study of *The Protestant Ethic and the Spirit of Capitalism* (London, 1930).

activities — science, technology and the economy. (GW. X. 15) All other cultural activities are said to be made subservient to and dependent upon this three-fold basis of bourgeois society. Here Tillich ostensibly stands with Marx against Hegel and Weber alike. However, this alliance is finally illusory. For it is the *spirit* of capitalism which is being attacked by Tillich and not the social conditions which — in Marx's view — produce the ideology of capitalism. This is implied in Tillich's characterisation of bourgeois society as an *attitude*. Tillich's critique of Marx in the same work further substantiates this interpretation.

Although Tillich accepts much of Marx's critique of bourgeois society, there is a sense in which Tillich turns Marx on his head, as Marx had turned Hegel on his head. The question is whether this results in a return to Hegel pure and simple. Tillich no doubt would have us conclude that it does not. For, in his view, both Marx and Hegel would have been transcended (*aufgehoben*), each having been corrected in the light of the other. In contrast both to Hegel and to Marx, Tillich could have claimed that he regards the history of culture neither merely as a progressive objectivisation of spirit nor merely as a drama of dialectical materialism. In contrast to Hegel and in apparent agreement with Marx, Tillich interpreted the period from the enlightenment through the nineteenth century as having its real foundation in the economic conditions of existence: it is a period determined by the rise of capitalism. (cf. CA, 20ff) Although the 'foundation' for that particular period, and for all capitalist societies, is located in the material conditions of existence, this does not in Tillich's view necessarily hold for all societies in all times and places: 'The relative truth of social dialectics, rooted in economic conflicts, cannot be denied, but truth becomes error if this kind of dialectics is raised to the status of a law for all history. Then it becomes a quasi-religious principle and loses any empirical verifiability [*sic*!].' (ST. III. 330) According to Tillich, Marx was mistaken in generalising what is true of capitalist societies as if it were true of non-capitalist societies as well. In fact, Tillich argued that by pointing to the material conditions of existence as the real basis of all societies, Marx had betrayed the extent to which he, too, was captive to the spirit of capitalism. Tillich interpreted what he saw as the revolt against the capitalist spirit in the late-nineteenth and early-twentieth centuries as a rejection not merely of a particular economic foundation of society — namely, capitalism — but as a rejection of any economic system as an adequate foundation. In the various trends sketched in *Die religiöse Lage* Tillich saw a full-scale rebellion against the self-sufficiency of materialism and a renewed quest for establishing a new society upon a spiritual (*geistige*) foundation.⁵⁶ Whether in a particular instance 'material' or 'spiritual', the 'foundation' of a society gives rise to and is expressed in the cultural life of that society — in its values, its belief systems, its arts and technology, its sciences and its philosophies, its political and its economic systems. In this regard Tillich concurs with both Hegel and Marx: culture is the direct and immediate expression of its underlying 'foundation'. I shall suggest in the next section of this chapter that this aspect of Tillich's culture theory betrays the fastness with which he was held captive by that same model of cultural unity which held Hegel and Marx alike captive.

Tillich's intention would seem to have been to embrace and criticise both Hegel and Marx in terms of the other. By allowing that in some societies the 'foundation' of its culture is economic, Tillich ostensibly stood with Marx over against Hegel. By insisting that in other societies the foundation is spiritual, Tillich stood with Hegel over against Marx. And he stood with Weber and Troeltsch against both when he claimed that neither theory has universal applicability. Yet the particular mode of Tillich's attempted *Aufhebung* of Hegel and Marx betrays the extent to which he in certain respects remained within the idealist tradition.

If it were the case that Tillich never escaped the idealist theory of culture, this would clearly be contrary to his stated intention. For he noted on more than one occasion that the marxian critique of that tradition must be absorbed before any advance is made in the development of an adequate theory of culture. For instance, in his important transitional essay on 'Die geistige Welt im Jahre 1926', he declared, 'It is no longer permissible since Marx to speak of the cultural situation without mentioning the social situation as well'. (GW. X. 95) Yet it is doubtful that even there he had really absorbed the radical nature of Marx's critique. For in many cases when Tillich 'mentions' the social situation, he tends to 'spiritualise' it, in the sense that he tends to transform, say, the capitalist society into the spirit of the capitalist society. The very title of his article — 'Die geistige Welt im Jahre 1926' — gives the game away. Likewise in *Die religiöse Lage der Gegenwart* 'the real foundation' is translated into an ideological construct. Nor is one given cause to believe that Tillich had really assimilated the

---

⁵⁶ This is how Tillich regarded expressionism in art and literature, existentialism and vitalism in philosophy, depth psychology and even quantum mechanics!

marxian critique of the idealist tradition when he asserts that the history of ideas is separable from general history. (GW. X. 26) The extent to which Tillich remained captive to idealism, even in those places he was writing ostensibly under marxian influence, is suggested also by his having described 'the capitalist economic system' as the 'symbolic expression of the bourgeois spirit'! (GW. VI. 39)

In the *Systematic Theology* the process runs its full course until, step by step, the 'situation' is reduced to *philosophy*. First, 'situation' is translated from the actual conditions under which people live at a given time and in a given place to their 'self-understanding': '"Situation", as one pole of all theological work, does not refer to the psychological or sociological state in which individuals or groups live. It refers to the scientific and artistic, the economic, political, and ethical forms in which they express their interpretation of existence'. (ST. I. 3–4) That is to say, 'situation' is transformed into *ideology*. The next step is to reduce each of these various forms of expression to philosophy. This, too, is done explicitly. Having noted that one of the tasks of the theologian is to relate theology to the 'other forms of knowledge', Tillich says, 'The point of contact between scientific research and theology lies in the philosophical element of both, the sciences and theology. Therefore, the question of the relation of theology to the special sciences merges into the question of the relation between theology and philosophy.' (ST. I. 18; cf. TC, 113; RGG. IV. 1201f) The context makes clear that the term 'sciences' does not mean only the natural and physical sciences.[57] The context further suggest that 'merges into' is to be interpreted more strictly as 'is reduced to'. Thus it is that, at one level at least, 'culture' is reduced in Tillich's methodology to 'the philosophical element' in the various ideological interpretations of human culture.

If culture is reduced to philosophy, one is given added cause to fear that Tillich has narrowed, rather than broadened, the scope of the problem of the structure of relations between religion and culture. On both fronts there would seem to be a clear retreat so that Tillich tends to speak, not so much of the correlation of culture and religion – as he might have done in the early twenties – nor even of society and christianity – as he might have

---

[57] Nor does the German translator understand Tillich to be restricting his comments to the *Naturwissenschaften*: 'Der Beziehungspunkt von wissenschaftlicher Forschung und Theologie liegt in dem philosophischen Element, das sowohl die Wissenschaften als auch die Theologie enthalten.' STd. I. 26.

done in the late twenties and early thirties — but of the correlation of philosophy and theology. This reduction, it would seem, betrays in part the extent of Tillich's continued indebtedness to the first two strands of the German conception of *Kultur*.

3. Culture as 'Complex Whole'

The second strand seems both to be tied to the first and to anticipate the third. Hegel's philosophy of history seems to show how closely the notion of culture as *Geistesleben* is tied to the enlightenment conception of the progress of human culture, whereas the earthy character of Herder's conception of the *Volksgeist* points forward to more recent anthropological conceptions of culture. The anthropologically orientated usage of the word 'culture' has been somewhat unflatteringly described by Gombrich as its 'sterilised' meaning.[58] I take it that he meant this as no compliment to the purity of their discipline. If he should be complaining that the acerbic anthropologists have maliciously robbed the word 'culture' of the richness of meaning which it might be thought to have only within the humanities, then the worry is somewhat misplaced. For the word 'culture', even within scientific anthropology, continues in many cases to carry with it much that is associated with the first two strands identified in this chapter. One is made aware of the continued influence of the idea of the progress of human culture (*cultura animi*) every time an anthropologist speaks even casually of 'primitive culture' or whenever someone writing as recently as Clifford Geertz talks about man's self-creation and self-completion through his culture. The continued effects of the second strand — culture as *Geistesleben* — are felt whenever an anthropologist speaks grandiloquently of 'the superorganic' (Kroeber) or when anthropologists attempt to apply psychological categories to whole societies, as in many 'culture and personality' studies, or whenever one refers glibly to something called 'national character'. And it may be the case that the peculiar history of the word 'culture' has played at least an indirect role whenever an anthropologist has attempted to conceive culture as a totality, as a whole.

When an anthropologist speaks of the unity of a whole culture, he assumes fairly tight connexions between some extraordinarily different

---

[58] *Op. cit.*, p. 2.

sorts of entities, processes, activities and institutions. Gustav Klemm made an early attempt to define the culture of national groups (*Volkskörper*) in terms of their 'customs, knowledge and skills, domestic and public life in time of peace and in time of war, religion, science and art.'[59] Writing possibly under the influence of Klemm,[60] Tylor formulated his above-mentioned definition of *culture* as a 'complex whole'. He did not explicitly claim that his was to be regarded as an exhaustive definition and, indeed, his choice of phrases would seem to suggest that he regarded it simply as enumerative. He would seem to have allowed that there are yet other sorts of things which constitute this complex whole called 'culture'. If one were to add to Tylor's list such items as the economic structure of society, technology and other aspects of material culture, together with the various institutions which support the fabric of society, then it would become even clearer that it is a problem of some proportions to attempt to speak, as Tylor recommended, of a culture as a 'complex whole'. What sense might it make to speak of the quite different sorts of things which constitute a culture as forming together a 'complex unity' or an 'organic whole'? What sort of assumptions would count as warrants for making connexions between these very different kinds of things which would justify talk of the unity of a whole culture?

'We have learned', observes Tilich, 'that cultures are wholes, and that we cannot compare parts of them with parts of others, but must understand the significance of the particulars in the light of the whole.' (MB, 26) This lesson is said to have been learned 'partly through the insight that a living reality is a structured unity, a *Gestalt*, and not a mechanical composite.' Tillich, unfortunately, does not go on to clarify what he means by *Gestalt*, nor how being a 'structured unity' differs from being a 'mechanical composite'. One is left in no doubt, however, that in respect to cultures Tillich believes it preferable to ascribe organic properties, rather than 'merely' mechanical properties.[61]

---

[59] *Allgemeine Kulturgeschichte der Menschheit* (Leipzig, 1843). Later he reduced this to their customs, beliefs and forms of government. See *Allgemeine Kulturwissenschaft* (Leipzig, 1854).

[60] A claim made by A. L. Kroeber in *An Anthropologist Looks at History* (Berkeley, 1963), p. 87.

[61] The background of Tillich's understanding of *Gestalt* is perhaps to be found in *Das System der Wissenschaften* (1923; repr. GW. I). Its ramifications for *Lebensphilosophie* are never far below the surface in part four of the ST.

Since there is no compelling reason to think that Tillich is using the word *Gestalt* is some idiosyncratic sense, it might be reasonable to assume that the term is being used in its normal 'gestaltist' sense. The gestaltist's claim is popularly understood as 'the whole is greater than the sum of its parts'. Some might regard this claim as extravagant. But the gestaltist's claim is capable of at least two different interpretations. One might construe it in such a way that the 'whole' is regarded as something other than and in addition to the several parts which constitute it. If so construed, it would be difficult to see why this claim should not be dismissed simply as a category mistake. Yet, the claim is capable of being understood in another way, a way which need not involve one in a category mistake. The gestaltist's emphasis would seem to be on the organic unity of the several parts, a unity that enables them to do something collectively which none is able to do individually and which is not simply the sum of their individual skills. They are mutually adaptive so that new and frequently highly complex tasks can be performed and they are sometimes mutually supportive so that the organism is more able to survive external threats to its existence. The gestaltist's claim of 'structural unity' undoubtedly expresses insight into the way the various elements of certain — especially organic — structures affect one another. The claim need not involve a confusion of categories. Whether a claim appropriate to *organic* wholes is also applicable to *cultural* wholes is another question. The metaphor has had appeal for many, including Tillich.

When Tillich offers grounds for his assertion that the very different components which make up a culture constitute a 'structured unity', however, he appeals not so much to the metaphor of an organism as to a metaphor borrowed from art. The list of individual components varies in Tillich's writings,[62] but he characteristically claims that each component of a given

---

[62] When talking about the components of culture, Tillich may simply enumerate them or he may sometimes schematise them. If the latter, he tends with some consistency to divide culture into two spheres, the one theoretical and the other practical. (Cf., e.g., GW. I. 230, 350ff; X. 20; ST. III. 57ff) The two basic cultural acts are said to be *language* (representing the theoretical sphere) and *technology* (representing the practical). Those aspects of culture which are said to comprise each sphere may vary in Tillich's writings. Even so, cultural activities such as art and literature, science and metaphysics tend to comprise the theoretical sphere; such elements as personal and social ethics, the state and the law, technology and material artifacts tend to comprise the practical sphere. The listings for the practical sphere are more various than the listings for the theoret-

culture shares in and expresses a common 'style', the style of the culture. Through the analysis of this common style one gains access to that which is said to give unity to a culture, namely, its *substance*. (TC, 42–3; ST. III. 60; GW. IX. 22)

Tillich's having appealed to both metaphors when referring to the unity of a culture is curious. The unity appropriate to an organism and the stylistic unity appropriate to various works of art would seem to have little in common. The attractiveness of both metaphors to Tillich may in fact betray the largely hidden influence of someone else for whom both organic and stylistic metaphors held considerable attraction. In an easily overlooked footnote, Tillich intimates that the concept of 'the style of a culture' is borrowed from Oswald Spengler, the dilettantish and somewhat eccentric author of the best-selling volumes on 'the decline of the west' which appeared at the end of the first world war.[63] One could perhaps understand why such a work might have appealed to the young Tillich in 1918. It is more difficult to understand why he seems to have continued throughout his life to regard Spengler as a figure of significance.[64]

The use of 'style' in the interpretation of cultures is by no means original with Spengler. Indeed, his own use of that concept was clumsy and heavy-handed in comparison to its use by Jacob Burckhardt, the culture historian at Basel who first made extensive use of 'style' as a key to interpreting cultures.[65] Spengler's usage also loses the freshness and vitality of Nietzsche's occasional and largely informal concept of style. In his *Unzeitgemässe Betrachtungen*, for instance, Nietzsche had characterised the

---

ical. (Cf. GW. X. 20 and ST. III. 66) This fact may not be wholly insignificant, for it suggests that Tillich had a clearer conception of what constitutes the 'theoretical' or ideological side of culture than of what constitutes its 'practical' side.

[63] RV. 285. The reference does not appear in the most accessible English translation of the article to which the footnote is appended. See S. Hook (ed.), *Religious Experience and Truth* (London, 1962), pp. 301ff. Nor does it appear in the version reprinted in Tillich's collected works. GW. V. 196ff.

[64] Even in his last writings Tillich still held, as in an address included in *The Future of Religions*, that Spengler was a figure to contend with. (FR, 69; cf. GW. XIII. 137, ST. III. 374)

[65] See, e.g., *Die Kultur der Renaissance in Italien* (Basel, 1860). Cf. Eva Schaper, 'The Concept of Style: The Sociologist's Key to Art?', *British Journal of Aesthetics*, IX (1969), 246–57.

culture of a people as 'the unity of the artistic styles in all manifestations of the life of that people.'[66] Even though Spengler is neither more skillful than Burckhardt nor more sensitive than Nietzsche, *his* particular use of the notion of 'style' is the one which seems to have caught Tillich's imagination. For that reason, we attend to Spengler, rather than to Burckhardt or to Nietzsche.[67]

In the *Untergang* Spengler attempted to develop a new approach to the philosophy of history, an approach which he called, although not entirely to his own satisfaction, 'a morphology of world history'.[68] Our restricted purpose does not require that we attend directly to the problem of relations between cultures in Spengler's methodology, problematic though that aspect of his thought is; we are more specifically concerned with the sort of bond which is required to account for the 'profound, formal connexion' which he reckoned to exist between individual attitudes, activities and institutions of any single culture. According to Spengler the various aspects of a given culture form an organic unity: expressions of art in a given culture, consequently, must be seen in relation to that culture's form of government; religious views, in relation to technology; economic system, in relation to epistemology. There is said to be an 'unmistakeable connexion', for instance, linking together in organic unity the nude statue, the city-state and the development of coin-currency. But, one asks, what is the nature of this 'unmistakeable connexion'? Is he claiming that they are among themselves *causally* conncted so that the development of coin-currency in some way occasioned the appearance of the nude statue?! This would be easily falsifiable in principle, if not in fact. But such is not what Spengler claimed. He did not hold that their *active interaction* binds the various aspects of culture together. Rather, the single spiritual [*seelischen*] principle which is given immediate and direct expression in each indepen-

---

[66] *Werke*, ed. K. Schlechta (Darmstadt, 1966), vol. I, p. 233; cf. p. 142.

[67] That is was from Spengler, rather than from Burckhardt or Nietzsche, that Tillich acquired the notion of the style of a culture is indirectly supported by the total absence of that notion from *Kirchliche Apologetik*, which was written some six years before the first volume of the *Untergang* appeared. Obviously, 'silence' does not prove the influence of Spengler; had the concept of style played a significant role in KA, however, it would have disproved that Tillich borrowed the concept originally from Spengler.

[68] *The Decline of the West* (London, 1932), vol. I, p. 5.

dent element is held to be the cause of their 'unmistakeable connexion'.[69] And this spiritual principle is for Spengler unique to individual cultures, so that there is no over-arching, progressive self-manifestation of a world-soul in universal history; nor is there a universal history of mankind. Rather, each culture is born of its own distinct idea, appropriate to 'its own soul', uniquely embodied in its own activities, institutions and artifacts, and identifiable by their stylistic unity. Indeed, there is no access to the culture's soul except through the 'style' of the culture.

For a single style characterises the history of each distinct culture: 'in the general historical picture of a Culture there can be but one style, *the style of the Culture*'.[70] Yet, there are a number of styles which can be distinguished within the history of the West alone. One thinks, for instance, of gothic, baroque, rococo, romantic styles. Spengler terms these 'style-phases', rather than distinct styles, reserving the latter for such *styles* as 'Chinese' and 'Egyptian': 'Gothic and Baroque are simply the youth and age of one and the same vessel of forms, the style of the West as ripening and ripened'.[71] Styles pass through the same phases as cultures so that the history of a culture is the history of the phases of its particular style.

If we enquire what in Spengler's view the 'style' of a culture looks like, we find that he treats culture styles typologically. This is not necessarily a fatal defect. For typologies, if used properly, can be heuristically useful. Difficulties do arise, however, in the particular way Spengler handles his typologies. For he treats types as prime phenomena, rather than as abstractions and heuristic devices. To put it bluntly, in Spengler's hands, the style determines the artist and not the artist the style. For the 'style' of a culture is the direct and necessary expression of the 'soul' of that culture: any work of art *in* a given culture which is not produced in the 'style' *of* that culture, does not belong properly *to* that culture since it does not express that culture's soul. (We ignore for the moment the circularity of that argument.) This enables Spengler to exclude anomalies and exceptions by definition: the theory stands, in his view, untouched by the existence of counter-examples.

If we enquire similarly what in Tillich's view the 'style' of a culture looks like, we likewise find that he treats culture-styles typologically: 'The

---

[69] *Ibid.*, I, p. 47.
[70] *Ibid.*, I, p. 205.
[71] *Ibid.*

theme of cultural history [*Geistesgeschichte*] is the conflict between theonomy and autonomy'. (GW. I. 388) Tillich's typological use of 'autonomy' and 'theonomy' may bear in certain respects a resemblance to Spengler's typological use of the 'Apollinian' and the 'Faustian' styles, but it is the dissimilarities which are more striking. Autonomous and theonomous 'styles' are in Tillich's account actively competitive within a single culture, so that one or the other at any given time might represent 'the spirit of the age', 'the style of the culture'; neither represents in a straightforward sense the 'spirit' of the 'people' in every phase of their development. Indeed, Tillich seems rather to hold that this dialectic is universal in the sense of operating at all times and in all places within every culture history and not merely within European culture history.

In the context of an argument that cultural analysis[72] is a theological resource of frequently unrecognised importance, Tillich asserts that the key to a theological understanding of a cultural product is its 'style'. He acknowledges that the term 'style' is associated primarily with the fine arts, but claims that its range of applicability extends to other aspects of culture as well. For it is not uncommon to speak of a style of dress, or a style of thought or even a style of life.[73] In addition, however, Tillich insists that an entire culture or a whole period of cultural history may be characterised by its own style which distinguishes it from other cultures and epochs: 'The style of a period expresses itself in its cultural forms, in its choice of objects, in the attitudes of its creative personalities, in its institutions and customs'. (ST. I. 40) Nor is this coincidence of styles within a period or a group mere happenstance, for groups and epochs are in some sense substantially distinct. (ST. III. 324–6; GW. IX. 22) It would not make sense, reasons Tillich, to speak of historical periods or culturally distinct groups were it not the case that the category of substance is applicable to periods and groups; and 'if a history-creating situation is called a substance, this means that there is a point of identity in all its manifestations'. (ST. III. 325) Both the distinctness of cultures from other cultures and the unity which links together individual elements within a single culture are caused by the particular culture's substance, which 'is unconsciously present in a culture, a group, an individual, giving the passion and driving power to him who

---
[72] 'Kulturgeschichte' (STd. I. 50).
[73] For a more thorough treatment of some of the different senses in which we use the word 'style', see A. L. Kroeber, *Style and Civilizations* (Ithaca, New York, 1957), pp. 2ff.

creates and the significance and power of meaning to his creations'. (ST. III. 60) To illustrate his point, Tillich says it is substance which gives a language its expressive ability.

> This is the reason that translation from one language to another is fully possible only in those spheres in which form is predominant over substance (as in mathematics) and becomes difficult or impossible when substance is predominant. In poetry, for example, translation is essentially impossible because poetry is the most direct expression of the substance through an individual. The encounter with reality on which one language is based differs from the encounter with reality in any other language, and this encounter in its totality and its depth is the substance in the cultural self-creation of life. (*ibid*)

The style which characterises the cultural functions of a period or a group is the key which unlocks that period's or that group's 'encounter with reality'. For substance expresses itself in the style of cultural creativity. (GW. IX. 22) Historic periods and cultural groups are, in short, organic wholes which may be interpreted according to the common stylistic patterns evidenced in the individual aspects of the culture of the period or the group. From such almost isolated remarks as these, it becomes clear that Tillich held that cultures are united by their 'controlling idea' which is exhibited in the 'stylistic' unity of that culture's or that age's activities, products and institutions. The controlling idea, however, which underlies and is expressed in each aspect of a culture is the source of its unity. It is the cement which binds the culture together.

Though it may differ in detail, Tillich's theory of culture unity is another instance, of those theories which hold that the unity of a culture derives from some more fundamental power or factor which gives rise to and is expressed in individual cultural activities. Proponents of such theories may call this factor the group's basic 'idea', 'spirit' or 'soul', 'primal vision' or 'intuition'. Talk of the 'interconnexions' between and among the various spheres of a culture may figure in their accounts, even prominently, but the status of such interconnexions in these theories of culture unity is unclear. For there need be no direct link between the various aspects of a culture in order for the whole culture to be unified, since its unity is guaranteed apriori from the basic factor's direct and immediate manifestation in each individual aspect of the culture.

Such schemes of culture unity can be represented in the following diagram in which X stands for the basic factor and the lower case letters represent the individual aspects of a culture — art, technology, science, law, religion, economic system, etc.:

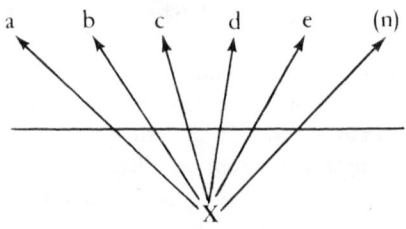

The value of X varies from theory to theory, but in any case it is the driving force of the culture and the source of its 'unity'. Hegel called it the 'idea'; Herder, the 'spirit'; Spengler, the 'soul' of the culture.[74] Tillich called it the 'substance' or the 'driving force' of the culture or the age. Access to the X is through and only through its forms of expression: a, b, c, d, e, . . . (n). Tillich is quite explicit that this is his view, though he does not seem to realise that this makes his theory highly problematic. Among other things, it makes testing the theory impossible: there is no way to get hold of and to examine the X which is said to underlie the whole of the culture. Nor is the existence of anomalies and exceptions allowed to count decisively against such theories. The problem of anomalies is handled in several different ways in such theories. First, and most crudely, the exception is forced into the pattern of the total culture. And there is more than one example of this technique in Spengler's *Untergang*! Nor is it entirely unknown in Tillich's writings. One thinks, for instance, of the sometimes implausible allies detected by Tillich in *Die religiöse Lage* in the battle against the spirit of capitalism! Second, one could exclude the exception by definition: since it is

---

[74] It might be thought by some that Marx, no less than Hegel and Herder and Spengler, should stand indicted here as well. Leaving aside his earlier, more philosophical writings, there is an obvious formal similarity between his Überbau/Unterbau account and the accounts of spirit/manifestation in the writings of Herder, Hegel and Spengler. Yet, there is an important difference. Marx's theory is in principle subject to empirical investigation in a way that those 'idealist' accounts are not. The economic conditions of existence are in principle accessible in a way that the 'world spirit' or 'soul of the people' simply is not.

not in the style of the total culture, it is not an expression of that culture's spirit or soul and is therefore not part of the culture or age in question, even though it occurs in it. Here the circularity of the argument is patently obvious. And it is a circularity into which Tillich stands in danger of falling in *Die religiöse Lage* when he speaks of the difficulty of determining which phenomena of an age 'really' express the spirit of the age. Third, there is one other way of handling the problem by stipulating that only those cultures which are perfectly (or nearly so) united stylistically are 'really' cultures. Nor was it only Spengler who resorted to such devices. At least one anthropologist has constructed a similar line of argument.[75] But in none of the three cases has the problem of individual anomalies — not to mention groups of anomalies which exhibit a kind of stylistic pattern of their own distinct from the culture's 'style' — been adequately accounted for or explained satisfactorily. Indeed, the problem of anomalies is to some extent a product of the theory. The difficulty arises in the first place by such theorists attempting to trace the unity of a culture to a single source which is other than and in addition to the phenomena of the culture in question, i.e. to a force or power which underlies and gives structure and unity to the several aspects of the culture.

A second difficulty encountered by such approaches to culture unity is the problem of accounting for cross-cultural influence. For instance, the influence of western technology in traditional, non-western cultures — such as Japan — poses difficulties for any approach which regards the style of a culture as primary and underived, as an expression of that culture's own, unique X. Or one might mention the influence of primitive art on the late-impressionists of France and the early-expressionists of Germany as posing a similar difficulty for such accounts. Tillich has less difficulty accommodating cross-cultural influence at one level than some since he held that the 'human condition' is universal, even though there is no 'universal history' in the enlightenment sense. Not surprisingly, it is this aspect of Spengler's theory which Tillich from the first most forcefully rejected. (GW. XIII. 137 ff)

Finally, the overarching difficulty for this approach is that the visible is explained in terms of the invisible, the problematic in terms of the obscure. The inability of proponents of such theories to agree as to the value to be

---

[75] See E. Sapir, 'Culture, Genuine and Spurious', *The American Journal of Sociology*, XXIX (1924), 401 ff.

substituted for X further weakens their case and raises questions about the enterprise's likely fruitfulness. The questionableness of such theories lies not so much in *what* is to be identified as the unifying factor, as in the fact *that* the unity of culture is explained in terms of some single factor, whether mental or material, whether simple or complex. And this single factor is held to be something which all the individual facets of a culture have in common.

For reasons already given, Tillich's theory or culture unity must be classified with such theories. It is, to that extent, not only incomplete in detail, but also defective in principle and in need of revision. Does it make no sense to speak holistically of 'the style of a culture' or even of 'the unity of a culture'? Is it not possible to conceive cultures as a 'complex whole', 'a structured unity'? Although it will not be possible here to give a full defence, I want to suggest nonetheless that it might be possible to give a different account of the nature of culture unity, an account which would allow Tillich to conceive a culture as a 'totality' and even to regard its 'stylistic pattern' as a key to its interpretation.

One consequence of the class of theories which has been considered above is that the very diverse things which constitute a culture cannot be treated in terms of their own individuality and complexity. Economic structures, customs, ideologies, institutions, artifacts and social relationships must all be treated as if they were of a similar character. They must all be reinterpreted in such a way that, contrary to all appearances and our experience of them, they all have a similar logical standing. They must all become in the same sense expressions of some common factor or vehicles of some hidden meaning. Such theories do violence not only to the complexity which is clearly a feature of cultures conceived as a whole. But they also do violence to the complexity of each of those individual elements which constitute a culture, whether the economy or religion. Leaving aside the economy, which not even economists can claim to understand, religion has several logically dissimilar dimensions. It includes doctrines of different sorts, myths of various kinds, ethical injunctions, ritual behaviour and different styles of experience, all embodied variously in social institutions of some complexity. No theory of culture unity which disregards the different sorts of things which constitute a culture, nor the different strata of each constituent element, can be regarded as an adequate theory of culture unity. Whatever sense it might make to speak of the 'style' of a culture, that style cannot be defined in terms of something which every aspect of that culture has in common. Nor is it clear *why* 'the style of a culture' must be defined in terms of that which all its individual elements have in common. It might be defined as the particular pattern produced by the actual interrelationships which exist at any time among the diverse components which make up a culture. That is to say, the style or pattern of a particular culture could be conceived as its total structure, rather than as that which all its individual elements have in common. The 'style' of a culture, which in any case would be no more than partial and subject to constant modification as the individual elements interact in ever new kinds of ways, would on this view be a consequence of the criss-crossing and overlapping of the various elements of that culture. The source of unity of a culture, according to this account, would be reducible without remainder to the actual, observable interaction of its several parts. This would have several consequences.

First, it could not be assumed apriori that a culture *must* exhibit a common 'style'. The culture of a highly differentiated and pluralistic society may in fact exhibit a number of different 'styles', some complementary and others competitive. If one were given to paradox, one might say that it is the style of such a culture to have no single 'style'. Nor could it be assumed, secondly, that every element of a given culture must connect up with every other element. Not only might there be different degrees of interaction, there might be no direct interaction between some elements. There is bound to be an element of incompleteness in relations between the individual elements of a culture.[76] Third, there would seem to be no reason to assume that those which do connect up are all connected in the same sort of way. Nor would there seem to be any reason to assume that each individual element must have the same role or function in every culture. It might be suggested, for instance, that the *constitution* has a very different function in Great Britain, the Federal Republic of Germany and the United States. There would seem to be no compelling reason to think that what is true of this aspect of culture would be less true of the remaining aspects. Finally, determining 'the style of a culture' would be a painstaking task of tracing the patterns and relations among the several components of that culture. It would have to be constructed, if at all, case by case.[77]

---

[76] Cf. Geertz's observation that 'cultural analysis is intrinsically incomplete. And, worse than that, the more deeply it goes the less complete it is.' *The Interpretation of Cultures*, p. 29.
[77] The most thorough-going and convincing attempt by an anthropologist to re-

This suggests that, although it might be *empirically* possible to describe culture as a whole, it might not be *technically* possible. One complaint one might make about the way Tillich analysed 'the present situation' derives from his tendency to make too sweeping generalisations based on too little evidence. In *Die religiöse Lage der Gegenwart*, for instance, Tillich makes a number of penetrating observations about current trends in thought. But he claims too much when he makes wider generalisations about 'the present situation'. He writes on occasion almost as if he regarded Weimar culture as standing in unified rebellion against the values of *bürgerliche Gesellschaft*. This view of 'the Weimar style' would express at best a hope. If there is any generalisation which holds for Weimar culture and society, it is surely that there was precious little agreement about anything — a fact which must already have been clear to Tillich by the time he wrote that volume. It would be more nearly right to stress that 'a socio-cultural history of the 1920's is a mosaic consisting of an endless number of stones, large and small'.[78] One cannot deny that the 'stones' selected by Tillich were part of the Weimar mosaic. Yet one can complain that he ignored completely ever so many other stones, which 'were as much part of the *Zeitgeist* as the Bauhaus, *The Magic Mountain*, Professor Heidegger and Dr. Caligari'.[79] Perhaps it would be better if theologians, like anthropologists, learned to be content with a more piecemeal approach to cultural analysis, even if their aim were ultimately to describe the 'style' of a whole culture. Perhaps it would be better if the over-grand 'problem of religion and culture' were broken up into a number of smaller, more manageable issues, each of which would need to be addressed in its own terms. What then would become of Schleiermacher's dilemma, of Tillich's method of correlation? The dilemma would remain, though it would become more concrete: in any given interaction between any aspect of religion and any other aspect of culture, would it be possible to conceive a relationship in which there could be a genuine and thorough-going reciprocity that would threaten the autonomy of neither the one nor the other? Does Tillich's concept of correlation contribute to the answer to this question? That we must determine in part three.

---

formulate the concept of 'the style of a culture' along similar lines was made by Kroeber. See esp. *Style and Civilization* and *An Anthropologist Looks at History*.
[78] Walter Laqueur, *Weimar: A Cultural History, 1918–1933* (London, 1974), p. 34.
[79] *Ibid.*, p. 35.

PART THREE
TWO MODELS OF A CORRELATIVE RELATION

CHAPTER FIVE
QUESTIONING, ANSWERING AND THE CONCEPT
OF CORRELATION

When explaining the sort of relation between religion and culture which was to be called a correlative relation, Tillich typically turned to one of two sets of metaphors: 'questioning' and 'answering' as in a conversation between discussion partners; or 'form' and 'content' (*Gehalt*) as in his frequently cited formula that 'the form of religion is culture and the substance [*Gehalt*] of culture is religion'. In the *Systematic Theology* especially he tended to combine the two and rarely ever to distinguish betwen them. They were joined perhaps for the first time in his 1947 article on 'The Problem of Theological Method':

> The method of correlation is especially the method of apologetic theology. Question and answer must be correlated in such a way that the religious symbol is interpreted as the adequate answer to a question, implied in man's existence, and asked in primitive, pre-philosophical, or elaborated philosophical terms . . . The form of the questions, whether primitive or philosophical, is decisive for the theological form in which the answer is given. And, conversely, the substance of the question is determined by the substance of the answer. Nobody is able to ask questions concerning God, revelation, Christ, etc., who has not already received some answer. So we can say: With respect to man's ultimate concern the questions contain the substance of the answers, and the answers are shaped by the form of the questions.[1]

Even so, each metaphor has in the development of Tillichs' thought a largely independent origin and history. In this and the next chapter these two sets of metaphors are to be examined separately with a view toward determining their respective roles in the formation and extension of Tillich's theory of correlation. I shall hope to show that these two pairs of metaphors function

---

[1] *JRel*, XXVII (1947), p. 25. But, cf. PE, 92–3.

as 'submerged models' or 'conceptual archetypes', in the sense given those phrases by Max Black.[2]

Black shows that the logic of 'model' is manifold and dependent upon the specific sense in which the term is used. He distinguishes five main senses of 'model', each of which has its own set of rules governing its proper use: scale models, analogue models, mathematical models, theoretical models, and submerged models or 'conceptual archetypes'.[3] Not all the five main uses of 'model' are equally relevant to our discussion of Tillich's two models of a correlative relation. For instance, mathematical models need not be discussed at all, despite their importance in the debate among philosophers of science as to the function and status of models.[4] Of the remaining four main senses of the term, theoretical models and 'conceptual archetypes' are most important for the argument of this chapter. Scale models and analogue models are relevant only to the extent that an understanding of their proper use enables one better to understand the proper use of theoretical models. And when 'conceptual archetypes' or 'submerged models' are forced to the surface and made explicit, that use of 'model' is reducible without remainder to a theoretical model.

Despite the significant differences among the five senses of 'model' identified by Black, there are certain similarities which should be noted before turning briefly to the individual senses of the term. First, the model and its original do not correspond exactly in every detail, whatever the sense in which 'model' is being used. Mary Hesse usefully distinguishes those features of a model which are analogically positive, those which are analogically negative, and those which are analogically neutral in the sense of not known, the latter being important primarily in theory-extension.[5] Second, it is in no case possible simply to 'read off' features of the model directly without supplementary validation. This is a consequence of the analogical relationship

---

[2] Cf. the chapter 'Models and Archetypes' in Max Black, *Models and Metaphors* (Ithaca, NY, 1962).

[3] In addition to these five main uses, Black mentions two other common uses: 'model' as a type of design, such as a Model 'T' Ford, and 'model' as an exemplar, such as a 'model husband'. There are still other common uses of 'model' which are not mentioned by Black. One thinks of an artist's model or of a fashion model. This serves to suggest something of the wide variety of ways in which we ordinarily use the term 'model'.

[4] See, e.g., R. B. Braithwaite, *Scientific Explanation* (Cambridge, 1953), pp. 88ff.

[5] See *Models and Analogies in Science* (2nd. ed.; Notre Dame, 1966).

between the model and the original. A given property is not proved to be a feature of the 'original' simply because it is a feature of the model, although its being a feature of the model might in some circumstances lead one to make the appropriate measurements to determine whether it is in fact a feature of the phenomenon of which the model is thought to be a model. What then are the major differences which distinguish the main senses of 'model'?

Scale models and *analogue models* are both constructable representations of some real or imaginary 'original'. But each stands in a different kind of relationship to that original. Clearly an hydraulic model of an economic system does not correspond to that system in the same way that a scale model of the QE-II corresponds to the Cunard liner by that neame. Whereas scale models represent as faithfully as practicable specific details of the original in the same geometric proportions in a smaller or larger or even similar scale, analogue models reproduce in a different medium only the 'web of relationships' which characterises the original. As such, the class of possible analogue models for any one 'original' is obviously going to be greater than the class of possible scale models for the same entity. Likewise, not only can a large number of different kinds of analogue models be constructed for a single phenomenon, a single analogue model can also be applied to a number of different sorts of phenomena sharing a similar structure of relationships. The risk of misreading an analogue model is correspondingly much higher than the risk of misreading a scale model. This being the case, independent confirmation of readings made from analogue models is most essential. For, as Black rightly warns, 'analogue models furnish plausible hypotheses, not proofs.'[6] But, it should be reminded, this is true of all senses of 'model' and not merely of analogue models.

Unlike scale models and analogue models, *theoretical models* need not be constructable. They need only be capable of description. This feature brings with it its own liabilities, as well as assets. The primary asset of a theoretical model is that its correspondence with the original need only be extensive enough to allow the 'reading off' of a sufficient number of analogies with the 'original'. What the user of theoretical models gains in flexibility, he loses in controls against excess. The necessity to construct scale and analogue models forces a strictness which is greatly diminished in the case of theoretical models. For example, James Watson mentions that more than one promising model of the structure of DNA had to be abandoned when the measurements

---

[6] *Op. cit.*, p. 223.

taken from the constructed model failed to correspond within the acceptable limits to the measurements demanded by the raw data gained elsewhere, for instance, from the results of X-ray photography.[7] The user of a theoretical model has no such recourse to direct measurements to act as a control against excess. Consequently, he must be even more cautious in the use of his model and must to an even greater extent rely upon independent tests for control. No model, especially not a theoretical model, is self-authenticating.

The final sense of 'model' is termed by Black the implicit model or the *conceptual archetype*, by which he means 'a systematic repertoire of ideas by means of which a given thinker describes, by *analogical* extension, some domain to which those ideas do not immediately and literally apply.'[8] He cites the much-discussed and sometimes controversial work of Kurt Lewin as a paradigmatic case of the systematic use of an implicit model.[9] Although Lewin disclaims the use of models, he frequently uses a vocabulary in his work in the social sciences which is indigenous rather to the physical sciences. Black regards such terms as 'visible symptoms of a massive archetype awaiting to be reconstructed by a sufficiently patient critic.'[10] Although Black is not opposed in principle to the use of implicit models and seems even to have high regard for Lewin's theories, he warns against implicit models being 'permanently insulated from empirical disproof' by virtue of the tendency to use them metaphysically: 'The more persuasive the archetype, the greater the danger of its becoming a self-certifying myth.' On the other hand, Black adds, 'a good archetype can yield to the demands of experience; while it channels its master's thought, it need not do so inflexibly.'[11] Black seems to be suggesting that at least in the case of conceptual archetypes there can and perhaps even should be a kind of reciprocal relation between model and original. Though this runs somewhat counter to the usual sort of relation between model and original,[12] it is in line with Mary Hesse's recommendations as to the role of models in the extension of theories. She, no less than Black, is determined to keep the use of models in check. It would appear that another way in which possible abuse of conceptual archetypes

---

[7] *The Double Helix* (Harmondsworth, 1968).
[8] *Op. cit.*, p. 241.
[9] Cf. *Field Theory in Social Science* (New York, 1951).
[10] *Loc. cit.*
[11] *Ibid.*, p. 242.
[12] That is to say, if A is a model of B, B is not a model of A.

could be countered would be to make them explicit. That is to say, they should be developed openly and systematically as theoretical models.

With this end in view, I shall attempt in these two chapters to analyse Tillich's two main models of a correlative relation. Tillich himself did not clearly distinguish the two. Nor have his critics generally seen the distinction between the 'question-answer' model and the 'form-content' model.[13] Thus, an element of ambiguity has characterised much of the critical discussion of Tillich's method of correlation. Some of the persistent objections to Tillich's notion of correlation have been directed ostensibly against his 'question-answer' model of a correlative relation. However, a few of the most unwelcome features ascribed by critics to that model are, as we shall see, rather more accurately to be regarded as features of the 'form-content' model of correlation. By analysing the two models separately, it is hoped that we shall be in a stronger position critically to assess Tillich's concept of correlation. It is not sufficient, however, to treat the two models in complete separation. Since they tend to be mixed in Tillich's actual usage of them, it will be necessary to see them in connexion with each other.

In chapter six, I shall hope to sort out certain aspects of the relationship between Tillich's two models of correlation, with a view toward determining whether they present competing accounts of the structure of relations between religion and culture. I shall argue that, while not directly competitive, neither of the two models on its own satisfies both the conditions of a correlative relation laid down above in chapter two. Although it might satisfy the reciprocity condition, 'questioning and answering' is by itself too shapeless to be an adequate model of correlationship; and, although it might satisfy the autonomy condition, the dialectic of 'form and content' as developed in Tillich's later writings on correlation cannot be regarded on its own as sufficiently dialectical to satisfy the reciprocity condition. It might be thought therefore that, although each on its own is insufficient, in combination the two metaphors would meet both conditions. I shall argue that this, regrettably, is not the case. In addition, I shall seek to show that there is within Tillich's elaboration of each metaphor a certain amount of tension, so that a far from consistent picture emerges in his writings as to

---

[13] It is one of the virtues of Robert Scharlemann's study of Tillich's thought that he detected a difference between what I am referring to as Tillich's two models of a correlative relation. *Reflection and Doubt in the Thought of Paul Tillich* (New Haven, 1969), pp. 113ff.

what he would allow to count as a correlative relationship between religion and culture. This holds equally, though not for the same reasons, for each of the two models.

In the present chapter we look first at the role of questioning and answering in the development of Tillich's thought, with particular reference to its function as a model of a correlative relation. We shall then attempt to determine the adequacy of his model, paying attention to some of the more interesting objections which have been raised against it. A similar pattern has been adopted for the sixth and final chapter in which the role and adequacy of 'form and content' are discussed.

The Role of Questioning and Answering in the Development of Tillich's Thought

Tillich typically endeavoured to explain the sort of relationship which in his view obtains between 'the human situation' or 'the cultural context' and 'the christian message' by calling attention to its similarity to the sort of relationship which he thought to exist between questions and answers generally. In order to understand why Tillich came to speak of the relationship between religion and culture in these terms, it is useful to trace Tillich's attempt almost from the beginning to construct a 'genuinely' dialectical theology, a theology in which question and answer, 'yes' and 'no', belong inseparably together.[14]

In twentieth-century religious thought the phrase 'dialectical theology' is almost uniformly associated with Karl Barth and his small circle of fellow-rebels against the then-prevailing protestant liberalism in Germany.[15] But Tillich, too, regarded himself a dialectical theologian, though of a quite different sort.[16] Nor can it be denied that, in one way or another, dialectic is

---

[14] These two pairs of terms, though not strictly speaking parallel, are typically treated by Tillich as if they were. Cf. K&B, 15f; GW. VII. 247ff.

[15] Much of the important material relating to the development of 'the dialectical theology' has been usefully collected and published in two volumes as *Anfänge der dialektischen Theologie*, ed. J. Moltmann (Munich, 1962, 1963).

[16] The intricate relationship between Tillich and the dialectical theology has never been properly sorted out, though a beginning has been made by H. Förster, *Die Kritik Paul Tillich's an der Theologie Karl Barths* (Göttingen, 1964). Regarding the method of correlation, see pp. 80–137.

made to play an important role (or, rather, roles) in Tillich's theology. And *correlation* was clearly intended by Tillich to furnish the methodological foundation for what in the preface to *The Protestant Era* he termed his 'neo-dialectical' theology, which in contrast to 'the supernaturalism of later Barthianism' is said by Tillich to be 'truly dialectical'. (PE, xxiv, xxii)

The restriction of the criticism to *later* Barthianism is not insignificant. Tillich had been early attracted to Barth and had regarded him as an ally: 'When Barth's commentary on Romans was published, a wide circle of theologians of the same age attached themselves to the school for which Barth had prepared the way. Some did so publicly, and some − like [Tillich] − in a "subterranean" group of fellow-laborers.' (GW. VIII. 254) Tillich is reported to have told Barth at their first meeting that he regarded the commentary on Romans as a 'genuine symptom' of the dawning of a new age of theonomy.[17] It is not clear that Barth altogether shared that estimate.

They met, probably for the first time,[18] in the spring of 1922, about a year before their largely unproductive interchange on 'paradox' in successive issues of *Theologische Blätter*. (GW. VII. 216ff) The meeting occurred in

---

[17] *Karl Barth − Eduard Thurneysen Briefwechsel*, vol. II: 1921−1930 (Zürich, 1974), p. 64.

[18] In a private letter (see below, note 20), Tillich implies this was their first meeting. But, Kenneth Schedler is of the view that Barth and Tillich had become acquainted in 1919 through their association with the 'religious socialism' movement. See *Natur und Gnade* (Stuttgart, 1970), p. 150ff. It is noteworthy that Martin Rade sent the following postcard to Barth (29. 8. 1921) regarding Tillich's chances of becoming Ragaz's successor at the University of Zürich: 'Wie stehts um Ragazens Nachfolge? Wäre eine Möglichkeit, daß Lic. Tillich aus Berlin berufen werden könnte? Du kennst ihn ja. Seine Aussichten sind bei uns [in Germany] sehr schlecht trotz der dem[okratisch]-soz[ial]dem[okratischen] Republik, die wir haben. Rag[az] selbst meine ich müßte mit einem solchen Nachfolger wohl zufrieden sein. Aber hat er noch Einfluß? Wer besetzt? *An wen könnte ich mich mit einiger Aussicht auf Erfolg wenden?* Ich möchte keine Dummheit begehn u[nd] nicht schaden. Vielleicht kannst Du die Anregung einfach weitergeben.' (Original in Karl-Barth-Archiv, Basel) Barth replied to Rade 1 September 1921: 'Die Situation in Zürich ist nach den letzten Nachrichten, die ich darüber habe, so dass allgemeine Ratlosigkeit herrscht. Der Name von Tillich ist unter vielen Anderen auch schon genannt worden. Er hat aber jedenfalls ein doppeltes Ressentiment gegen sich bei der Fakultät *und* bei der (berufenden) Zürcher Regierung und ev[entuell] beim mitredenden Publikum: 1. als Religiös-Sozialer (dies scheint bes[onders] die Fakultät grimmig abzulehnen, auch Ragaz soll gesagt haben, er

Göttingen and was arranged – in view of subsequent events, perhaps ironically – by Emanuel Hirsch, at the time the most senior and certainly the most well-known of the three.[19] Barth's contemporary account of their meeting has long been available in the Barth-Thurneysen correspondence. But it has not been widely known that Tillich, too, recorded his immediate impressions of that meeting in a private and as yet unpublished letter to his close friend and brother-in-law, Alfred Fritz.[20]

Tillich's account agrees in substance with Barth's especially regarding Hirsch's persistent attempts to polarise the two. It was apparently possible for them to have a serious discussion only when they managed to get away from Hirsch for a walk together! They talked mainly about philosophy of history, though Tillich confesses – and in his letter Barth concurs – they found little about which to agree. As a 'supranatural eschatologist' Barth was said to have had no interest in history and to have found Tillich's notion of 'theonomy' dangerous. If that were the case, Tillich countered, than Barth's own notion of 'act of faith' must likewise be dangerous (cf. GW. XII. 191 f), a point which Tillich implies Barth conceded. 'Finally', reports Tillich, 'we made the following pact: he will endeavour to rationalise his supranatural

---

wünsche keinen r[eligiös]-s[ozialen] Nachfolger). 2. als *Deutscher* (unsere 'führenden Kreise' früher kritiklos offen für Alles, was von draussen kam, sind jetzt ganz westlich orientiert und werden deutsche Berufungen tunlichst vermeiden. Ragaz selber traue ich es durchaus zu, dass auch er Tillich als Deutschen nicht möchte.) Am Besten wendest du dich an Walter Koehler o[der] Oswald Mayer. Die ganze Geschichte ist sehr ungut. (Original in Martin-Rade-Archiv, UB, Marburg) I am grateful to Dr. Christoph Schwöbel for having called this to my attention.

[19] Although two years younger than Barth and Tillich, Hirsch had been *Ordinarius* in Göttingen since 1921. Tillich became *Ordinarius* through his appointment at Dresden und Leipzig in 1925. In the same year, Barth became *Ordinarius* in Münster. Barth had been 'honorary professor' at Göttingen since 1921, but this post was listed as 'außerhalb der Fakultät'. See W. Ebel, *Catalogus Professorum Gottingensium, 1734–1962* (Göttingen, 1962). See also W. Trillhaas, 'Karl Barth in Göttingen' (1970; repr. in *Perspektiven und Gestalten des neuzeitlichen Christentums*, Göttingen, 1976, pp. 171–84).

[20] The letter is undated and is marked 'Bei Goslar im Speisewagen. Sonntag Nachmittag'. On internal evidence and in comparison with a letter which Barth wrote to Thurneysen concerning Tillich's visit to Göttingen, the letter can be precisely dated as Sunday, 2 April 1922. See *Barth-Thurneysen Briefwechsel*, II, 64–7.

formulas and I will endeavour to balance [*kompensieren*] my rational formulas with supranatural ones; he will proclaim the essential meaning of the Unconditioned as a biblical theologian, and I shall do so as a cultural theologian.'

'Die Überwindung des Religionsbegriffs in der Religionsphilosophie' appeared later that year in *Kant-Studien*.[21] It might be thought that in it Tillich was upholding his end of the bargain by arguing, amongst other things, that 'God is known only through God!' (GW. I. 388) Tillich also went out of his way in that article to call attention to the similarities which he saw to exist between his own views and those of Barth and Gogarten (GW. I. 367f), an act of generosity which possibly had the unintended effect of leading Harnack to count Tillich among 'the theologians who are contemptuous of the scientific theology'![22] That article, however, which originated as an address to the Berlin chapter of the Kant-Gesellschaft delivered on 25 January 1922, was written well before the meeting with Barth. It is in fact evidently the 'unpublished address' mentioned by Barth and Tillich alike in their respective letters. In view of its highly dialectical character, it is perhaps not surprising that Barth could at that time have regarded Tillich an ally, albeit with reservations, and could even have commended Tillich's forthcoming book on philosophy of religion to his own publisher to show Tillich's connexion with the dialectical theologians.

Their pact was short-lived, however, and Tillich's book was published instead by Vandenhoeck and Ruprecht of Göttingen. Nor has *Das System der Wissenschaften*, in which Tillich self-consciously assumed for himself the mantle of Troeltsch,[23] generally been understood as demonstrating Tillich's close ties to the dialectical theology.

The very next year Tillich began contrasting his own use of dialectic with Barth's usage. In return, Barth politely protested that he did not really understand what Tillich was talking about (!) and then proceeded 'to understand Tillich better than he understands himself'. (GW. VII. 226ff) At the end of his riposte to Barth, a reply which Barth scathingly dismissed in a

---

[21] Vol. XXVII (1922), 446–69; repr. GW. I. 367–88.
[22] Harnack's postcard to Barth is published in the *Barth-Thurneysen Briefwechsel*, II, 135.
[23] GW. I. 112: 'Während der Drucklegung traf mich die Nachricht von dem plötzlichen Tode Ernst Troeltschs. Sein leidenschaftliches Streben war es, zum System zu kommen. Dem Dank, den ich ihm schulde auch für die Wirkung, die seine Arbeit auf die geistigen Grundlagen dieses Buches gehabt hat, möchte ich dadurch Ausdruck geben, daß ich das Buch seinem Andenken widme.'

letter to Thurneysen,[24] Tillich expressed the fear that the way Barth and Gogarten use dialectic 'leads unintentionally beyond the dialectical position to a very positive and very undialectical supranaturalism, that from the "yes" and "no" of relations between God and world which are essential to every dialectic emerges a simple "no" against the world, whose destiny it is most definitely always to remain impracticable and at some point to be transformed unexpectedly into an all the more positive and undialectical "yes".' (GW. VII. 243)

As Barth turned increasingly to the production of his dogmatics, first *christliche* and then *kirchliche*, Tillich felt his early suspicions to have been confirmed.[25] Soon after his emigration to the United States, he wrote a wideranging attack on Barth entitled 'What is Wrong with the "Dialectic" Theology?' (1935; GW. VII. 247–62) Amongst other things, Tillich there argued that the so-called dialectical theology is not truly dialectical at all, but supranaturalistic and paradoxical. He nowhere rejected *in toto* Barth's theological programme and often acknowledged its importance, especially for the then-current *Kirchenkampf*.[26] Evenso, in that article and indeed elsewhere, Tillich regularly contrasts Barth's so-called dialectical theology with his own correlation-theology, the latter being 'truly dialectical'.

Tillich's thought was from the beginning in some sense dialectical. His first sketch of a systematic theology was dialectical in the sense that the term is popularly, if misleadingly, associated with Hegel. In part one of the system of 1913, Tillich asserted that the necessary contradiction between the absolute standpoint ('intuition') and the relative standpoint ('reflexion') is resolved in the theological standpoint, based as it is in the paradox. Tillich attempted to clarify this move in the following way:

---

[24] *Barth-Thurneysen Briefwechsel*, II, 203.

[25] See also Theodor Siegfried's critique of Barth's *Prolegomena zur christlichen Dogmatik*, a critique which was published as volume one of *Das Wort und die Existenz: Eine Auseinandersetzung mit der dialektischen Theologie* under the title *Die Theologie des Worts bei Karl Barth* (Gotha, 1930). Later professor at Marburg, Siegfried was a member of Tillich's Kairos-Circle in Berlin and contributed articles to the two symposia published by that group. *Kairos: Zur Geisteslage und Geisteswendung*, ed. P. Tillich (Darmstadt, 1926), pp. 93–231, and *Protestantismus als Kritik und Gestaltung*, ed. P. Tillich (Darmstadt, 1929), pp. 71–101.

[26] See, e.g., 'Um was es Geht: Antwort an Emanuel Hirsch', *Theologische Blätter*, XIV (1935), cols. 117–20.

The absolute and the relative standpoints are related to one another in such a way that the relative standpoint is both produced and destroyed by the absolute standpoint. This contradiction demands to be resolved for the sake of the absoluteness of the absolute standpoint. For it can only prove itself to be absolute by showing that it does not go on endlessly producing and negating its contradiction; it must show that it takes the contradiction up into itself positively, yet without depriving itself of its dialectical independence. The absolute standpoint must therefore without prejudice to its absoluteness lower itself to the relative standpoint and raise the relative up into itself. Intuition must enter into the sphere of reflexion, of particularity, of contradiction, in order to guide reflexion through itself and beyond itself. This relationship is 'the paradox'. (§ 22)

In the second and specifically dogmatic part of the 1913 sketch of a systematic theology, Tillich states explicitly that the theological paradox is to be understood christologically: 'In Jesus of Nazareth the theological paradox — that is, the unity of the absolute and the relative in the sphere of the relative — is actualised in a single individual.' (§ 37) This paradox, as it is expressed in the symbol of the cross (§§ 39—42), is the criterion by which is to be measured the work of the theologian no less than that of all the other cultural spheres. Tillich stressed here, as later, that 'the theological system stands under the paradox, which is established by it and realised in it. But the theological system is not the absolute system, no more so than is the system of the sciences from which it proceeds and to which it returns. . . .' (§ 72) Tillich had from the beginning, and well before the first world war, the firm conviction that God is in heaven and man is on earth, even when he is a theologian.[27]

Tillich's thought was also in other respects dialectical from the outset. When in 1912 he was examined for his *Licentiat* in theology, he defended ten theses, the last of which constitutes perhaps his earliest statement on the kind of relationship he envisaged between religion and culture: 'The church can faithfully fulfill its apologetic task to the cultured only to the extent that it aspires neither to the vindication and defense of the church's teachings nor to the definition and control of boundaries between faith and knowledge,

---

[27] Cf. K. Barth, *Römerbrief* (2nd. ed.; repr. Zürich, 1968), p. XIII.

but aspires rather to exposing the living and dialectical relation of the present cultural situation to christianity'.[28]

Curiously linked here are the notion of the dialectical interplay between christianity and culture and the apologetic task of the church. *Prima facie,* apologetics and this sort of dialectic would not seem to be wholly compatible. The usual meaning of *apologetics* is, as in an adversary system of justice, the defence of a particular position in the face of an accusor; and the usual meaning of *dialectic* is 'a co-operative inquiry carried on in conversation between two or more minds that are equally bent, not on getting the better of the argument, but on arriving at the truth.'[29] Even so, in both the *Kirchliche Apologetik* and the *Systematic Theology*, apologetics and dialectic are inextricably bound up together in Tillich's methodology.

How, then, does he propose to hold the two together?

The very structure of the *Systematic Theology* suggests the way he came to regard the connexion between the two. Each of its five parts consists of the analysis of certain 'questions' implied in the human situation, on the one side, and their 'answers' implied in the christian message, on the other. *Correlation* is defined by Tillich principally as the sort of relation which ought to obtain between certain kinds of philosophical questions and corresponding theological answers. (ST. I. 60; II. 13) One point at which dialectic and apologetics make contact is clearly to be found in the much-discussed and frequently misrepresented question-answer schema which defines in part the structure of the *Systematic Theology*.

Despite its centrality in Tillich's usual formulations of the method of correlation, this question-answer schema is last in time among the elements which constitute the concept of correlation. All the most important components of that concept were operative in Tillich's thought prior to his having adopted the question-answer structure for his theological system. Even so, one would not be justified in inferring from its lateness in time that this component is a less important element of the concept of correlation than those which had been present earlier in Tillich's writings. The

---

[28] I am grateful to Wilhelm Pauck for having called this to my attention and for having supplied me with a copy of it. This and the other nine theses are also printed in Hermann Brandt, *Gotteserkenntnis und Weltentfremdung* (Göttingen, 1971), p. 257f. But, see M. Satrom, *Der Begriff der Religion im Werk Paul Tillichs* (Marburg, 1973), pp. 194–5.

[29] F. M. Cornford, *Plato's Theory of Knowledge* (London, 1960), p. 30.

question-answer schema might as a matter of fact be less important than some other components, but this would not follow from its being such a late addition. Nor are the component elements simply coupled together in the concept of correlation as are the individual carriages of a train, the one after the other, separable at any point. Components of the concept of correlation were joined in a way rather more analogous to the mixing of paints: the addition of each new component modified the shade, if not changed the colour, of the whole. In what follows I shall attempt to show that important transformations occur in Tillich's conception of the relationship between religion and culture as a result of his having come to adopt the question-answer schema in terms of which the method of correlation is formulated.

Although last in time in its specific role in the method of correlation, 'questioning' and 'answering' – or 'dialectic' – as an apologetic technique is rooted in Tillich's earliest reflections on the theological task as recorded especially in the *Kirchliche Apologetik* (cf. GW. XIII. 34ff). Having been prepared in 1912–1913, this document substantiates in some respects Tillich's later claim that his own 'dialectical' position had been arrived at independently of any contact with Barth. (GW. I. 368) There is another striking feature of the *Kirchliche Apologetik* which should not go unmentioned in view of the not uncommon opinion that Tillich's earliest interests were more nearly philosophical than theological, and more theoretical than practical: namely, the concern exhibited in that work for the life of the church and the church's mission. This concern is evidenced, for instance, by the inclusion of a surprisingly detailed if somewhat naive programme for the training of professional church apologists, a programme which Tillich together with his close friend Carl Richard Wegener went some distance toward implementing in Berlin. (GW. XIII. 59ff, cf. pp. 543ff; OB, 60–1) That apologetics was regarded by Tillich from the beginning as a function of the church is underscored by his proposal in *Kirchliche Apologetik* that apologists be ordained and given full ministerial status, somewhat on the order of foreign missionaries. Apologetics, reasons Tillich, is a sort of 'home missions', an aspect of the 'inner mission' of the church. (GW. XIII. 37, 44, 57f) But our main interest in that work lies elsewhere, in what is there termed by Tillich simply 'the dialectical method'. (GW. XIII. 40)

It will be recalled that Tillich had argued in his 1935 article cited above that Barth's theology could not be dialectical, because in dialectical theology 'Yes' and 'No' belong 'inseparably together', whereas in the so-called dialectical theology they are 'irreconcilably separated'. (GW. VII. 247) Though Tillich does not there clarify what is meant by their 'belonging together', he does state in his introduction to *The Protestant Era* that 'dialectics is the way of seeking for truth by talking with others from different points of view, through "Yes" and "No", until a "Yes" has been reached which is hardened in the fire of many "No's" and which unites the elements of truth promoted in the discussion.' (PE, ix) This is not merely a 'belonging together' in the sense that polar opposites, such as say 'up' and 'down', mutually imply each other. This is 'belonging together' in the sense of a mutual affecting, a relationship of reciprocity. Though written over thirty years later, these lines are a not inaccurate summary of the 'dialectical method' sketched in *Kirchliche Apologetik*.

In that early work the conversational character of apologetics is emphasised. The apologist is said not to be an authoritative schoolmaster tutoring ignorant pupils. (GW. XIII. 39) Possessing truth only in a relative way, he enters discussion with the 'cultured' as a partner, as a fellow-seeker after truth. (GW. XIII. 40–1) With truth alone as the object of the apologist's 'dialogue', he stands ready to rethink and to modify his own position, as well as critically to test the position of his discussion-partner. (GW. XIII. 40) He is able to enter the conversation as a partner, rather than as a teacher, because of his realisation that truth is not his private possession and because of his conviction that no truth is ultimately incompatible with christianity. (GW. XIII. 41–2) So, according to this early 'dialectical method', a final affirmative "Yes!" emerges through the give and take of mutual criticism. Tillich is in no doubt that this final "Yes!" will be a christian "Yes!", and he is firmly convinced at this point that all spiritual or cultural tendencies must finally find their goal in christianity (GW. XIII. 41; cf. XII. 96), which alone is said to have power to give unity to a fragmented culture. (GW. XIII. 36ff, esp. 38)

Even though he does not continue explicitly to talk of questioning and answering, similar views are echoed elsewhere in Tillich's early writings. It would not be unreasonable to suggest that most of Tillich's early writings presuppose this understanding of the dialectical character of the theological task. It is precisely this questioning and being questioned, answering and being answered, which gives vitality (as well as persuasiveness) to many of Tillich's writings in the 1920's, written as they were from the 'boundary' between religion and the other spheres of culture. (Cf. RV, 11ff) One thinks especially of his essays on religious socialism in which Tillich submits christianity to the radical critique of marxism without allowing marxism itself to go unchallenged by an equally radical critique. (Cf. GW. II. 91ff, 159ff, 219ff) And, indeed, the truly dialectical character of Tillich's thought is more easily seen when he is dealing concretely with issues than when as in the *Systematic Theology* he manipulates abstract concepts like 'philosophy' and 'theology'. Questioning and being questioned; answering and being answered – this is the essence of the dialectical method followed by Tillich from the outset. 'Question and answer, Yes and No in an actual disputation – this original form of all dialectics is the most adequate form of my own thinking.' (K&B, 15–6)

In fact, this 'dialectical method' can be regarded in an important sense as a first step in the direction which would lead eventually to the 'method of correlation'. There are of course intermediary steps and, as we shall see, not all in the same direction! For it would be just as much a mistake to assert that the sort of questioning and answering formalised in the method of correlation is entirely continuous with this early dialectical method as it would be to deny there is any connexion whatever between them. There is a gradual but unmistakeable modification in the application of the dialectical principle in Tillich's writings subsequent to his brief and only reluctantly accepted appointment as *Extraordinarius* at Marburg in 1924–1925.

A decisive factor in this change may have been Tillich's having come into contact there with the work of Martin Heidegger.[30] The latter was at the time preparing to publish his *Sein und Zeit*, the first and only volume of which appeared in the spring of 1927 in the *Jahrbuch für Phänomenologie und phänomenologische Forschung*, a journal edited at the time by Edmund Husserl.

Although he once asserted there is no way to determine once-for-all what is to be expected of philosophy, Heidegger characteristically conceived

---

30 Although apparently acquainted with each other's presence, Tillich and Heidegger seem never to have met personally at Marburg: 'the only "conversation" Tillich seems to have had with him [Heidegger] was by way of points made in the course of lectures, transported back and forth from classroom to classroom by student gossip.' Wilhelm and Marion Pauck, *Paul Tillich: His Life and Thought*, vol. I (New York, 1976), p. 98. See also Hannah Tillich, *From Time to Time* (London, 1974), pp. 116–7. On the intellectual ferment at Marburg during the period when Tillich would have been there, see the eyewitness account of H.-G. Gadamer, 'Martin Heidegger und die Marburger Theologie' in *Zeit und Geschichte*, ed. E. Dinkler (Tübingen, 1964), pp. 479ff.

the fundamental task of philosophy as the clarification of the question of the structure and meaning of being-itself.[31] He approaches the question of being through an analysis of the structure of human existence. Man puts himself to the question. Yet it is not human existence as such which is the object of philosophy. The analysis of human existence is the way of getting at the question of being-itself. This presupposes that to ask the question of any particular kind of existence is implicitly to ask the question of being-itself, that any question of the form 'what *is* x?' implies the question of *is*-ness, of being-itself.[32] This essentially metaphysical concern with being-itself distinguishes Heidegger from the more straight-forward 'existentialists'. And it should be recalled that Heidegger repudiated the claim that his philosophy is existentialist. This concern with being-itself, and with non-being, further tends to ally Heidegger's 'radical' philosophy with the classical tradition of metaphysical philosophy, especially that which is exemplified in and stems from the Plato of the *Sophist* and more especially, perhaps, the pre-Socratics, whose dark sayings Heidegger was so fond of quoting. Although Heidegger does return to some of the preoccupations of classical philosophy, he cannot be said *merely* to have returned: Kant was regarded by him as a figure who must be reckoned with by any metaphysician. And his respect for Kant is evidenced throughout his metaphysical writings, but especially in *Kant and the Problem of Metaphysics*. For Heidegger, as for Kant, the bounds of sense cannot be transgressed. Heidegger holds that the philosopher's access to being-as-such must be indirect, through the phenomenological analysis of human existence. Why *human* existence? Man is the only being (*Seiendes*) who is self-conscious in the sense that he recognises he 'is' and someday will 'not be'. Man is the questioner and he asks what it is 'to be' and 'not to be', not out of detached interest but out of concern with his own existence. Although man is the only appropriate starting-point of philosophy, the object of philosophical analysis is not man, but being-itself. Being-itself, however, is not accessible

---

[31] For what follows, I am dependent mainly on *Sein und Zeit* (2nd. ed.; Halle, 1929), *Einführung in die Metaphysik* (Tübingen, 1953), and of course *Kant und das Problem der Metaphysik* (Bonn, 1929). I have also benefitted from Heidegger's recently published Marburg lectures on logic: *Die Frage nach der Wahrheit* (Frankfurt, 1976).

[32] This would seem to be the distinction meant by *existenziell* and *existenzial* in *Sein und Zeit*, p. 12.

to a phenomenological analysis: it cannot be sought; it must disclose itself. These are the limits of philosophy. Beyond this point, says Heidegger, it would be transcended.

The parallels between these, and numerous other uncited, but characteristically Heideggerian ideas and Tillich's philosophical theology are unmistakeable and need not be laboured. (See esp. ST. I. 163ff) One must urge caution, however, in inferring from such parallels that Tillich's ideas were derived from Heidegger. There is in fact no consensus regarding the extent of Tillich's indebtedness to Heidegger. Without denying that Tillich was influenced by Heidegger, it must be remembered that behind the work of both men stands a common philosophical heritage and a similar reading of that heritage which pre-dates their having come into contact with one another (however indirectly) in 1924–1925. To make the point one need only recall the impact upon each independently of the pre-Socratics, the mediaeval mystics, Schelling, Kierkegaard and Nietzsche. (cf. also OB, 56f) Even so, Tillich explicitly acknowledged his debt to Heidegger more than once and this ought not be ignored.[33]

Whatever the extent of Tillich's general indebtedness to Heidegger, 'questioning' and 'answering' gain a new and ultimately different significance in Tillich's work after his time at Marburg. I suggest it is at least possible that this different significance, which was in any case a gradual development, reflects one aspect of Heidegger's influence on Tillich. It will be recalled that Tillich implies he came to a different understanding of the relationship between philosophy and theology as a result of his contact with Heidegger. (GW. XII. 36)

So far as I have been able to determine from the material at my disposal, whether published or unpublished, the first example of this new use of 'questioning' and 'answering' after Tillich left Marburg occurs in the prologue to his lectures on epistemology delivered at the Technical Institute in Dresden, where Tillich had become *Ordinarius* in 1925. Tillich called the course 'The Structure of Religious Knowledge'. In what is available of that series of lectures, one becomes aware that Tillich is in the process of modifying his earlier 'dialectical' method to accommodate his new understanding of the object of philosophy as the clarification of the question of

---

[33] Nor should it go unnoticed that Tillich came to count *Sein und Zeit* among the ten books which had most influenced the direction of his thought. GW. XIV. 222.

being-as-such. Even so, the role of 'questioning' and 'answering' had not by then become sufficiently regularised for one to be able yet to speak of 'the method of correlation'. This degree of standardisation would not be reached until several years later, until after Tillich's emigration to the United States. That its development had already been begun, however, is clear from the Dresden lectures.

Tillich's lectures on *Die Gestalt der religiösen Erkenntnis*, delivered in 1927–1928, invite comparison with his only slightly earlier essay on the philosophy of religion in Dessoir's *Lehrbuch der Philosophie*. (1925; GW. I. 297–364) For both in that article and in his lectures on epistemology Tillich addresses similar issues, including the nature of the boundary line beyond which ontology or metaphysics would pass over into theology and *vice versa*. Even though the subject matter is similar, the perspective in each is quite different. The notion of philosophical 'questioning' and theological 'answering' which is so central in the Dresden lectures is totally absent both from the article on the philosophy of religion and in *Das System der Wissenschaften*, in both of which the relationship between theology and philosophy is worked out primarily in terms of the dialectic of form and *Gehalt* and the dialectic of autonomy-theonomy. In those works the point at which philosophy passes over into theology and *vice versa* is the point at which the two are synthesised: '. . . there is in both the doctrine of revelation and in philosophy a point at which the two are one. To find this point and from there to create a synthetic solution is the decisive task of the philosophy of religion.' (GW. I. 299) The location of that point is to be determined by an analysis of the place of philosophy and the place of theology in the general system of the sciences. Such an analysis reveals that philosophy's extremity is the point at which it is one with theology, so that it is possible for Tillich to speak there of theology as a special sort of metaphysic, a metaphysic which expresses the power and unity of meaning, a metaphysic in touch with its depth, a theonomous metaphysic. (GW. I. 251ff, 278ff)

The character of the 'boundary' between philosophy and theology is of a different sort in the Dresden lectures. For Tillich there addresses the problem of the transition from philosophy to theology in terms of the transition from raising ontological questions to receiving theological answers. Man necessarily asks the question of the meaning of his existence. Implied in this question, however, is the question of being-itself. This, says Tillich following Heidegger, is the question addressed by the philosopher.

But, he continues, this time in contradistinction to Heidegger, to ask the question of the meaning of being also inevitably raises the question of that which lies beyond or transcends being (*das Jenseits des Seins*). Although the philosopher can, even must, raise this question, it is not within his power to form an answer. The philosopher qua phisosopher can lead from the ontological analysis of being-itself to the point where the question is asked about that which transcends being, but he can go no further without ceasing to be a philosopher. He cannot transgress 'the bounds of sense', cannot pass from the phenomenal to the noumenal.[34] When confronted with the question of *das Jenseits des Seins* the philosopher must remain silent. If he does not remain silent, he ceases to be a philosopher and becomes instead a theologian. That is to say, he can address that question only upon the basis of a disclosure of that which transcends being, or what Tillich later called the power and ground of being. For Tillich, as for Heidegger, the 'answer' to the question of the meaning of being cannot be deduced from the analysis of human existence: it must disclose itself. For this reason, if for no other, one must conclude that the complaint made by John Heywood Thomas[35] and others to the effect that Tillich distinguishes philosophy and theology merely by definition is to some degree misdirected. This is not to say, of course, that there are consequently no difficulties in Tillich's attempt to distinguish between them!

The problem arises as to how the philosopher can even broach the question of the transcendent if the answer to that question can come only from something which lies beyond the grasp of man, from *Jenseits des Seins*. Tillich's reply to this question is instructive and, although a full consideration of it is beyond the scope of the present work, what he has to say about it in his Dresden lectures should at least be cited in the present context: 'Man can ask in earnestness for the transcendent only if the transcendent has already spoken. The voice may be faint, but it is nonetheless operative in ontology at every point . . . And that means that, rather than the theological's being grounded in the ontological, the ontological is grounded in the theological . . . For it is neither being-itself nor human existence as such which is primary, but that which transcends

---

[34] It would seem that in 'die Frage nach dem Sinn vom Sein' both Tillich and Heidegger presuppose the critical philosophy of Kant.
[35] See esp. his 'Correlation of Philosophy and Theology in Tillich's System', *LonQuartHolR*, CLXXXIV (1959), 47ff.

being.'[36] Despite heideggerian echoes in this quotation from *Die Gestalt der religiösen Erkenntnis,* Tillich's critique of Heidegger is implicit especially in the last sentence. According to Heidegger, the existential is grounded in the ontological. According to Tillich, the ontological in which the existential is grounded is itself grounded in the theological. As he had done earlier with marxist philosophy, he has now taken heideggerian philosophy and turned it back upon itself. He has with heideggerian tools criticised heideggerian philosophy, thereby carrying through with 'socratic irony' (cf. GW. XIII. 40) the programme projected in *Kirchliche Apologetik.* Even so, these lectures mark the beginning of an important modification of that earlier dialectical principle, the magnitude of which does not become apparent in Tillich's published writings until well after his emigration.

Indeed, were it is not for the existence of this partial manuscript of his Dresden lectures, it would not be known for certain that Tillich had entertained such ideas an early as 1927, though there are indirect hints in his writings as early as 1925. For instance, in a lecture delivered first to a group of Marburg students in December 1924 Tillich developed the theme of apologetics as the art of 'answering' (GW. XII. 81ff), a theme which became a leading motive in subsequent writings, including the *Systematic Theology.* (cf. ST. III. 195) In addition, the 'boundary' theme is introduced in his collection of esays entitled *Religiöse Verwirklichung* (cf. RV, 11–14) and developed extensively especially in the first essay entitled 'Die protestantische Verkündigung und der Mensch der Gegenwart' in which is stressed the limits of human possibility owing to the brokeness of his existence. (RV, 25–42) And in one of the articles contributed by Tillich to the second edition of *Religion in Geschichte und Gegenwart* he lays stress on the importance of radical questioning in philosophy. (RGG. IV. 1198–1204) In another he remarks that philosophy asks the radical question, *die Frage nach der Frage.* (RGG. IV. 1231) Yet, in the latter case, his account of dialectical relations between philosophy and theology is substantially more similar to the approach of his article in Dessoir's *Lehrbuch* than to that of the Dresden lectures. Nonetheless, in the chapter in *Religiöse Verwirklichung* on 'Christologie und Geschichtsdeutung' – a lecture originally delivered at Dresden and Leipzig – Tillich wrote in words that clearly anticipate later developments, 'Geschichte und Christologie gehören

---

[36] See below, p. 274.

zusammen wie Frage und Antwort. Wir wollen darum so vorgehen, daß wir zunächst die geschichtsphilosophische Frage entfalten, um dann den Sinn der christologischen Antwort aufzuweisen.' (RV, 111) This is, so far as I know, the first time this particular sense of 'questioning and answering' appears in Tillich's writings. Almost as noteworthy as its occurrence there is its absence from other works of the same period, including both Tillich's 1928 inaugural lecture at Frankfurt on the theme 'Philosophie und Schicksal' which appeared first in *Kant-Studien* (1929; repr. GW. IV. 23– 35) and also his *Protestantismus als Kritik und Gestaltung,* the second book of the Kairos-Circle which appeared the same year. (Repr. GW. VII. 29–53)

The pattern which emerges at this point in the development of Tillich's thought is far from tidy. Nor is this entirely surprising. For it is consistent with Tillich's own account of the way he gradually came to accept an 'existentialist' way of relating philosophy and theology: 'It took years before I became fully aware of the impact of this encounter [with Heidegger's philosophy] on my own thinking. I resisted, I tried to learn, I accepted the new way of thinking . . .' (K&B, 14) The lectures at Dresden, given not long after his having left Marburg, show Tillich trying out, perhaps for the first time, ideas which would only later be assimilated into his concept of correlation. And there is evidence that at this time Tillich himself was not entirely clear which way such thoughts would lead. (Cf. RGG. IV. 1233) That direction becomes clearer only after his emigration and then in two articles published in 1935: 'What is Wrong with the "Dialectic" Theology?', to which reference has already been made, and 'Natural and Revealed Religion', to which we now turn.

In addition to his contact with that 'new way of thinking' which he learned at Marburg, there is another decisive factor involved in Tillich's eventually having adopted this new usage of 'questioning and answering', rather than simply continuing his earlier 'dialectical principle' as found in the *Kirchliche Apologetik.* I refer to the gradual but inevitable erosion in the late 1920's of Tillich's confidence in the future of Germany and the eventual collapse of the Republic in the wake of 1933, together with the attempt by Hirsch and others to synthesis christianity and the new politics. It is not, I think, insignificant that after 1933 Tillich was much more reluctant to speak of the synthesis in time and space of religion and culture, of theology and

---

[37] *Christendom,* I (1935), 159–70.

philosophy: 'Philosophy and theology are not separated, and they are not identical, but they are correlated, and their correlation is the methodological problem of a Protestant theology.' (PE, xxii) Nor is it insignificant that the two articles in which the new use of 'question' and 'answer' occurs concern issues raised in the respective attempts of Barth and to a lesser extent Hirsch to define the proper structure of relations between theology and philosophy, religion and culture. The connexion is explicitly made in 'Natural and Revealed Religion':

> Because the Christian churches failed to criticize and to transform the historical and religious experience of the German people by the ultimate criterion, given in revelation, a new pagan tribe-religion has arisen which denies revelation in calling itself revelation. And because the Christian churches in Germany and beyond Germany have lost at the same time the transcendent criterion, given in revelation, and the concrete reality of human life and human experience now we have in Germany a cleavage between that tribe-religion which wants to make itself understandable to the German masses and that transcendentalism of Karl Barth which wants to safeguard Christianity and revelation without any connection with the present situation. It is a conflict of a paganized natural theology without a superstructure of revelation and a supernatural theology of revelation without a substructure of natural theology. This example shows clearly the practical importance of a problem which seems to be very abstract and sophisticated.[38]

In response to this situation, Tillich shifts the field of revelation from nature to history[39] and then denies that there are two sorts of theology: 'There is only *one* theology — it is a theology which interprets human religious experience by revelation as criticism and transformation of human religious experience.'[40] But this apparent 'methodological monism', as he terms it, is more dialectical than it at first seems, as Tillich seeks to explain by recourse to the metaphor (*Gleichnis*) of questioning and answering: 'Revelation is an answer which is understandable only if there has been a question. Answers without preceding questions are meaningless. Therefore the questioning [*sic*]

---

[38] *Ibid.*, pp. 165–6.
[39] *Ibid.*, p. 166.
[40] *Ibid.*, p. 167.

for revelation must precede revelation, but this questioning [sic] is not possible without a certain knowledge of the subject for which the question is asked. That means: the questioning [sic] for revelation presupposes revelation, and conversely: they are dependent on each other.'[41] Thus it is that the beginning of the history of religion is a question implying an answer and an answer implying a question.' This is very similar to the ideas sketched first in *Die Gestalt der religiösen Erkenntnis*, which had been prepared by Tillich some seven years earlier.

The trend in Tillich's subsequent writings, including the *Systematic Theology*, is quite clear. The question-answer schema, originating as it did in the earlier 'dialectical method', is increasingly formalised and increasingly detached from the context of actual conversations between apologists and the *Gebildeten*, or even theologians and philosophers generally.[42] In the *Systematic Theology* it is more often philosophy and theology than philosoph*ers* and theolog*ians* who 'converse' with one another, with Tillich manipulating the abstractions in such a way that they move inexorably toward 'the christian answer' in every case. The result may well be judged in its own way 'dialectical', but it is not dialectical in the same way that the method sketched in the *Kirchliche Apologetik* is supposed to be dialectical.[43] Nor is it dialectical in at least one important sense claimed for the method of correlation by Tillich: it is not sufficiently reciprocal. But, we must ask, is this defect – as so often claimed – simply a consequence of his having used questioning and answering as a model of a correlative relation? I shall show that it is not.

Questioning and Answering as a Model of Correlation

Having traced the development of the use of 'questioning' and 'answering' in Tillich's thought, it remains in this section of the chapter to establish the *status* of 'questioning' and 'answering' as a model and then to test its *adequacy* as a model of a correlative relation.

Questioning and answering play a role in Tillich's methodology almost from the first and 'correlation' appears as a technical term of relation in his

---

[41] *Ibid.*, p. 169.
[42] Though see G. B. Hammond, *Man in Estrangement* (Nashville, 1965), p. 3.
[43] As we shall see in the next section, however, there are difficulties with the precise sense of 'dialectic' also in that work.

writings as early as 1924, but it is not until some nine years later that the two are used in conjunction with one another. 'Correlation' is first explained explicitly in terms of questioning and answering in the 1935 Dudleian Lecture referred to above. At the time he gave that lecture, however, Tillich may not have sorted out in his own mind the precise standing of questioning and answering as regards the concept of correlation. That is to say, he seems not yet to have decided whether it is to be regarded as having an 'as if' or an 'as is' status. For in that lecture he introduced the notion of the questions implied in human existence and the answers implied in divine revelation as 'a simile which, I think, is more than a simile'[44] or, in German, '. . . ein Gleichnis . . ., das aber mehr als nur ein Gleichnis ist' (GW. VIII. 56) And even in the *Systematic Theology* he seems to be aware that, as regards the divine-human correlation at least, it is not possible to speak literally of human questions and divine answers: '*Symbolically speaking*, God answers man's questions, and under the impact of God's answers man asks them.' (ST. I. 61; ital. added) Even though it is not entirely clear what Tillich means here by 'symbolically' — for he uses that word in more senses than he acknowledges! — it would not be unreasonable perhaps to suggest that questioning and answering is being put forward as a metaphorical or analogical way of describing the relationship between revelation and its reception in what Tillich, following Brunner, called 'the divine-human encounter'. (cf. GW. XII. 346ff)

But this is only one of the several sorts of relations which are described by Tillich as correlative relations and which are sometimes explained in terms of the question-answer model. As regards some of these other senses of 'correlation', he tends to use the model without such qualifications. He uses it as if it were a literal account of relations between, say, philosophy and theology or psychoanalysis and theology (cf. TC, 125) or the human/cultural situation generally and the christian message. Even in these cases, however, the fact that he typically refers to the questions *implied in* the human/cultural situation and the answers *implied in* the christian message may suggest that he wants to stop short of assigning the question-answer model a literal status as regards relations between culture and religion.

Yet, one is at a loss to find a single instance in the *Systematic Theology* where Tillich specifically calls attention to aspects of the question-answer model which are to be regarded as what Mary Hesse would call

---

[44] 'Natural and Revealed Religion', pp. 168f.

'analogically negative features'. Tillich would seem to have held that this model and its 'original' stand in a one-to-one correspondence with one another so that any feature of the model is also a feature of any correlative relation between, say, philosophy and theology or art and theology. Two additional considerations must be taken into account, however.

First, Tillich nowhere sketches his 'model' in full detail. Those details which he does present are obviously selected having in mind their suitability for his specific purposes. We are, after all, dealing with a 'submerged model' or a 'conceptual archetype', not a full-blown theoretical model of the sort one might expect to find explained in *Nature* or some such periodical. Consequently, what we in effect find in Tillich's writings is *a selectively developed model in which only the main analogically positive features are spelled out*. It does not follow from this, however, that analogically negative features are nowhere implied in his writings. For instance, even though Tillich not infrequently writes as if the relationship between existential/cultural questions and theological answers generally were similar to relations between questions and answers generally, it is perhaps more nearly true to Tillich's intention to qualify this in two ways. Both ways serve to sharpen up and make explicit certain analogically negative features of the question-answer model of a correlative relation. (i) Despite what he sometimes says, Tillich is not in fact setting out a theory of relations between, say, philosophy and theology generally: he is intent only on correlating certain sorts of philosophical questions with certain sorts of theological answers. (ii) Nor is he setting out to base his theory of relations between philosophy and theology on a general theory of relations between all kinds of questions and all kinds of answers. Both these points are to be considered shortly.

Secondly, through the years Tillich came to modify his model so that it more accurately, in his view at least, reflected the details of the 'original'. This is amply illustrated in the previous section of this chapter. And some of the things which Tillich says in the *Systematic Theology* about relations between questions and answers generally would seem to have been dictated rather more by the demands of his understanding of relations between, for example, the human existential situation and divine revelation than by the demands of a comprehensive theory of the various sorts of relations which exist between all kinds of questions and all kinds of answers. For instance, on occasion he insists, and for explicitly theological reasons, that some kinds of existential questions must be reformulated before they can be answered theologically. (Cf. ST. III. 228) One might further suggest that Tillich's arguments against 'idolatry' and 'demonic distortions' constitute in effect arguments against particular ways *zu fragen nach*, not so much in the sense of asking a grammatical question as in the sense of undertaking a quest or making a search.

This, however, raises a considerable difficulty. For in the *Systematic Theology*, Tillich would seem to have conflated two very different sorts of activities in the particular ways he used the phrase 'the question of x'. He would seem to have held that 'the question of x' includes both forming a question about x and undertaking a quest for x. 'The question of God', for instance, means both undertaking a quest for God and forming a question about God or even the word 'God'. But these clearly are not identical activities, a point made as well by Alistair M. Macleod in his study of *Tillich: An Essay on the Role of Ontology in his Philosophical Theology*.[45] One might wonder, though Macleod apparently did not, how Tillich could possibly have so confused two such different sorts of activity. Without in any sense excusing this confusion, in fairness to Tillich, it should be remembered that their distinction is more easily blurred in German than in English. For either sort of activity could be spoken of as 'eine Frage nach x'. To make the point, I offer the following parallel passages from the American and the German editions of Tillich's *Systematic Theology*:

a) The experience of this situation leads to *the quest for* a morality which fulfills the law by transcending it . . . (ST. III. 50)
 Die Einsicht in diese Situation führt zu *der Frage nach* einer moralischen Motivation . . . (STd. III. 64)

b) Humanism itself leads to *the question of* culture transcending itself. (ST. III. 86)
 Der Humanismus selbst führt zu *der Frage nach* einer Kultur, die sich selbst transzendiert. (STd. III. 107)

c) *If one asks* what the guilt of the tragic hero is, the answer must be that he perverts the function of self-transcendence by identifying himself with that to which self-transcendence is directed . . . (ST. III. 94)
 Wenn *die Frage nach* der Schuld des tragischen Helden gestellt wird, lautet die Antwort . . . (STd. III. 115)

d) Religion is not the answer to *the quest for* unambiguous life, although the answer can only be received through religion. (ST. III. 106)

---

[45] (London, 1973), pp. 31ff.

Aus all dem folgt, daß Religion nicht die Antwort auf *die Frage nach* unzweideutigem Leben ist . . . (STd. III. 129f)

e) *The question of* unambiguous life is latent everywhere. All creatures long for an unambiguous fulfillment of their essential possibilities; but only in man as the bearer of the spirit do the ambiguities of life and *the quest for* unambiguous life become conscious. (ST. III. 107)

Daher ist *die Frage nach* unzweideutigem Leben überall latent vorhanden. Alle Geschöpfe sehnen sich nach einer unzweideutigen Erfüllung ihrer essentiellen Möglichkeiten. Aber nur im Menschen als dem Träger des Geistes werden die Zweideutigkeiten bewußt erlebt und daher auch *die Frage nach* unzweideutigem Leben bewußt gestellt. (STd. III. 130)

Each of these passages expresses a different sense of asking a question or making a quest, but in every case the relevant phrase is rendered in German as *die Frage nach*. This is the case even in example *e* where both 'the question of' and 'the quest for' appear in the same English passage. These phrases clearly do not have the same meaning, yet their identification is essential for moves made by Tillich when he speaks of relations between existential questions and revelatory answers, so that questions about God can be regarded as instances of the quest for God.[46]

Many of the most persistent criticisms of Tillich's concept of correlation have been directed ostensibly against his question-answer model of a correlative relation. As has been remarked above, however, some of the objectionable features ascribed to that model are rather more accurately to be regarded as features of the form-content model. As such, they will be taken up in the next chapter. Nonetheless, two sorts of criticism which have been levelled against the question-answer model proper may be distinguished.

First, a large number of commentators have complained that in his actual attempts to make correlations between existential questions and theological answers *either* 'message' illicitly dominates 'situation' *or* 'situation' illicitly dominates 'message' so that the resulting relationship does not satisfy both the conditions of a correlative relation as set forth above in chapter two. George Tavard suspects that Tillich is possibly guilty of both sorts of error! In his review of the third volume of the *Systematic Theology,*

---

[46] This problem need not be pursued further, however, as it has been treated in some detail by Macloed, *loc. cit.*

Tavard speaks of the 'deep imbalance' in Tillich's thought, 'which is so dominated by the desire to correlate situation and message that one often wonders whether the question is guided by the answer to be given in faith and which is known before the question is asked, or on the contrary the answer is so regulated by the question that it loses some of the originality of the Christian Revelation.'[47]

Nor are these criticisms entirely without foundation. There are undeniably occasions in the *Systematic Theology* when the theological 'answers' are dictated more by Tillich's philosophical assumptions than by the explicit demands of 'the christian message'; and there are other occasions in the *Systematic Theology* when the philosophical questions, putatively derived from a purely phenomenological analysis of the human/cultural situation, are directed rather pointedly and predictably toward the christian theological 'answer'.[48] Such criticisms, valid as they be in many cases, are not in and of themselves decisive for settling the question of the adequacy of Tillich's question-answer model of a correlative relation. For these sorts of objections have to do more with the skill with which Tillich applies his method of correlation to concrete problems than with the soundness of the concept of correlation conceived in terms of the question-answer model.[49] To these sorts of criticism, Tillich quite legitimately replied that no method is immune from misapplication: 'The method of correlation is not safe from distortion; no theological method is. The answer can prejudice the question to such a degree that the seriousness of the existential predicament is lost. No method is a guaranty [sic] against such failures.

---

[47] *Commonweal* (7 February 1964); repr. *JRel*, XLVI (1966), 224–5.

[48] Examples of the first kind can be found in K. Hamilton, *The System and the Gospel* (London, 1963). One example of the second kind has already been discussed above in chapter three, namely, Tillich's claim that everyone is necessarily religious. Bernard Martin offers another example: 'What is the entire first half of the second volume of his *Systematic Theology* if not a reiteration – in philosophical terminology, to be sure – of the classical Christian doctrine of sin?' *Paul Tillich's Doctrine of Man* (London, 1966), p. 33.

[49] Martin suggests that questioning and answering does not even describe what goes on within Tillich's own thought: 'Whatever the relation between philosophy and theology may be in Tillich's constructive work . . . it is not appropriately to be described as that of "question-and-answer". The method of correlation as he defines it is . . . a largely misleading description of his own procedure.' *Ibid.*, pp. 35f.

Theology, like all enterprises of the human mind, is ambiguous. But this is not an argument against theology or against the method of correlation.' (ST. II. 16; cf. ST. III. 4) Even granting Tillich's point, however, such criticisms may not be entirely irrelevant to an assessment of the adequacy of the question-answer model of a correlative relationship between culture and religion. Such 'distortions' may in fact be symptoms of more serious difficulties, that is, of defects inherent within the model. The sort of relations which obtains between questioning and answering might not serve as an adequate model of the sort of relations which obtains between culture and religion. Nor has everyone who has criticised the relationship between philosophical questioning and theological answering in the *Systematic Theology* restricted the scope of his critique to Tillich's ability to carry through his proposed method with skill and sensitivity.

Some have complained — and this constitutes the second sort of criticism — that the model is defective not merely in application but in principle. Some examples of this sort of criticism are quite superficial and betray a failure to interpret the relationship between philosophical questioning and theological answering in the light of Tillich's theory of religious knowledge. (cf. TC, 10ff; GW. IV. 107ff) Not uncommonly it is alleged that the question-answer model implies a limitation of God's transcendence: 'No answer is acceptable unless the question has been asked. There is the supposition that without divine aid a man is capable of asking all the questions corresponding to the answers of the divine kerygma.'[50] But this is clearly *not* Tillich's meaning. As we have seen already, he characteristically emphasised that man's ability to form the question of God is possible only because God is already in some sense 'known': 'The question of God is possible because an awareness of God is present in the question of God. This awareness precedes the question.' (ST. I. 206) This is consistent with Tillich's characteristic emphasis upon what he called 'the protestant principle', which — simply stated — is as follows: '. . . in relation to God, God alone can act and . . . no human claim, especially no religious claim, no intellectual or moral or devotional "work", can reunite us with him.' (ST. III. 224; cf. pp. 243–5) Standing in this case firmly within the protestant tradition, Tillich held that 'in relation to God, everything is by God.' (ST. III. 133; cf. p. 135) Such an objection further rests on an inversion of Tillich's method of correlation. Tillich typically stresses that

---

[50] Albert Zabala, *Myth and Symbol* (Paris, 1959), p. 317f.

the christian message contains the answers to *all* man's questions of an ultimate sort, whereas this objection requires an inverted reading of that claim so that Tillich is said further to hold that the christian message is able to 'answer' *only* those questions. This interpretation possibly rests on a misunderstanding of Tillich's claim that 'man cannot receive an answer to a question he has not asked.' (ST. II. 13) But, when seen within the full context of Tillich's theology, it becomes clear that he is there stressing *human* limitaion, and not in any sense curtailing divine freedom in dealings with men.[51]

But there is a more significant criticism that is sometimes put to effect that Tillich's notion of correlation is itself either incoherent or logically self-contradictory in the sense that it is impossible successfully to satisfy the minimum conditions of a correlative relation within the terms of the question-answer model as expounded in the *Systematic Theology*. This objection is forcefully made, for instance, by Douglass Lewis in his unjustly neglected article on 'The Conceptual Structure of Tillich's Method of Correlation'[52] Lewis argues that Tillich's stress on the logical *independence* of question and answer, philosophy and theology, in the sense that each is said to operate in its own 'realm of discourse', precludes the possibility of any truly theological statement being regarded as an 'answer' to any truly philosophical question. 'If philosophy and theology really operate in different realms of discourse, . . . then one cannot raise questions in one realm of discource and answer them from another . . .'[53] A question formed in one realm and an answer formed in another realm can never stand in a correlative relation to one another 'for they derive their meaning from two different logical contexts.' Yet, this is precisely what Tillich's method of

---

[51] Nor is Zabala alone in this sort of misunderstanding of the kind of relation which in Tillich's view holds as between existential questions and their answers implied in the christian message. See, e.g., Karl Barth's 'Introductory Report' in A. J. McKelway, *The Systematic Theology of Paul Tillich* (Richmond, 1964), pp. 11ff. For a summary and assessment of Barth's critique of the method of correlation, see H. Förster, *op. cit.*, pp. 128–35. Jochen Buchter, by way of contrast, makes a helpful distinction between the *ontological* priority of the 'answer' and the *apologetic* priority of the 'question'. See *Die Kriterien der Theologie im Werke Paul Tillichs* (Bonn, 1975), p. 107; see also p. 221.

[52] *Encounter*, XXVIII (1967), 263–74.

[53] *Ibid..*, p. 269.

correlation would seem to require and this requirement is judged by Lewis to involve Tillich in 'a direct logical contradiction'.

To drive his point home, Lewis offers the following analogy: 'Raising questions out of philosophy, psychology, physics, or some other non-theological context and answering them out of a theological context is like a physicist asking: "What is the (physical) source of the light of the world?" and the theologian answering: "Jesus Christ is the light of the world".' Even though Lewis has not perhaps selected a very imaginative example, no-one would want to disagree with him when he claims that this question and this answer 'are most clearly not logical correlates and never can be, for they derive their meaning from two different logical contexts.' In order for any statement to be an answer to a given question, on this view, that statement must belong to the same 'logical context' or 'realm of discourse' as the question. This would mean that, for instance, where theology and philosophy are distinct realms as Tillich sometimes claims, no theological statement can coherently constitute an answer to any philosophical question. The basis for this charge lies in Tillich's claim that some sorts of philosophical questions are answerable by and only by theological statements, even though philosophy and theology are regarded as distinct realms.

It is perhaps worth underscoring that Tillich is not claiming that every sort of philosophical question can be answered by and only by theological statements. Lewis and others would seem to have assumed that Tillich intends the method of correlation to be universally applicable to all sorts of philosophical questions and all sorts of theological statements. But this cannot be Tillich's meaning, for he sets out at some length the sorts of philosophical questions which are said to be capable of being correlated with theological answers. On occasion he explicitly refers to philosophical *solutions* to philosophical puzzles and even to philosophical *answers* to philosophical questions. (ST. III. 334−5 *et passim*) Although he does not infrequently speak as if he were recommending a general theory of relations between philosophy and theology, it is more accurate to say − as Tillich himself seems to imply − that only some sorts of philosophical questions stand in a correlative relation to their theological answers. For instance, philosophical or scientific questions which express a 'preliminary concern' would not in Tillich's view stand in a correlative relation to theological answers. Nor do casually asked questions so stand: the questions must be asked 'in earnest'. (STd. III. 256f; cf. ST. III. 223) The example intended by

Lewis as a *reductio ad absurdum* does not actually conform to the kinds of question which in Tillich's view would be capable of correlation with a theological answer. In Tillich's language, the question in Lewis's example expresses a 'preliminary concern' and not an 'ultimate concern'.

But this does not meet Lewis's objection in full. He holds that Tillich has involved himself in a 'logical contradiction' for claiming that *any* given philosophical question is answerable by and only by a theological answer, and not just for putatively claiming that *every* single philosophical question is so answerable.

Yet, the view of 'the logic of questions' presupposed in Lewis's charge is too simple, as is his view that theological statements constitute a single 'logical context'. For questions and answers are related in a variety of ways in ordinary language and no one sort of relation can legitimately constitute the only sort of relation allowable. In short, the logic of questions is manifold. Some of the different kinds of relations between questions and answers are to be found cursorily discussed in Waismann's posthumously published *Principles of Linguistic Philosophy*[54] and also in Wittgensteins's *Philosophical Investigations*[55] which stands behind many of the ideas expressed in Waismann's book. Much work no doubt remains to be done by logicians and philosophers of language before the complex 'logic of questions' is mapped out satisfactorily.[56] All that is required here, however, is to determine whether there exists a counter-example to those adduced by Lewis.

The issue is whether there are any occasions when questions formed in one distinct 'realm of discourse' are incapable of finding an answer from within that realm but can be answered nonetheless by reference to another realm. Lewis clearly holds, not only that it is wrong to hold that some *philosophical* questions are answerable by *theology*, but also that it is wrong to hold that any question from *one* realm is answerable from another realm. A counter-example to that offered by Lewis may be found in Waismann's *Principles of Linguistic Analysis*, in which he shows that giving an 'answer'

---

[54] London, 1965.
[55] Oxford, 1958.
[56] Waismann was keenly aware that his own remarks on 'the logic of questions' were tentative and preliminary: 'The problem is no easy one, and we approach it with the diffidence it deserves.' *Op. cit.*, p. 387. Cf. also the more recent collection *Questions*, ed. Henry Hiż (Dordrecht, 1977).

to the question, 'How does one trisect an angle?', involves shifting the goal of the search until the original goal finally disappears, though in a way that satisfies the questioner who is led with his consent at every stage from one sort of symbolism to another.[57] That is to say, it is a question which can not be answered from within the 'realm' it originated and which can be answered only by shifting to another 'realm': '. . . not every question can find an answer within the world of thought which gave it birth, . . . it is sometimes necessary for something quite fresh to happen, for man to pass to a new course of thought before the way to its solution can be opened up.'[58] To that extent, Tillich would seem to be given indirect support at least from Waismann.

Note the moves made in the following passage, bearing in mind of course that the technique is actually being applied to ends not shared by Tillich. According to Waismann, some sorts of philosophical questions or perplexities appear to be real problems, but are in fact 'evoked only by the mists in which our concepts are sunk':

> The [metaphysical] philosopher [such as Bradley, etc.] contemplates things through the prism of language and, misled by one or other of its aspects, for example by some analogy, suddenly sees things in a new strange light. We can cope with these problems only by turning back towards the focal point of his disquiet, that is, towards language itself. What we do then is to light up the mental background from which the question has detached itself; in a clearer perception of the world of our concept the question itself vanishes. Not that it has been answered in the usual sense of the word. Rather we have removed the factors that prompted the question by a more profound and penetrating analysis. The essence of this process is that it gradually leads the questioner on to some new aspect – and leads him consenting. It is just as with the case of our search for a method of trisecting the angle: our goal shifts until it finally disappears. We cannot constrain anyone who is unwilling to follow the new direction of a question; we can only extend the field of vision of the questioner, loosen his prejudices, guide his gaze in different directions: but all this can be achieved only with his consent.[59]

---

[57] Waismann, *op. cit.*, pp. 398–400, *q.v.*
[58] *Ibid.*, p. 413.
[59] *Ibid.*, pp. 416–7. Cf. also pp. 3 ff.

Though directed specifically against the philosophical tradition in which Tillich, broadly speaking, also stood, there are striking similarities — as well as equally striking dissimilarities! — between the technique of philosophical dialectic (apologetic?) recommended here by Waismann and the technique of apologetic dialectic recommended by Tillich as early as the *Kirchliche Apologetik*. In both cases we have examples of techniques of mediation between two different 'logical contexts' and in both cases the questioner is led from one way of seeing things to another way in order to find an answer to his query. Implied in both cases is the conviction that the questioner is in principle incapable of arriving at an 'answer' from within the logical context in which his question was formed.

At this point, however, the differences in the two techniques become more obvious. There is in each an important difference in attitude toward the sort of question which is in principle unanswerable from within its own context. Waismann regards such questions as improper in the sense that they betray a limited understanding of the scope and nature of a discipline ('How does one trisect an angle?') or a certain lack of clarity owing to one's having been 'misled' by one or another aspect of 'the prism of language'. Consequently, there can be no answer to such questions 'in the usual sense' of the word *answer*. One can only endeavour with great patience to remove 'the factors that prompted the question by a more profound and penetrating analysis'.

With Tillich it is quite different. The kinds of questions which he endeavours to correlate with theological answers are regarded by him as genuine and proper questions. They are questions which man qua man not only can ask but indeed necessarily must ask (cf. ST. I. 204–10), even though he is not able to form an answer from within 'the existential situation' in which the question was produced. Nor are they the sort of questions of which it could be said that 'the goal of our search disappears in proportion as the meaning of the problem is made precise', as Waismann says of the sort of questions he has in mind.[60] These are differences which are not by any means insignificant; nonetheless, these differences do not affect the point at hand.

The similarities are sufficient to show that what Tillich sets out to do in the *Systematic Theology* with questions and answers is not nonsense. Tillich's procedure there is in principle neither incoherent nor self-contra-

---

[60] *Ibid.*, p. 400.

dictory. But it is problematical as regards its ability to satisfy the two conditions of a correlative relation which were identified above in chapter two: namely, the reciprocity condition and the autonomy condition. Is it possible wholly within the terms of the question-answer model of correlation to have between religion and culture a thoroughly reciprocal relationship which nonetheless allows each to remain in some sense autonomous from the other?

In order to answer this question, reference must first be made to a tension which exists within 'the dialectical method' as it is explained in the *Kirchliche Apologetik*. Two basically different and ultimately competing views of the dialectical interplay of religion and culture are intertwined in that work. The first may be termed *dialectic as reciprocity* because the two co-equal discussion partners mutually influence one another in the dialogue between religion and culture, between the apologist and the 'cultured'. As suggested in the previous section of this chapter, this is the use of dialectic which tends to prevail in the *Kirchliche Apologetik*. And it would not be unfair to mention that this sense of dialectic is most compatible with what Tillich beginning in 1919 came to refer to as 'cultural theology'. In both cases the theologian is said to act as a free-agent, so that the discussion is entirely open-ended and there is no way to predict beforehand where it will lead. Any procedure in which this sense of dialectic were employed would afford a thorough-going reciprocity between the two partners. But it would provide no guidelines, much less criteria, for the direction and object of the 'conversation'. It is on its own too shapeless to be an adequate model of a correlative relation. The sort of relationship implied between religion and culture in any such procedure would satisfy the first but not the second condition of a correlative relationship.

Yet this is clearly not the sort of procedure one finds being used in Tillich's later writings, including the *Systematic Theology*. Nor, incidentally, is it the sort of procedure followed in the quotation above from Waismann's *Principles of Linguistic Philosophy*! Their procedures more nearly resemble the other sense in which 'dialectic' is used in the *Kirchliche Apologetik*. This second sort of usage can be called the *didactic use of dialectic* since one partner assumes the role of teacher and leads the other to knowledge which either is not otherwise available to him or which, as tends to be the case in the *Kirchliche Apologetik* itself, is extracted from him by socratic midwifery, so that the discussion partner comes to see that he has been 'really' religious all along. (cf. GW. XIII. 49) According to this second use of dialectic, the apologist may be seen as one who skillfully and patiently leads the cultured despiser of religion from one way of seeing things to another, though with his consent at every stage. In any case, the apologist speaks from a specific if unacknowledged standpoint and to a definite if unannounced end, namely the persuasion of the other person. This use of dialectic, which is more susceptible to Barth's critique of the ethics of apologetics[61] than is the later method of correlation, corresponds roughly to that which would be appropriate in what Tillich early termed 'church theology'. Here a definite shape is given to the 'dialogue' between religion and culture, the apologist and the cultured, but the element of reciprocity is as a consequence greatly diminished, if not largely eliminated.

The concept of a correlative relation implied in the so-called 'method of correlation' must be classed ultimately with the second, rather than with the first, sort of dialectic, and not merely because correlation is – as indicated above in chapter two – the principle of mediation between 'the christian message' and 'the present cultural situation'. For, despite Tillich's frequent claims to the contrary, the element of reciprocity is much restricted in the method of correlation, the shape of which can hardly be regarded open-ended. In the next chapter it will be shown that this is partly a result of Tillich's having become increasingly concerned after his emigration that aspects of his earlier 'cultural theology' offered little protection against the assimilation of 'message' into 'situation'. There are other factors as well, most of which are more closely connected with Tillich's form-content model than with his question-answer model of correlation.

---

[61] See *Kirchliche Dogmatik*, II/1 (Zürich, 1958⁴), pp. 102ff.

CHAPTER SIX
FORM, CONTENT AND THE CONCEPT OF CORRELATION

*The Role of 'Form' and 'Content' in the Development
of Tillich's Thought*

When Tillich states, as he not infrequently does, that the *form* of the existential question determines the *form*, but not the *content*, of the christian answer, a good deal more is being claimed than is at first apparent. For it is not merely the case — at least not in the most obvious sense — that the form of words in which the existential question is phrased is supposed to determine the form of words in which is phrased the christian answer, but not the content of that answer. If that were the case, then we would have to do with simply another aspect of 'the logic of questions and answers'. But, as will soon become apparent, what Tillich has to say about 'form' and 'content' cannot be treated simply as another aspect of that problem. Consequently, the problem of the relationship between 'form' and 'content' must be examined separately from that of the relationship between 'questioning' and 'answering', even though Tillich may not himself always separate the two sorts of problems.

Implied, rather, is the more characteristically Tillichian distinction between *cultural* 'form' and *religious* 'content'. This distinction is arguably among the most central, if not also most obscure, in his thought. It derives from the dialectic of *Form—Inhalt—Gehalt*. With the introduction of this particular dialectic into our study, we plunge into those dark depths of Tillich's thought where, if not all, certainly most of the cows are black.

This peculiar use of 'form' and 'content' is perhaps most recognisably associated with Tillich in the shape of the now familiar dictum, implied and all but explicitly stated in 'Über die Idee einer Theologie der Kultur' (esp. GW. IX. 21−2), that 'culture is the form of religion and religion is the substance of culture'. The earliest variation of this statement, which is in any case expressed in several different ways in Tillich's earlier writings (cf. GW. IX. 37; I. 329; XII. 43), is apparently to be found in 'Kirche und Kultur' (1924): '. . . der tragende Gehalt der Kultur ist die Religion, und die notwendige Form der Religion ist die Kultur.' (GW. IX. 42) It will be recalled from the previous chapter that this is the essay in which the word *correlation* makes its first appearance in Tillich's writings as a special term of relationship between religion and culture. (GW. IX. 32) Even so, Tillich does not there directly link 'correlation' with the dialectic of form and content (cf. GW. IX. 37), at least not in the way he had come to do so by the time he wrote the first volume of his *Systematic Theology*, in which the dialectic of form and content is as regards 'correlation' at least regularly associated with the dialectic of questioning and answering. And in the 'restatement' of the method of correlation offered in the introduction to the second volume of that work, the dialectic of form and content is expressed rather in terms of the triadic relations between and among 'form', 'material' and 'substance' (ST. II. 14—16), a point easily overlooked if one had not already been alerted to the significance of that conceptual triad in Tillich's thought through a careful study of its course of development. This 'shift' in Tillich's account of 'correlation' — which is not in one sense a shift at all — makes even more explicit than elsewhere the intimate connexion between his talk of 'form' and 'content' in the *Systematic Theology* and his earlier discussion of *Form, Inhalt* and *Gehalt*. (cf. also ST. I. 178ff; III. 60)

In one way or another this dialectic is to be counted among the most persistent threads woven into the fabric of Tillich's thought, to borrow David Kelsey's metaphor.[1] Although in the course of Tillich's development it underwent from the time of its first appearance in 1919 not inconsequential variations of shade and hue, if not also texture as well, that same thread is detectable in almost all Tillich's subsequent writings on religion and culture. This includes both major attempts to express his thought systematically, *Das System der Wissenschaften* and, of course, the *Systematic Theology*.

In the earlier work, the *Form—Gehalt* dialectic was used to explain the sort of 'theonomous unity' which it was held ought to obtain between religion and culture generally. Any sort of relationship short of this total synthesis was regarded there as an instance of 'the disruption of meaning' which that *System* was designed to overcome.[2] In the latter work, however, a very similar dialectic of form-content (though the actual terms used vary from place to place) is employed to apparently different ends to explain the now desired 'correlative' relationship between religion and culture, a rela-

---

[1] *The Fabric of Paul Tillich's Theology* (New Haven, 1967).
[2] For a summary of some of the main parts of *Das System der Wissenschaften*, see J. L. Adams, *Paul Tillich's Philosophy of Culture, Science and Religion* (New York, 1965), pp. 116—82.

tionship which expressed 'the interdependence of two independent factors'. (ST. II. 13)

The ideal of 'theonomous metaphysics' outlined in *Das System der Wissenschaften* thus ostensibly yields to the ideal of the correlation of philosophy and theology in the *Systematic Theology*.[3] And even Tillich on occasion remarked that the method of correlation was designed to *replace* the earlier and, in his later view, less satisfactory method of the theonomous 'elevation' of metaphysics. (GW. VII. 25) It would perhaps be closer to the actual state of affairs, however, to say that correlation more nearly *displaced* theonomy as the central methodological category in Tillich's system. For theonomy did not simply disappear from his repertoire of concepts after he had adopted the so-called method of correlation. 'Correlation' and 'theonomy' continue to be used side by side in the *Systematic Theology*.

This fact possibly constitutes a serious difficulty for the unity of Tillich's system of thought. For, even though similar sorts of assumptions are at work and the same dialectic used in their formulation, the concepts of theonomy and correlation *prima facie* at least would seem to imply different understandings of the relationship between religion and culture. One aim of this section is to determine, through an analysis of the varying roles played by 'form' and 'content' in the development of Tillich's thought, whether these ostensibly *different* accounts are also *incompatible* accounts of the relationship between religion and culture.

Whilst it plays a central if varied role in Tillich's two published systems, the dialectic of *Form−Inhalt−Gehalt* plays no such part in his first sketch of a system, the seventy-two theses on systematic theology prepared in 1913. In fact, the dialectic of *Form−Inhalt−Gehalt* is explicitly to be found in none of Tillich's writings known to me, whether published or unpublished, which were written before the first world war.

Nor is this insignificant.

For it bears out to some extent Tillich's claim to have formulated that conceptual triad immediately after the war under the immediate impact of certain paintings, mainly those done in an expressionistic style. (GW. IX. 22f; XII. 21f) It might have been otherwise. Similar sorts of terms had been

---

[3] This has been a common interpretation of Tillich's developing thought. See, e. g., J. M. van Hook, *Paul Tillich's Conception of the Relation between Philosophy and Theology* (PH. D. diss., Columbia, 1966), pp. 67−73, and G. D. Kaufmann, 'Can a Man Serve Two Masters?', *ThToday*, XV (1958), 59−77.

widely used in German idealism, by Fichte in his 1794 *Grundlage der gesamten Wissenschaftslehre* as well as by Schelling and Hegel alike in their respective philosophies of art.[4] A similar dialectic is used to different ends by Martin Kähler in his *Die Wissenschaft der christlichen Lehre*.[5] One would be unwise to deny that their usage of similar concepts had considerable influence on Tillich, whether directly or indirectly. The fact remains, however, that Tillich did not in any of his writings prior to 1914 use such a dialectic, even though it was for him so central in all his writings and many of his lectures (cf. GW. XIV. 296f) after that war. And it remains a fact that Tillich himself attributed the particular way he developed the relationship between *Form, Inhalt* and *Gehalt*, not to his acquaintance with the writings of those philosophers, but to his war-time encounter with the visual arts. Despite the similarity of Tillich's use of the terms *Form* and *Gehalt* to the uses made of those or similar terms by the philosophers of idealism – similarities which have been established and rightly stressed in some previous studies of Tillich's thought[6] – the dissimilarities are equally striking and can be accounted for in some measure by the decisive influence upon Tillich of expressionism and other related movements in art, especially 'die neue Sachlichkeit'.

At one time expressionism was seen narrowly as a German movement in art, a misconception early encouraged by certain German artists and critics.[7] It is now seen more properly within a wider, international context. Indeed, the term itself was apparently first used by the French painter Hervé in a private exhibition in 1901 at the Salon des Indépendants in Paris; and even in Germany the term was first used in connexion with the

---

[4] *Johan Gottlieb Fichte's Sämtliche Werke*, ed. J. H. Fichte, vol. I (Berlin, 1845–1846), pp. 91ff, *et passim*. *Schellings Werke*, ed. Manfred Schröter, vol. III: *Schriften zur Identitätsphilosophie, 1801–1806* (Munich, 1927), pp. 377ff, and also Ergänzungsband III: *Zur Philosophie der Kunst, 1803–1817* (Munich, 1959), esp. pp. 391ff. G. W. F. Hegel, *Werke in 20 Bänden* (Frankfurt, 1969–71), vols. XIII–XV, especially the section on romantic art in vol. XIV, pp. 127ff.

[5] 3rd. ed.; Leipzig, 1905, pp. 12ff, *et passim*.

[6] See, e. g., G. F. Sommer, *The Significance of the Late Philosophy of Schelling for the Formation and Interpretation of the Thought of Paul Tillich* (Ph.D. diss, Duke, 1960), pp. 58ff. But, see below, note 19!

[7] Kirchner, especially, comes to mind. See also H. Hilderbrandt, *Die Kunst des 19. und 20. Jahrhundert* (Potsdam, 1924), pp. 357–8.

paintings of Cézanne, van Gogh and Matisse![8] Be that as it may, the expressionistic movement in Germany, which can be said to have begun by 1905 with the formation of the *Bruecke* group,[9] soon became distinguishable in fundamental respects from their French counterparts, the Fauves.[10]

That this is in fact the case is persuasively argued by Bernard Myers.[11] Myers grants that the works of the French Fauves and the German expressionists bear superficial resemblances and also that they were both influenced by similar sorts of art (impressionist, primitive, mediaeval). Their aims, however, are profoundly different and their sources are used to serve different ends. 'The French distort and destroy form for analytical or synthetic purposes, whereas the German's distortions and deformations have as their purpose the emotional or psychological truth, the symbolic significance that lies beneath . . .'.[12] This difference can be seen in the use made of techniques developed by van Gogh. 'For the French his technique was important for its freedom of handling, brilliance of color, and combination of emotional decorative qualities. To the Germans the art of van Gogh meant an emotional frenzy and passion, a sympathy for humanity, and an ability to represent the essentials of a given mood through distortions of form, local color, and space'. To the German expressionists, it was van Gogh's ability 'to give many of his subjects transcendental meaning far beyond the immediate fact' which proved influential.[13] The expressionists used such techniques in order to bring out the hidden significance or 'inner meaning' of the subject matter. This tendency gives to much of their work its symbolical, even mystical or religious, quality which was so admired by the young Tillich, so that of it he could in 1919 say, 'Here a strong religious concern strives toward expression . . .'. (GW. IX. 23)

In his address on the notion of a theology of culture, Tillich painted in bold strokes only his picture of a theonomously unified culture. More details are added to this early sketch in several subsequent writings, including most ambitiously his rather forbidding *Das System der Wissen-*

---

[8] See F. Whitford, *Expressionism* (London, 1970), and B. Myers, *Expressionism: A Generation in Revolt* (London, 1963).
[9] Formed in Dresden by Kirchner, Pechstein and others.
[10] Matisse, Rouault, etc.
[11] *Op. cit.*
[12] *Ibid.*, p. 94
[13] *Ibid.*, p. 92.

schaften[14] and the more humanly proportioned 'Religionsphilosophie'.[15] But the earlier, if also more 'enthusiastic' (Cf. PE, 56), account in 'Über die Idee einer Theologie der Kultur' is in some ways the more directly useful for our present purposes. There his 'aesthetic model' is more explicit than in the later works, where it tends to be more 'submerged'.

The key concept of the address is perhaps *theonomy*, a term which had tended to be used since the eighteenth century at least in a largely pejorative sense in reference to heteronomy enforced by ecclesiastical authority.[16] It required not a little courage to advocate a new theonomy in a paper read to the Kant-Gesellschaft! And, not surprisingly, in his address Tillich was at pains to disclaim that his vision of a religiously imbued culture would represent in any sense a return to a sort of heteronomy, whether in thought or action or imagination. (cf. RGG. V. 1128–9) But, one might wonder, how is it possible for religion to be a dimension of every sphere of culture, providing its direction and values (cf. ST. III. 249 ff), and yet not violate the autonomy of that culture? In attempting to answer such a question, Tillich brought the distinction between *Form* and *Gehalt* to bear upon the notion of theonomy: '. . . the autonomy of the functions of culture is grounded in their form, in the rules of their use, whereas theonomy is grounded in their *Gehalt*, in the reality which is represented or realised through those rules'. The following formula is then offered: 'the more the form, the more the autonomy; the more the *Gehalt*, the more the theonomy'. (GW. IX. 19) But, according to Tillich's account, there is no such thing as 'pure form' or 'pure *Gehalt*', even if he elsewhere identifies 'the God above God' with 'pure *Gehalt*'. (GW. IX. 323) In order to visualise the relationship between form and *Gehalt*, the reader is invited by Tillich to imagine a line segment, one end of which is pure form and the other pure *Gehalt*. Along the line itself, however, the two are always united. For there is no form which forms nothing, nor is there any formless *Gehalt*.

---

[14] The contemporary reviews of this work show that German scholars were not sure what to make of the young Tillich's difficult and at times opaque thought. See, e. g., F. Büchsel, 'Die Stellung der Theologie im System der Wissenschaften', ZSysTh, I (1924), 399–411; A Dell, 'Der Charakter der Theologie in Tillichs System der Wissenschaften', ThBlätter, II (1923), 235–45; K. Leese, *Christliche Welt*, XXXVII (1926), 317–25, 371–5.

[15] For an exposition of this work, see J. L. Adams, *op. cit.*, pp. 183 ff.

[16] But, see M. Kähler, *Die Wissenschaft der christlichen Lehre*, and also Ludwig Ihmels *Theonomie und Autonomie* (Leipzig, 1903)!

But what precisely does Tillich means by *Gehalt*?[17] One is actually given very little help in 'Über die Idee einer Theologie der Kultur'. True, Tillich does draw certain distinctions with a view toward defining *Gehalt*. For instance, he says that *Gehalt* is 'something other than' *Inhalt*: 'By *Inhalt*, we understand the material as it objectively is [*das Gegenständliche in seinem einfachen Sosein*], which is taken up through form into the spiritual-cultural sphere. By *Gehalt*, however, one is to understand the meaning, the spiritual substantiality, which alone gives significance to form. *Gehalt* is grasped in an *Inhalt* by means of form and brought to expression'. (GW. IX. 20) From such statements one might feel confident in inferring that *Inhalt* is in Tillich's view primary to the extent that it is the 'stuff' which has meaning (*Gehalt*) and which is structured or shaped in a particular way (*Form*), that *Gehalt* is simply that which formed stuff signifies or means. It is somewhat perplexing, therefore, to find in the next sentences Tillich, having just introduced his triad of *Form*–*Inhalt*–*Gehalt*, proceeding to reduce it to a dialectic of form and *Gehalt*. He does this first by assimilating *Inhalt* into form and then by greatly reducing the significance of *Inhalt*, if not eliminating it altogether:

> *Inhalt* is the contingent element, *Gehalt* the essential one and form the mediating agent. The form must be appropriate to the *Inhalt*, so that no antithesis occurs between cultivation of form and cultivation of *Inhalt*. Rather, they stand together on one side, whereas the cultivation of *Gehalt* stands on the other. The shattering of form by *Gehalt* is identical with *Inhalt*'s becoming insignificant and unessential. Form loses its necessary connexion with *Inhalt*, because *Inhalt* is lost sight of in comparison with the overwhelming intensity of *Gehalt*. Thereby form becomes somewhat detached, or free-floating, so that it is related directly to *Gehalt* and loses its natural and necessary relationship to *Inhalt*. In this way it becomes form in a paradoxical sense in that it allows its own natural connexion to be shattered by *Gehalt*. (GW. IX. 22)

---

[17] Virtually all interpreters seem to be agreed that Tillich's conception of *Gehalt* is among the most diffuse in his early work. Tillich's notorious lack of precision in the way he uses key terms is nowhere more evident than in the case of *Gehalt*. Note the numerous ways the terms is used, e. g., in GW. IX. 35, 318, 321, 323; GW. I. 116 et passim; GW. XII, 112; STd. III. 75–6.

Even laying aside the easy and almost anthropomorphic way Tillich here talks about highly abstract concepts, this passage is on any account obscure. One turns perhaps to other writings for clearer statements. And although one finds numerous other statements, some of which are highly picturesque in their use of exended metaphor (cf. GW. IX. 318), they do not in and of themselves greatly clarify the matter at hand.

The situation becomes clearer only when Tillich turns to specific and relatively concrete examples. Of the examples adduced, those drawn from the visual arts are consistently the most vivid and to the point. In some cases[18] Tillich explicitly states that what he says about the other spheres of cultural life is derived from what he says about the arts.

In a short and explosive paragraph in his 1919 address, Tillich stresses the way expressionistic painters have distorted natural 'form'[19] in order to express more intensely the inner and largely hidden 'meaning' of the object represented.[20] The aim of these expressionists may be, as their name suggests, positive and affirmative, but in Tillich's view the form-destroying aspect of their work tended to dominate the form-creating aspect. In this particular style of painting *Inhalt* in the sense of outward appearance or *äußere Tatsächlichkeit* is regarded as a barrier to be broken through: 'Nature has been stripped naked, its hidden depths laid bare'. (GW. IX. 23) 'Beauty is not among those concepts which figure prominently in expressionist art theory (cf. GW. IX. 318); and even though some expressionistic paintings may achieve striking beauty, 'the scream' remains for many the symbol of expressionism.[21] To some extent, this would seem to hold for

---

[18] Both in 'Über die Idee einer Theologie der Kultur', GW. IX. 22–3, and elsewhere — see, e. g., GW. II. 35ff; GW. IV. 88ff.

[19] By 'form' Tillich would seem in this case to mean line, colour, shape, composition. By 'form' in art, Schelling — on the other hand — had meant the *forms* of art, i. e., music, painting, poetry, etc. This alone makes any easy identification between Tillich's theory of art and Schelling's theory impossible.

[20] What Tillich here says of expressionistic art is very closely akin to what Hegel said of romantic art. The object of art, according to Hegel's estimate, is the expression of the inner meaning of nature in sensuous form. But art is not mere form. It aims at a more perfect and a more transparent apprehension of spiritual meaning than is available through natural form: the 'real Gehalt of appearances is released through art'. This aim is most perfectly achieved, according to Hegel, in romanticism; according to Tillich, in expressionism.

[21] Nor is this symbol limited to the visual arts, where it is best known in association

Tillich as well, at least at the time he wrote this address. For he could not have had in mind paintings like Franz Marc's *Liegende Stier* (cf. GW. IX. 320) when he remarked, 'In the depths of all existence dwells horror and this horror seizes us in the paintings of the expressionists . . . which seems to me to be deepened by a sense of guilt, not in a strictly ethical sense, but much more in a cosmic sense, the guilt of sheer existence . . .'. One might be tempted to infer from such thoughts as these that even at this stage in his development Tillich held that in expressionistic art one has 'the question of existence' raised but not capable of being answered. This is not the case, however. The context makes clear that the expressionists are struggling for the 'answer' as well. It is in part this struggle which gives their work the religious quality it is seen by Tillich to have.[22]

Having declared the religious concerns of recent art, Tillich then proceeds by analogy in succeeding paragraphs to talk about the religious significance of recent philosophy, social and political theory. In those areas as well little significance is attached to subject matter or 'content'. Tillich talks instead of the direct and immediate relationship between form and *Gehalt*. (GW. IX. 23–7)

This reduction, though it does not go entirely unchecked, remains decisive for Tillich's thought in several respects. For instance, it allows him later to assert that it is not the 'subject matter' (i.e. *Inhalt*) of a work of art which makes it 'religious' art, but rather the *Gehalt* which is brought to expression in it. (Cf. GW. IX. 318; X. 34 f) He extends this analogy to other areas as well, including philosophy. (ST. III. 203 f) As I shall hope to show in the second section of this chapter, that reduction also helps explain some of the moves made by Tillich in his discussion of the relationship between christology and historiography. The influence of expressionism upon Tillich can be seen in these respects at least to have continued in his writings well after the demise of that movement in German art history.

---

with Munch; the symbol has also been applied to the literary arts. See W. H. Sokel, *The Writer in Extremis* (Stanford, 1959).

[22] It is not wholly clear whom Tillich had in mind when he remarked that 'the religious meaning of this art is explicitly affirmed by its representatives'. (GW. IX. 23) He may well have had in mind writings such as W. Kandinsky's *Über das Geistige in der Kunst* (Munich, 1912). If so, one should be aware that Kandinsky's theory of art is far removed from Tillich's. Another possibility might be G. F. Hartlaub, *Kunst und Religion* (Leipzig, 1919). For Tillich's review of the latter volume, see GW. IX. 312 ff.

Expressionism as a specific movement was short lived.[22a] By the mid-twenties it had divided in two main directions. As their initial restraint gave way to excess and loss of control, expressionism yielded on the one side to styles of painting in which there was greater and greater independence from the natural objects portrayed. These styles became increasingly abstract and non-representational, though nonetheless highly disciplined in the use of line, colour, composition. One thinks here mainly of certain of those artists who joined the Bauhaus: Kandinsky, Klee, and then later, Albers. Expressionism gave way on the other side to counter-movements in which there was a determined drive toward a more tightly controlled 'realism' in art. This was by no means a unified reaction.

A call for a return to some sort of 'realism' was sometimes made by those who wished to revive earlier, pre-expressionistic types of realism. But their intention should not be interpreted simply as a retreat from the new situation in which Germans found themselves following the war. If anything, the opposite is the case. There was a widespread feeling that the expressionists themselves were not prepared to face the harsh facts of the 'real world'. One thinks, for instance, of the indictment by von Keyserling against expressionism as 'rarefied studio art' incompatible with the conditions of a people just emerging from war.[23] An effort was made by some, and not merely the members of the *Novembergruppe* either, to put art to work in the service of social and political reform. There was a growing use made of the 'revolutionary realism' of the poster by certain politically active artists, such as Käthe Kollwitz. Whilst their art was highly 'expressive', it owed little to the expressionistic movement as such. There were other artists, however, who tried both to recover something of earlier sorts of realism and also to fulfill the basic aims of expressionism. The movement in German art which most clearly exhibits this two-fold attempt was known as *die neue Sachlichkeit*. Its proponents included Grosz, Dix, and perhaps most importantly, Max Beckmann.

The phrase 'die neue Sachlichkeit' was first applied to their art, not by the artists themselves, but by G. F. Hartlaub, who wanted to distinguish their art from expressionism. Hartlaub saw their work as 'related to the general contemporary feeling in Germany [circa 1925] of resignation and

---

[22a] See R. Samuel and R. H. Thomas, *Expressionism in German Life* (Cambridge, 1939).
[23] Cited in O. Nagel, *Käthe Kollwitz* (London, 1971), p. 39.

cynicism after a period of exuberant hopes (which had found an outlet in Expressionism). Cynicism and resignation are the negative side of the *Neue Sachlichkeit*; the positive side expresses itself in the enthusiasm for the immediate reality as a result of the desire to take things entirely objectively on a material basis without immediately investing them with ideal implications'.[24]

Tillich, too, shared in this new mood. It can be seen in retrospect to have had important consequences for the particular direction his own thought took after about 1925, especially for his understanding of the relationship between cultural 'form' and religious 'content'. The method of correlation is an eventual consequence of this change in direction.

In the early years after the first world war, the situation in Germany appeared to Tillich uncertain, but hopeful. It was a time 'pregnant with meaning', a time in which (in his preferred terminology) the conditioned forms of life were being shattered by unconditioned meaning, by an overwhelming upsurge from the depths, by the breakthrough of the eternal into time. Despite the uncertainty of the economic, political and social spheres generally, it was for him and many others a time of great expectations. By 1925 or so, however, the situation had changed. The economic and political situation had been stabilised somewhat, to be sure; but it had also become clear to most people, whether in regret or in relief, that there would be no fundamental reform of social institutions under the Weimar government. Nor would there be, as Tillich – following Troeltsch – had earlier hoped, a theonomous unification of cultural beliefs and values. The particular kairos had passed and the opportunity had been missed, or largely so.

Looking back over the first quarter of the century, a time which had been for Germany more than for most countries one of rapid social change, Tillich wrote that the new year signaled in all spheres of cultural life a time to catch one's breath: 'not a pause from productive [intellectual] work – there is none – but a pause in the restlessness of transience, of pressing forward, of rushing further away from one's starting point, from the stresses of the turn of the century'. (GW. X. 94) The pause was interpreted by Tillich as both an expression and a consequence of a growing disillusionment and disquietude.

Tillich, no less than those about whom he was there speaking, was much affected by this gradual change of mood which occurred in the mid-1920's.

---

[24] Cited in F. Whitford, *Expressionism*, p. 174.

Among those factors which gave him pause was his growing realisation that his own earlier efforts had been in many respects naively utopian: 'Was it not all ultimately romanticism, intoxication, utopianism?' (GW. VI. 41; but cf. PE, 59–60!) It had by then become clear to him that the old order, which he called 'the spirit of capitalist society', had been too strong and persistent ('Its demonic power was too great') to be defeated by 'romanticism, passion and revolution'. (GW. VI. 41; cf. GW. X. 116–20)

Tillich's virtual repudiation of his own earlier work led, not to despair, but toward a new sense of realism, a *neue Sachlichkeit*, which he called at the time 'belief-full realism' or *gläubiger Realismus*. In adopting this as a description of his thought, Tillich intended thereby to express his growing concern for the concrete and the actual, the *inhaltlich*, rather than merely the abstract and the ideal. In a little-known address entitled 'Gläubiger Realismus' which was delivered to a youth group in 1927, Tillich warned that 'the world of concepts can gain independent existence for itself and obscure the factual world like a fog. Thereupon, concepts are derived from other concepts, concepts are disposed of through other concepts – all without new or original perception'. (GW. IV. 77) A fresh and direct approach to reality was said to be required, an approach which Tillich set out to define in this and other writings from the same period.

The first important sketch of this new approach is found in the second and better-known piece entitled 'Gläubiger Realismus' which appeared first in the *Theologische Blätter*.[25] This article makes explicit that the call for a 'gläubiger Realismus' is connected with recent trends in German painting, notably the emergence of a *neue Sachlichkeit*. Tillich begins his address with an almost nostalgic reference to the by then almost totally dissipated movement known as expressionism. In expressionistic paintings, 'cosmic meaning and depth were drawn out of things. Their outer forms were shattered in order to lay bare their inner significance. A metaphysical blood flowed from the colours over the gray of the real world. Bold hopes were awakened for a rebirth of myth and ritual. And the revolutionary developments in all other cultural and social spheres seemed to justify these artists' visions'.[26] But, Tillich notes, sometime around 1922 paintings began to

---

[25] In a revised form, it appeared in translation in *The Protestant Era* (pp. 66–82); this version was used also for the *Gesammelte Werke* (IV. 88–106). In what follows, I have used the original version, as it appeared in the *ThBlätter*, VII (1928), cols. 109–18.

[26] *Ibid.*, col. 109.

appear which, though in their own way revolutionary, owed little to expressionism and which, in contrast to that movement, placed stress upon the empirical reality of things. These paintings soon attracted the attention even of those people who had been drawn to specifically expressionistic art. It was clear to Tillich that this 'new realism' was in no sense merely a revival of the realism of the nineteenth century. For the artists of the new realism were seen to be interested in more than just the 'surface' of things:

> The empirical reality of the object was searched for anew, not for its own sake, but as an expression of objective *Gehalt*, of its inner power. The older realism had deprived things of their *Gehalt*, their [inner] power, for the sake of their outer form; expressionism had destroyed the outer form in order to express their inner *Gehalt*; the new realism gives unqualified attention to the outer form of things, but in order to reveal in and through it their inner power. Consequently, such works of art exhibit a characteristic and sometimes disquieting ambiguity as between the empirical and the transcendent. The unconscious will of such artists aspires toward a belief-ful realism.[27]

Just as Tillich had once attributed religious intentions to the earlier expressionistic artists, he now saw in the work of the neo-realists a religious tendency, albeit an unconscious and ambiguous one. And just as his earlier understanding of the relationship between form and *Gehalt* 'in other fields' had been moulded considerably by the influence of expressionistic works of art, his newer understanding was similarly moulded by the belief-ful realism exhibited in the works of these artists.

In the remainder of the article Tillich distinguishes various sorts of realism, only some of which approach to a 'belief-ful realism' or what he would come to call, following a suggestion by James Luther Adams, a 'self-transcending realism'. (PE. 67; cf. GW. XII. 355) The defective and inadequate forms of realism are described as instances of *ungläubiger Realismus* or what he would later call 'self-limiting' or 'self-sufficient realism'. (PE. 67) The phrases adopted latterly suggest more graphically that which distinguishes *gläubiger Realismus* from *ungläubiger Realismus*, namely the different orientation of each toward 'external reality'. Such phrases further show more surely the links between theonomy, *gläubiger Realismus* and

---

[27] *Ibid.*, cols. 109–10.

correlation. Theonomy was, of course, for Tillich a particular sort of autonomy, a self-transcending autonomy in contrast to a self-sufficient autonomy.[28] Professor Adams's translations show more clearly the links which exist in this direction. In doing so, however, firmer links are established between theonomy and correlation: for correlation is said by Tillich to form part of the strategy of a self-transcending realism. In the 1947 article on 'The Problem of Theological Method', Tillich announced almost at the outset that 'the methodological remarks made in this paper describe the method actually used in my attempts to elaborate a theology of "self-transcending Realism" (gläubiger Realismus), which is supposed to overcome supra-naturalism as well as its naturalistic counterpart'.[29]

The direction of Tillich's movement is seen to be from theonomy in its earlier and 'utopian sense' to *gläubiger Realismus* and then to the method of correlation. This movement runs roughly parallel to the tendency toward a new *Sachlichkeit* in Tillich's writings from the mid-1920's to his emigration. This tendency is exhibited in part by Tillich's becoming increasingly concrete in his approach to matters so that he speaks increasingly, for instance, of the problem of the relationship between christianity and society (cf. GW. IX. 47ff), rather than the more abstract problem of the relationship between religion and culture in general.[30]

The influence of developments within the visual arts certainly played a major role in the modification of Tillich's theory of relations between cultural form and religious content (*Gehalt*). In would be oversimple, however, to suggest that these developments account in full for the direction of Tillich's thought after about 1925. For the situation is clearly more complex than that. In addition to the influence of art and the factors already discussed in the previous chapter, I should like to call attention to two others: first, Tillich's opportunity to offer for the first time courses specifically in christian theology as a result of his call to Marburg in 1925;

---

[28] See above, chapter two, pp. 34–9.
[29] *JRel*, XXVII (1947), p. 16. Later, in the ST he added – almost certainly as an afterthought – 'theological dualism' to those inadequate approaches which are said to be superseded by the method of correlation. ST. I. 65f; cf. ST. II. 5ff.
[30] This shift is rightly stressed by E. Amelung in *Die Gestalt der Liebe* (Gütersloh, 1972). Whether a similar 'concreteness' is exhibited in Tillich's writings after 1933 is another issue. In general, it may be said that concreteness as regards matters political and social is largely lacking in Tillich's later works.

and, second, the effect upon him of the putative misuse by Hirsch and others of certain key concepts used as well by Tillich and the religious socialists.

Tillich's having begun lecturing specifically on systematic theology first at Marburg perhaps helps account for a major shift of emphasis in many of his subsequent writings leading up to 1933. For thereafter he tends to write increasingly explicitly as what he would no doubt earlier have termed a *church theologian*. This is not to say that he wrote correspondingly less as a *cultural theologian*. Rather, it is the case that after about 1926 in addition to his characteristic themes in cultural theology one begins to encounter for the first time in his post-war writings a sustained discussion of more specifically doctrinal themes, at times in conjunction with and as an extension of long-standing topics, such as kairos. Given that the concept of correlation is intended principally as a means of relating within the context of church theology the christian message and modern culture, such a shift of emphasis is of considerable importance for our understanding of the development of Tillich's concept of correlation. That such a shift in fact occurred is supported in part by Tillich's tendency in his writings between 1927 and 1933 to lay greater stress upon christology than he had done in those published between 1919 and 1926. This, too, can be regarded as an aspect of the new 'Sachlichkeit' in his writings after 1926!

Even though their consideration may have been expected in view of the nature of the topics being discussed, christological themes are noticeably absent from the address 'Über die Idee einer Theologie der Kultur' and, more surprisingly, from the various essays on the concept of 'Kairos' which were published prior to 1926 or so.[31] That a shift of some sort is under way may be suspected from the initial article on 'Gläubiger Realismus' (1927; GW. IV. 77—87). Even so, one would have to read with that article at least one other published in the same year in order to get a more clearly defined picture of the christological character of that shift. In the article on 'Die Idee der Offenbarung' Tillich argued that an object is a medium of revelation not in itself, not in its 'empirical character', but only in its character as

---

[31] It should be recalled that this included, not only the first pamphlet of the Kairos-circle entitled *Kairos: Zur Geisteslage und Geisteswendung* (1926; cf. GW. VI. 29—41), but also the article on 'Kairos und Logos', though the subtitle more clearly identifies the object of that article: 'eine Untersuchung zur Metaphysik der Erkenntnis'. (GW. IV. 43—76)

'bearer'. That being the case, Tillich concludes, no object can be regarded as in itself revelatory. Rather, revelation breaks through the conditioned structures without being bound to them. This sounds familiar enough to anyone who knows Tillich's writings from the early 1920's. But the differences are as important as the similarities. First, Tillich speaks here of *revelation* whereas he had typically spoken earlier of *the unconditioned*. Second, and more to the point, he here relates his general argument specifically to christology in a way he simply never did in his earlier writings. (GW. VIII. 36 q.v.) Whilst most assuredly built upon foundations laid in his earlier writings (including those having to do with the *Form—Inhalt—Gehalt* dialectic), this specifically christological application nonetheless represents a significant movement toward explicitly doctrinal themes.

This shift in emphasis was firmly and unmistakeably established when, in an article written especially for his collection entitled *Religiöse Verwirklichung*, Tillich argued that no-one can deal with the main issues of a philosophy of history without dealing with the christological issue (GW. VI. 83). In weighing the significance of this shift, one must bear in mind that Tillich himself had been writing not a little since 1919 on philosophy of history with hardly any direct consideration at all of the christological question! In those writings, it was not so much the kairos in the distant past as the present kairos which had so obviously caught his imagination, and the imagination of his comrades in the closing days of the first world war. Indeed, Tillich had in those writings — following perhaps Troeltsch — quite explicitly rejected any notion of a *Heilsgeschichte*. So it is a not inconsiderable reversal when in this piece on 'Christologie und Geschichtsdeutung' Tillich came to describe Jesus Christ as *the centre of history* from which the whole of history gets its meaning. (GW. VI. 87f, 93f) This new centre of Tillich's philosophy of history gains fresh significance when, as we shall see shortly, in his open letter to Hirsch, he speaks of Jesus Christ as *the final criterion* against which every other historical moment (*Stunde*) is to be measured.[32] Jesus Christ subsequently comes to be identified by Tillich as *the* kairos in relation to which all the others are to be assessed. (cf. GW. VI. 137—9; ST. III. 369—72; PE, xv) It is clearly only a short step beyond such statements to say as well that Jesus Christ[33] is

---

[32] Cf. also the remarks in OB, 43, 50.
[33] Perhaps more accurately, the *symbol* 'Jesus as the Christ'.

the content of the christian faith or that the kerygma is the substance and criterion of all theological statements.

One looks in vain for similar sorts of statements in Tillich's writings, published or unpublished, which can be dated between 1919 and 1926. Even though some of his papers prior to the first world war are clearly essays in church-theology, this is not true of those written after that war. Indeed, it is really only after 1926 that Tillich can be seen to begin writing again explicitly as a church theologian. Evidence for this is in part the re-orientation of the doctrine of kairos, so that the kairos is identified with the appearance of the Christ.[34]

That re-orientation had already begun by the time that Tillich delivered his lectures on 'the structure of religious knowledge' at Dresden. The distinction is drawn there for the first time in what is available of Tillich's writings between a general and a special sense of kairos. (§§ 147–8) Readers of *The Protestant Era* might be expected to protest at this point that christology is a central theme already in the article on 'Kairos' which appeared originally in 1922. Attention could be called to the passage in that article where Tillich distinguished three meanings of the word 'kairos':

> 'Kairos' in its *unique* and universal sense is, for Christian faith, the appearing of Jesus as the Christ. Kairos in its *general* and special [sic] sense for the philosopher of history is every turning-point in history in which the eternal judges and transforms the temporal. Kairos in its *special* [sic] sense, as decisive for our present situation, is the coming of a new theonomy on the soil of a secularized and emptied autonomous culture. (PE, 46f)

And, it could be claimed, in the sections which follow, Tillich makes clear that the christological kairos is the criterion against which all other kairoi are to be measured.

One cannot deny that this passage occurs in the article entitled 'Kairos' which was printed in *The Protestant Era*. A similar passage occurs as well in the German translation of the same article which is printed in the *Gesammelte Werke*. (GW. VI. 24) But, no such passage appears in the original

---

[34] A similar point has been made by Theodor Mahlmann in 'Eschatologie und Utopie in geschichtsphilosophischen Denken Paul Tillichs', *NeueZSysTh*, VII (1965), 364–5.

version of 'Kairos' which was published in *Die Tat*.³⁵ In fact, the distinction between kairos in the unique sense and kairos in the general sense does not occur at all in that article. Nor is this surprising. Such a distinction would have been quite alien to Tillich's thought at that stage. Before allowing the article 'Kairos' to be reprinted in *The Protestant Era*, however, Tillich rewrote it extensively in order to accommodate later developments. Among these must be counted the identification of 'kairos in its unique sense' with the appearance of Jesus as the Christ. As it happens Jesus Christ is mentioned only once in the 1922 article, and then in passing.³⁶ The 'Kairos' article is in no way a counter-example. The fact that Tillich thought it necessary to rewrite it before allowing it to be republished actually strengthens my point. The fact that he rewrote it in just the ways which he did also supports the view that christology gains an importance in Tillich's later writings that it did not have in his earlier essays on the philosophy of history and culture. It also lends support to the view that Tillich's thought became more specifically theological after his emigration.

If the claim were to be sustained that Tillich has 'always' been 'in some sense' a church theologian,³⁷ other grounds would have to be adduced than the one cited in the quotation above from *The Protestant Era*. I have elsewhere suggested that such grounds do exist and are to be found in the

---

³⁵ XIV (1922), 330–50. The August issue of *Die Tat: Monatsschrift für die Zukunft deutscher Kultur* was devoted entirely to the theme of 'religious socialism' and had Carl Mennicke as its editor. It included articles by Mennicke, Wilhelm Loew, Hans Hartmann, Eduard Heimann, Emil Fuchs and Günther Dehn, as well as Tillich.

³⁶ *Ibid.*, p. 330. Cf. GW. VI. 10. It is unfortunate that Amelung, in his otherwise fine study of Tillich's theology of culture, seems to have relied uncritically on the version of 'Kairos' which was reprinted in the GW. Cf. *Die Gestalt der Liebe*, pp. 66–73.

³⁷ A claim made by Amelung against Mahlmann's thesis that Tillich can be reckoned as a 'church theologian', *ein Theologe der Kirche,* from the time that the kairos was identified with the appearance of the Christ. (See above, note 34) In reply, Amelung warns, 'One should not overlook the fact that the following sentence is to be found already in the Kairos-article of 1922·: "Kairos in its *unique* and universal sense is, for the christian faith, the appearance of Jesus as the christ". (GW. VI. 24) . . . Tillich was in this sense always a church theologian'. We have seen, however, that this passage is a later addition to the text and is no basis for interpreting Tillich's standpoint in 1922!

Kirchliche Apologetik.³⁸ Nor would I wish now to deny that Tillich was in the sense suggested there a church theologian from the outset. But I would want in addition to stress that this side of his programme was by no means dominant between 1919 and 1926. His writings of that period show him primarily to be a cultural theologian. This is as true of *Das System der Wissenschaften* as it is of the other writings. Nor is it perhaps insignificant that he tends to speak there, not of the relationship between *philosophy* and *theology* (as he does in the *Systematic Theology*), but rather of the relationship between *autonomous* philosophy and *theonomous* philosophy. And, in this connexion, one should also recall from the previous chapter Tillich's 'pact' with Barth.³⁹ Nor should one ignore the almost total absence of specifically doctrinal content in Tillich's publications between 1919 and 1926.

But if it is the case that Tillich was a church theologian from the outset in addition to his being a cultural theologian, it is also the case that after 1926 Tillich was a cultural theologian as well as a church theologian. Indeed, the tension between these two motives creates certain difficulties in the way Tillich executes his theological programme. This is the case especially in the areas where those two concerns overlap, such as the problem of the relationship between religious 'content' and cultural 'form'.

There is, however, yet another factor which contributed to the way Tillich came to use 'form' and 'content' in his concept of correlation: namely, the attempt by Hirsch and others to employ to quite different ends notions similar to those used by the religious socialists in their philosophy of kairos.

Tillich and Hirsch had been close friends since their student days at Berlin, though even there later differences were perhaps foreshadowed by Tillich's having been more attracted to Schelling and Hirsch's having turned rather to Fichte.⁴⁰ And even after the first world war, to which each had reacted so strongly but in ways which led in completely opposite directions, they continued to remain close friends despite their spirited and at times almost violent disagreements about matters touching on religion and politics. Tillich in fact came to speak of 'die spannungsreiche Einheit unserer

---

38 Cf. *JThSt*, XXV (1974), 232.
39 See above, pp. 160–4, esp. p. 162f.
40 See E. Hirsch, *Christliche Freiheit und politische Bindung* (Hamburg, 1934), p. 46. The correspondence between Hirsch and Tillich during the first world war has been edited by H.-W. Schütte (Berlin and Schleswig-Holstein, 1973).

persönlichen Freundschaft und sachlichen Gegnerschaft'.[41] Throughout the 1920's, however, they maintained the courtesy early established of sending to one another copies of their new publications. Tillich having earlier given Hirsch a copy of his pro-socialist interpretation of *Die religiöse Lage*, Hirsch could hardly be expected to resist sending Tillich a copy of his own interpretation of *Die gegenwärtige, geistige Lage*, a book which may be regarded as in part a riposte to Tillich's earlier work. Indeed it comes to light that Hirsch had actually hoped with that book to 'convert' Tillich to the cause of the *deutsche Christen*.[42] The actual effect was otherwise. If anything, it drove Tillich further toward Barth![43]

From his place of exile in New York, Tillich sent Hirsch a 15,000 word reply in the form of a personal letter, which was then published in the *Theologische Blätter* as 'Die Theologie des Kairos und die gegenwärtige geistige Lage'.[44] The letter, which is intended in large measure as a defense and restatement in the light of 1933 of the kairos-doctrine, begins with the apparently dangerous claim that virtually all the basic categories used in Hirsch's new book had been taken over from the religious-socialist move-

---

[41] 'Die Theologie des Kairos und die gegenwärtige geistige Lage', *ThBl*, XIII (1934), col. 305. (= 'Theologie des Kairos').

[42] E. Hirsch, *Christliche Freiheit und politische Bindung*, p. 20.

[43] Cf. 'Um was es geht', *ThBlätter*, XIV (1935), cols. 117–20.

[44] Vol. XIII (1934), cols. 305–28. Only some aspects of the debate can be considered here. There is, unfortunately, no proper study of all aspects of this controversy. D. Hopper's account of what he calls 'the Hirsch affair' in *Tillich: A Theological Portrait* (Philadelphia, 1968) is plagued with several errors of fact and judgment. For instance, he refers to Hirsch as 'an early participant in the German Religious-Socialist movement' who 'throughout the 1920's . . . proved to be an influential proponent of the views of Religious Socialism.' (p. 69) It would be interesting to learn what evidence Hopper has for this claim; he cites none. Nor does he seem to have been aware of such books as *Deutschlands Schicksal*, which would have clarified Hirsch's position considerably! It may be that Hopper has confused E. Hirsch with M. Hirsch, who was a member of the Neuwerk-Kreis. More interesting is the article by G. Schneider-Flume entitled 'Kritische Theologie contra theologisch-politischen Offenbarungsglauben: Eine vergleichende Strukturanalyse der politischen Theologie Paul Tillichs, Emanuel Hirschs und Richard Shaulls', *EvangTh*, XXXIII (1973), 114–37. 'The Hirsch affair', unfortunately does not fall within the scope of Klaus Scholder's history of *Die Kirchen und das Dritte Reich*, vol. I: *Vorgeschichte und Zeit der Illusionen 1918–1934* (Frankfurt, 1977). Will it perhaps be considered in volume two?

ment, the movement which Hirsch had opposed so bitterly 'for the past fourteen years'.[45] At this putative about-face, Tillich expresses mock joy, adding quickly that his sense of joy is dampened somewhat both by the fact that Hirsch has intentionally disguised his adoption of the categories of religious socialism and also by the fact that the particular way he has used them deprives them of their 'most profound meaning'.[46] Tillich seeks to support each of these claims in turn, the latter of the two being by far the more important for our present purposes.

Tillich's first point is largely ironic and polemical,[47] as is his subsequent rebuke that, far from being an existentialist philosopher, Hirsch remains an 'enthusiastic idealist'.[48] His second point is more substantial, however, concerning as it does the proper role of the cultural 'situation' in theology and contributing as it does to a not unimportant 'clarification' (Tillich's word) of his own notion of the correlative relationship between cultural form and religious content.

In the process, Tillich also sets out to show in what respects he stands with Hirsch against Barth and in what respects he stands with Barth against Hirsch. Tillich thereby anticipates to some extent arguments which he would develop in writings shortly to appear, including 'Was ist falsch in der dialektischen Theologie?',[49] 'The Totalitarian State and the Claims of the Church'[50] and 'Natural and Revealed Religion'.[51]

Tillich begins by reminding Hirsch, himself the author of a major and influential book on *Die Reich-Gottes-Begriffe des neueren europäischen Denkens*[52] which had been reviewed by Tillich in the same journal,[53] that Jesus's proclamation of the kingdom of God was inherently eschatological.

---

[45] Col. 306.
[46] Col. 306.
[47] Hirsch, not unexpectedly, bristled at the charge of plagerism. See *Christliche Freiheit und politische Bindung*.
[48] Col. 316.
[49] *Die Christliche Welt*, L (1936), cols. 353–64; originally in *JRel*, XV (1935), 127–45; repr. GW. VII. 247–62.
[50] *Social Research*, I (1934), 405–33; repr. GW. X. 121–45.
[51] *Christendom*, I (1935), 159–70; repr. GW. VIII. 47–58.
[52] Göttingen, 1922. On the connexion of that book to Hirsch's 'political' writings – esp. *Deutschlands Schicksal* – see his own remarks in 'Meine Wendejahre (1916–21)', *Freies Christentum*, nr. 12 (1 Dec 1951), 5f.
[53] *ThBlätter*, I (1922), cols. 42–3.

By 'eschatological' Tillich seems to have meant that the kingdom is paradoxically both present and 'not here'. The hiddeness of the kingdom, a notion which (though Tillich fails to mention it) had been as attractive to Hirsch in his earlier work as it had been to the dialectical theologians, is then said by Tillich to 'belong inseparably to the notion of kairos, both in primitive christianity and in religious socialism'.[54] According to Tillich, this eschatological emphasis

> allies us [i.e., the religious socialists] with Barth to the extent that we deny with him the tangible presence of the divine in a finite object or event; it separates us from Barth because the eschatological has for him a supranatural character, but for us it is paradoxical. We do not set the transcendent in an undialectical opposition to history, but believe rather that it can be understood as genuine transcendence only if it can be regarded as that which ever and again breaks into history, shakes it violently and turns it upside down. In this view of things, you and we stand together in agreement. The theology of the kairos stands exactly in the middle between the theology of the new national lutheranism and the dialectical theology. It regards the latter as a deviation toward the abstract-transcendental, the former as a deviation toward the demonic-sacramental. Against both, it advocates the prophetic and primitive christian paradox that the kingdom of God comes in history but nonetheless remains beyond history.[55]

That at least is how things are said to have stood prior to 1933. That had been the strategy of the religious socialists; but their strategy had to be altered owing to more recent events. Tillich, admitting that such a position was neither constructed for nor suited to the then-current church struggle, makes forcefully clear to Hirsch that for the duration of that conflict he would 'stand on that side which defends the eschatological over against the assault of a demonised sacramentalism' which simply equates the presence of the kingdom with historical events.[56] The cost of the one may be high,

---

[54] 'Theologie des Kairos', col. 312.
[55] *Ibid*.
[56] Tillich allows that in this conflict one must choose either the one side or the other; there could be no mediation. He possibly intended to remind Hirsch of his own words: 'there is no middle way; there is only an either/or'. *Die gegenwärtige, geistige Lage*, p. 133.

but the cost of the other was seen to be even higher. Tillich then accuses Hirsch of having 'perverted the prophetic-eschatological purpose of the kairos-doctrine into a priestly-sacramental consecration of an actual occurrence' and in so doing of ascribing absolute value to something finite.[57] Tillich protests that this is really a perversion of the kairos doctrine and not merely an unwelcome but nonetheless legitimate application of it.[58] It is not wholly clear, however, that Tillich had convinced even himself.[59] For there then follows what is for us the most crucial section of Tillich's 'open-letter'.

Tillich queries whether Hirsch is entirely clear about the sort of relationship which exists for him between current events and his theology. In particular he queries whether such events are regarded by Hirsch as a source of revelation alongside the biblical witness. He states that this would seem to be the case in *Die gegenwärtige, geistige Lage*. But, rather than simply prosecute Hirsch, Tillich turns this query into an occasion for self-examination. He asks himself 'whether there is any way such a conception can be justified in terms of the notion of kairos'.[60] Answering his own question negatively, and yet at the same time pushing further in self-examination, Tillich continues, 'I do not myself see how, but I grant you however that in previous years we did not deal sufficiently with the problems which present themselves here and that, as a result, such misguided interpretations [of kairos] have not been ruled out with sufficient clarity. To the extent that recent events and their precipitation in your book force us to clarify these issues, I am – despite all my criticisms – truly grateful'.[61]

The 'clarifying' remarks which then follow amount to more than *mere* clarification. They represent in some measure a shift in Tillich's understanding of the relationship between culture and religion, 'situation' and 'message', a shift toward the position expounded eventually in the first volume of the *Systematic Theology*:

> The concept of revelation has two sides which must be clearly distinguished. On the one hand, revelation is manifest only as a

---

[57] 'Theologie des Kairos', cols. 312–3.
[58] *Ibid.*, col. 318.
[59] Cf. also 'The Present Theological Situation in the Light of the Continental European Development', *ThToday*, VI (1949), 303–4.
[60] 'Theologie des Kairos', col. 318.
[61] *Ibid.*; cf. also col 319.

'revelatory correlation'. Revelation is not a concept which can be thought about objectively; it is actualised, rather, only insofar as it is revelation for someone. But, and this is the other side, when it is actualised in a correlation, it is exclusive. It cannot tolerate other revelations alongside itself; it can only allow other situations in which men enter into the revelatory correlation. Every new situation alters the correlation, but it does not alter the revelation . . . Revelation is that to which I am able unconditionally to submit myself as the final criterion of my thought and action. The kairos, the historical moment, can therefore never of itself constitute revelation. It can do no more than announce the arrival of a new revelatory correlation. It sign-posts the moment in which the meaning of revelation discloses itself anew for knowledge and action, in which for instance the ultimate criterion of truth is manifest afresh over against a particular historical structure [*Zeitkonstellation*], as for instance the cross of christ over against demonic capitalism or demonic nationalism.[62]

Even though none of the ideas presented is wholly alien to Tillich's earlier writings, their total effect here and throughout the 'open letter' is considerably different. It soon becomes evident that we have here to do not merely with a sharpening of focus so that the detail is more precise, but rather with a shift of focal point so that what was formerly peripheral to the vision is now central and vice versa.

The resulting effect is in three main respects different from that achieved in the earlier writings on kairos and theonomy. Each of these respects reflects an attempt by Tillich to rescue his 'theology of kairos' from Hirsch's alleged abuse of it.

First, certain new elements which had been introduced in his writings around 1927 are here developed further and in one case at least extended significantly. Tillich had already begun writing more directly as a church theologian and he had also already begun substituting for the earlier abstract term *Gehalt* the more specifically theological term *revelation*, and he had also already begun to stress the importance of christology. This has been interpreted as part of the turning toward a new 'Sachlichkeit' in Tillich's writings, as part of his formulation of a *gläubiger Realismus*. Although

---

[62] *Ibid.*, col. 318. Cf. ST. I. 126 ff.

anticipated perhaps in the seventh of his *Zehn Thesen* concerning the church and the third Reich (cf. GW. XIII. 178), the identification of the cross of Christ as the 'final criterion' of all thought and action against which all others are to be measured would seem to occur for the first time in his 'open letter' to Hirsch.[63] Such specification represents an important step leading eventually to the much later identification of the kerygmatic symbol of 'Jesus the christ' as that which makes christian theology christian through history and across cultures.

Although this criterion is lacking in his earlier writings on kairos, writings which seem to imply that theological criteria vary from time to time and are given in the situation itself (cf. GW. VII. 216ff, 240ff), this particular development is not entirely unprepared for in his Dresden lectures.[64] Nor is it entirely unprepared for in his earlier speculations about form and *Gehalt*. In his earlier writings the presence of powerful *Gehalt* was regarded as that which makes an object or event 'religious'. Henceforth, the presence of the symbol 'Jesus as the christ' as final criterion of theological statements makes a given theology a christian theology. Related as it is to earlier comments on the relationship between form and *Gehalt*, specifying this criterion does nonetheless represent a new development in Tillich's thought: for, critics had already complained that Tillich had not given sufficient thought to the rules governing theological judgments about the kairos.[65] It may be the case that Tillich had already begun to take such criticisms seriously. So, there is little indication to that effect in his published writings between 1928 and 1934. It would seem, rather, that only after Hirsch's alleged 'misuse' of the concept of kairos did Tillich seek to 'clarify' this 'ambiguity' in his methodology. In his book, Hirsch (following his beloved Kierkegaard) stressed largely the risk-character of all theological judgments about the 'present moment': without hope of objective or rational proof, one must dare to affirm the presence of God in the reawakening of Germany.[66] This proposal is surely not so far removed from that made by Tillich to Barth some ten years earlier that 'each age has the task to create anew the eternal meaning of all ages out of its own life and in its own words'. (GW. VII. 240; but cf. 220f) Admitting,

---

[63] 'Theologie des Kairos', cols. 318—9, *et passim*.
[64] See esp. §§ 60ff.
[65] See G. Kuhlmann, *Brunstäd und Tillich* (Tübingen, 1928), pp. 26ff.
[66] *Die gegenwärtige, geistige Lage*, pp. 102ff, 139f *et passim*.

as before, that risk and resolve are inherent in the theological interpretation of 'the present', Tillich in addition came to stress that they are not in themselves constitutive of that which makes christian theology christian. Christian theology is christian in virtue of the preservation of the message of the cross as its criterion; but christian theology is relevant to the times in virtue of the theologian's skill in interpreting the situation at hand.[67] Tillich tends in his open-letter to refer to these two poles of theology as 'revelation' and 'kairos'. He would later come to speak of them as 'message' and 'situation'.

Nor is such a change of terminology insignificant. It tends to confirm what one only suspects upon the basis of this letter, namely, that it is not only Hirsch who is guilty of emptying kairos of its 'profoundest sense'. In Tillich's earlier writings kairos is defined as 'the fulness of time', as 'time pregnant with meaning', in distinction to 'clock time' or chronos. Not every sort of age is a kairos. Only some moments can be described as being 'filled with unconditional *Gehalt* and unconditional demand'. (GW. II. 94) Kairos does not in those writings designate merely a *Lage*; it is 'the right time'. In the open letter to Hirsch, however, kairos is defined almost casually, as for instance in the long citation above, as 'the historical moment', the suggestion being that it is *any* historical moment, and not just moments of a particular sort. Indeed, the word kairos is used throughout the letter interchangeably, not only with *Stunde* (Hirsch's preferred term), but also with the more sterile term *Lage*.[68] Kairos is not here, as in earlier writings, the dialectical unity of 'situation' and 'import'; in the open letter to Hirsch it is regarded as the 'situation' itself. In terms of the dialectic of form and *Gehalt*, kairos is no longer the moment when *Gehalt* bursts through form, breaking up the old and establishing the new 'form'; rather, it is now *the 'form' itself*. This change of usage implies a kind of separation between form and *Gehalt* which is uncharacteristic of Tillich's earlier writings.

This separation suggests the third respect in which the open letter constitutes more than mere clarification of already held views. One of its more striking features is Tillich's having introduced for the first time in any of his writings, published or unpublished, the notion that 'revelation' and 'kairos' exist *on different levels* or *auf verschiedenen Ebenen*.[69] Tillich states that he

---

[67] 'Theologie des Kairos', col. 319.
[68] *Ibid*, cols. 318f *et passim*.
[69] *Ibid*., col. 319.

formulated this sharp distinction in an effort to show in what respects Hirsch's use constituted a misuse of the kairos-concept. The two levels, it is said, must never be confused. They must remain distinct if christian theology is both to remain christian and also to gain contemporaneity. Being governed by revelation 'makes a theologian a theologian'; competence in interpreting the times gives his work contemporary relevance. The fatal error of Hirsch's book is said by Tillich to be that these two different levels are not clearly distinguished, so that the situation as such (i.e. the kairos) is regarded as a source of revelation.

Tillich's intention in introducing the term *level* is unmistakeable, as is his intention in making the cross of Christ the criterion against which all theological judgments are measured. He clearly wanted thereby to preserve that which makes christian theology christian, or put another way, to protect the freedom and autonomy of theology against demonic heteronomy. Nor is this concern simply absent from Tillich's earlier writings. This can be easily illustrated by reference to a distinction which occurs both in the open letter to Hirsch and in an article entitled 'Grundlinien des religiösen Sozialismus' which Tillich had published in 1923.[70] In both articles, Tillich distinguishes between what he calls the *reservatum religiosum* and the *obligatum religiosum*. But the distinction is used in each article to different ends. Comparing the use made of this distinction in 1923 and in 1934 will give some indication of the effect which the concept of levels had on the development of Tillich's thought.[71] In the earlier article, Tillich argues that religion always has a double relationship to culture and that this follows from the double-sided character of religion itself: 'It contains within itself a "No", a *reservatum religiosum*, and a "Yes", an *obligatum religiosum*'. (GW. II. 96) When confronted with demonically distorted cultural forms, religion withdraws into itself for protection (*reservatum religiosum*). This is said to be a permanent and necessary feature of religion's relationship to culture, so that no simple identification of the two is possible. But it is only one side of their relationship. If religion neglects its *obligatum religiosum*, it in effect abandons the 'world' to self-

---

[70] *Blätter für Religiösen Sozialismus*, IV (1923), 1–24. Repr. GW. II. 91–119. For a brief exposition and analysis of the 'Grundlinien', see Amelung, *Die Gestalt der Liebe*, pp. 74–85.
[71] For what follows I am dependent upon Eric Schwerdtfeger, *Die politische Theorie in der Theologie Paul Tillichs* (Marburg, 1969).

destruction. Since religion is itself in some sense part of the 'world', this contributes as well to its own self-destruction. Consequently, the proper orientation to culture must include both the 'No' of the *reservatum* and the 'Yes' of the *obligatum* in dialectical unity. The stress in the open letter to Hirsch lies elsewhere. There Tillich stresses, not their unity, but their disparity as regards 'levels'. This has important consequences for the subsequent direction of Tillich's theological development. The insight which Tillich owed to Hirsch — that revelation and kairos lie on different levels — undermines any sort of synthesis between religion and culture such as might have been proffered in some of Tillich's earlier writings. Where Tillich had earlier stressed the dialectical unity of cultural 'form' and religious 'substance', he would increasingly come to stress their distinctness and their disparity. Or as he would put it later as regards philosophy and theology, 'Neither is a conflict between theology and philosophy necessary, nor is a synthesis between them possible' for there is no 'common basis' for either conflict or synthesis. (ST. I. 26f) They operate on different levels.

Whereas Tillich had earlier on sought to establish within his philosophy of religion the mutual immanence of cultural form and religious content, after 1933 he sought to define their differences and to mediate between them within the context of his theological system. If the symbol of the one approach is *theonomy*, the symbol of the other is *correlation*; and 1933 marks in some sense the divide between the two.

The divide, however, is neither so absolute nor so dramatic as this suggests. That it is not so absolute has been shown both in this and in the previous chapter. Tillich's thought is not so easily divided. Just as the concept of correlation is to be found in Tillich's writings prior to 1933, the concept of theonomy continues to play a major rôle thereafter. Nor is the divide so dramatic as this suggests. As Tillich himself observed of a later but nonetheless overlapping period: 'It was not a dramatic change in mind that I experienced during the past decade [1939—49] — such a change is hardly to be expected in the sixth decade of one's life — but a slow, often conscious, always effective transformation in various respects'.[72]

Even though Tillich was writing there neither about his concept of correlation in particular nor about the decade after 1933 exactly, his comments are also at least partially appropriate to the sort of development exhibited in his writings between 1933 and 1943. During those years he adjusted with

---

[72] 'Beyond Religious Socialism', *ChrCent*, LXVI (1949), 732.

more or less success to a new intellectual and social environment. (cf. TC, 159ff; OB, 91ff; GW. XIII. 187ff) But he also slowly incorporated into his thought the experience of one who had realised that religious socialism had failed utterly. (cf. GW. XIII. 227ff, esp. 235f; VII. 247ff) The kairos was past. Instead of a time 'pregnant with meaning', one now lived in a spiritual vacuum or, at best, a 'sacred void'. 'Instead of a creative *Kairos*, I see a vacuum which can be made creative only if it is accepted and endured and, rejecting all kinds of premature solutions, is transformed into a deepening "sacred void" of waiting'.[73] In this new situation the main principles of religious socialism were no longer applicable, at least not 'in the forseeable future'. No new theonomy could be foreseen.

Tillich had no doubt been moving toward such a conclusion for many years, beginning perhaps as early as 1926. Nor should one in this connexion fail to note that the word 'theonomy', which had most certainly been among the most central concepts in Tillich's earlier writings on religious socialism, does not occur at all in Tillich's last major work prior to his emigration. Not once. And this despite its title: *Die sozialistische Entscheidung*. (1933; repr. GW. II. 219–365; cf. esp. 353f) Whilst insisting that the socialist principle alone has the power to create a future for the west, Tillich is in the circumstances understandably diffident as to the immediate prospects of socialism. One can only wait in expectation. But then, he says in conclusion, 'Expectation is the symbol of socialism'. (GW. II. 365)

In the spiritual vacuum, the sacred void, one waits in expectation for a new kairos which contains within itself the possibility of a new theonomy. But, what kind of theology does the theologian do in the meantime?

In the face of this sort of question, final shape was given to what he eventually called his method of correlation. In seeking an answer to that question, however, Tillich no longer turned, as he had earlier, to the visual arts. There, too, one is confronted with a sort of sacred void or spiritual vacuum in which the radical questions of human excistence are asked, but not answered. (TC. 68f) Even his beloved expressionists are portrayed increasingly as representing the ambiguities and brokeness of human existence. (cf. STd. III. 90f) The works of such artists as van Gogh, Munch, Picasso, Braque and others are now seen as expressing principally

---

[73] *Ibid.*, p. 733. Cf. PE, 60. See also 'Das geistige Vacuum', *Das sozialistische Jahrhundert*, II (1948), 303–5.

'the horror of emptiness', 'disruptiveness, existential doubt, emptiness and meaninglessness', 'the human situation in its depths of estrangement and despair', 'the dissolution' of man's mental and even physical world, a world in which he is no longer at home.[74] Art of this sort 'puts the religious question radically, and has the power, the courage to face the situation out of which this question comes, namely the human predicament'. Such artists raise the question implied in the existence of 'the autonomous man who has become insecure in his autonomy'. (PE. 192) Such artists raise, but can not answer, that question.

> Theonomy is the answer to the question implied in autonomy, the question concerning a religious substance and an ultimate meaning of life and culture. Autonomy is able to live as long as it can draw from the religious tradition of the past, from the remnants of a lost theonomy. But more and more it loses this spiritual foundation. It becomes emptier, more formalistic, or more factual and is driven toward skepticism and cynicism, toward the loss of meaning and purpose. The history of autonomous cultures is the history of a continuous waste of spiritual substance. At the end of this process autonomy turns back to the lost theonomy with impotent longing, or it looks forward to a new theonomy in the attitude of creative waiting until the kairos appears. (PE. 46)

This quotation, coming as it does from the heavily rewritten fourth section of an article which appeared first in 1922, suggests certain says in which Tillich sought to adapt older views to accommodate more recent developments in his thought. Not the least conspicuous of these was his method of correlation. Thus, it raises yet again the issue of the relationship between correlation and theonomy.

This particular quotation, when taken on its own and in isolation from any other writings by Tillich, suggests that in his view theonomy is an empirical possibility so long as culture lives from its 'spiritual foundation'. And there are many occasions within the *Systematic Theology* itself when Tillich clearly implies that theonomy is such a possibility. There are other occasions, however, when he qualifies this judgment and strongly protests that theonomy is *not* an 'empirical condition'. Rather, it is an

---

[74] All quoted from 'Existentialist Aspects of Modern Art', *Christianity and the Existentialists*, ed. C. Michalson (New York, 1956), pp. 137ff.

eschatological symbol of which there are only fragmentary realisations or 'anticipations' within human culture and history. (PE, 59; ST. III. 250ff, 140, *et passim*) What Tillich once referred to as 'the most precise statement of theonomy' (PE, 57) – namely, 'culture is the form of religion and religion is the substance of culture' – then becomes an *ideal* statement of the *essential* unity of religion and culture. (cf. ST. III. 157f) Under the 'conditions of existence', however, that unity does not and cannot fully obtain; nor can it be wholly irradicated. (ST. III. 250; cf. ST. I. 202–10) Under such circumstances, the principle of correlation is operative. And the method of correlation, from this point of view, provides for a mediation between autonomous cultural 'forms' and theonomous religious 'content' (*Gehalt*) from which they are estranged but not separated.

Interpreted in this way, the apparent antinomy in Tillich's mature thought between theonomy and correlation is in principle resolved. The notion of theonomous unity is an expression of the *essential* or ideal unity of cultural 'form' and religious 'content' (*Gehalt*), whereas the notion of correlation expresses their *existential* or actual estrangement. It follows from this that in principle at least correlation and theonomy imply different but not competing accounts of the structure of relations between cultural 'form' and religious 'content'. Whilst the apparent antinomy may be resolved in principle, it does not follow that therefore there remain no difficulties in the way Tillich actually uses 'theonomy' and 'correlation' within his theological system. For there clearly are difficulties in especially that area where the two overlap.

The problem of the relationship between 'church theology' and 'cultural theology' can also be resolved in principle. In 'Über die Idee einer Theologie der Kultur', church theology and cultural theology are so opposed to one another in aim and interest that they are in important respects clearly competitive. Even so Tillich claims that the two enterprises are complementary and should ideally be synthesised in the work of each theologian. (GW. IX. 27ff) I suggested that in Tillich's early work at least *theonomy* can be regarded as the methodological principle of a 'cultural theology' and in his later work *correlation* as that of a 'church theology'. If it is the case, as I have attempted to show, that theonomy and correlation do not in his later work imply competing explanations of the structure of relations berween religion and culture, can it be shown that cultural theology and church theology also serve compatible ends? The apparent antimony between Tillich's early conception of theonomy and his later conception of correlation is resolved in part at least because his conception of theonomy is in important respects modified through the years.

The scope and aims of 'cultural theology' are also modified, but not just in the ways that 'theonomy' is modified. By the time Tillich published the first volume of his *Systematic Theology*, 'cultural theology' is subsumed under and brought into the service of 'church theology'. (ST. I. 39f q.v.) The object of cultural theology is now regarded as the analysis and description of the 'situation' addressed by the christian theologian. In effect, the formulation of the questions implied in human existence is the primary task of the cultural theologian. (cf. ST. II. 14–5; cf. PE, 60) Consequently, the aims and objectives of 'cultural theology' and 'church theology' can no longer be regarded as competitive. Indeed, what Tillich speaks of in the *Systematic Theology* as 'apologetic theology' can be regarded as his own 'personal union' (cf. GW. IX. 29) of cultural theology and church theology in such a way that the fundamental symbols of the christian religion are shown to answer the questions implied in human existence. As in the case of theonomy and correlation, the apparent antinomy between the two sorts of theology is in principle resolved, even if there remain difficulties as to the way he relates the two in practice.

There are other difficulties in Tillich's theory of correlative relations between cultural forms and religious content. Two of the most crucial for our estimate of Tillich's success in resolving Schleiermacher's dilemma are dealt with in detail in the following section.

Form and Content as a Model of Correlation

Having traced the development of some ways that 'form' and 'content' came to be used in Tillich's writings, we must on that basis now establish the *status* of 'form' and 'content' as a model, determine its *role* vis-à-vis the question-answer model, and then test its *adequacy* as a model of a correlative relationship.

Earlier I mentioned that it would be tempting to speak of form and content as an 'aesthetic model' of correlation. This would clearly not be appropriate in the way that it might be appropriate to speak of questioning and answering as a 'conversational model'. For the connexion between Tillich's concept of correlation and his theory of art is clearly more oblique than is its connexion with his understanding of dialectic. On the basis of the evidence offered in the previous section, the connexion would seem to be as follows: 'correlation' is sometimes explained by Tillich in terms of a particular sort of relationship between 'form' and 'content'; this use of 'form' and 'content' can be understood as an expression of the typically Tillichian stress upon cultural 'form' and religious 'content' (*Gehalt*), as in the slogan with which he is associated, that 'culture is the form of religion and religion is the substance [*Gehalt*] of culture'; this formula derives from his theory of art and is extended by analogy to the other realms of culture generally; what is meant by that slogan is subsequently modified to accommodate in part a changed understanding of the relationship between 'form' and 'content' in art; one consequence of this modification is the notion of a *gläubiger Realismus*; the method of correlation is intended as the methodological expression of *gläubiger Realismus*; therefore, and in this sense, the relationship between 'form' and 'content' in Tillich's concept of correlation is at least obliquely related to his theory of art. But, one must ask, is that connexion sufficiently direct to allow one to speak of form and content as an aesthetic model? One must grant that art played a unique role in the formation, extension and modification of Tillich's understanding of relations between cultural form and religious content. Even so, it has been shown that a number of other factors conditioned the eventual shape of the relations between 'form' and 'content' in Tillich's concept of correlation. A more intimate connexion will be established between art and Tillich's view of what would count as the 'content' of the christian message in any correlation between 'message' and 'situation'. In respect to christology one is clearly justified in speaking of an 'aesthetic model'. Art may have played still a greater rôle in the development of Tillich's understanding of relations between cultural form and religious content.

That the visual arts had of least a heuristic role in Tillich's initial formulation of his dialectic of form and *Gehalt* is quickly established by reference again to his address on the notion of a theology of culture. His account there of the sort of 'analysis' a theology of culture should undertake begins with a consideration of the expressionistic movement, and for two reasons: first, 'because this appears to me to be an especially impressive example of the . . . relationship between form and *Gehalt* and secondly because the very definitions of those notions were fashioned directly under its influence'. (GW. IX. 22f; OB, 27–8, q.v.; cf. GW. IX. 345ff) Yet the importance of the visual arts for the way Tillich used those notions did not cease with their initial definition. Works of art became a favourite source for illustrative material from the beginning of his teaching career. He later recalled having 'used pictures in my lectures [at the University of Berlin] in order to show in other realms of life, especially philosophy, the relationship of form and substance, the possibility of breaking the surface form of reality in order to dig into its depths . . .'. Then Tillich added somewhat tellingly, 'and I must confess that I have not learned from any theological book as much as I learned from these pictures of the great modern artists who broke through into the realm out of which symbols are born'.[75]

But, as hinted even in this passage, art was not for Tillich merely a means of *illustrating* certain philosophical problems. It is more nearly *paradigmatic* for his conception of the relationship between form and *Gehalt* 'in other realms'. In an unpublished paper entitled 'Contemporary Art and the Revelatory Character of Style', for instance, Tillich wrote that after the first world war the visual arts 'soon became for me a realm of human activity from which I derived categories both for my philosophical and my theological thought. Beyond this' – he continues – 'I used in my early lectures on the history of the philosophy of religion analogies in the visual arts to illuminate the character of philosophical concepts'. The trend in Tillich's early works is to extend his conception of relations between *Form*, *Inhalt* and *Gehalt* from the visual arts exclusively to cultural life generally until, as in *Das System der Wissenschaften*, it becomes (together with *Denken*, *Sein* and *Geist*) the controlling dialectic in terms of which all areas of knowledge are organised.

Even though no effort has been made to indicate the full extent of that influence, the material presented in the previous section would seem to be sufficient to support a claim that the visual arts played a unique role not only in the formation and extension of Tillich's conception of the relationship between form and *Gehalt*, but also in the modification of that conception from around 1925. We have seen, however, that the influence of the visual arts is not the only factor which must be taken into account when explaining subsequent developments in Tillich's dialectic of form and *Gehalt*. Two such factors were considered at length in the first section of this chapter. That the form-content model did on occasion yield to the demands of experience is surely a point in its favour. An important point. For, as Max Black has no doubt rightly warned, one of the dangers of using models in the sense of conceptual archetypes is that they may become permanently insulated from

---

[75] *Ibid.*, p. 144. Tillich made this point in a number of places, including 'Art and Ultimate Reality', *Cross Currents*, X (1960), 10.

criticism and correction. Whatever difficulties his particular usage of 'form' and 'content' may create for his concept of correlation, Tillich's evident willingness to reshape his understanding of the relationship between 'form' and 'content', kairos and revelation, is in principle to be commended. And it has already been shown that the continued presence of the earlier understanding of the relationship between cultural form and religious content alongside the newer understanding in Tillich's *Systematic Theology* is not as serious a difficulty as one might at first suppose.

What sort of theology does the model serve? Just as the question-answer model is capable of two widely different uses, the form-content model is equally capable of being brought into the service either of what Tillich had earlier called cultural theology or into that of church theology. The mere distinction between cultural form and religious content does not in and of itself dictate the shape such a 'model' will be given. As used in Tillich's writings prior to about 1925, the form-content model is somewhat more suited to the aims of a cultural theology to the extent that stress is placed there upon the 'break-through' (*durchbrechen*) of the 'unconditioned' *from within* conditioned forms. And the truly cultural theologian is said in such circumstances to be 'open not only for every sort of form, but also for every new spirit'. (GW. IX. 29) A form-content model of the relationship between religion and culture, when interpreted in this way, is clearly not an equally suitable foundation for a church theology. Like the earlier form of the conversational model, it lacks sufficient shape and direction. After about 1925, however, a different sort of emphasis begins to make itself known in Tillich's writings. The stress shifts to the 'intrusion' (*hereinbrechen*) of divine revelation *from beyond* the conditioned form of human existence. And a little later the christological confession 'Jesus is the Christ' comes to be spoken of as the criterion according to which the spirits are tested, the guardian which protects that which makes christian theology christian. When reinterpreted in this way, form and content are now clearly more suited to 'church theology' than to 'cultural theology'. It is principally in the second sense that Tillich spoke of the *correlation* between cultural 'forms' and religious 'content'. That being the case, we must ask whether the form-content model satisfies both the criteria of a correlative relationship.

It was argued in the previous chapter that, construed in one way, the strength of the question-answer model of correlation lay in the thoroughgoing reciprocity it allowed between the two discussion partners. Yet, on its own it failed to provide convincing guidelines for the direction and goal of the "dialogue" between religion and culture, such that it failed adequately to protect the 'christianness' of christianity. The weakness of the question-answer model, however, is the strength of the form-content model to the extent that, in its later usage, the christian "substance" is sharply distinguished from the cultural "form" of its expression. Tillich is clearly intent on preserving 'the essential and unique character' of the christian message. (cf. ST. I. 7) But, the strength of the question-answer model is in this respect the weakness of the form-content model to the extent that in it the element of reciprocity is greatly diminished, if not eclipsed altogether. For genuine reciprocity is virtually precluded by the form-content distinction in the sense that the religious substance is made immune from cultural critique or influence and, in addition, autonomous cultural forms are made immune from religious critique. This latter point follows from his early insistence that religion is 'neutral' or 'indifferent' (GW. IX. 16) as regards its cultural form of expression. Within the framework of Tillich's theory of relations between cultural form and religious content there can be no specifically religious form.[76]

Tillich's over-riding intention in making the distinction between the unchanging content of the christian message and the changing forms of cultural expression is clear and unambiguous. He was seeking to account for the interaction between christianity and culture or 'message' and 'situation' and yet to protect the autonomy of each. (cf. ST. I.8) To protect culture from religious tutelage, autonomous cultural forms are made immune from religious critique. To protect theology from cultural tutelage, religious substance — 'the eternal message' — is made immune from cultural critique or influence (cf. ST. I. 64), even if — as I shall show shortly — this immunity is sometimes bought at too high a price.

When used in combination with the question-answer model, the form-content model has the effect of restricting greatly if not eliminating altogether the reciprocity normally associated with 'Question and answer, Yes and No in an actual disputation ...'. (K&B, 15) Despite Tillich's persistent talk about the 'mutual dependence' of questioning and answering in the method of correlation, reciprocity is finally illusory. There is no mutual interaction on the same 'level' or in the same 'dimension': form does not mutually affect form; content does not mutually affect content.

---

[76] On the consequences of this for Tillich's theology of culture, see Amelung, *Die Gestalt der Liebe*.

Neither singularly nor in combination do the two sets of metaphors enable Tillich to satisfy the two conditions of a correlative relation. On its own the question-answer model fails to satisfy the autonomy condition; on its own, the form-content model fails to satisfy the reciprocity condition; the particular way they are combined by Tillich in his account of the method of correlation does not satisfy the reciprocity condition.

Nor can it simply be assumed that the form-content model convincingly and adequately satisfied even the autonomy condition. For undisputably serious difficulties are created by the sort of conditions which Tillich stipulates must obtain in order for, say, christian theology to remain christian through history and across cultures. So that the christian message will not be derived from or simply reduced to 'merely' another aspect of the cultural situation, Tillich stipulates that the *content* of the christian message must be independent of that situation. It must be independent both in the sense that it be based on revelation and in the sense that it not be in any way dependent upon non-theological judgments. Even laying aside the issue whether and in what sense christianity need appeal to 'revelation' as a source of its 'content', two issues remain regarding his insistence that an 'unchanging content' or an *ewige Gehalt* must characterise any theology which is to be judged a christian theology. First, what constitutes that 'content'? Second, must there be such a 'content', however it is to be defined, in order for a christian theology to remain 'what it is'? Each of these questions is to be considered in turn.

Before turning to them directly, however, a brief remark or two is required regarding the sense of the word 'unchanging' in the phrase 'unchanging content'. For it is not always altogether clear in Tillich's writings in precisely which sense it is being insisted that the 'content' of christianity must remain *unchanged*. In what follows, however, I shall assume that it was his view that the content of christianity remains unchanged so long as it does not undergo a change from one kind to another. This sense of 'unchanging' would seem to be implied, for instance, in the section on 'the dynamics of revelation' in the *Systematic Theology*. (ST. I. 126–8 q.v.) For although the original revelation of 'Jesus as the Christ' is said there to be 'the permanent', 'unchanging' and 'immovable point of reference' in all christian theology, Tillich allows in addition that 'the act of referring is never the same, since new generations with new potentialities of reception enter the [revelatory] correlation and transform it'. (ST. I. 126) So, he would seem to allow that some sorts of change are legitimate, namely, the sorts which occur within the constellation which he calls 'dependent revelation'. Other sorts are not regarded as legitimate. He is driven in that same section to ask whether change in the sense of development can ever lead to change in the sense of a change of kind. (ST. I. 128 q.v.) And it is this second sort of 'change' which Tillich seeks to avoid when he insists that christian theology must preserve intact the unchanging content of the christian message.

But what constitutes this content?

Tillich is by no means consistent regarding what is to count as the 'content' of the christian message, owing partly perhaps to his tendency after his emigration to use the one word to do the job of two German words: *Inhalt* and *Gehalt*. Even so, in his mature writings, he most frequently specifies that this 'content' is somehow to be identified with the primitive baptismal formula 'Jesus is the Christ'. We have already had occasion to mention that this confession in his view constitutes both a sufficient and necessary expression of the essence or the unchanging substance of christianity. It makes christianity 'what it is'. (cf. ST. II. 97)

The symbol 'Jesus as the Christ' is, of course, only one of the central symbols of the christian religion. Given all its various symbols, why is this particular one to be regarded as constitutive of 'the christian message'? Tillich says it expresses the central paradox of christianity (ST. II. 90−2), namely, that a moment in time has eternal significance, that Jesus as the christ is 'the point of identity between the absolutely concrete and the absolutely universal'. (ST. I. 15−16) Consequently, 'Jesus as the Christ' is not one symbol amongst other symbols: it is '*the* answer of Christianity' (ST. II. 93 but cf. STd. II. 103), 'the only possible foundation of a Christian theology which claims to be *the* theology' (ST. I. 17), the 'fixed core' and 'substance' of the christian faith[77]. (HCT, xiv; ST. II. 145)

In view of the importance attached to the symbol 'Jesus is the Christ' as that which makes christianity christian, as the 'unchanging point of reference' in christian theology, it is necessary to enquire further into its character and role in Tillich's theology.

---

[77] Kelsey explains this ambiguity in terms of competing aesthetic theories which he detects in Tillich's writings on 'the biblical picture of Jesus as the Christ'. See *The Fabric of Paul Tillich's Theology,* pp. 105f *et passim*. There is much to be said for Kelsey's analysis, though one wishes he had related his argument to the problem of the ambiguous role of *Inhalt* in the dialectic of *Form-Inhalt-Gehalt*. This would have enabled him to see more clearly that the ambiguity he detects is by no means restricted to Tillich's account of 'the biblical picture'.

Tillich says that the symbol has two main aspects, neither of which can be slighted without christianity's ceasing to be 'what it is': the 'Jesus-character' of Jesus as the christ and the 'Christ-character' of Jesus as the christ. (ST. II.142ff) On Tillich's account, the requirement to do justice both to the concrete, historical foundation of christianity (*Jesus* is the christ) and to the universal, transhistorical significance claimed for that foundation (Jesus is *the christ*) inheres in any attempt to do christian theology. The problem of the relationship between christology and historical enquiry is one point at which the tension between the 'particularity' and the 'universality' occasioned by this dual requirement has been especially noticeable in Tillich's theology. An antinomy would seem to run through Tillich's attempt to define the proper relationship between christology and historical research, such that his talk about an 'unchanging point of reference' in christian theology becomes highly problematic.

On the one hand, Tillich insists vigorously that the foundation of christian faith ("Jesus is the Christ") is both an historical fact and 'the believing reception of Jesus as the Christ'. The whole theological enterprise is said to be undercut unless both these elements are preserved in the symbol 'Jesus is the Christ'. (ST. II. 98—9) For the basic christian assertion is that 'essential God-Manhood has appeared within existence and subjected itself to the conditions of existence without being conquered by them'. In order to conquer existential estrangement, the power of 'new being' must be manifest in an actual person: otherwise the New Being would remain a quest and an expectation and would not be a reality in space and time. 'Only if the [*sic*] existence is conquered in *one* point — a personal life, representing existence as a whole — is it conquered in principle . . .'. Elsewhere Tillich states emphatically that the foundation of christianity would be denied if the factual element in it were denied. (ST. II. 107) He frequently emphasises that Jesus of Nazareth, the bearer of the power of new being, was in fact an individual, historical person existing in space and time and in comparison with whom all mythological divine figures are abstract expressions of the hope of new being, but not its bringer. It is precisely the concreteness of the biblical picture of a man, Jesus of Nazareth, as bringer of this power which gives the symbol 'Jesus as the Christ' its universal significance. (ST. II. 151) Tillich shows no patience whatever with what he takes to be Hegel's view that faith in Christ is faith in a personified ideal. In his unpublished lectures on Hegel delivered at the University of Frankfurt, Tillich argued that this view above all else was responsible for the collapse of the Hegelian school.[78] This side of Tillich's christology cannot be adequately expressed by the phrase 'new being' alone. It must be expanded to 'the new being in Jesus as the Christ' inasmuch as 'new being' apart from 'Jesus of Nazareth' is abstract and a-historical, and, therefore, not a sufficient summary of 'the biblical picture of Jesus as the Christ'. (ST. I.49f)

On the other hand, Tillich insists equally vigorously that historical research can neither give nor take away the foundation of the christian faith. (ST. II. 113) That is to say, no statement or combination of statements about the past *arrived at by historical enquiry* is allowed to count decisively for or against the truth of the 'foundation' of christian faith. Tillich consistently argued throughout his career that christian faith demands a foundation which is certain in the sense of being incorrigible and that historical enquiry is incapable of providing such a foundation since historical knowledge can never attain to more than a high degree of probability. For this reason, 'the historical Jesus' cannot be the foundation of faith; rather, 'the biblical picture of Jesus as the Christ' constitutes faith's foundation. This move on Tillich's part created difficulties for his approach from which he was never able to extricate himself.

In 'Die christliche Gewißheit und der historische Jesus',[79] an unpublished paper which was written in 1911, in the wake of the collapse of 'the quest of the historical Jesus' and the short-lived ascendency of the 'Christ-myth' movement,[80] Tillich considered the consequences for christian theology if historians were to conclude that Jesus of Nazareth had never existed. Having distinguished between the confession 'Jesus is the Christ' and the contingent proposition 'Jesus, the Christ, existed', Tillich there argued that faith in the christ of the biblical picture is authenticated by the presence of the transforming power of the Spirit and does not depend, either as a matter of empirical fact or as a matter of logical necessity, upon the incertitude of historical

---

[78] *Vorlesungen über Hegel* (Univ. of Frankfurt, WS 1931–2; 440 pp. typescript), pp. 72–3, 75ff.

[79] Tillich-Archiv.

[80] The first edition of A. Schweitzer's *Geschichte der Leben-Jesu-Forschung* was published in 1906 and A. Drews's *Die Christusmythe* appeared in 1909. Kierkegaard's *Philosophical Fragments* appeared in German translation only in 1910, although it had been published in Denmark in 1844. Troeltsch's study of *Die Bedeutung der Geschichtlichkeit Jesu für den Glauben* was published in 1911, the same year in which Tillich prepared his theses on the historical Jesus.

enquiry into the existence of Jesus of Nazareth. Indeed, such dependence is regarded as a form of heteronomy and, therefore, contrary to the protestant doctrine of justification. Nor is this radical bifurcation between confession of the christ and statements about Jesus restricted to Tillich's earliest writings. Shortly before his death, Tillich commented that even if 'the biblical picture' were a fabrication of Mark the evangelist, it would still be a valid expression of the power of new being, for Mark would then have been 'the bearer of the Spirit through whom has created the church and transformed . . . many in all generations, somehow including myself'.[81] Clearly this lack of specificity as regards the actual bringer and bearer of the new being creates not inconsiderable difficulties for any theologian who would make 'Jesus the Christ' the 'immovable reference' of christian theology, 'the substance and criterion' of all theological statements.

One possible solution to this difficulty would be to postulate more than one way of acquiring knowledge of the past such that there could be both a 'scientific' way (namely, historical research) and a way of faith. If it were further granted that each of these ways is independent of the other, then it might be possible for faith to claim to be certain on its own grounds as to the truth of a given statement about the past (such as 'Jesus of Nazareth existed') without submitting itself to the alleged uncertainties of historical research. Whilst he did on occasion come very close to such a view (cf. R&R, 364), Tillich in the main rejected this alternative as untenable: faith is not able to bestow certainty upon statements about the past which historical research is incapable of giving them.[82] Despite his characteristic refusal to adopt such a view, it is less than clear whether he successfully avoided the procedure in practice. For Tillich does insist that faith can guarantee 'its own foundation' and that its foundation is in some sense historical or that it at least entails an historical proposition. Although faith is said not to be able to guarantee that Jesus of Nazareth ever lived, it is said to be able to guarantee 'the fact to which "Jesus of Nazareth" refers', namely that the power of new being became actual in an individual, historical person. Although admittedly less

---

[81] 'Rejoinder', *JRel*, XLVI (1966), 192. Tillich's remarks are in response to D. M. Smith's essay in the same number entitled 'The Historical Jesus in Paul Tillich's Theology', pp. 131–48.

[82] This distinguishes Tillich from, e. g., the American theologian John Knox. See the latter's *The Church and the Reality of Christ* (London, 1963), and *Limits of Unbelief* (London, 1970), pp. 70 ff.

specific than the statement that the power of new being became actual in Jesus of Nazareth, even the more modest claim that this power became actual in 'a personal life' remains or entails a contingent proposition about the past. Despite his protestation to the contrary, Tillich is thereby committed to the view that faith is capable of guaranteeing on its own grounds at least one statement about the past.

That an historical person corresponds to the biblical picture of Jesus as the Christ is said to be guaranteed by what Tillich earlier termed an 'imaginative intuition' or *fantasiemäßige Anschauung* and later an *analogia imaginis* 'between the picture and the actual personal life from which it has arisen'. (ST. II. 115) Tillich's argument would appear to run as follows: the power of new being cannot have become actualised except in and through an individual person; this power *is* actual in the biblical picture of Jesus as the Christ; there must therefore have been an individual person who corresponds to the symbol 'Jesus as the christ', whether or not his name was Jesus of Nazareth.[83]

For reasons which I have offered in an article published elsewhere, this simply will not do.[84] Yet, of greater interest at the moment is determining *why* Tillich could give such arguments without realising their utter inadequacy, or their implications for his insistence that christianity has in Jesus the christ an 'immovable point of reference'. I would suggest that such arguments are in important measure derived from the relationship between *Form, Inhalt* and *Gehalt* developed first in his theory of art.

It must be stressed, however, that this is not the only factor guiding Tillich's thought. To be reckoned with as well is undoubtedly the influence upon him of his former professor at Halle, Martin Kähler.[85] Kähler, in fact, actually adumbrated something like the *analogia imaginis* in his still-influential pamphlet entitled *Der sogenannte historische Jesus und der geschichtliche, biblische Christus*. Having argued at an earlier point in the pamphlet that the biblical picture [*Bild*] of Jesus could not be merely an

---

[83] For a study of some of the various aspects of the analogia imaginis in Tillich's theology, see K.-D. Nörenberg, *Analogia Imaginis: Der Symbolbegriff in der Theologie Paul Tillichs* (Gütersloh, 1966).

[84] 'Is Jesus Necessary for Christology', in *Christ, Faith and History*, ed. S. W. Sykes and J. P. Clayton (Cambridge, 1972), pp. 154 ff.

[85] See H. Leipold, *Offenbarung und Geschichte als Problem des Verstehens* Gütersloh, 1962) and the more recent study by H.-G. Link, *Geschichte Jesu und Bild Christi* (Neukirchen, 1975).

Form, Content and the Concept of Correlation   233

idealised composite portrait of the highest hopes of man or merely 'the loftiest poem of mankind',[86] Kähler added, 'We encounter precisely the historical [*geschichtliche*] Christ, not as an ideal to be realized in the remote future by scientific investigation nor as the fluctuating result of the biographers' disputations, but, rather, within a tradition which possesses the inherent power to convince us of its divine authenticity'.[87] This inherent power is said by Kähler to make Jesus the christ 'directly accessible' and to make it impossible to differentiate the historic [*geschichtliche*] christ from the biblical picture of Jesus as the christ. Likewise, for Tillich, it is the inherent power of the biblical picture which is said to guarantee that an actual person corresponds to that portrait.

There is an additional and perhaps even more important factor which must be taken into account, namely, Tillich's tendency to treat aesthetically or 'symbolically' the biblical picture of Jesus. This is not so of Kähler, who – though not the naive 'biblicist' he is frequently taken to be – nonetheless tended on the whole to be more literal and more conservative in his handling of the 'biblical picture' than was his student Tillich.

In view of what was said earlier in this chapter about the influence upon the young Tillich of German expressionism, it should have come as no surprise to learn that he explicitly identified the biblical picture of Jesus as an expressionistic portrait. (ST. II. 115–6) Aspects of Tillich's particular interpretation of the biblical picture, as well as some of the moves which he makes using the *analogia imaginis*, become more intelligible when seen in relation to the aesthetic model. The component elements of the biblical picture would appear to correspond in the following way to the components of artistic creations: 'a personal life' may be regarded as the form of the biblical picture; 'Jesus of Nazareth' and specific information about his life and teachings, that is, biographical material, supply its content in the sense of *Inhalt*; and 'the power of New Being' must I think be understood as the portrait's *Gehalt*. Those individuals who have been grasped by this power in and through the biblical picture can certify the experience of the powerful *Gehalt* of new being, although they cannot certify the objective factuality of the specific content of that picture: ' The concrete biblical material [in the biblical picture of the Christ] is not guaranteed by faith in respect to external factuality [i. e.

---

[86] *The So-Called Historical Jesus and the Historic Biblical Christ* (Philadelphia, 1964), pp. 53, 78–9.
[87] *Ibid.*, pp. 121–2.

Inhalt]; but it is guaranteed as an adequate expression of the transforming power [i. e. *Gehalt*] of the New Being in Jesus as the Christ'. (ST. II. 115) Just as it is not content or subject matter (*Inhalt*) which makes a piece of art a medium of religious meaning, it is likewise not the specific content which makes the biblical picture of Jesus as the christ a medium of the power of new being.

This then is the significance of the aesthetic model employed by Tillich in his *analogia imaginis*: it is intended as a means of holding together the claim that the foundation of christian faith is historical and the claim that the foundation is in principle unfalsifiable. For falsification of any aspect of the specific, factual content (in the sense of *Inhalt*) of the biblical picture would not entail the falsification of the picture itself, as long as 'power' (in the sense of *Gehalt*) continued to be mediated through it. This being the case, what becomes of Tillich's claim that 'Christianity is what it is through the affirmation that Jesus of Nazareth, who has been called "the Christ", is actually the Christ, namely, he who brings the new state of things, the New Being'? In Tillich's own words, it is not 'the historical Jesus' which is the foundation of christian faith, but the *symbol* of Jesus as the christ. One commentator has not inaccurately described 'the biblical picture' in Tillich's theology as a *verbal icon*: this characterisation pinpoints nicely the almost wholly aesthetic function of the symbol 'Jesus as the christ' in Tillich's thought.[88]

But, can a christian theology trade exclusively in such a currency? One must ask what is the cash value of that symbol in the light of Tillich's unwillingness or inability to support it with hard reserves which can be mined only by historical research? Is not autonomy being purchased at too high a price? For the confession 'Jesus is the Christ' cannot be more certain than is warranted by the evidence for the empirical propositions entailed by that claim. For recent theology, this is no doubt a 'hard saying'.

For instance, it is not sufficient to say that one can be certain that the power of new being became actualised in a 'personal life' and then express indifference as to whether his name was 'Jesus of Nazareth'. For, if one cannot specify with some certainty the *particular* person in whom existential estrangement is alleged to have been conquered, what warrant is there for the claim that it has been conquered in an individual person? If it is the case, as Tillich claims, that the 'power of new being' is effective in the biblical picture as such, then why is it thought necessary that in addition it must have

---

[88] Kelsey, drawing on the work of the literary critic W. K. Wimsatt.

been actualised originally by an individual, historical person — whatever his name — whose likeness the 'picture' is? For it would not follow solely from the fact that someone discovers creative power in 'the biblical picture' that an actual person is portrayed there. Nor would it follow that it is also a good likeness! A fictional character in literature may be powerful without being a portrayal of an actual person. Indeed, a fictional creation is often more powerful precisely because it is a composite of characteristics of several individuals or because it epitomises common human experiences. Even though a character may expand one's self-awareness, challenge one's life-style, or make whole new dimensions of existential possibilities available to one, that would not 'certify' the existence of an actual, individual person who corresponds to the fictional creation of the author's imagination. This does not, of course, preclude the possibility that the character in question was in fact a 'portrait' of an actual individual. It may even be a good likeness. Indeed, this is a common enough occurrence in literature and drama. But whether this were the case could be determined only by the marshalling of convincing evidence in support of such a claim. Whether there is sufficient evidence to support the claim that the portraits in the gospels of 'Jesus as the Christ' are good likenesses of Jesus of Nazareth is of course a separate and unresolved issue in the research into christian origins. Tillich's particular stance on the relationship between christology and historiography, however, clearly creates insurmountable difficulties for any theologian who claims that both aspects of the confession 'Jesus is the Christ' must be preserved in order for christianity to remain 'what it is' and who furthermore claims that the appearance of the power of new being in Jesus of Nazareth (or whoever) is the 'unchanging point of reference' for any theology which would be christian.

Even if this particular difficulty were resolved, however, a problem would still remain for Tillich's identification of the 'unchanging content' of christian theology in that the confession 'Jesus is the christ' is not in itself sufficient to establish the christian quality of a given theology. For the crucial difficulty is not so much that of simply referring to Jesus as the christ, but rather more that of the way in which such a reference is made. And the plain fact is that even what is to count as referring to Jesus as the christ has not, does not now and is not likely ever to mean the same thing to all christian theologians.

The bare requirement merely to refer to 'Jesus as the christ' is consequently not sufficient for the weight that 'foundation' must support in Tillich's methodology. In addition, it would seem that in practice Tillich has in mind, not merely referring, but rather *referring in a particular way*: for, as mentioned already, he insists that both the 'Jesus-character' and the 'christ-character' of that symbol must be preserved in any genuinely christian theology. Though in itself problematic, this then enables Tillich to rule out certain sorts of ways of referring to Jesus as inadequate ways of referring to the original revelation upon which the christian religion is founded. And the effective casualties include not only the *deutsche Christen,* but a number of others as well — including the author of *Das Wesen des Christentums,* Adolf von Harnack! (ST. II. 146)

After 1933 Tillich may have called into question *what* is allowed to count in other theological systems as the 'unchanging substance' of the christian message, but he never to my knowledge called into question *that* there must be such an 'ewige Gehalt' or 'eternal content' to serve as a criterion against which all instances of christian theology are to be measured and in virtue of which certain theologies are to be classified as *christian* theologies. Whilst not perhaps as naive as those who have held that there is a set of unchanging doctrines or practices in virtue of which a theology is a christian theology, Tillich did nonetheless share with them an important and, in his case at least, inadequately examined assumption. This assumption, given expression in the particular way he talked about the relationship between 'form' and 'content', can be paraphrased in the following way: *all instances of christian theology must have some property in common in virtue of which they are to be regarded as instances of christian theology.* I have already suggested that this assumption, introduced by Tillich as a means of protecting the self-identity of christian theology under very trying circumstances, precludes his concept of correlation being thoroughly reciprocal, such that the second condition of a correlative relationship is not fulfilled. But, more positively, and with the assistance of aspects of Wittgenstein's later philosophy, I shall now attempt to show that Tillich's notion of correlation could be revised in such a way that both conditions of correlationship would be met. For I believe it to be in large measure Tillich's 'essentialist' views about what makes christian theologies christian which prevented his successfully resolving the methodological dilemma outlined in chapter two.

By 'essentialism' I mean the view that all instances of a given general term must have in common some property in virtue of which they may be regarded as instances of that term. This view is also sometimes called 'realism'.[89] Even though neither term is wholly satisfactory and both terms

---

[89] E. g., by J. R. Bambrough.

are used by Tillich in other contexts, it was thought that 'essentialism' is the less unsatisfactory of the two.

The later philosophy of Ludwig Wittgenstein represents, amongst other things, a notable attack against essentialism in this sense. In what follows I shall hope to show that some remarks to be found in this later philosophy, especially those regarding 'family resemblances', have a bearing on the issue whether individual theologies must have something in common in order to be classified as christian theologies, even though Wittgenstein himself never applied those remarks to this particular issue. I shall argue – over against Tillich – that christian theology does not require an unchanging content (whatever value is given to the word 'content') in order to remain genuinely christian because 'family resemblance' would be sufficient in order for individual theologies to be regarded as instances of christian theology.

An important feature of Wittgenstein's attack upon essentialism is the view that philosophy proceeds by analysis of individual, concrete cases. He frequently condemned our craving for generality, or 'our contemptuous attitude toward the particular case'. In the earlier of *The Blue and Brown Books*, which together constitute important preliminary studies for the *Philosophical Investigations*, Wittgenstein states that this illicit craving arises from a number of philosophical confusions, including the tendency always to look for something in common to all the entities which we subsume under a general term, when similarity is sometimes sufficient. 'We are inclined to think that there must be something in common to all games, say, and that this common property is the justification for applying the general term "game" to the various games; whereas games form a *family* the members of which have family likenesses'.[90] Here is introduced perhaps for the first time Wittgen-

---

[90] L: Wittgenstein, *The Blue and Brown Books* (2nd. ed.; Oxford, 1969), p. 17. Among the other confusions singled out by Wittgenstein is the idea that the meaning of every word is an entity or an image corresponding to the word, when the meaning of some words is the use to which they are put in language games. *Philosophical Investigations* (2nd. ed.; Oxford, 1958), § 43. Despite Wittgenstein's careful limitation of his theory to only some sorts of cases, a few philosophers have attempted to extend this into a general theory of linguistic meaning. See, e. g., W. P. Alston, *Philosophy of Language* (Englewood Cliffs, 1964). Some – notably John Heywood Thomas – have accused Tillich of subscribing to an 'entity'-theory of meaning. This is too-simple on two counts: namely, the inadequacy of attempts to extend Wittgenstein's 'use'-theory into a general theory and, secondly, the inadequacy of any attempt to reduce Tillich's concept of

stein's notion of family resemblances. For our purposes it is not irrelevant that the notion first appears in a context which makes clear it was intended in some way to illuminate the problem of universals or of general terms.

In the whole of his later writings, Wittgenstein sketched in broad strokes only his theory of family resemblances, a metaphor often used in conjunction with other metaphors, such as 'language games'.[91] Owing partly to Wittgenstein's style and to what has been euphemistically termed his 'economy of expression', as well as to his tendency to elucidate metaphor with metaphor, the remarks on family resemblances are subject to varied interpretation.[92] Nor is there any consensus among Anglo-American philosophers as to the significance of 'family resemblances'. What Wittgenstein accomplished, if Wittgenstein accomplished anything, by means of this notion is by no means agreed. A few have claimed that thereby Wittgenstein 'solved' the traditional philosophical problem of universals.[93] Some acknowledge its applicability to some cases but not to others, at times appealing to Wittgenstein's own warnings against the 'craving for generality'.[94] Others have claimed that Wittgenstein has offered nothing new, that he is merely reiterating or possibly extending Hume's resemblance theory of universals.[95] Still others

---

symbol to too simple a view of meaning. For a generally perceptive analysis of Tillich's theory of language and symbols, see W. L. Rowe, *Religious Symbols and God* (Chicago, 1968).

[91] Owing to the fairly specific focus of this chapter, it has not been necessary to deal directly with 'language-games' in Wittgenstein's philosophy. For critical accounts of the use – and abuse – of this side of Wittgenstein's thought in recent philosophy of religion, see Kai Nielson, 'Wittgensteinian Fideism', *Phil*, XLII (1967), 191–209, and P. J. Sherry, *Religion, Truth and Language Games* (London, 1977).

[92] See, e. g., the articles and the now somewhat dated bibliography in G. Pitcher, ed., *Wittgenstein: The Philosophical Investigations* (London, 1968).

[93] Most boldly by J. R. Bambrough in 'Universals and Family Resemblances' (1960–1; repr. Pitcher, op. cit., pp. 186–204, from which references are to be made). See also D. F. Pears, 'Universals', *Logic and Language*, 2nd series, ed. Anthony Flew (London, 1953), pp. 51–64, and John Wisdom, 'Metaphysics and Verification' (1938; repr. *Philosophy and Psycho-analysis*, Oxford, 1953, pp. 51–101).

[94] M. Hodges, 'Wittgenstein on Universals', *PhilStud*, XXIV (1973), 22–30; A. J. Ayer, *The Problem of Knowledge* (Harmondsworth, 1967), pp. 10–2.

[95] R. I Aaron, *Theory of Universals* (Oxford, 1967²), pp. 67ff, 168.

have queried whether it is possible to say what would be a 'solution' to *the* problem of universals.[96]

Whether the notion of family resemblances actually does *solve* the problem of universals — or even whether it is possible to solve such a problem, if it is a single problem — it is clear that the notion was introduced by Wittgenstein as an instrument to be used in relation to at least one of the cluster of problems traditionally subsumed under 'the problem of universals'.[97] For he explicitly identifies family resemblances with the problem of classifying particular entities under a general term.[98] And it is this aspect of the problem which ties in with one of the features of Tillich's concept of correlation, namely, the assumption that particular theologies must have something in common in order to be christian theologies. And it is only this connexion which is relevant for the argument being developed here.

Clearly our task would be lighter if it could be convincingly shown that Wittgenstein's account of 'family resemblances' were capable of extension as a general theory, as for instance Renford Bambrough has claimed. For if his notion of 'resemblances' could account for all general terms, then it would account for any general term, including 'theology'. Can a case be made for the extension of 'family resemblances' to include all sorts of general terms? 'When I claim that Wittgenstein solved the problem of universals', explains Bambrough, 'I am claiming that his remarks can be paraphrased into a doctrine which can be set out in general terms and can be related to the traditional theories [of universals], and which can then be shown to deserve to supersede the traditional theories'.[99] By the 'traditional theories', he means *realism* or 'essentialism' and *nominalism*. In a highly compressed section, to which the reader is referred, Bambrough summarises clearly and concisely in

---

[96] A. R. Manser, 'Games and Family Resemblances', *Phil*, XLII (1967), 210–25; R. J. O'Shaugnessy, 'On Having Something in Common', *Mind*, LXXIX (1970), 436–40; and, by implication, J. Teichmann, 'Universals and Common Properties', *Analysis*, XXIX (1969), 162–5.

[97] J. Teichmann writes, 'I agree with Bambrough that many things said by Wittgenstein about meaning bear quite directly on questions concerning Universals. How could discussion of meaning *not* bear on questions about Universals?' *Op. cit.*, p. 162.

[98] *Philosophical Investigations*, § 67; *Blue and Brown Books*, pp. 17, 19.

[99] 'Universals and Family Resemblances', p. 198.

what ways he regards 'family resemblances' as having superseded those two theories.[100]

Within the strictures imposed upon it by Bambrough – strictures not always perceived clearly by all his critics – the attempt to re-state 'family resemblances' as a general theory is indeed possible, but perhaps ironically it obscures Wittgenstein's most important contributions to the discussion about general terms.

Why this is so can be clarified by reference to one of the examples adduced by Bambrough in support of his claim: 'In the sense in which, according to Wittgenstein, games have nothing in common except that they are games, . . . *brothers have nothing in common except that they are brothers*. It is true that brothers have in common that they are male siblings, but their having in common that they are male siblings is their having in common that they are brothers, and not their having in common something in addition to their being brothers'.[101] This generalisation can be stated in the following form: X's have nothing in common (in virtue of which they are X's) except that they *are* X's. This is so, though it expresses a tautology.[102] More importantly, however, it obscures the situation rather than clarifies it. And it obscures the problem by failing to make clear that the problem of universals is fundamentally a metaphysical or an ontological problem.

Philosophers have sometimes treated the so-called 'problem of universals' as primarily an ontological problem and at other times as primarily a linguistic problem. In modern analytic philosophy, the latter tends to be case, though not exclusively so. Rather than asking, 'Do universals exist?', the modern philosopher tends to ask, 'How do we use general terms?' There are advantages to this linguistic approach to the matter. For one need not get involved at all in the classical debate regarding the 'existence' of universals. General terms obviously exist and language could not function otherwise. So the issue is shifted from the ontological to the linguistic. But the matter cannot rest there. For even though one sort of metaphysical puzzle is avoided by this move, there nonetheless remains an ontological

---

[100] *Ibid.*, pp. 198–9.
[101] *Ibid.*, p. 194.
[102] See J. Teichmann, *loc., cit.*

dimension to the problem of universals, even when the problem is linguistically conceived.[103]

This dimension is begging for attention in Bambrough's generalised form of Wittgenstein's notion. For if we say that 'X's have nothing in common except that they are X's', then we have to ask what it is to *be* an X. And that, according to Wittgenstein, cannot be generalised. For the conditions under which particular games are classifiable as 'games' are very different from the conditions under which particular brothers are classifiable as 'brothers'. The aspect of the problem of universals addressed by Wittgenstein is the problem of identification and classification. And that is what Bambrough obscures. In doing so, he obscures precisely those points where Wittgenstein made a significant contribution. That contribution is two-fold. First, Wittgenstein shows that no general theory of universals is required. Secondly, he shows that in some cases, but not necessarily all cases, resemblance between entities is sufficient for them to be classified under the same general term.

Since Wittgenstein's comments cannot be *usefully* extended into a general theory of the nature of universals, we must enquire further whether *theology* is among those concepts which can be regarded as family resemblance concepts. To deal with this question, we must consider some of the central features of family resemblance concepts and determine whether theology has any of those features. There are two features in particular which would seem typically to characterise family resemblance concepts. First, *family resemblance analysis is most suitable for the identification and classification of highly complex entities, concepts, processes and functions.* One is tempted almost to postulate the rule that the more complex the phenomenon in question, the more suitable family-resemblance analysis as a means of explaining the grounds for subsuming the individual entities, etc., under the single general term. There would be certain difficulties with such a rule, however, in that one could no doubt imagine a highly complex entity each distinct property of which was essential. Whether or not such a rule would obtain in all such cases, it is not perhaps accidental that the examples

---

[103] 'The substitution of a question about language for a question about entities does not always get rid of a metaphysical problem, and it has not yet been shown that a linguistic reformulation of the problem of universals removes the whole of the metaphysical puzzle.' D. D. Raphael, 'Universals, Resemblance, and Identity', *ProcArisSoc,* LV (1954–5), 132.

adduced by Wittgenstein tend themselves on the whole to be highly complex. Nor does he anywhere known to me cite a single logically simple concept as being amenable to family-resemblance analysis.[104] These would not seem to be among those sorts of things envisaged by Wittgenstein as 'forming a family' or as exhibiting 'family resemblances'.

There are, however, certain other sorts of examples also passed over by Wittgenstein which would seem to show great promise as 'family-resemblance' concepts. Bambrough, for instance, cites to good effect the problem of taxonomy in biology.[105] But one might also have thought that certain examples from among the social and historical sciences would be likely candidates for such analysis. Wittgenstein does not to my knowledge ever adduce such examples, however. But, then, examples of this sort are in any case rare in his writings generally. These would not seem to be the particular sort of problems which perplexed him. Whilst he did not himself cite such examples, it would not perhaps be unreasonable to suggest that religious traditions (such as christianity) or religious activities (such as theology or worship) might be amenable to family resemblance analysis, and this in part because they are examples of highly complex historical and cultural phenomena.[106]

Recognition of the extent of this complexity is one of the fruits of modern historical criticism of the traditions which collectively constitute christianity and its theological heritage. This may perhaps be taken for granted. Nor is it a judgment with which Tillich would quarrel, even though he would still wish to insist in addition that despite the complexity of its history, theology — e.g. — must have the primitive kerygma as 'the substance and criterion of each of its statements'.

But christian theology is complex in another sense as well: namely, it is linguistically complex. And this sort of complexity creates more serious difficulties for Tillich's position than the other sort, owing to his tendency to treat all theological statements and all religious symbols as having a similar logical status. But this is not the case. Theological statements are not all of the same sort, nor do all the symbols and other terms used by theo-

---

[104] One must be mindful, of course, that Wittgenstein called into question any too facile an understanding of what is to count as a 'simple' or a 'composite' concept. Cf. *Philosophical Investigations*, §§ 46 ff.
[105] *Op. cit.*
[106] Cf. above, part two.

logians have a similar logical standing. Numerous examples could be cited. However, one need perhaps only recall the very different sorts of statements which appear even in the traditional creeds to be reminded that this is the case. Furthermore, the use of even the most central and straightforwardly 'religious' of religious symbols, such as 'God', is thought by some to exhibit 'a manifold and inconsistent logic'.[107] Given the linguistic complexity of theology, what does it mean to claim that each theological statement has as its 'substance and criterion' the symbol 'Jesus is the Christ'? Indeed, that symbol too is on its own linguistically complex. If we even begin to unpack it, we find that its components are not all logically of the same type. For instance, as shown above, it implies both a empirical, historical judgment *and* a theological judgment, the latter of which cannot simply be read off from the empirical judgment but which nonetheless entails it. Determining the logical status of the symbol 'Jesus is the christ' in fact would seem to remain one of the pressing demands for theology today.[108]

Even if it were granted, and it would seem that it must be, that religious traditions and religious activities are complex phenomena, one might still wish to deny that they are best approached as family-resemblance concepts. For being complex might be a necessary condition for such amenability, in the sense that a logically simple entity cannot be thought amenable; but it would not be a sufficient condition, in the sense that one could construct a logically complex concept each component of which was constitutive.

There is, however, a second typical feature of phenomena susceptible to family-resemblance analysis: namely, *the absence of any single property common to all their instances which bind them together*. Wittgenstein characteristically introduces a new metaphor in order to illustrate the sort of 'criss-crossing and overlapping' which unifies the individual instances subsumed under the same family-resemblance concept: he likens the principle of unity to a *rope*. 'What ties the ship to the wharf is a rope, and the rope consists of fibres, but it does not get its strength from any fibre which runs through it from one end to the other, but from the fact that

---

[107] The thesis of a study by M. Durrant of *The Logical Status of 'God' and the Function of Theological Sentences* (London, 1973).
[108] This is certainly one dimension of the recent debate in Britain over *The Myth of God Incarnate*, ed. J. Hick (London, 1977).

there is a vast number of fibres overlapping'.[109] Family-resemblance concepts are unified in the way that a rope is unified and are extended in the way that ropes are extended. The unity is not contingent upon any one property which is present in each of its instances: the unity derives from the complicated network of overlappings. But it does not follow from this that the concept is not *really* unified, nor does it follow that its unity is arbitrary or a mental fiction.

There are limits and the limits are real: not everything is allowed.

For there is involved what has been usefully termed a 'quorum factor'.[110] Parliamentary bodies typically require a quorum of members to be present before business can be conducted. No one particular member need be present, as long as the agreed percentage of other members is present. Likewise, with the features which need be present in each entity, etc., classifiable under a given family-resemblance term: no one feature need be present in any single entity, etc., though a sort of 'quorum of features' must be present. One cannot formulate a valid generalisation regarding even what percentage must be present which would be applicable for all concepts that are family-resemblance concepts, for – following Wittgenstein – each case must be considered separately.

This suggests a second reason why 'theology' might usefully be regarded as a potential family-resemblance term: every attempt to identify that single fact which all instances of christian theology (or, more extravagantly, every theological proposition) are said to have in common in virtue of which they are christian theologies has failed and is bound to fail. There simply is no a-historical, a-cultural 'unchanging content' or 'ewige Gehalt' to be found, no matter how it is defined. That this is the case is agreed even by those who would have us reopen afresh the quest for the historical 'essence' of christianity.[111] It might be suggested that the past history of such attempts to define an 'essence' (in the sense of that which all instances of christianity have in common) has been the history of an ever-receding object, which though no longer to hand (as in Tillich's case) is grasped all the more strongly out of the not illegitimate fear that its loss would mean the loss of that which makes christian theology christian or, more generally, that

---

[109] *Blue and Brown Books*, p. 87. Cf. *Philosophical Investigations*, § 67.
[110] By J. Hospers in *An Introduction to Philosophical Analysis* (2nd. ed.; London, 1967).
[111] See S. W. Sykes, 'The Essence of Christianity', *RelSt*, VII (1971), 291 ff.

which makes christianity christian. But, if not available, neither is it necessary for there to be something in common to all instances of christian theology in order for them to be classified legitimately as instances of christian theology. For christian theologies may be more usefully regarded as 'forming a family' the individual members of which are related to one another through 'a complicated network of similarities, overlappings and criss-crossings'.

But this would not mean that the class of possible christian theologies is entirely open, in the sense of being boundless or arbitrary. There would remain something like a 'quorum factor' to be reckoned with, though that factor would be less straightforward if it were applied to historically developing traditions than if it were applied to relatively fixed parliamentary bodies. Even so, looking at christian theology as a family-resemblance concept would have other advantages. It would allow one to do justice to the richness of the several traditions which make up christianity and to do so in a historically honest way so that no artificial unity is imposed nor radical surgery prescribed, whether the surgeon be a Kierkegaard or a Harnack or a Pius X.

Family resemblance analysis would do this in three ways.

First, family resemblance analysis would allow one to distinguish clearly between *describing* christianity (or christian theology) in terms of its complex network of inter-relationships, on the one side, and *drawing boundaries* for particular purposes, on the other. Family resemblance analysis is, on Wittgenstein's own account, 'purely descriptive'.[112] This corresponds to and is consistent with his frequently cited dictum that philosophy 'leaves everything as it is'.[113] Even so, Wittgenstein makes allowance for those occasions when it may be necessary to set limits 'for a special purpose'.[114] He insists that it is not the drawing of the boundary or the limiting of the definition which makes a concept (e. g., game, pace) usable generally; nonetheless, he allows – albeit parenthetically and here without elaboration – that boundaries and definitions may be required in order to make a given concept usable 'for that special purpose'.[115] There are no doubt numerous sorts of purposes which might be served by drawing such

---

[112] *Blue and Brown Books*, p. 125.
[113] *Philosophical Investigations*, § 124.
[114] *Ibid.*, § 69.
[115] *Ibid.*

boundaries. For instance, one might wish to refer to board games and no others; or one might want to sketch a specimen plant for use in a gardening book to illustrate the effects certain insects or diseases have on plants generally; or one might want to establish a range of standard colours so that manufacturers could then produce different kitchen appliances in matching colours. In each case, the boundaries would have been drawn for different sorts of purposes. But in no case would the drawing of boundaries have been required in order for the concepts 'game', 'plant' or 'colour' to have been usable — *except for that special purpose.* And in no case is the particular group of games or the specimen plant or the standard colour to be equated with what is common to all games, all plants, or all colours — but this is to anticipate a second possible advantage of family-resemblance analysis for theology.

The distinction drawn by Wittgenstein between describing and defining (or drawing boundaries) would enable one to distinguish between two different sorts of ways in which such phrases as 'the christian tradition' or 'christian theology' or even 'christianity' could be used. For such phrases and terms could be used in either a purely descriptive sense or in a theologically-charged normative sense. If, on the one hand, one wanted to delineate in a purely descriptive way what counts as 'the christian tradition' or 'christian theology', then one would offer an account of 'the complicated network of similarities, overlappings and criss-crossings' which obtain among the various strands of what we term collectively 'the christian tradition' or 'christian theology'. 'For a special purpose', on the other hand, one might want to offer a normative judgment as to what is to count as *'the* tradition' or, to use a phrase more common within protestant liberalism, 'the *essence* of christianity'. And there are no doubt numerous 'special purposes' which could be served by offering such a judgment. For instance, in reply to the query of a foreign student for whom christianity is a little known 'other' (!) religion, one might attempt as best one could to encompass in a few sentences the characteristic beliefs and practices of the christian religion. Nor is it entirely fanciful to imagine a similar conversation occurring between an Irish catholic christian and an Irish protestant christian. The zealot's desire to effect 'a critical reduction to principles' might be another special purpose served by specifying the centre of 'the tradition'. Or a leading motif from within the christian tradition (such as the trinity, *sola gratia*, the kingdom of God, the *kenosis* of the christ, etc.) might be employed as the fundamental principle from which a systematic theology or even a new religious movement is generated. Or again, in the face of an uncommonly forceful attempt to subvert christianity to other than religious ends, one might wish emphatically to reaffirm certain central doctrines which seem under threat. So there might be numerous 'special purposes'. Nor is there any compelling reason why these 'purposes' should not be served *so long as one realises that what one is doing when drawing such boundaries is quite different from what one does when describing christianity or the christian tradition in an 'objective' way.*

The distinction between the two sorts of activity is not infrequently blurred, if not confused altogether, in theological discussion, even among those who lay great stress on 'the tradition' or 'the essence of christianity'. Although he purported to be engaged only in the latter sort of exercise (i. e., describing objectively), Harnack for instance was in fact more nearly involved in the former, more normative sort when in Das Wesen des Christentums he marched his undoubtedly obedient students Sherman-like through the history of christianity. The difference between these two ways of speaking about 'christianity' is more cleanly drawn by Troeltsch in his analysis of the concept 'essence of christianity'.[116] It is to be regretted that Tillich seems not fully to have appreciated the enormous importance that analysis had for any subsequent attempt to determine what makes christianity (or christian theology) christian, the result being that in this respect if no other Tillich stands nearer Harnack than Troeltsch, despite his sometimes trenchant criticisms of the former.

As we have seen earlier in this chapter, problematic as it is, the kerygmatic symbol 'Jesus as the Christ' is proposed by Tillich as the criterion against which all theologies should be measured in order to determine whether they are to be classified as christian theologies. I suggested in an earlier chapter that this symbol becomes for Tillich the principle of interpretation by means of which he seeks to give a definite shape to the christian tradition. By its use, he draws boundaries for a special purpose. Nor is it a purpose which need be disallowed. Even so, Tillich does nonetheless claim more for this symbol — a symbol which he sometimes equates with 'the content of the christian message' — than is warranted by the history of christian theology and in so doing he makes a mistake similar to that which Harnack had made. Tillich looks for that which makes christian theology christian in that which all christian theologies are said to have in common.

---

[116] Repr. *Gesammelte Schriften*, vol. II (Tübingen, 1913), 386—451.

In advocating such a procedure, Tillich — like Harnack — in effect confuses the purely descriptive task of the historian (and the Wittgensteinian philosopher?) and the more strictly normative task of the theologian. And he thereby confuses the hermeneutical principle adopted in his latter capacity with that which makes instances of christian theology instances of christian theology. It may be the hermeneutical principle adopted which makes a given christian theology the particular christian theology it is, but it is the complex structure of inter-relations between it and the others which makes a given theology a christian theology.

The other two points may be stated more briefly. Second, family resemblance analysis would not require one to seek the basis for the unity of the christian tradition in the lowest common denominator of all its aspects, in that which all its instances share 'in common'. Seeing christian theology as a family resemblance concept would allow one to view christian theology in its full complexity, both historical and linguistic. And it would allow one to assimilate into one's conception of 'the christian tradition' even those diverse elements which are self-contradictory and mutually exclusive — including for instance the various senses in which the symbol 'Jesus as the christ' has been used in christian theologies. In a family resemblance analysis of instances of christian theology, the 'network' of relations as such would become the basis for its unity and integrity. And what is true for theology is also true of the christian religion considered in all its aspects, a point supported above in the chapters on religion and culture.

Third, family resemblance analysis would allow one to do greater justice to the evident development within the christian theological tradition and to its ability to assimilate within itself elements of genuine novelty — whether derived from secular or from other religious sources — but in such a way that its own integrity is not threatened nor its own autonomy undermined. And it would allow one so to do by eliminating the need for an 'unchanging content' as the basis for the autonomy and integrity of theology.

Conclusion: The Dilemma Resolved?

It may be suggested in conclusion that treating 'christian theology' as a family resemblance concept would allow one to do justice to the undoubtedly legitimate *motives* which led Tillich to formulate the concept of correlation but to do so without being restricted to the demonstrably inadequate and self-defeating *means* he himself employed. Tillich's concept of correlation could be regarded as contributing to the resolution of Schleiermacher's dilemma if and only if the two conditions of correlationship were both fulfilled, that is, if and only if it enabled one to establish between christianity and culture a relationship in which there could be a genuine and thorough-going reciprocity which would threaten the autonomy neither of religion nor of culture. In order to protect the autonomy of christian theology from cultural assimilation, thereby fulfilling one of the two conditions of correlationship, Tillich exempted the 'content' of the christian message (by which he meant that which all christian theologies have in common in virtue of which they are christian theologies) from any sort of cultural influence. But, that being the case, Tillich in effect violated the other condition of a correlative relationship between religion and culture, namely, the reciprocity condition.

As it stands, therefore, Tillich's concept of correlation does not contribute to the resolution of the dilemma set by Schleiermacher.

But, family resemblance analysis would allow one to reformulate his concept of correlation in such a way that both the requisite conditions were fulfilled. By eliminating the need to posit an 'unchanging content', even a vaguely defined and elusive one, as the means of protecting the self-identity of christian theology in the face of the threat of total assimilation into 'die gegenwärtige, geistige Lage', family resemblance analysis would allow a correlative relationship between religion and culture to be dialectical in the full sense of 'reciprocal'. Yet, it would do so in such a way that the autonomy of each would be preserved, in the sense that neither would be reduced to the other. Each would remain in some sense 'self-directed'.

Not that this 'solution' would simply remove the problem of the self-identity of christian theology through history and across cultures. The notion of self-identity is more, rather than less, complex within the framework of a family-resemblance approach. One could specify no single property ' in common' in virtue of which instances of theology might be regarded as instances of christian theology. One could form no generalisations. One could only proceed case by case, tracing the criss-crossings and overlappings which exhibit the unity of the individual instances. This approach would afford no short-cuts. Nor would it offer guarantees against possibly illicit 'correlations' between aspects of christianity and aspects of culture.

One could only look and see.

APPENDICES

APPENDIX 1

SYSTEMATISCHE THEOLOGIE (1913)

Tillich's first known sketch of a systematic theology was composed in December 1913. No complete manuscript of that sketch seems to have survived, although the Tillich-Archiv has a copy of Tillich's outline of the main points covered in his 1913 systematic theology. This outline includes the titles of the seventy-two propositions, but not the propositions themselves. For them we are dependent upon a transcript of the 1913 sketch made by Tillich's close friend Carl Richard Wegener shortly before Tillich reported for military duty in 1914. There are good grounds for accepting Wegener's transcription as being reasonably reliable. It varies only in small detail from the outline by Tillich which is extant. All such variations are enclosed below in ⌐ ¬ and are explained in footnotes. Wegener added a few words to propositions 35 and 36. But, his having enclosed his additions in square brackets suggests a carefulness which gives added credence to his transcription. Wegener copies each proposition on a separate page, thereby allowing himself ample space to raise queries or make comments of his own. Such additions are generally in a different colour ink or in pencil and are easily distinguishable from Tillich's propositions. Wegener's comments, which are not reproduced below, seem to have been written at various times. Some cannot have been made before 1919. For instance, to § 32 Wegener adds in round brackets, 's. "Vorsehung", Wilamowitz: Plato I, 597'. The reference is to Ulrich von Wilamowitz-Moellendorff's *Platon*, the first volume of which was entitled 'Leben und Werke' and was published by the Weidmannsche Buchhandlung (Berlin) in 1919.[2] Even if all the comments

---

[1] Wegener had collaborated with Tillich in Berlin in the planning of the so-called 'Vernunft-Abende' and the production of the *Kirchliche Apologetik*. GW. XIII. 34ff; see also pp. 543ff, and OB, 60−1. On the relationship between Tillich and Wegener, see Wilhelm and Marion Pauck, *Paul Tillich: Life and Thought*, vol. I (New York, 1976).

[2] There are other such examples. In his notes to § 1, for instance, Wegener makes reference to 'Simm. LA 109', which I take to be Simmel's *Lebensanschauung*, a volume which appeared in 1918.

were based on conversations with Tillich (which I doubt), they could not be assumed to be based on conversations which transpired before the first world war. One should perhaps err on the side of caution and disregard altogether Wegener's notes.

SYSTEMATISCHE THEOLOGIE

⌜Einleitung: Orientierung über den Stand der Probleme⌝ [3]

ERSTER TEIL (§§ 1–28)

Die Begründung des theologischen Prinzips in dem wissenschaftlichen Prinzip überhaupt. Fundamentaltheologie

I. Der absolute Standpunkt: Intuition (§§ 1–15)
  a. Der systematische Anfang des Denkens

§ 1. *Die Wahrheit*
Prinzip der Wahrheit ist die Wahrheit selber.

§ 2. *Wahrheit und Wahrheitserkenntnis*
In der absoluten Wahrheit sind die Gegensätze: ideell und reell; abstrakt und konkret; formell und material; aufgehoben.

§ 3. *Das Denken*
Der absoluten Wahrheit steht gegenüber die absolute Identität von Denken und Wahrheit als Prinzip des Denkens.

  b. Die systematische Entwicklung des Denkens

§ 4. *Prinzip und System*
Das Prinzip, als lebendiges betrachtet, ist System.

§ 5. *Der Begriff*
Die lebendige Einheit einer bestimmten Mannigfaltigkeit ist der Begriff. Insofern das Denken den lebendigen Begriff setzt, ist es Intuition.

§ 6. *Das Unbegreifliche*
Das Unbegreifliche ist der Begriff, er ist sich selbst Voraussetzung und Grenze.

---

[3] Appears in Tillich's outline, but not in Wegener's transcription.

c. Das vollendete System
i. Die Organisation des Systems der Wissenschaften

§ 7. Natur und Geist

Das System der Wissenschaften ist der Inbegriff aller möglichen Stellungen des Denkens zur Wahrheit; seine Organisation ist gegeben durch die beiden Grundverhältnisse des Denkens zur Wahrheit: Natur und Geist.

§ 8. Der Mensch und die Freiheit

Der Mensch ist das Gleichgewicht von Natur und Geist – oder die Freiheit.

§ 9. Die Philosophie des Geistes

Die Philosophie des Geistes ist das System aller Stellungen des Geistes zur Natur.

Entsprechend den Grundstellungen des Geistes zur Natur gliedert sich das System der Geistesphilosophie in Kultur-, Moral- und Religionsphilosophie.

Die Geistesphilosophie enthält drei Momente: sie ist immer zugleich phänomenologisch, historisch und normativ, gemäß der Bewegung des Begriffs vom Allgemeinen durch das Bestimmte zum Vollkommenen.

ii. Die Religionsphilosophie

§ 10. Religionsbegriff und Gottesbegriff

Die Religionsphilosophie ist derjenige Teil der Geistesphilosophie, in welchem der Geist sich der absoluten Wahrheit gegenüber zugleich als Geist bestimmt und aufhebt, d. h. in welcher der Geist die absolute Wahrheit als Gott anschaut. Gott ist das Absolute vom Standpunkt des Geistes, der als religiöser sein dialektisches Verhältnis zur Wahrheit durchschaut hat. Daraus ergibt sich für die Religion, daß sie zugleich Bewußtsein der Freiheit dem Absoluten gegenüber und Gebundenheit an das Absolute ist; und für den Gottesbegriff, daß Gott persönlich ist, wie der Geist, der in persönliche Beziehung zu ihm tritt, daß Gott das persönlich gewordene Absolute ist.

§ 11. Die wissenschaftliche Begründung des Gottesgedankens

Die wissenschaftliche Begründung des Gottesgedankens ist identisch mit der Ableitung des religionsphilosophischen Prinzips aus dem wissenschaftlichen Prinzip überhaupt.

§ 12. Religion, Sittlichkeit und Kultur

Die *Kultur* ist der Inbegriff aller auf das Gegebene gerichteten Geistesfunktionen. Das *Sittliche* ist demgemäß nicht eine Funktion des

Geistes neben anderen, sondern das Bewußtsein um den absoluten Wert des Kulturorganismus für den individuellen Geist. Die *Religion* aber bewirkt einerseits – insofern sie als Freiheitsbewußtsein Gott wie einem bestimmten Gegebenen gegenübersteht – eine eigentümliche religiöse Kultur, andererseits – insofern sie als Abhängigkeitsbewußtsein alles Gegebene Gott gegenüber aufhebt – ein Bewußtsein über den negativen Charakter alles Handelns dem Absoluten gegenüber. Die Einheit des absoluten sittlichen Wertbewußtseins und des religiösen Relativitätsbewußtseins alles kulturellen Tuns ergibt die subjektive *Religiosität*.

§ *13. Die konkrete Religion und das Heilige*
Aus der Verbindung des religiösen Prinzips mit einer bestimmten Kulturstufe zu einer eigentümlichen religiösen Kultur entsteht die konkrete Religion.

Sie ist konkret, insofern sie Gott in konkreten Formen und Handlungen vorstellt, d. h. eine bestimmte Mythologie bildet und die Gegenwart Gottes in konkreten Gegenständen aus Natur und Geschichte erlebt, d. h. bestimmte Objekte für heilig erklärt. Die Bejahung einer konkreten Mythologie und die Anerkennung bestimmter Objekte als heilig ist der Glaube oder die konkrete religiöse Funktion.

§ *14. Das Idealreich und die absolute Religion*
Wie am Ende des Naturprozesses der Mensch als vollendetes Naturwesen steht, so steht am Ende des Geschichtsprozesses der vollkommene Zustand, das Idealreich. Im Idealreich ist also auch die Religionsgeschichte zu ihrem Ziel gelangt: die absolute Religion ist verwirklicht.

§ *15. Das absolute System und die Mystik*
Insofern das vollendete System die Aufhebung aller Gegensätze bedeutet, ist es absolute Mystik.

II. Der relative Standpunkt: Reflexion (§§ 16–21)

§ *16. Die Reflexion*
Dem absoluten Standpunkt steht gegenüber der Standpunkt der Relativität oder Reflexion, d. h. derjenige Standpunkt, für den die Einheit des absoluten Systems aufgehoben ist und der Widerspruch herrscht.

§ *17. Der Kampf der Methoden und die Skepsis*
Mit dem absoluten System zerfällt die absolute Methode. Es erhebt sich der Kampf der *Induktion* gegen die *Deduktion*. Da aber keine für sich die

Wahrheit erreichen kann, so ist der prinzipielle *Zweifel* das Resultat dieses Kampfes.

§ *18. Optimismus und Pessimismus*[4]

Die negative Durchsetzung des absoluten Standpunktes gegen die Selbstbehauptung des Individuellen ist das Sterben des Einzelnen in der Natur und die Auflösung der Einheit des Geistes.

§ *19. Die Selbstzerstörung der Kultur*[5]

§ *20. Die Auflösung der Religion*

§ *21. Die Katastrophe der Mystik*

III. Der theologische Standpunkt: Das Paradox (§§ 22−28)

a. Das abstrakte Moment des theologischen Prinzips: Rechtfertigung

§ *22. Das Paradox*

Der absolute und der relative Standpunkt stehen so einander gegenüber, daß der relative von dem absoluten zugleich getragen und zerstört wird. Dieser Widerspruch verlangt um der Absolutheit des absoluten Standpunktes willen eine Überwindung; denn nur darin kann er sich als absolut erweisen, daß er seinen Widerspruch nicht ins Unendliche zugleich schafft und vernichtet, sondern dadurch, daß er ihn positiv in sich aufnimmt, ohne ihn doch seiner dialektischen Selbständigkeit zu berauben. Der absolute Standpunkt muß sich also unbeschadet seiner Absolutheit zu dem relativen herablassen und ihn zu sich erheben. Die Intuition muß in die Sphäre der Reflexion, der Einzelheit, des Widerspruchs eingehen, um die Reflexion durch sich selbst hinauszuführen. Dieses Verhältnis aber ist das Paradox.

§ *23. Das theologische Prinzip*[6]

§ *24. Die Rechtfertigung*

Das Urteil Gottes, durch das ein bestimmter Einzelstandpunkt zugleich absolut verneint und absolut bejaht wird, ist die Rechtfertigung; insofern dies Urteil absolut und ohne Veraussetzung in dem Beurteilten geschieht, ist es Prädestination.

---

[4] The words 'Leiden und Tod' are crossed through in Tillich's handwritten outline and replaced (Tillich?) by 'Optimismus und Pessimismus', the words which appear in Wegener's copy.

[5] Propositions 19−21 are missing in Wegener's transcription.

[6] Missing in Wegener's draft.

b. Das konkrete Moment des theologischen Prinzips: Jesus Christus

§ 25. *Glaube und Geschichte*

Das Urteil, daß in Jesus von Nazareth das Absolute sich herabgelassen hat zum Relativen und das Relative zurückgekehrt (ist) zum Absoluten, ist der Inhalt des konkreten Moments des theologischen Prinzips. In diesem Urteil ist naturgemäß ein geschichtliches und ein Glaubensurteil verbunden.

§ 26. *Die historische Theologie*

Die Verknüpfung des theologischen Prinzips mit einem bestimmten historischen Urteil macht die Begründung dieses Urteils durch eine spezielle historische Theologie notwendig.

Entsprechend den drei Abschnitten des in Christus begründeten Geschichtsverlaufes gliedert sich die historische Theologie in alttestamentliche, neutestamentliche und kirchengeschichtliche Wissenschaft.

§ 27. *Die Quellen der Dogmatik*[7]

c. Das absolute Moment des theologischen Prinzips: ⌜Die Vollendung⌝[8]

§ 28. *Die Vollendung*

Der Gegensatz von abstraktem und konkretem Moment des theologischen Prinzips ist aufgehoben im absoluten. Insofern jedoch der theologische Standpunkt dem absoluten gegenübersteht, ist das absolute Moment nicht als realisiert gesetzt, sondern als im Begriff realisiert zu werden; es ist das Moment der Selbstaufhebung des theologischen Standpunktes und seiner Rückkehr zum absoluten.

ZWEITER TEIL (§§ 29–49)

Die Entfaltung des theologischen Prinzips zu einem System religiöser Erkenntnis. Dogmatik

I. Der Hervorgang der Welt aus Gott bis zum vollendeten Widerspruch[9] (§§ 29–36)

a. Gott und die Welt (Allmacht und Liebe)

---

[7] Missing in Wegener's copy.
[8] These words do not appear in Tillich's handwritten outline.
[9] In Tillich's outline, the words '(Gott der Vater)' follow.

Appendix 1: Systematische Theologie (1913)

§ 29. *Der lebendige Gott (Trinität)*
Gott ist der lebendige: er ist die Einheit der unendlichen Mannigfaltigkeit.

§ 30. *Der allmächtige Gott (Schöpfung)*
Der Inbegriff alles Einzelnen als Einzelnes ist die Welt. Insofern Gott das Einzelne im Unterschied von sich setzt, ist er der allmächtige Schöpfer, insofern das Einzelne schlechthin gebunden bleibt an Gott, ist er der allmächtige Herr.

§ 31. *Die freie Liebe Gottes (Der Mensch)*
Der Mensch ist dasjenige Einzelwesen, in dem die konkrete Einheit des göttlichen Lebens vollkommen zur Darstellung kommt. Dadurch ist er Abbild Gottes des Sohnes und Gegenstand der freien göttlichen Liebe.

Insofern der Mensch Einzelwesen ist, steht er in den Formen der Einzelheit, ist unfrei; insofern der Mensch absolutes Einzelwesen ist, erhebt er sich über die Formen der Einzelheit, ist frei.

§ 32. *Die allmächtige Liebe Gottes (Vorsehung)*
Während die freie Liebe Gottes dem Menschen Freiheit gibt, sich auch gegen die Liebe Gottes zu behaupten, führt die allmächtige Liebe Gottes über den Gegensatz der Einzelwesen hinaus ihren Weltplan zur Vollendung: die Verwirklichung des Reiches Gottes. Dieses Tun ist die göttliche Vorsehung.

b. Gott und die Sünde (Heiligkeit und Zorn)

§ 33. *Der heilige Gott und die Sünde*
Sünde ist die Selbstbehauptung des Einzelwesens als Einzelwesen und die Ablehnung der Gemeinschaft der göttlichen Liebe. Dem Sünder gegenüber wird die allmächtige Liebe Gottes zur heiligen Liebe, die den Sünder zugleich verneint und bejaht.

§ 34. *Die Sündhaftigkeit und der Zorn Gottes*
Die Einsicht, daß für den theologischen Standpunkt die Sünde schon immer Voraussetzung ist, führt zur Anerkennung eines allgemeinen Zustandes der Sündhaftigkeit, aus dem die Einzelsünde folgt.

Der göttliche Zorn oder das negative Moment der göttlichen Liebe ist in diesem Zustand der Sündhaftigkeit und durch ihn wirksam zur Zerstörung des gottwidrigen Einzelwesens.

c. Gott und die Geschichte (Gerechtigkeit und Gnade)

§ 35. Die Gerechtigkeit Gottes und die Geschichte der Menschheit
In der Geschichte der Menschheit betätigt die heilige Liebe ihr relatives Verhältnis zum Standpunkt der Sündhaftigkeit: sie bejaht den Einzelnen, insofern er in die Einheit des göttlichen Lebens zurückkehrt; sie verneint ihn, insofern er sich selbst im Gegensatz dazu behauptet: [insofern] ist [sie] göttliche Gerechtigkeit.[10]

§ 36. Die Gnade Gottes und die Geschichte der Offenbarung
In der Geschichte der Offenbarung betätigt die heilige Liebe ihr absolutes Verhältnis zu dem Standpunkt der Sündhaftigkeit: sie verneint und bejaht zugleich den Einzelnen absolut, ungeachtet seiner positiven und negativen Relativität: [So] ist [sie] göttliche Gnade.

II. Das Eingehen Gottes in die Welt des Widerspruchs (§§ 37–43)[11]

a. Die Herrlichkeit Jesu Christi (Offenbarung)

§ 37. Die Einheit Gottes und des historischen Jesus
In Jesus von Nazareth ist das theologische Paradox, d. h. die Einheit des Absoluten und Relativen auf dem Boden des Relativen, in einem Einzelwesen verwirklicht. Die Einheit Gottes und des historischen Jesus ist bedingt von Gott aus durch das vollkommene Eingehen des konkreten Momentes Gottes in den Zustand der Sündhaftigkeit, von Jesus aus durch die vollkommene Aufhebung seiner Selbstheit in die Einheit des göttlichen Lebens.

§ 38. ⌐Die Offenbarung der Herrlichkeit des Christus in Jesu Wort und Werk⌐[12]
Jesus offenbart seine gottmenschliche Herrlichkeit durch seine maßgebende Verkündigung und einzigartige Verwirklichung des theologischen Prinzips.

b. Die Niedrigkeit Jesu Christi (Versöhnung)

§ 39. Das Kreuz Christi als Tat der heiligen Liebe
Das Kreuz Christi ist das vollendete Nein und das vollendete Ja zum Standpunkt der Sündhaftigkeit; denn am Kreuz kommt die Sündhaftigkeit

---

[10] The emendations in square brackets in §§ 35–6 are from Wegener.
[11] The words '(Gott der Sohn)' follow in Tillich's handwritten outline.
[12] The following is to be found in Tillich's own outline: 'Die Offenbarung der Herrlichkeit Jesu Christ in seinem Wort und Werk'.

und der Zorn Gottes, zugleich die Gnade Gottes, welche die Schuld trägt, zur Vollendung.

§ 40. *Das stellvertretende Leiden Jesu Christi*[13]

§ 41. *Die Versöhnung der Menschheit mit Gott*
Durch das Kreuz Christi wird der Widerspruch von Gott und Menschheit aufgehoben, die Versöhnung beider begründet.

c. Die Erhöhung Jesu Christi (Wiedergeburt)

§ 42. *Die Auferstehung Christi*
Der Widerspruch der Herrlichkeit Jesu mit seiner Niedrigkeit wird aufgehoben durch seine Erhöhung. Als der, welcher den Standpunkt der Einzelheit überwunden hat, hat er auch die Vernichtung der Einzelheit, den Tod, überwunden und kehrt zurück in die Einheit mit Gott. Die Form, in der die Überwindung des Todes vorgestellt wird, ist systematisch gleichgültig.

§ 43. *Die Wiedergeburt oder Erlösung*[14]

III. Die Rückkehr der Welt zu Gott
bis ⌜zur⌝ vollendeten Einheit (§§ 44–49)[15]
a. Die Rückkehr der Menschheit zu Gott (Soteriologie)

§ 44. *Die Einheit Gottes und des erhöhten Christus*
Durch die Erhöhung Christi ist die Spannung überwunden, in der sich die Einheit Gottes und des historischen Jesus verwirklichte und deren Vollendung das Kreuz war. Dennoch ist nicht die unmittelbare Einheit des ewigen göttlichen Lebens gesetzt, sondern in die Einheit ist das Moment der Einzelheit als selbständiges mitaufgenommen: Christus bleibt Mensch auch als Erhöhter und führt durch den Geist die Menschheit zurück zu Gott [Trinität].[16]

---

[13] Proposition missing in Wegener's transcription.
[14] Proposition missing in Wegener's copy.
[15] Rather than 'zur', one finds 'zu der' in Tillich's outline. In addition, the words '(Gott der Geist)' complete the heading.
[16] The word 'Trinität' appears in square brackets and is, therfore, probably an emendation by Wegener.

§ 45. Die Einheit der Menschheit in dem erhöhten Christus[17]

Die Überwindung des Zustandes der Sündhaftigkeit, die durch das Eingehen Gottes in diesen Zustand prinzipiell geschehen ist, verwirklicht sich durch die Vereinigung der Menschheit mit dem erhöhten Christus in einem Organismus, dessen Lebensprinzip der von Christus ausgehende Heilige Geist ist (Kirche). Die Wirkung des Heiligen Geistes ist vermittelt durch die Botschaft von der Gnade Gottes in Christo (das heilige Wort) und die Anschauung dieser Gnade in der heiligen Handlung (Sakrament).

§ 46. Kirchengeschichte und Weltgeschichte
(Grundlegung der theologischen Ethik)

Während in der Kirchengeschichte das theologische Prinzip eingeht in alle Seiten des Reflexionsstandpunktes, bewegen sich in der Weltgeschichte alle Seiten des Reflexionsstandpunktes auf das theologische Prinzip hin. Beide Bewegungen beeinflussen sich wechselseitig, kommen aber, als auf dem Boden der Relativität stehend, ins Unendliche zu keiner absoluten Einheit.

b. Die Rückkehr der Natur zu Gott (Eschatologie)

§ 47. Die Aufhebung des Standes der Sündhaftigkeit (Das Ende)

Die Aufhebung des Standes der Sündhaftigkeit ist bedingt durch die Rückkehr der Natur, als der Grundlage aller Einzelheit, zu Gott. Dieselbe geschieht durch das Sterben der Naturwesen während des Naturprozesses und erreicht ihre Vollendung mit der Erschöpfung aller in der Natur liegenden Möglichkeiten zu neuer Produktion.

§ 48. Die Vollendung der Einzelpersönlichkeit (Auferstehung und Gericht)

Durch die Menschwerdung und Erhöhung des Sohnes Gottes hat die Einzelpersönlichkeit als Einzelpersönlichkeit eine ewige Bejahung in Gott erlangt; dementsprechend bedeutet das Sterben für sie nicht Aufhebung, sondern Vollendung. Doch ist das Werk der Vollendung abhängig von dem Maß, in dem der Einzelmensch sich über den Zustand der Sündhaftigkeit erhoben hat, nicht aber von einem bestimmten Weg dieser Erhebung.

c. ⌐Der absolute Zustand (Reich Gottes)⌐ [18]

§ 49. Das ewige Leben (Trinität)

Das ewige Leben ist die ewige Gemeinschaft des Einzelnen untereinander

---

[17] The term '(Kirche)' follows in Tillich's manuscript.
[18] The entire heading is missing from Tillich's handwritten outline.

und mit Christus in der Einheit mit Gott. Es ist der absolute Zustand, verwirklicht als Reich Gottes: die ewige Einheit der Mannigfaltigkeit, verwirklicht in Freiheit und Liebe.

DRITTER TEIL (§§ 50–72)
Die Anwendung des theologischen Prinzips auf das Geistesleben der Menschheit. Theologische Ethik

 I. Die Anwendung des theologischen Prinzips auf das religiöse Leben
(§§ 50–56)
  a. Das objektiv-religiöse Leben: die Kirchen
   § 50. Die Kirche und die Kirchen
Die Kirche wird durch Verbindung mit dem geschichtlichen Leben Einzelkirche.
 Die Einzelkirche ist in dem Maße eine adäquate Darstellung der Kirche, in welchem das theologische Prinzip in ihr wirksam ist.

   § 51. Das kirchliche Leben und das kirchliche Amt
Das Leben der Kirchen hat seinen Grund in der Verkündigung der göttlichen Gnade durch Wort und Sakrament, sein Ziel in der Darstellung der Kirche Christi durch die Gemeinschaft ihrer Glieder untereinander und mit Christus, seine Organe grundlegend in den Trägern des geistlichen Amts, dann auch in allen, die sich in den Dienst des kirchlichen Lebens stellen.

   § 52. Kirchliche und weltliche Organisation
Dem Verhältnis von Kultur und Geistesleben entsprechend hat jede Kirche die Tendenz, mit den gesellschaftlichen Organisationen Synthesen einzugehen. Dem Verhältnis von theologischem Prinzip und Religion entsprechend ist die Kirche prinzipiell frei von jeder Synthese dieser Art und hat sie aufzuheben, wo die Absolutheit des theologischen Prinzips durch sie verdeckt wird.

  b. Das subjektiv-religiöse Leben: die Frömmigkeit
   § 53. Die Entstehung der christlichen Frömmigkeit: Bekehrung
Die subjektive Teilnahme an der Kirche ist ihrer Entstehung nach betrachtet Abkehr von der Sphäre der Sündhaftigkeit (Buße) und Hinkehr zu Gott (Glaube). Entsprechend dem theologischen Prinzip handelt es sich dabei aber

nicht um zwei aufeinanderfolgende Akte, sondern um einen einheitlichen (Bekehrung), in welchem beide Seiten sich gegenseitig bedingen. Eine zeitliche Fixierung des Bekehrungsaktes widerspricht dem Rechtfertigungsgedanken.

§ 54. *Die Entwicklung der christlichen Frömmigkeit: Heiligung*
Was in der Bekehrung als grundsätzliche Tat erscheint, wird in der Heiligung als Entwicklung betrachtet: als fortschreitende Loslösung von der Sündhaftigkeit und immer innigere Vereinigung mit Gott; während jedoch die Bekehrung als prinzipieller Akt das absolute Moment in der christlichen Frömmigkeit ist, bleibt die Heiligung immer relativ, entsprechend der Voraussetzung des Paradox.

§ 55. *Die Gestaltungen der christlichen Frömmigkeit: Individualisierung*
Entsprechend dem Gegensatz von abstraktem und konkretem Moment im theologischen Prinzip gestaltet sich die christliche Frömmigkeit entweder von dem einen oder von dem andern Moment aus: beide Formen sind gleichberechtigt, können aber nur so lange als christlich gelten, als sie sich nicht in exklusiven Gegensatz zu dem andern Moment stellen, sondern ihn implicite in sich tragen. Eine absolute Form der Frömmigkeit ist niemals möglich.

c. Die subjektiv-objektive Form des religiösen Lebens: ⌈Kultus⌉ [19](Dogma)

§ 56. *Der Kultus*
Die Religion als Aktualität ist Kultus (Gottesdienst). Die Grundformen des Kultus sind Gebet und Andacht. Im Gebet wird der Einzelne vor Gott gebracht, in der Andacht wird die Gegenwart Gottes im Einzelnen und über allen Einzelnen angeschaut; im Kultus der Gemeinde verbinden sich Gebet und Andacht zum öffentlichen Gottesdienst, in dem die Gemeinde ihren Besitz zugleich darstellt und erneuert (Bekenntnis und Erbauung).

II. Die Anwendung des theologischen Prinzips auf das sittliche Leben
(§§ 57–67)

a. Die Erhebung der sittlichen Persönlichkeit über das Unmittelbare
(das absolut Sittliche)

§ 57. *Das sittliche Prinzip: Autonomie und Heteronomie*
Während die konkret-heteronomen Erklärungen des Sittlichen die Absolutheit der sittlichen Kategorien zerstören, wird die abstrakt-autonome

---

[19] The word 'Kultus' does not appear in Tillich's manuscript.

Erklärung durch die Relativität der sittlichen Urteile unmöglich gemacht. Die spekulative Synthese, nach der das Sittliche Selbstbestimmung der Freiheit ist, zerfällt vor der Kritik der Reflexion in ihre beiden Elemente. Durch das theologische Prinzip wird das Sittliche als die Einheit von Freiheit und Liebe im Paradox begriffen.

§ 58. Das sittliche Handeln: Gesetzesmoral und ⌈Persönlichkeitsmoral⌉[20]
Aus dem Gegensatz von abstrakt und konkret ergibt sich für den Reflexionsstandpunkt bezüglich der Form des sittlichen Handelns der Gegensatz von Gesetzesethik und Persönlichkeitsethik. Beides ist unmöglich, denn das Gesetz bleibt dem Willen fremd und der relativen Persönlichkeit steht die sittliche Norm gegenüber. Durch das theologische Paradox wird aus der Gesetzesethik Ethik der Gnade und aus der Persönlichkeitsethik Geistesethik und damit die Einheit beider gesetzt.

§ 59. Die sittliche Bildung: Asketismus und Ästhetizismus
Für die Frage nach der sittlichen Bildung ergibt sich aus der abstrakten Betrachtungsweise die Forderung, alles Relative zu verneinen und sich ausschließlich dem Absoluten hinzugeben (Askese); aus der konkreten Betrachtungsweise die Forderung, alles Relative zu bejahen, ohne sich Einem absolut hinzugeben (Ästhetizismus). Aber die Askese gibt nicht die Freiheit und der Ästhetizismus verhindert die Liebe.

Die Einheit des Ja und Nein im theologischen Paradox stellt die Aufgabe, für alles Relative vom Absoluten aus zugleich ein Nein (Freiheit) und ein Ja (Liebe) zu haben.

§ 60. Die Grenzen der sittlichen Persönlichkeit und die sittliche Liebe
Wo das sittliche Streben ausschließlich auf die Bildung der sittlichen Persönlichkeit gerichtet ist und auch die Liebe Mittel zu sittlichen Vollendung wird, entsteht die egozentrische Verkehrung der Ethik. Davon kann nur diejenige Liebe befreien, die auch in sittlicher Beziehung nicht sich, sondern den anderen sucht.

b. Die Rückkehr der sittlichen Persönlichkeit in das Unmittelbare
(das konkret Sittliche)

§ 61. Die natürliche Gemeinschaft: Familie
Das sittliche Problem der Familie ist in dem Gegensatz von natürlicher

---

[20] The word 'Geistesmoral' is crossed through and replaced by 'Persönlichkeitsmoral' in Tillich's handwritten outline.

Gebundenheit und geistiger Selbständigkeit des Einzelnen der Familie gegenüber begründet.

Die Lösung des Problems liegt in der Einheit der erziehenden und unbedingt verzeihenden Liebe.

§ 62. *Die rechtliche Gemeinschaft: Staat*

Das sittliche Problem des Staates ist in dem Gegensatz von sittlicher Naturordnung, die der Staat in sich verkörpert, und sittlicher Freiheit des Einzelnen begründet.

Die Lösung des Problems liegt in der Einheit von wirkendem und leidendem Verhalten des Einzelnen dem Staate gegenüber.

§ 63. *Die soziale Gemeinschaft: Gesellschaft*

Das sittliche Problem der Gesellschaft liegt in der Aufgabe begründet, den relativen gesellschaftlichen Beziehungen einen absoluten Gehalt zu geben.

Gelöst wird das Problem durch die wirksame Anerkennung der absoluten sittlichen Würde einer jeden Persönlichkeit ohne Aufhebung der Relativität der gesellschaftlichen Beziehung.

§ 64. *Die religiöse Gemeinschaft: Kirche*

Das sittliche Problem der Kirche für den Einzelnen ist in dem Gegensatz von objektiver und subjektiver Religiosität (Kirchlichkeit und Frömmigkeit) begründet.

Gelöst wird das Problem durch die Einheit von Kritik und lebendiger Anteilnahme am kirchlichen Leben oder von Wahrhaftigkeit und tragender Liebe, wie sie möglich ist durch die Einheit von Absolutem und Relativem im theologischen Prinzip.

§ 65. *Die geistige Gemeinschaft: Freundschaft*

Das sittliche Problem der Freundschaft ist in dem Gegensatz von unmittelbarer Sympathie und bewußter geistiger Gemeinschaft begründet.

Die Lösung des Problems liegt in der religiös begründeten Treue als Einheit von Erinnerung und Erwartung; diese Einheit ist [nämlich][21] unzerstörbar allein durch die gemeinsame Beziehung auf Gott.

§ 66. *Die vollkommene Gemeinschaft: Ehe*

Voraussetzung der Ehe ist die Lösung des sexuellen Problems im Sinne des monogamischen Prinzips.

---

[21] The word 'nämlich' was added to the text by Wegener.

Das sittliche Problem der Ehe ist die Absolutheit der Gemeinschaft zwischen zwei relativen Persönlichkeiten.

Gelöst wird das Problem durch die Paradoxie des Vertrauens als Einheit von Glaube, Liebe und Hoffnung, entsprechend den drei Momenten des theologischen Prinzips.

§ 67. Die Grenzen der sittlichen Gemeinschaft und die sittliche Wahrhaftigkeit

Wo das sittliche Streben ausschließlich auf die Teilnahme an der sittlichen Gemeinschaft gerichtet ist und diesem Ziel die Selbständigkeit der sittlichen Persönlichkeit geopfert wird, entsteht die Ethik der Unwahrhaftigkeit. Davon kann nur diejenige Wahrhaftigkeit befreien, die nach Analogie des Rechtfertigungsurteils gebildet ist und trotz aller Relativität die absoluten Kategorien anwendet.

III. Die Anwendung des theologischen Prinzips auf das kulturelle Leben (§§ 68–72)

§ 68. Technik und Reich Gottes

Die dialektische Not der sachlichen Kultur ist die Knechtung des Geistes an die Welt durch Beherrschung der Welt.

Das theologische Prinzip rechtfertigt die sachliche Kulturarbeit (Technik), indem es die Offenbarung Gottes in ihr anschaut, sie in den Dienst des Reiches Gottes stellt und ihre ewige Bedeutung für das vollendete Gottesreich erkennt.

§ 69. Staat und Kirche

Die dialektische Not des Staates ergibt sich aus seinem notwendigen Anspruch, Träger des gesamten Kulturgehaltes zu sein, und seiner Unfähigkeit, aus sich selbst einen Gehalt zu schöpfen. Das theologische Prinzip rechtfertigt den Staat, indem es in ihm das Abbild der Einheit des Gottesreiches bejaht, indem es ihm mittels der Kirche den geistigen Gehalt gibt und die ewige Einheit von Staat und Kirche erkennt.

§ 70. Humanität und Liebe

Die dialektische Not der Humanität ist darin begründet, daß sie persönlich begründeten Mängeln nur mit sachlichen Mitteln abhelfen kann und dadurch dauernd neue Mängel schaffen muß.

Das theologische Prinzip bejaht die Humanität als Kampf gegen die Sündhaftigkeit, bejaht und vertieft sie durch die Liebe und stellt die endliche Einheit von Humanität und Liebe in Aussicht.

§ 71. Kunst und Kultus

Die dialektische Not alles Ästhetischen ist darin begründet, daß die ästhetische Anschauung bei dem Stoffe festhält, in dem sie das Ewige schaut.

Sie wird gerechtfertigt von dem theologischen Prinzip abstrakt als Überwinden des Stoffes, konkret, weil sie Trägerin der Andacht und selbst Andacht werden kann und ihren ewigen Wesen nach dem Kultus gleich Anschauung Gottes in allem Konkreten und über allem Konkreten ist.

§ 72. Wissenschaft und Dogma

Die dialektische Not der Wissenschaft und ihre Erlösung durch das theologische Prinzip ist der Inhalt der gesamten systematischen Theologie. An dieser Stelle tritt das theologische System selbst unter das Paradox, das von ihm begründet und durchgeführt ist. Auch das theologische System ist nicht das absolute System, so wenig wie das System der Wissenschaften, aus dem es hervorgegangen ist und zu dem es wieder zurückkehrt, um den ganzen Kreislauf von neuem zu beginnen.

APPENDIX 2

DIE GESTALT DER RELIGIÖSEN ERKENNTNIS (1927–1928)

Tillich's lectures on religious epistemology at Dresden constitute his second extant sketch of a systematic theology.[1] The propositions which Tillich dictated to his students during the winter semester 1927–8 were typed up, partially corrected by hand, and preserved in two notebooks. The one is named 'Grundlegung' and the other 'Aufbau'. It may be that Tillich had planned eventually to publish a volume based on the lectures. He did, in any case, write out the introduction to the prologue, adding footnotes which suggest that he expected the text to be read by persons other than himself. This introduction is printed first, followed by the propositions available. The footnotes in German are found in Tillich's typescript; those in English are my own.

Einleitung: Sinn und Weg des Prologs

Es soll erst gegangen und dann nach der Möglichkeit des Gehens gefragt und dann wieder gegangen werden. So wird vielleicht vermieden, daß die Methoden die Sachfragen überwuchern. Wird aber zuerst gegangen, so müssen Stücke des Weges benutzt werden, der nachher wieder gegangen wird; diese Stücke erscheinen zweimal. Das zweite Mal in Einheit mit dem Ganzen, das erste Mal als Hinführung zu dem Ort, an dem das Ganze steht. Nicht alle Stücke sind dazu geeignet, sondern nur diejenigen, in denen die schaffende Potenz des Ganzen selbst Gegenstand ist. Die schaffende Potenz des Ganzen aber ist der Mensch, der erkennende, der religiös erkennende Mensch. Er ist, wie alle Wirklichkeit Gegenstand der religiösen Erkenntnis; aber er ist im Unterschied von aller (uns gegebenen) Wirklichkeit auch Träger der religiösen Erkenntnis. Darum ist es angemessen, zweimal von ihm zu reden, einmal in der Sache selbst, und einmal in der Hinführung zur Sache. Denn der religiös erkennende Mensch ist der Ort, an dem die Sache steht, von der geredet werden soll.

[1] See above, chapter one, pp. 25–31.

Doch ist das Reden beide Male verschieden. Das zweite Reden vom Menschen und seiner religiösen Erkenntnis steht im Zusammenhang des Ganzen und hat die methodische Besinnung hinter sich. Das erste Reden ist losgelöst, ohne Voraussetzung und ohne methodischen Zwang. Es ist ein unmittelbares Reden und geschieht vor dem mittelbaren, methodisch geleiteten Reden. Es ist nicht etwa Einleitung zu diesem. Es ist ein Reden von der Sache selbst, aber vor der Sache. Und darum ist es Prolog. ‚Prolog‘ hat mehr von der Sache als ‚Einleitung‘; die Einleitung dient nur, der Prolog ist auch selbständig.

Ein Prolog ist angemessen, wenn die Sache, von der geredet werden soll, keinen festen Ort im Bewußtsein der Hörenden hat. Von vielen Gegenständen kann sofort gesprochen werden: ihr Ort steht fest, sie sind jederzeit zur Hand. Einige Gegenstände aber stehen noch nicht oder nicht mehr zur Hand, so die religiöse Erkenntnis. Ihr Ort muß erst gezeigt werden, muß erst wieder sichtbar werden. Die meisten kirchlichen Dogmatiker selbst der letzten Zeit meinen, daß ihr Gegenstand für die sie Hörenden noch zur Hand wäre, noch einen festen Ort in ihrem Bewußtsein hätte. Das ist nicht mehr oder nur noch in engsten Kreisen der Fall. Bei den weitaus meisten ist der Ort des Gegenstandes ‚religiöse Erkenntnis‘ oder gar ‚Selbstbesinnung der religiösen Erkenntnis‘ das Fragwürdige noch vor jeder inhaltlichen Frage. Dem gibt der Prolog Ausdruck. Nicht als ob er die Fragwürdigkeit mit einem Schlage aufheben könnte. Vielmehr erkennt er sie an, steht selbst in ihr. Der Prolog ist das Bekenntnis des Redenden, daß er nicht außerhalb der Geisteslage seiner Gegenwart steht, daß er mit ihr verbunden ist und an ihrer Fragwürdigkeit mit trägt. Aus ihr heraus aber gibt er Antworten, Hinweise auf den Ort; nicht kategorisch: sondern tastend, vorstoßend, wegsuchend – mit aller sprachlichen und sachlichen Vorläufigkeit, die solche Haltung zur Folge hat. Der Prolog ringt um die Möglichkeit dessen, was nachher als Wirklichkeit ausgebreitet werden soll. Er sucht zu zeigen, daß religiöse Erkenntnis eine menschliche Möglichkeit ist[2], eine Möglichkeit, die so tief wie nur irgend eine, ja tiefer als jede andere, im menschlichen Sein und damit im Sein selbst verwurzelt ist; freilich an dem Punkt, wo das Sein über sich hinausweist auf ein Jenseits seiner selbst, und damit die menschliche Möglichkeit als menschliche aufhebt.

---

[2] Ohne die Einschränkung am Ende dieses Satzes würden diese Worte das Gegenteil der Wahrheit sagen. Das muß bei jeder Polemik gegen den ontologischen Weg berücksichtigt werden.

Appendix 2: Die Gestalt der religiösen Erkenntnis (1927–1928)

Vom Menschen kann auf doppelte Weise geredet werden. Er kann aufgefaßt werden als ein Gegenstand unter anderen Gegenständen, als ein Seiendes unter anderem Seiendem. Es kann das Sinsgebiet aufgewiesen werden, dem er angehört, die allgemeinen Merkmale, die ihm von dort her zukommen, wie die besonderen, die ihn unterscheiden. So kann der Mensch als Lebewesen unter anderen, als seelisches, als soziales, als geschichtliches Wesen betrachtet werden; er kann Gegenstand der Biologie, Psychologie, Soziologie, Ethnologie werden. Jede dieser Betrachtungen kann Wesenserkenntnis des Menschen, kann Anthropologie werden. Aber keine dieser Betrachtungen kann den Ort aufzeigen, an dem religiöse Erkenntnis entspringt. Denn sie alle machen den Menschen zu einem ‚Gegenstand', zu einem durch Gesetze bestimmten Seienden, einem Ding unter Dingen. Sie sind berechtigt dazu, denn das menschliche Sein ist auch durch Dinggesetze bestimmt. Aber sie irren, wenn sie meinen, auf diese Weise den Ort der religiösen Erkenntnis aufweisen zu können. Die Versuche etwa, auf dem Wege der Religionspsychologie an ihn heranzukommen, haben den Zugang zur Sache für Jahrzehnte verschüttet. Und die soziologisch-ethnologischen Bemühungen um das gleiche Ziel haben kein besseres Ergebnis gehabt. Wohl ist Religion, wenn sie ist, bestimmt durch die Gesetze, die jene Wissenschaften erkennen. Aber niemals kann sie aus jenen Gesetzen abgeleitet werden. Ihr Ort im menschlichen Sein wird verfehlt, sobald der Mensch Gegenstandsgesetzen unterworfen wird. Der Ort der Religion ist das vor-gegenständliche Sein des Menschen.

Damit aber erhebt sich eine neue Möglichkeit den Menschen zu betrachten, eine Anthropologie ungegenständlicher Art, ein Versuch das menschliche Sein zu erfassen, nicht wie ein Seiendes unter anderem Seiendem, sondern im Hinblick auf das Sein selbst, als eine, ja als *die* Antwort auf die Frage nach dem Sein. Eine solche Anthropologie könnte man als ontologische Anthropologie neben die wissenschaftliche stellen. Sie fragt, was ist das Sein des Menschen im Hinblick auf das Sein selbst oder (was das gleiche besagt) im Hinblick auf den Sinn des Seins? Wie kommt im Menschen der Sinn des Seins zur Anschauung seiner selbst? Und was bedeutet es für das menschliche Sein, daß in ihm sich der Sinn des Seins erfüllt? Solche Fragen sind einer gegenständlichen Beantwortung nicht zugänglich. Werden sie beantwortet, so spricht in den Antworten das Sein sich selbst aus. Es reflektiert nicht über seine Form, sondern es zeugt von seinem Sinn. Ontologie ist Zeugnis. Sie ist Zeugnis, obgleich ihre Form wissenschaftlich ist. Denn die wissenschaftliche Form ist nicht die produktive

Kraft der Ontologie. Das ist ‚die Ideenschau', die etwas anderes ist als ‚Intuition' oder gar ‚intuitive Methode' (ein höchst bedenklicher Begriff), die vielmehr Sich-Aussprechen des Seins über seinen Sinn ist[3]. Wo aber des Sein seinen Sinn unmittelbar ausspricht, da verlieren die gegenständlichen Begriffe, die mit der wissenschaftlichen Form gegeben sind, ihren eigentlichen, nämlich gegenständlichen Charakter. Sie erhalten mythische Qualität. Ontologie spricht mit wissenschaftlichen Begriffen im Element des Mythos. Daß sie im Element des Mythos lebt, macht ihr die reine Wissenschaft zum Vorwurf. Und auch eine Philosophie, die gegenständliche Erkenntnis des Seienden sein wollte, mußte die Ontologie auszuscheiden versuchen. Wir wissen, daß es ihr nie wirklich gelungen ist; denn die ontologische Anschauung der Dinge ist mit dem Wesen des Menschen unlöslich verknüpft. – Umgekehrt macht die Religion, gelegentlich auch die Kunst, der Ontologie zum Vorwurf, daß sie sich gegenständlicher Begriffe bedient. Aber in einer Zeit gegenständlicher Welt-erfassung und -gestaltung würde die ontologische Aussprache des Seins-Sinnes ihren Ernst einbüßen, bediente sie sich anderer Mittel, als derer, die die Geisteslage zur Verfügung stellt[4]. Darum tritt mit Beginn der wissenschaftlichen Begriffsbildung die Ontologie notwendig aus dem Stadium des ungebrochenen in den des

---

[3] Ohne diese Voraussetzung müßte eine ontologische Theologie wie sie hier und weiterhin versucht wird, unbedingt abgelehnt werden. Der Versuch, an die religiöse Möglichkeit des Menschen durch gegenständliche Wesensschau heranzukommen, muß nicht nur mißlingen, sondern bedeutet die Aufhebung der religiösen Möglichkeit. Denn er bedeutet das Abschneiden der das Religiöse kennzeichnenden Beziehung zum Jenseits des menschlichen Seins.

[4] Den Vorwurf gegen ontologisches Denken in der Theologie, daß es dem Ernst des Religiösen nicht gerecht würde, kann dieses zurückgeben. Es heißt die Gegenwart, den geschichtlichen Augenblick und damit die konkreten Aufgaben nicht ernst nehmen, wenn man in einer Zeit radikal gegenständlicher Denkformung ungebrochen mythische Begriffe als verständlich voraussetzt und ohne Selbstbesinnung über ihre Vernehmbarkeit mit ihnen arbeitet. Das heißt, im Sinne des Pharisäismus ‚den Menschen unerträgliche Lasten auflegen' – Lasten intellektueller Bejahung, die man selbst nicht zu tragen braucht, weil man ihren belastenden Charakter nicht oder – wie es häufiger ist, – nicht mehr merkt. Dieser Versuch trifft die neuere Theologie in weitem Ausmaße. Ihr gegenüber war die ältere jetzt so allseitig abgelehnte liberale Theologie williger, mitzutragen und darin – christlicher.

gebrochenen Mythos⁵. Der Mensch muß sich, wenn er den Sinn seines Seins ausspricht, wenn er zeugt vom Sinn des Seins überhaupt, wenn er also ontologisch redet, der abstrakt gegenständlichen Begriffe bedienen. Aber er kann sich ihrer, wenn er wirklich ontologisch redet, nur bedienen als Ausdruck seines urständlichen, d. h. vorgegenständlichen Seins, also als Mythos. So entsteht notwendig im Sinnleben der Menschheit jenes eigentümliche doppelsinnige Gebilde der Ontologie, das von zwei Seiten bekämpft, scheinbar überwunden, immer neu sich erhebt. Jenes Gebilde, das ein erstaunliches, selten verstandenes Wahrzeichen der Doppelsinnigkeit unseres Daseins ist; derjenigen Gestalt des menschlichen Daseins nämlich, in der über der Tiefe unseres ungegenständlichen Seins sich die Gegenstände greifende und begreifende Rationalität erhebt. Weil dieses aber unser Schicksal ist, darum können wir die Ontologie nicht verbannen, können ihren Doppelsinn nicht in Eindeutigkeit zwingen, wie es die rationale Metaphysik versuchte, der Kant den Garaus gemacht hat⁶.

Auf ontologischem Wege also soll der Ort aufgesucht werden, an dem religiöse Erkenntnis entspringt. Auf ontologische Weise soll vom Menschen geredet werden, nicht auf gegenständlich-wissenschaftliche. Dabei kann es nun geschehen, daß das Reden vom Menschen an einen Punkt gelangt, wo es nicht mehr Reden vom Menschen ist, sondern entweder Schweigen oder Reden vom Jenseits des Menschen. Der Ort, an dem religiöse Erkenntnis entspringt, könnte sich als ein ‚raumloser' Ort herausstellen, als das Jenseits jedes möglichen Ortes. Wenn es so wäre, so wäre die Ontologie zur Theologie geworden, so wäre das Zeugnis vom Sinn des Seins zu einem Zeugnis über das Jenseits von Sein und Sinn geworden. So aber ist es. Die Frage nach dem Sinn des Seins, die der Mensch an sein eigenes Sein stellt, treibt sinngemäß zu der Frage nach dem Jenseits von Sein und Sinn. Antwort auf diese Frage wäre religiöse Erkenntnis; aber solche Antwort liegt nicht im menschlichen Sein, nicht im Sein überhaupt. Sie ist nicht Gegenstand eines ontologischen, sondern, wenn überhaupt eines profetischen Zeugnisses. Der Ontologie bleibt die Aufgabe, bis an diesen Punkt heranzuführen, wo möglicherweise profetisches Zeugnis und damit religiöse Erkenntnis

---

5   Über die Begriffe ‚gebrochener' und ‚ungebrochener Mythos', s. meinen Aufsatz über ‚das religiöse Symbol' in *Blätter für deutsche Philosophie*, Bd. I, Heft 4. und den Artikel ‚Mythos' in *R.G.G.*, zweite Auflage.
6   Über den hier vorausgesetzten Begriff vergl. mein *System der Wissenschaften*. Göttingen 1923, S. 128 u. 153.

entspringt. Sie soll die Anschauung des vorgegenständlichen menschlichen Seins bis zu der Stelle treiben, an der das menschliche Sein über sich hinausweist, die ontologische Frage zur theologischen wird.

Aber der Prolog kann hier nicht stehen bleiben. Denn er soll ja nicht nur von dem möglichen, sondern auch von dem wirklichen Ort religiöser Erkenntnis reden. Er soll nicht nur auf den Ort der Frage sondern auch der Antwort hinführen. Er muß also voraussetzen, daß jene Möglichkeit, auf die das ontologische Zeugnis hinweist, irgendwann und irgendwo Wirklichkeit geworden ist. Und er muß zeigen, wie solche Wirklichkeit aussieht und wie in ihr religiöse Erkenntnis entspringen kann. Er wiederholt nicht profetisches Zeugnis, sondern er beschreibt die Form, in der es erscheint, gleichsam die Ränder des Ortes, der selbst das Jenseits jedes Ortes ist und nicht beschrieben werden kann. Die Beschreibung dieses Randes, an dem das Jenseits des Ortes ‚Ort' wird, an dem das Jenseits des menschlichen Seins menschliches Sein wird, an dem Erkenntnis religiöse Erkenntnis wird — die Beschreibung dieser Stätte der Berührung ist das Ziel des Prologs. Eine solche Beschreibung ist freilich nicht mehr ontologisch. Das Ontologische ist in ihr gebrochen und zum Theologischen geworden. Gegenstand ist nicht das menschliche Sein, sondern das Jenseits des Seins, erscheinend im menschlichen Sein. Daß so etwas möglich ist, muß vorausgesetzt werden. Es kann nicht anders als vorausgesetzt werden. Denn Prolog ist Vorwegnahme, ist Reden von der Sache vor der Sache.

Im Prolog führt der Weg von der Ontologie zur Theologie. In Wahrheit ist das Theologische die Voraussetzung des Ontologischen. Das[s] die Ontologie bis zu dem Punkt führt, wo sich die Frage erhebt nach dem Jenseits des Seins: das ist nur möglich, weil hinter ihr die schon vernommene Antwort steht. Nach dem Jenseits seiner selbst kann der Mensch im Ernst nur fragen, wenn das Jenseits schon gesprochen hat. Dieser Spruch kann abgeklungen sein, aber er wirkt nach in jedem Schritt der Ontologie. Das menschliche Sein so sehen, daß es zu der Frage treibt nach seinem Jenseits, das kann nicht rational erzwungen werden, das ist nur möglich auf dem Boden ursprünglichen Zeugnisses vom Jenseits des Seins. Der methodische Weg des Prologs schlägt also die entgegengesetzte Richtung ein als der sachliche Weg des Lebens. Und das bedeutet: nicht das Theologische gründet sich auf das Ontologische sondern das Ontologische auf das Theologische, wenn auch der Weg der Hinführung notwendig der umgekehrte ist. Denn nicht das Sein, auch nicht das menschliche Sein ist das erste, sondern das Jenseits des Seins.

Appendix 2: Die Gestalt der religiösen Erkenntnis (1927–1928)

BAND EINS: GRUNDLEGUNG

Erster Teil: Hinführung

A. *Prolog: Der Ort der religiösen Erkenntnis*

Einleitung: Sinn und Weg des Prologs

§ 1. Aufgabe des Prologs ist es, den Ort zu zeigen, an dem religiöse Erkenntnis entspringt. Er führt in einer ontologischen Betrachtung des menschlichen Seins bis zu dem Punkt, wo die Frage entsteht nach dem Jenseits des Seins und die Antwort auf diese Frage vernommen werden kann.

I. Das menschliche Sein als Ort der religiösen Frage

1. Die Bedrohung des Seins im menschlichen Sein

§ 2. Das menschliche Sein ist Erhebung des Seins über seine Unmittelbarkeit oder Erhebung des Sinnes des Seins über das bloße Sein.

2. Die Bedrohtheit des menschlichen Seins

§ 3. Mit der Erhebung des Seins über sich selbst im menschlichen Sein steht der Mensch in der Freiheit. Freiheit ist Freiheit des Seins von sich selbst, und damit Möglichkeit des Nichtseins. In dieser Möglichkeit ist die Bedrohtheit der menschlichen Lage begründet.

3. Die Sicherungen des menschlichen Seins

§ 4. Der menschliche Lebensprozeß ist ein ständiges Ringen um Sicherung gegen die Bedrohtheit des menschlichen Seins, gegen die Drohung des Nichtseins. Die Sicherungen können vital oder geistig, und im Geistigen profan oder religiös oder heroisch sein.

4. Die menschliche Grenzsituation

§ 5. Mit dem Zerbrechen jeder durch Freiheit gesetzten Sicherung kommt es zur Erkenntnis der unbedingten Bedrohtheit des menschlichen Seins oder zur menschlichen Grenzsituation.

II. Die Erscheinung des Jenseits des menschlichen Seins als Ort der religiösen Antwort und die religiöse Erkenntnis

1. Das Jenseits von Sein und Freiheit

§ 6. In der menschlichen Grenzsituation erhebt sich die Frage nach einer nicht durch Freiheit gesetzten Sicherung oder nach dem Jenseits von Sein und Freiheit.

2. Die Gestalt der Gnade

§ 7. Das Jenseits von Sein und Freiheit erscheint auf dem Boden des Seins als Gestalt der Gnade. Die Gestalt der Gnade verwirklicht sich in Seinsgestalten als deren transzendentes Bedeuten.

3. Der Wandel in der Gestalt der Gnade

§ 8. Die Gestalt der Gnade ist an keine Seinsgestalt gebunden. Sie ist ausdrücklich gemeint in den religiösen Formen. Sie kann verborgen sein in den profanen Formen. Sie wandelt sich einerseits mit dem Wandel der Seinsgestalten, an denen sie erscheint, andererseits mit der Art und Kraft ihres Erscheinens.

4. Die Erkenntnis aus der Gestalt der Gnade

§ 9. Religiöse Erkenntnis ist Erkenntnis aus der Gestalt der Gnade. Ihr Gegenstand ist das Sein im Hinblick auf das Jenseits des Seins. Sie wandelt sich entsprechend dem Wandel der Gestalt der Gnade, zu der sie gehört.

B. Der Ort der Selbstbesinnung der religiösen Erkenntnis: Einleitung
1. Die Anlässe zur Selbstbesinnung der religiösen Erkenntnis

§ 10. Anlaß zur Selbstbesinnung der religiösen Erkenntnis sind Spannungen in der Gestalt der Gnade und der zu ihr gehörigen Erkenntnis. Solche Spannungen entstehen entweder fremd-religiös durch die Begegnung mit einer fremden Religion oder inner-religiös durch Gegensätze in der eigenen Religion oder außer-religiös durch rationale Kritik und Formschöpfung.

2. Die gegenwärtige Aufgabe der Selbstbesinnung der religiösen Erkenntnis

§ 11. Jede Selbstbesinnung der religiösen Erkenntnis vollzieht sich auf dem Boden einer konkreten Gestalt der Gnade. Das Christentum, der konkrete Ort, der hier versuchten Selbstbesinnung, hat in seiner theologischen Arbeit alle Anlässe zur Selbstbesinnung in sich aufgenommen. Die gegenwärtige Lage der christlichen Theologie zwingt zu einer neuen Durchdenkung ihrer Probleme infolge des Auftretens entscheidender neuer Spannungen in jeder der drei Richtungen.

Appendix 2: Die Gestalt der religiösen Erkenntnis (1927–1928) 277

3. Die Gegenstände der Selbstbesinnung der religiösen Erkenntnis

§ 12. Erster und maßgebender Gegenstand der Selbstbesinnung sind die Inhalte der religiösen Erkenntnis. Zweiter und abgeleiteter Gegenstand der Selbstbesinnung ist das Wesen der religiösen Erkenntnis. Dritter rein formaler Gegenstand der Selbstbesinnung ist das Wesen der Selbstbesinnung selbst.

4. Der Ausgangspunkt der Selbstbesinnung der religiösen Erkenntnis

§ 13. Die Erkenntnisse jeder Stufe der Selbstbesinnung sind in jeder anderen enthalten. Ausgangspunkt und Durchführung richten sich nach dem jeweiligen Arbeitsziel. Sollen die Inhalte der religiösen Erkenntnis dargestellt werden, so ist es zweckmäßig, die beiden anderen Gegenstandsgruppen als Grundlegung zusammenzufassen.

5. Der Name der Selbstbesinnung der religiösen Erkenntnis

§ 14. Die traditionellen Namen für die Arbeit an der Gestalt der religiösen Erkenntnis (insbesondere Dogmatik und Glaubenslehre) sind durch ihre kirchenrechtlichen Belastungen in der gegenwärtigen Lage unbrauchbar. Der Name ‚Gestalt der religiösen Erkenntnis' ist ein Versuch, die Sache symbolkräftig für unsere Lage zum Ausdruck zu bringen.

6. Der Charakter der Selbstbesinnung der religiösen Erkenntnis

§ 15. Die Selbstbesinnung hat einerseits den Charakter der jeweiligen religiösen Erkenntnis, auf der sie ruht. Sie hat andererseits den Charakter der jeweilig zur Verfügung stehenden Methode. Und zwar überwiegt die methodische Seite bei der Betrachtung des Wesens der religiösen Erkenntnis, der konkrete Standort bei der Betrachtung der Gestalt der religiösen Erkenntnis, ohne daß eine Seite von der anderen getrennt werden könnte.

Zweiter Teil: Das Wesen der religiösen Erkenntnis

A. Die Besinnung auf das Wesen der religiösen Erkenntnis

I. Die methodische Haltung der Wesenserkenntnis:
Das Allgemeine und das Einmalige

1. Sache und Wissenschaften von der Sache

§ 16. Die Selbstbesinnung auf das Wesen der religiösen Erkenntnis muß ihren Weg aus der Sache bestimmen ohne Rücksicht auf das gegenseitige Verhältnis der Wissenschaften, die sich der Sache zuwenden; vor allem ohne Rücksicht auf Gegenüberstellungen fixierter Begriffe von Theologie und Philosophie.

2. Das Problem des Allgemeinen in der Selbstbesinnung der religiösen Erkenntnis

§ 17. Das Wesen ‚Religiöse Erkenntnis' vereinigt untrennbar in sich ein abstrakt-allgemeines und ein konkret-einmaliges Element. Das Verhältnis beider Elemente zueinander ist das Grundproblem der Methode der Wesenserkenntnis.

3. Die Grundhaltungen der Wesenserkenntnis

§ 18. Geistige Wesenheiten sind dynamisch in der Existenz, nicht statisch jenseits der Existenz zu erschauen. Ihre Erkenntnis geschieht aus dem konkreten Lebenszusammenhang mit ihnen und hat darum subjektiv den Charakter der Entscheidung, objektiv den Charakter des Schicksals.

4. Wesenserkenntnis und existentielles Erkennen

§ 19. Sofern die konkrete Wesenserkenntnis notwendig mit einer Entscheidung verbunden ist, hat sie existentiellen Charakter, d. h. sie hat die Möglichkeit, eine Entscheidung über Sein und Nichtsein des Erkennenden zu enthalten. Es gibt keinen grundsätzlichen Gegensatz zwischen Wesenserkenntnis und existentieller Erkenntnis, weil es keine Erkenntnis ohne Wesenserfassung gibt.

5. Das Universelle und das Generelle in der Wesenserkenntnis

§ 20. Der Wahrheitsanspruch der konkreten Wesenserkenntnis hat nicht den Charakter des Generellen, sondern den des Universellen. Das Universelle enthält die Einheit des Einmaligen und des Allgemeinen. Sowohl die Versuche des Idealismus, das Einmalige, als auch die Versuche des Nominalismus und der dialektischen Theologie, das Allgemeine auszustoßen, sind abzulehnen; damit fällt der Gegensatz von philosophischer und theologischer Wesenserkenntnis der Religion hin.

II. Der methodische Weg der Wesenserkenntnis: Das Rationale und das Intuitive

1. Das empirische Element der Wesenserkenntnis: Wesenserkenntnis und Religionsgeschichte

§ 21. Das konkrete Wesen ist geschichtliches Wesen. Seine Erfassung setzt ein lebendiges Stehen in der geschichtlichen Verwirklichung des Wesens voraus. Sie kann mit empirisch-historischer Selbsterkenntnis verbunden sein. Der Wesensbegriff aber kann nicht empirisch-historisch gewonnen werden. Die Mischgebilde von historischer und systematischer Betrachtung (Wesen der Religion, Wesen des Christentums als historische Begriffe) sind zu verwerfen.

2. Das intuitive Element der Wesenserkenntnis: Innere und äußere Wesensschau

§ 22. Das konkrete Wesen ist geistiges Wesen. Es wird erfaßt durch innere Selbstanschauung oder schlichtes Sich-aussprechen des menschlichen Seins in einem Sinngebilde. Die konkrete Wesensschau darf weder mit der phänomenologischen noch mit der psychologischen Gegenstandserkenntnis verwechselt werden.

3. Das kritische Element der Wesenserkenntnis: Wesen und Kategorie

§ 23. Das konkrete Wesen ist gültiges Wesen. Seine objektive Erfassung hat notwendigerweise kritischen Charakter. Sie hebt aus dem konkreten Gebilde die formalen Prinzipien heraus und mißt an ihnen die tatsächliche Erscheinung. Die Einheit von Kritik und Intuition ist das methodische Ideal der Wesenserfassung.

III. Die Aufgabe der Wesenserkenntnis im Zusammenhang der Grundlegung

§ 24. Es ist nicht Aufgabe der Grundlegung, ein ausführliches System der Religionsphilosophie zu geben, sondern nur diejenigen Seiten des Wesens Religion und religiöse Erkenntnis zu behandeln, die zur Grundlegung der Selbstbesinnung auf die Gestalt der religiösen Erkenntnis notwendig sind.

B. Entfaltung des Wesens der religiösen Erkenntnis
I. Allgemeine Charakteristik der religiösen Erkenntnis: Theologische Axiomatik

Einleitung: Wesen und Bedeutung einer theologischen Axiomatik

§ 25. Die allgemeine Charakteristik der religiösen Erkenntnis gibt Bestimmungen über das Verhältnis der Erkennenden zu seinem Gegenstand in der religiösen Erkenntnis. Die Sätze, in denen diese Bestimmung zum Ausdruck kommt, haben axiomatischen Charakter für jede religiöse Erkenntnis.

1. Das erste Axiom

§ 26. Religiöse Erkenntnis ist Erkenntnis dessen, was uns unbedingt angeht. Kein Satz enthält religiöse Erkenntnis, der nicht insofern von einer Sache spricht, als sie uns unbedingt angeht.

2. Das zweite Axiom

§ 27. Unbedingt geht uns an, was über unser Sein entscheidet. Kein Satz enthält religiöse Erkenntnis, der nicht insofern von einer Sache spricht, als sie über unser Sein entscheidet.

3. Das dritte Axiom

§ 28. Über unser Sein entscheidet, was die unbedingte Forderung an unser Sein enthält. Kein Satz hat religiöse Erkenntnis, der nicht insofern von einer Sache spricht, als sie die unbedingte Forderung an unser Sein enthält.

4. Das vierte Axiom

§ 29. Die unbedingte Forderung an unser Sein enthält, was die unbedingte Erfüllung für unser Sein enthält. Kein Satz hat religiöse Erkenntnis, der nicht insofern von einer Sache spricht, als sie die unbedingte Erfüllung für unser Sein enthält.

II. Die Grundlage der religiösen Erkenntnis: Theologische Phänomenologie

Einleitung: Die Erscheinung des Seins-Jenseits im Sein als Grund der religiösen Erkenntnis

§ 30. Grundlage der religiösen Erkenntnis ist die Erscheinung des Seins-Jenseits im Sein oder die Erscheinung des uns unbedingt

Angehenden für uns im Sein. (Satz der Notwendigkeit der Offenbarung)

    a. Die Merkmale der Erscheinung des Seins-Jenseits im Sein: Allgemeine Offenbarungslehre

        1. Die Erscheinung im Verhältnis zum Seienden überhaupt

§ 31. Die Erscheinung des Seins-Jenseits im Sein ist weder Vollendung noch Zerstörung der Seinsformen, sondern ihre Erschütterung und Umwendung. (Satz des Wesens der Offenbarung)

        2. Die Erscheinung im Verhältnis zum subjektiven und objektiven Sein

§ 32. Die Erscheinung des Seins-Jenseits im Sein ist nicht Mitteilung von Sachverhalten, sondern reale Vergegenwärtigung. Sie vollzieht sich weder nur im Objekt, noch nur im Subjekt, sondern in der Wechselwirkung beider.

        3. Die Erscheinung im Verhältnis zum natürlichen und geschichtlichen Sein

§ 33. Die Erscheinung des Seins-Jenseits im Sein hat immer geschichtlichen Charakter, ganz gleich, ob der Träger der Erscheinung ein Naturvorgang oder ein Geschichtsverlauf ist. (Satz der geschichtlichen Offenbarung)

    b. Die wesenserfüllte Erscheinung des Seins-Jenseits im Sein: Geistesgeschichtliche Offenbarungslehre

        1. Die Möglichkeit der wesensunerfüllten Erscheinung

§ 34. Die Erscheinung des Seins-Jenseits im Sein vollzieht sich immer in konkreter Form. Die Tatsache des Erscheinens ist unabhängig von Art und Wert der konkreten Form. (Satz der Grund- und Heils-Offenbarung)

        2. Die dämonische Form der wesensunerfüllten Erscheinung

§ 35. Die Erscheinung des Seins-Jenseits im Sein wird dämonisch, sofern der Träger der Erscheinung Unbedingtheit beansprucht. (Satz der dämonisierten Offenbarung)

        3. Die profane Form der wesensunerfüllten Erscheinung

§ 36. Die Erscheinung des Seins-Jenseits im Sein wird profan, sofern das transzendente Bedeuten des Trägers der Erscheinung aufhört. (Satz der profanisierten Offenbarung)

c. Die wesenserfüllte Erscheinung des Seins-Jenseits im Sein: Konkrete Offenbarungslehre

1. Das Kriterium der wesenserfüllten Erscheinung

§ 37. Die Erscheinung des Seins-Jenseits im Sein ist vollkommen, wenn in der konkreten Form der Erscheinung jede konkrete Form in Frage gestellt ist. (Satz der vollkommenen Offenbarung)

2. Die Wirklichkeit der wesenserfüllten Erscheinung

§ 38. Das Christentum beansprucht auf der vollkommenen Erscheinung des Seins-Jenseits im Sein zu beruhen. (Satz des Wesens des Christentums)

3. Der geschichtliche Charakter der wesenserfüllten Erscheinung

§ 39. Die vollkommene Erscheinung des Seins-Jenseits im Sein stellt sich dar als einheitliche Geschichte, deren Mitte die christliche Urtatsache ist. (Satz der Offenbarungsgeschichte)

4. Der konkrete und der universale Charakter der wesenserfüllten Erscheinung

§ 40. Sofern das Christentum den Anspruch erhebt, auf der vollkommenen Erscheinung des Seins-Jenseits im Sein zu beruhen, steht es einerseits über jeder seiner Verwirklichungen und kann sich andererseits wiederfinden außerhalb seiner eigenen empirischen Geschichte. (Satz der Absolutheit des Christentums)

d. Die Entstehung der religiösen Erkenntnis aus der wesenserfüllten Erscheinung des Seins-Jenseits im Sein

§ 41. Der innere Anlaß zur Selbstbesinnung der religiösen Erkenntnis auf christlichem Boden ist die Notwendigkeit, die vollkommene Erscheinung des Seins-Jenseits im Sein gegen Dämonisierung und Profanisierung zu schützen. (Satz des Wesens der christlichen Theologie)

III. Der Gegenstand der religiösen Erkenntnis

a. Der religiöse Gegenstand überhaupt: Theologische Gegenstandslehre

1. Das Jenseits von Sein und Freiheit oder das unbedingt Mächtige als religiöser Gegenstand

§ 42. Der religiöse Gegenstand oder das Jenseits von Sein und Freiheit hat für den Menschen den Charakter des unbedingt Mächtigen, das eben dadurch jede Bemächtigung oder Vergegenständlichung ausschließt. Es ist das Wesen des religiösen Gegenstandes, nicht Gegenstand werden zu können.

2. Das Verhältnis des religiösen Gegenstandes zu den übrigen Gegenständen: Positive Darstellung

§ 43. Der religiöse Gegenstand ist kein Gegenstand neben oder über anderen, sondern er ist das jede Gegenständlichkeit und damit jede Seinsmacht bedrohende und erfüllende Jenseits der Gegenständlichkeit.

3. Das Verhältnis des religiösen Gegenstandes zu den übrigen Gegenständen: Negative Darstellung

§ 44. Der religiöse Gegenstand wird dämonisiert, sofern er als ein Seiendes höherer Art gefaßt wird, er wird profanisiert, sofern er als die ideale oder vitale Einheit des Seienden gefaßt wird.

4. Die Anschauung des religiösen Gegenstandes als Gott

§ 45. Das Vorwort für den nichtgegenständlichen Gegenstand der Religion ist ‚Gott'. In der ursprünglichen und wesensmäßigen Auffassung dieses Wortes schwingt die Ungegenständlichkeit des in ihm Gemeinten mit. Die Vergegenständlichung Gottes zu einem höhern Wesen, dessen Dasein in Frage gestellt werden kann, bedeutet die Aufhebung des wesensmäßigen Sinnes des Wortes ‚Gott'.

5. Die Erscheinung des religiösen Gegenstandes und die Gestalt der Gnade

§ 46. Der religiöse Gegenstand ist religiöser Gegenstand nur sofern er erscheint. Als erscheinender ist er konkret und erfüllt, aber mit der Bestimmung, daß seine Konkretheit und Erfülltheit zugleich in Frage gestellt ist durch die Unbedingtheit seiner Transzendenz.

b. Der religiöse Erkenntnisgegenstand:
Theologische Erkenntnislehre, Erster Teil

1. Das Letztgemeinte der religiösen Erkenntnis

§ 47. Der religiöse Gegenstand ist immer auch Gegenstand der religiösen Erkenntnis. Sofern er den Charakter hat, ungegenständlich zu sein, kann religiöse Erkenntnis nur gedeutet werden als Selbsterfassung des Seins-Jenseits im Sein durch die religiöse Erkenntnis.

2. Der Aufbau der Gegenstände der religiösen Erkenntnis

§ 48. Allgemeiner Gegenstand der religiösen Erkenntnis ist das Jenseits von Sein und Freiheit in seinem Erscheinen auf dem Boden von Sein und Freiheit. Der allgemeine Gegenstand zerfällt in zwei Gegenstandsgruppen: 1. das Seiende im Hinblick auf das Jenseits seiner selbst, 2. das Jenseits des Seienden im Hinblick auf das Seiende, in dem es erscheint. Beide Gruppen gehören ursprünglich und wesensmäßig zusammen, sind aber für die tatsächliche religiöse Erkenntnis geschieden.

3. Der Gegenstandscharakter der religiösen Erkenntnisgegenstände

§ 49. Aus der Ungegenständlichkeit des religiösen Gegenstandes folgt, daß die Inhalte der religiösen Erkenntnis Vertretungen (Symbole) des unbedingt Transzendenten sind. Das gilt ausschließlich für die Gegenstände der zweiten Gruppe, während in denjenigen der ersten Gruppe Eigentlichkeits- und Vertretungscharakter verbunden sind.

IV. Das Vollziehen der religiösen Erkenntnis
a. Das religiöse Vollziehen überhaupt: Theologische Aktlehre

Einleitung: Die Wechselwirkung von religiösem Gegenstand und religiösem Vollziehen

§ 50. Das Wesen des Religiösen kann weder vom religiösen Gegentand noch vom religiösen Vollziehen aus, sondern nur von der Wechselbeziehung beider bestimmt werden. Gegenstand und Vollziehen sind nur mit einander gegeben.

1. Das Vollziehen jenseits von Sein und Freiheit oder das reine Ergriffensein

§ 51. Das religiöse Vollziehen ist ursprünglich und wesensmäßig weder ein Vollziehen des Seins noch der Freiheit sondern des Jenseits beider, also ein Vollzogenwerden oder ein reines Ergriffensein.

2. Das Verhältnis des religiösen Vollziehens zu dem übrigen Vollziehen: positive Darstellung

§ 52. Das religiöse Vollziehen steht nicht neben oder über den anderen Vollzügen sondern es ist das, in allen Vollzügen wirkende reine Ergriffensein.

3. Das Verhältnis des religiösen Vollziehens zu dem übrigen Vollziehen: negative Darstellung

§ 53. Das religiöse Vollziehen wird dämonisiert, sofern es als ein Vollziehen höherer Art gefaßt ist, es wird profanisiert, sofern es als die ideale oder vitale Einheit der übrigen Vollzüge gefaßt wird.

4. Die Anschauung des religiösen Vollziehens als Glaube

§ 54. Das Urwort für das nicht vollziehbare Vollziehen der Religion ist ‚Glaube'. In der ursprünglichen und wesensmäßigen Auffassung dieses Wortes schwingt die Unvollziehbarkeit des in ihm Gemeinten mit. Die Verselbständigung des Glaubens zu einem Vollziehen höherer Art, das als menschliche Leistung in Frage gestellt werden kann, bedeutet die Aufhebung des wesensmäßigen Sinnes des Wortes Glaube.

5. Die Erscheinung des religiösen Vollziehens und die Gestalt der Gnade

§ 55. Das religiöse Vollziehen ist möglich nur auf Grund eines Erscheinens des Jenseits von Sein und Freiheit oder einer Gestalt der Gnade. Als solches ist es konkret und erfüllt, aber mit der Bestimmung, daß es seine eigene Konkretheit und Erfülltheit zugleich in Frage stellt vor der Unbedingtheit des reinen Ergriffenseins.

b. Das Vollziehen der religiösen Erkenntnis: Theologische Erkenntnislehre, Zweiter Teil

1. Das religiöse Vollziehen und die religiöse Erkenntnis

§ 56. Da das religiöse Vollziehen auf einen Gegenstand gerichtet ist, so ist in ihm notwendig religiöse Erkenntnis enthalten. Es gibt keine vom religiösen Vollziehen losgelöste religiöse Erkenntnis, wie es umgekehrt kein erkenntnisloses religiöses Vollziehen gibt.

2. Der erkenntnistheoretische Charakter der religiösen Erkenntnis

§ 57. Die Erkenntnis des Sein[s]-Jenseits als Seins-Jenseits ist unbedingt und eigentlich, hat aber keinen Inhalt als diese Verneinung jedes Inhaltes. Die Erkenntnis des Seins im Hinblick auf das Seins-Jenseits ist bedingt und zugleich eigentlich und uneigentlich. Die Erkenntnis des Seins-Jenseits im Hinblick auf das Seiende, in dem es erscheint, ist bedingt und uneigentlich.

3. *Der Gewißheitscharakter der religiösen Erkenntnis*

§ 58. Die Gewißheit der religiösen Erkenntnis ist ihrem Wesen nach die Einheit von unbedingter und wagender Gewißheit. Unbedingte Gewißheit hat die Erkenntnis des Seins-Jenseits als solches. Wagende Gewißheit die Erkenntnis der konkreten Erscheinungsform des Seins-Jenseits im Sein. Wissenschaftliche oder praktische Überzeugungen enthält die religiöse Erkenntnis als solche nicht.

Dritter Teil:
Die Gestalt der religiösen Erkenntnis

A. *Die Besinnung auf die Gestalt der religiösen Erkenntnis*

Einleitung: Die Aufgabe der Besinnung
auf die Gestalt der religiösen Erkenntnis

§ 59. Vor dem Aufbau der Gestalt der religiösen Erkenntnis ist zu sprechen von den historischen Normen, der wissenschaftlichen Form und dem sozialen Ort der Gestalt der religiösen Erkenntnis.

I. Die geschichtlichen Grundlagen der Selbstbesinnung:
Theologische Normenlehre
a. Norm und Geschichte

1. *Der geschichtliche Charakter der Selbstbesinnung*

§ 60. Infolge des geschichtlichen Charakters der Erscheinung des Seins-Jenseits im Sein muß jede Selbstbesinnung auf die Gestalt der religiösen Erkenntnis in der Geschichte ihre Grundlage und ihre Norm haben. (Satz des historischen Charakters der Theologie)

2. *Innere und äußere Norm*

§ 61. Die innere Norm der Selbstbesinnung ist die vollkommene Erscheinung des Seins-Jenseits im Sein. Die innere Norm ist der Maßstab jeder äußeren geschichtlichen Norm, obwohl sie nur durch sie erfaßbar ist. (Satz des überhistorischen Charakters der Theologie)

b. Die ursprüngliche Verkündigung der vollkommenen Erscheinung des Seins-Jenseits als grundlegende Norm der Selbstbesinnung:
Theologische Schriftlehre

1. Die ursprüngliche Verkündigung als Norm und als Religionsgeschichte

§ 62. Die grundlegende äußere Norm der Selbstbesinnung ist die ursprüngliche Verkündigung von der vollkommenen Erscheinung des Seins-Jenseits im Sein. Sofern diese Verkündigung zugleich Zeugnis der urchristlichen Religionsgeschichte ist, hat sie keine normative Bedeutung für die Selbstbesinnung. (Satz der Autorität der Schrift)

2. Inhalt und Grenzen der ursprünglichen Verkündigung

§ 63. Die Urkunde von der ursprünglichen Verkündigung enthält gleichzeitig Elemente der Vorbereitung und der Auswirkung der vollkommenen Erscheinung des Seins-Jenseits im Sein. Diese Elemente sind untrennbar von der Verkündigung selbst, bewirken aber, daß die Grenzen der Urkunde grundsätzlich fließend sind. (Satz der Geltung des Kanons)

c. Die abgeleitete Verkündigung der vollkommenen Erscheinung des Seins-Jenseits als weiterführende Norm der Selbstbesinnung:
Theologische Traditionslehre

1. Die abgeleitete Verkündigung als Mittleres zwischen Gegenwart und ursprünglicher Verkündigung

§ 64. Die abgeleitete Verkündigung oder die kirchliche Tradition ist die lebendige Vermittlung zwischen der ursprünglichen Verkündigung und der Gegenwart. Es gibt keinen Zugang zur ursprünglichen Verkündigung außer durch die abgeleitete Verkündigung. (Satz der Schrift und Tradition)

2. Die abgeleitete Verkündigung als Zeugnis des Kampfes gegen Dämonisierung und Profanisierung der vollkommenen Erscheinung des Seins-Jenseits

§ 65. Die abgeleitete Verkündigung oder kirchliche Tradition ist weiterführende Norm der Selbstbesinnung, sofern sie Zeugnis ist des Kampfes gegen Dämonisierung und Profanisierung der vollkommenen Erscheinung des Seins-Jenseits. Ihre Entscheidungen sind maßgebend für die Selbstbesinnung, jedoch nur, soweit sie mit der inneren Norm übereinstimmen. (Satz der Autorität der Tradition)

d. Gegenwart und geschichtliche Norm: Theologische Rezeptionslehre

   *1. Die Aufnahme der geschichtlichen Normen
   im gegenwärtigen Bewußtsein*

§ 66. Das religiöse Bewußtsein der Gegenwart ist weder Gegenstand noch Norm, sondern Medium der Selbstbesinnung der religiösen Erkenntnis. (Satz des religiösen Bewußtseins)

   *2. Rezeption und Produktion religiöser Erkenntnis
   in der gegenwärtigen religiösen Gemeinschaft*

§ 67. Die Selbstbesinnung der religiösen Erkenntnis ist bestimmt durch die religiöse Gemeinschaft auf deren Boden sie sich vollzieht. Sie ist konfessionsgebunden ohne konfessionell sein zu wollen. (Satz der Konfessionalität der Theologie)

   *3. Rezeption und Produktion religiöser Erkenntnis
   in der gegenwärtigen profanen Gesellschaft*

§ 68. Die Selbstbesinnung der religiösen Erkenntnis ist bestimmt durch die profane Gesellschaft, auf deren Boden sie sich vollzieht. Sie ist zeitgebunden, ohne zeitgebunden sein zu wollen. (Satz der Zeitgemäßheit der Theologie)

   *4. Rezeption und Produktion religiöser Erkenntnis
   in dem gegenwärtigen Einzelnen*

§ 69. Die Selbstbesinnung der religiösen Erkenntnis ist bestimmt durch den Einzelnen, in dem sie sich vollzieht. Sie ist persönlichkeitsgebunden, ohne persönlich sein zu wollen. (Satz des individuellen Charakters der Theologie)

II. Die wissenschaftliche Form der Selbstbesinnung:
Theologische Methodenlehre

a. Der formal- und der material-wissenschaftliche Charakter
der Selbstbesinnung: Theologische Vernunftlehre

   1. Wissenschaft und Gestalt der Gnade

§ 70. Die wissenschaftliche Form wird in der Erscheinung des Seins-Jenseits im Sein nicht zerbrochen, sondern erschüttert und umgewendet. (Satz von Vernunft und Offenbarung)

2. Die Wissenschaft als ordnendes Prinzip in der Selbstbesinnung

§ 71. Die wissenschaftliche Selbstbesinnung auf die Inhalte der religiösen Erkenntnis hat die Aufgabe, den Wesenszusammenhang der religiösen Erkenntnisinhalte aufzudecken und prinzipiell und kritisch zur Darstellung zu bringen. Darin ist die wissenschaftliche Vernunft der religiösen Erkenntnis gegenüber nicht schaffend sondern ordnend. (Satz des organischen Gebrauchs der Vernunft in der Theologie)

3. Die Wissenschaft als schaffendes Prinzip in der Selbstbesinnung

§ 72. Jede Erfassung geistiger Wesenszusammenhänge ist zugleich ein Gestalten und Umgestalten derselben. Insofern ist die wissenschaftliche Vernunft produktiv den theologischen Inhalten gegenüber. Sie hat ein Recht dazu, sofern sie selbst teil hat an der Gestalt der Gnade. (Satz des produktiven Gebrauchs der Vernunft in der Theologie)

b. Die Selbstbesinnung auf die Gestalt der religiösen Erkenntnis im System der Wissenschaften: Theologische Wissenschaftslehre

1. Der normative Charakter der Selbstbesinnung

§ 73. Wissenschaftssystematisch gehört die Selbstbesinnung auf die Gestalt der religiösen Erkenntnis zu den konkret-normativen Geisteswissenschaften. Ihre Sätze enthalten weder individuelle noch generelle Feststellungen. (Satz des normativen Charakters der systematischen Theologie)

2. Das Verhältnis der Selbstbesinnung zur Metaphysik

§ 74. Die Begriffe, in denen sich die Selbstbesinnung auf die Inhalte der religiösen Erkenntnis niederschlägt, sind sachlich und geschichtlich in der Einheit mythischer und metaphysischer Schau begründet, doch so, daß auf dem Boden der vollkommenen Erscheinung des Seins-Jenseits das Mythische und Metaphysische miteinander und durcheinander gebrochen sind. (Satz des logischen Charakters der systematischen Theologie)

3. Das Verhältnis der Selbstbesinnung zur Ethik

§ 75. Die Selbstbesinnung auf die Inhalte des religiösen Erkennens steht in unlöslicher Wechselwirkung mit der Selbstbesinnung auf die Inhalte des religiösen Handelns. Es gibt keinen Satz der einen Richtung, in dem nicht Material der anderen Richtung aufgenommen wäre. Denn das religiöse Vollziehen ist die unlösliche Einheit eines praktischen und theoretischen Vollziehens. (Satz des Verhältnisses von Dogmatik und Ethik in der systematischen Theologie)

4. Das Verhältnis der Selbstbesinnung zu Historie und Exegese

§ 76. Sofern die Selbstbesinnung auf die Inhalte der religiösen Erkenntnis historische Grundlagen hat, steht sie in unlöslicher Wechselbeziehung mit den historischen Wissenschaften, die der Erforschung ihrer historischen Grundlagen zugewandt sind. (Satz des Verhältnisses von systematischer und historischer Theologie)

c. Der Aufbau der Gestalt der religiösen Erkenntnis:
Theologische Systemlehre

1. Sinn und Grenzen eines Systems der religiösen Erkenntnis

§ 77. Der systematische Charakter der Selbstbesinnung auf die Gestalt der religiösen Erkenntnis ist mit dem systematischen Charakter des Erkennens selbst gegeben. Er hat lediglich ordnende Bedeutung und ist begrenzt durch die ursprünglich religiöse Gegebenheit der Erkenntnisinhalte. (Satz des systematischen Charakters der systematischen Theologie)

2. Die Gegenstände des Aufbaus

§ 78. Das Seiende im Hinblick auf das Jenseits des Seins wird am zweckmäßigsten angeschaut als Natur, als Geschichte, und als übergreifende Einheit von Natur und Geschichte. Daraus ergeben sich die drei mythischen Symbole der Schöpfung, Erlösung und Vollendung als Hauptgegenstände des Aufbaus. (Satz der religiösen Zentralsymbole)

3. Die Prinzipien des Aufbaus

§ 79. Entsprechend der Doppelrichtung der religiösen Erkenntnis auf das Seiende und das Jenseits des Seins ist jeder Gegenstand so zu behandeln, daß zuerst das Seiende im Hinblick auf das Jenseits des Seins dargestellt wird, daß zweitens die so gewonnenen Vertretungsbegriffe zur Bestimmung des Jenseits des Seins in seiner Beziehung zum Sein gebraucht werden. Dadurch ist eine besondere Lehre von ‚Gott' innerhalb der Selbstbesinnung auf die Inhalte der religiösen Erkenntnis ausgeschlossen.

III. Die soziale Bedeutung der Selbstbesinnung: Soziologie der theologischen Erkenntnis
a. Der Zweck der Selbstbesinnung
1. Die Selbstgenügsamkeit des theoretischen Zweckes

§ 80. Zweck der Selbstbesinnung der religiösen Erkenntnis ist die tiefere Erfassung der Erscheinung des Seins-Jenseits im Sein unter Abwehr dämonischer und profaner Mißdeutungen. Der theoretische Zweck der Selbstbesinnung ist selbstgenugsam und bedarf keiner praktischen Ergänzung.

2. Die Einheit des theoretischen und praktischen Zweckes

§ 81. Praktischer Zweck der Selbstbesinnung der religiösen Erkenntnis ist die Herausstellung der Inhalte der religiösen Erkenntnis für eine Gemeinschaft zum Zwecke der Verkündigung und der Verteidigung. Praktischer und theoretischer Zweck sind unlöslich miteinander verbunden.

b. Die soziale Verantwortung der Selbstbesinnung
1. Die Bindung der Selbstbesinnung an eine konkrete Gestalt der Gnade

§ 82. Jede Selbstbesinnung auf die Inhalte der religiösen Erkenntnis ist sachlich gebunden an eine konkrete Gestalt der Gnade. Der Träger der Selbstbesinnung ist demgemäß verantwortlich gebunden an die religiöse Gemeinschaft, deren Inhalt die Verwirklichung der konkreten Gestalt der Gnade ist. (Satz des Bekenntnischarakters der Theologie)

2. Die Freiheit der Selbstbesinnung von jeder konkreten Gestalt der Gnade

§ 83. Sofern die vollkommene Erscheinung des Seins-Jenseits jede konkrete Gestalt der Gnade in Frage stellt, ist die Selbstbesinnung frei von der Bindung an die religiöse Gemeinschaft. Weder kirchenrechtliche noch sakramentale Bindung entspricht dem Wesen der vollkommenen Erscheinung des Seins-Jenseits im Sein. (Satz der Freiheit der Theologie)

c. Die soziale Doppelaufgabe der gegenwärtigen Selbstbesinnung
1. Die Aufgabe an der innerkirchlichen Gemeinschaft

§ 84. Die Selbstbesinnung auf die Inhalte der religiösen Erkenntnis hat gegenüber der religiösen Gemeinschaft die Aufgabe, an der Gestaltung und Wandlung der sie tragenden und einenden religiösen Symbole mitzuarbeiten.

2. Die Aufgabe an der außerkirchlichen Gesellschaft

§ 85. Die Selbtbesinnung auf die Inhalte der religiösen Erkenntnis hat gegenüber der außerkirchlichen Gesellschaft die Aufgabe, die in ihr wirkenden unter autonomen Formen verborgenen religiösen Symbole ans Licht zu stellen, und von der vollkommenen Erscheinung des Seins-Jenseits aus zu beurteilen.

3. Die Aufgabe an der Überwindung des Gegensatzes beider

§ 86. Die Selbstbesinnung auf die Inhalte der religiösen Erkenntnis hat die Aufgabe, durch wechselseitige Kritik und Ringen um einheitliche religiöse Symbole den Zwiespalt von religiöser Gemeinschaft und außerkirchlicher Gesellschaft zu überwinden, und beide zu einen im Hinblick auf die vollkomme Erscheinung des Jenseits von Sein und Freiheit.

BAND ZWEI: AUFBAU

Erster Teil: Das Seiende als Natürliches in der vollkommenen Erscheinung des Seins-Jenseits: Von der Schöpfung — Theologische Seinserkenntnis

A. Das Seiende als Wesensgemäßes in der vollkommenen Erscheinung des Seins-Jenseits: Von Gott und Welt in ihrer Verbundenheit

I. Das Seiende in seiner reinen Kreatürlichkeit: Der Urstand

a. Die Merkmale der reinen Kreatürlichkeit

1. Die Wirklichkeit des Kreaturseins

§ 87. In der vollkommenen Erscheinung des Seins-Jenseits erfährt jedes Seiende die Erschütterung seiner Selbstheit und Weltlichkeit und seine Hinwendung zum Seins-Jenseits. (Satz der Kreatürlichkeit des Seienden)

2. Mut und Schwermut als allgemeiner Ausdruck des Kreaturseins

§ 88. Die Einheit von schöpferischem Mut und seiner Grenze bewußter Schwermut ist der allgemeine Ausdruck des kreatürlichen Daseins.

Appendix 2: Die Gestalt der religiösen Erkenntnis (1927–1928)

3. Lust und Schmerz als seelischer Ausdruck des Kreaturseins

§ 89. In der Einheit von schöpferischer Lust und Todesschmerz kommt die Kreatürlichkeit des Seienden innerlich zum Ausdruck. (Erster Satz der Theodicee)

4. Die Gottesbeweise als Versuche begrifflichen Ausdrucks des Kreaturseins

§ 90. Die Beweise für das Dasein Gottes sind eine rationale und darum unsachgemäße Ausdrucksform für die Kreatürlichkeit des Seienden. In sachgemäßer Fassung sind sie Zeugnisse für die Erschütterung und Umwendung der Welterkenntnis. (Satz der Gottesbeweise)

b. Die Vollkommenheit des Kreatürlichen

1. Die Stufen des Kreatürlichen

§ 91. Das Seiende im reinen Stande seiner Kreatürlichkeit ist vollkommen in jeder seiner Stufen. Der christliche Schöpfungsgedanke ist die Überwindung der im Neuplatonismus zusammengefaßten heidnischen Stufenlehre.

2. Die Schöpfung aus Nichts

§ 92. Der symbolische Ausdruck für die Einheit von Kreatürlichkeit und Vollkommenheit ist der Satz von der Schöpfung aus Nichts. Dieser Satz darf nicht als Aussage über einen mythisch-metaphysischen Vorgang aufgefaßt werden.

II. Das Seins-Jenseits als Ursprung des Seienden: Die Macht Gottes

a. Die Anschauung des Seins-Jenseits als des unbedingt Selbstmächtigen

1. Die Einheit von Klarheit und Tiefe als Symbol für das Seins-Jenseits

§ 93. Gegenüber der Kreatürlichkeit des Seienden wird das Seins-Jenseits angeschaut als Einheit von Klarheit und Tiefe. Dabei ist Klarheit der Ausdruck für die Ungespaltenheit, Tiefe der Ausdruck für die Unerschöpflichkeit des Seins-Jenseits.

2. Die Einheit von Verschlossenheit und Selbstmitteilung als Symbol des Seins-Jenseits

§ 94. Das Verhältnis von Seins-Jenseits und kreatürlich Seiendem führt zuerst zu dem Symbol = Paar der Verschlossenheit und Selbstmitteilung des Seins-Jenseits. Dabei ist Verschlossenheit Ausdruck für das reine Gegenüber von Sein und Seins-Jenseits, Selbstmitteilung Ausdruck für das Teilhaben des Seienden am Seins-Jenseits.

3. Die Einheit von Herrlichkeit und Hingabe als Symbol für das Seins-Jenseits

§ 95. Das Verhältnis von Seins-Jenseits und kreatürlich Seiendem führt zweitens zu dem Symbol = Paar der Herrlichkeit und Hingabe des Seins-Jenseits. Dabei ist Herrlichkeit der Ausdruck für die Wesenserfüllende Forderung die vom Seins-Jenseits an das Seiende ergeht; Hingabe der Ausdruck für das tragende Teilhaben des Seins-Jenseits an der Kreatürlichkeit des Seienden.

b. Die Anschauung des Seins-Jenseits als des unbedingt Weltmächtigen

1. Die unbedingte Seinsmächtigkeit als Symbol des Seins-Jenseits

§ 96. Als das unbedingt-Seinsmächtige wird das Seins-Jenseits angeschaut einerseits sofern es Träger der unbedingten Seinsfülle ist, andererseits, sofern es des Seienden unbedingt mächtig ist. Der Begriff der Allmacht ist abzulehnen, weil er zu falschen, aus der kreatürlichen Situation herausführenden Reflexionen über Möglichkeiten und Nichtmöglichkeiten führt.

2. Die unbedingte Raum- und Zeitmächtigkeit als Symbol des Seins-Jenseits

§ 97. Die unbedingte Seinsmächtigkeit wird anschaulich als unbedingte Raum- und Zeitmächtigkeit. Im Symbol der Ewigkeit sofern es nicht als Unzeitlichkeit mißdeutet wird, kommt das unmittelbar zum Ausdruck, während der Begriff der Allgegenwart aus dem gleichen Grunde abzulehnen ist, wie der der Allmacht.

3. Der geistige Charakter der unbedingten Seinsmächtigkeit

§ 98. Entsprechend der Klarheit des Seins-Jenseits hat die unbedingte Seinsmächtigkeit geistigen Charakter. Sie ist geistige Seinsmächtigkeit. Der Begriff der Allwissenheit dafür ist aus dem gleichen Grunde abzulehnen, wie der Begriff der Allmacht.

c. Die Anschauung des Seins-Jenseits als des unbedingt Vollkommenen

1. Die vollkommene Lebendigkeit als Symbol für das Seins-Jenseits

§ 99. Während die Sphäre des Anorganischen kein Symbol gibt für das Seins-Jenseits, entspringt aus der organischen Sphäre das Symbol der

Appendix 2: Die Gestalt der religiösen Erkenntnis (1927–1928)

vollkommenen Lebendigkeit als Ausdruck für die Vollkommenheit des Seins-Jenseits.

2. Die vollkommene Innerlichkeit als Symbol für das Seins-Jenseits

§ 100. Die mit dem Lebendigen verbundene Innerlichkeit ergibt ein zweites Symbol für das Seins-Jenseits. Die Auffassung der Innerlichkeit als Persönlichkeit unterliegt Bedenken wegen der mit dem Persönlichkeitsbegriff verbundenen Besonderung. Notwendig ist dagegen die Idee der Einheit des Innerlichen als Symbol für das Seins-Jenseits.

3. Die vollkommene Wesenhaftigkeit als Symbol für das Seins-Jenseits

§ 101. Aus der alles Seiende tragenden Wesenswelt entspringt das Symbol der vollkommenen Wesenhaftigkeit des Seins-Jenseits. Die Bedeutung dieses Symbols beruht insonderheit auf der Abwehr aller dualistischen Versuche, die Wesenswelt in die wesenswidrige Existenz hereinzuziehen und mit dem Seins-Jenseits in Widerspruch zu stellen.

B. Das Seiende als Wesenswidriges in der vollkommenen Erscheinung des Seins-Jenseits: Von Gott und Welt in ihrer Getrenntheit

I. Das Seiende im Widerspruch mit seiner Kreatürlichkeit: Die Sünde

a. Das Wesen des Wesenswidrigen

1. Der allgemeine Charakter des Wesenswidrigen

§ 102. In jedem Seienden ist das Streben, in seiner bedingten Form Unbedingtheit zu erlangen. Dieses Streben bedeutet die Tendenz, die Tiefe des Seins-Jenseits zu besitzen, losgelöst von seiner Klarheit oder die Klarheit losgelöst von seiner Tiefe.

2. Die Selbstliebe

§ 103. Das wesenswidrige Streben des Seienden ist Selbstliebe oder der Wille die eigene Seinsmacht (das Selbst) zu haben losgelöst von der Macht des Anderen und der unbedingten Macht des Seins-Jenseits.

3. Die Begierde

§ 104. Die Selbstliebe drückt sich aus im Sinnlichen als Begierde oder als Wille, sich auf dem Boden des eigenen Selbst die unendliche Seinsfülle anzueignen.

4. Die Überhebung

§ 105. Die Selbstliebe äußert sich im Geistigen aus als Überhebung oder als Wille, die unendliche Form des Seienden zu benutzen zur Erhebung des eigenen Selbst an die Stelle des Trägers der Unbedingten Form.

5. Das Mißtrauen

§ 106. Das Streben des Seienden, Unbedingtheit zu erlangen ist negativ Abwendung vom Seins-Jenseits, innerlich angeschaut: Mißtrauen.

b. Die Erscheinung des Wesenswidrigen

1. Das Zerreißen der kreatürlichen Einheit

§ 107. Die Wesenswidrigkeit erscheint als Zerreißen der kreatürlichen Einheit, also als Zerreißen von Mut und Schwermut in Trotz und Verzweiflung, von schöpferischer Lust und Todesschmerz in isolierte Lust und isolierte Qual.

2. Die bürgerliche Gerechtigkeit

§ 108. Der Versuch die auseinandergerissenen Extreme auszugleichen, führt zur bürgerlichen Gerechtigkeit, in der die wesenswidrige Kreatürlichkeit zur Breite und Existenzmöglichkeit kommt.

c. Die Wirklichkeit des Wesenswidrigen

1. Die Einheit von Freiheit und Notwendigkeit im Wesenswidrigen

§ 109. Jeder Akt der Selbstliebe ist zugleich Ausdruck der Wesenswidrigkeit des Seienden überhaupt und Tat eigener Selbstmächtigkeit. Er ist zugleich notwendig und verantwortlich. (Satz der Erbsünde)

2. Die moralische und die tragische Auffassung der Wesenswidrigkeit

§ 110. Die moralische Auffassung des Wesenswidrigen kennt nur das Element der Verantwortlichkeit, die tragische Auffassung nur das Element der Notwendigkeit. Beide verfehlen die wirkliche menschliche Situation, wie sie sich umittelbar im Selbstbewußtsein ausspricht.

d. Der Ursprung des Wesenswidrigen

1. Die Angst der Kreatürlichkeit als Möglichkeitsgrund des Wesenswidrigen

§ 111. In jedem Kreatürlichen ist die Angst lebendig, sein Selbst zu verlieren und treibt es zur Verwirklichung der eigenen Selbstmächtigkeit. Die Angst der Kreatürlichkeit ist die Versuchung der Kreatürlichkeit.

Appendix 2: Die Gestalt der religiösen Erkenntnis (1927—1928)

2. *Die wesenmäßige Unableitbarkeit der Wirklichkeit des Wesenswidrigen*

§ 112. Es gibt keine Wesensnotwendigkeit des Wesenswidrigen. Da Erkenntnis Einung ist, so kann das Wesenswidrige niemals direkt erkannt werden, sondern immer nur indirekt als das im Erkennen Abgestoßene oder wesensmäßig Unerkennbare.

e. Die Wirkung des Wesenswidrigen

1. Die Zerspaltung

§ 113. Das Streben des Seienden auf dem Boden seines begrenzten Selbst Unbedingtheit zu erlangen, führt zur Zerspaltung des Selbst, sowohl des individuellen wie des sozialen.

2. Die Selbstzerstörung

§ 114. Der Wille des Selbst, seiner Zerspaltung zu entrinnen, treibt zur Selbstzerstörung des Selbst, durch den in wesenswidriger Krankheit und Tod sich auswirkenden verborgenen Todeswillen.

3. Die Sinnentleerung

§ 115. Die Loslösung von dem sinnerfüllenden Seins-Jenseits führt zur Sinnentleerung und dem damit verbundenen Verlust der vitalen Daseinsmöglichkeit.

4. Das Schuldbewußtsein

§ 116. Im Schuldbewußtsein wird die mit dem Wesenswidrigen verbundene Seinsauflösung als Gericht erlebt.

II. Das Seins-Jenseits als Verneinung des Seienden in der Wesenswidrigkeit: Die Heiligkeit Gottes

1. *Die Unzugänglichkeit als Symbol für das Seins-Jenseits*

§ 117. Auf dem Boden des Schuldbewußtseins wird das Seins-Jenseits angeschaut als das Unzugänglich-Zurückstoßende oder als das Jenseits einer unbedingten Kluft.

2. *Der Zorn als Symbol für das Seins-Jenseits*

§ 118. Auf dem Boden des Schuldbewußtseins wird das Seins-Jenseits angeschaut als das aktiv zur Selbstzerstörung Treibende. Das Symbol des Zornes für diese Anschauung ist wegen des im Zorn vorhandenen falschen Affektcharakters fragwürdig.

C. Das Seiende als Zusammen von Wesensmäßigem und Wesenswidrigem in der vollkommenen Erscheinung des Seins-Jenseits: Von Gott und Welt in dem Zusammen von Getrenntheit und Verbundenheit

I. Das Seiende in der Zweideutigkeit seines Kreaturseins: Welterhaltung und Weltregierung

a. Der Charakter der Zweideutigkeit des Kreatürlichen: Das Schöpferische und das Dämonische

1. Der allgemeine Begriff des Dämonischen

§ 119. Die Wesenswidrigkeit des Seienden hebt ihr schöpferisches Getragensein nicht auf. Die Verbindung des Schöpferischen mit dem Wesenswidrigen ist das Dämonische. Dämonie ist wesenswidriges Hervorbrechen des schöpferischen Grundes in den Dingen. Sie hat immer zugleich tragenden und auflösenden, formenden und formzerstörenden, göttlichen und widergöttlichen Charakter.

2. Das Dämonische in der vorgeistigen Wirklichkeit

§ 120. Das Dämonische in der Natur ist infolge der Fremdheit zwischen Natur und Geist nur von ferne und indirekt zu erfassen. Es wird angeschaut sowohl in der Zweideutigkeit der Naturelemente als auch in der eigentümlichen Doppelsinnigkeit mancher Pflanzen und vor allem Tiere.

3. Das Dämonische in der geistigen Wirklichkeit

§ 121. Dem Seelischen gegenüber ist Dämonie Zerspaltung der inneren Einheit, religiös angeschaut als Besessenheit. In der objektiv geistigen Sphäre ist Dämonie Herrschaft übergreifender zugleich tragender und zerstörender geistiger Gebilde.

4. Das Dämonische in der religiösen Wirklichkeit

§ 122. Auf religiösem Boden wirkt das Dämonische Heilige Sinnwidrigkeit in der Anschauung des Seins-Jenseits und in den Formen des auf das Seins-Jenseits gerichteten Handelns. Im Heilig-Zerstörerischen der religiösen Sphäre kommt das Dämonische zur Vollendung.

b. Die Erhaltung des Seienden in seiner Zweideutigkeit: Vorsehung und Schicksal

1. Das Ineinander von Wesensmäßigem und Wesenswidrigem in den Seinsformen

§ 123. Im Zusammenhang der Welt ist das Wesenswidrige so eingeordnet in das Wesensgemäße, daß die Welt erhalten wird und ihr Sinn, so wie der Sinn jedes Einzelnen in ihr zur Erfüllung kommen kann.

2. Die Zuordnung von Wesenswidrigkeit und Seinszerstörung

§ 124. Die Verflochtenheit von Wesensmäßigem und Wesenswidrigem macht eine bestimmte Zuordnung von Wesenswidrigkeit und Seinsauflösung unmöglich. Der Vergeltungsgedanke beruht auf einer falschen Isolierung von dem Gesamtstand der Wesenswidrigkeit.

3. Die moralische Weltordnung

§ 125. Im Hinblick auf die Gesamtzuordnung von Wesenswidrigkeit und Seinszerstörung, sowie im Hinblick auf die Möglichkeit einer Sinnerfüllung des Seienden trotz der Wesenswidrigkeit kann von einer moralischen Weltordnung gesprochen werden.

4. Wesenswidrigkeit und Sinnerfüllung

§ 126. Die Möglichkeit der Sinnerfüllung trotz der Wesenswidrigkeit in jedem Moment des Lebensprozesses ist der Inhalt des Vorsehungsgedankens. Der Begriff der Vorsehung ist fragwürdig, insofern er das Bild eines vorhergesehenen, fixierten Planes enthalten kann. Die wirkliche Sinnerfüllung aber ist aktuell und schöpferisch und neu gegenüber jedem im Lebensprozeß eintretenden neuen Element. In diesem dynamischen Vorsehungsgedanken ist der berechtigte religiöse Anstoß an dem statischen Vorsehungsgedanken überwunden.

5. Der christliche Schicksalsbegriff

§ 127. Jedes Seiende hat Schicksal, sofern es frei ist und als freies getragen und eingeordnet in das Ganze. Das absolut Notwendige und das absolut Freie hat kein Schicksal. Die dämonische Auffassung des Schicksals und der damit verbundene religiöse Protest gegen den Schicksalsgedanken sind in der vollkommenen Erscheinung des Seins-Jenseits überwunden.

c. Die Erscheinung des Wesens in der Zweideutigkeit des Kreatürlichen: Das Wunder

1. Wesen- und Existenzform der Dinge

§ 128. Durch die Zerspaltenheit des Seienden sind die es tragenden Wesensformen nicht aufgehoben. In der Existenz der Dinge sind Wesensmäßigkeit und Wesenswidrigkeit ineinander verflochten. Darum ist die Existenzform der Dinge variabel und sowohl der dämonischen Verzerrung wie der Überwindung des Dämonischen zugänglich.

2. Das Wesen des Wunders

§ 129. Wunder ist Erscheinen der reinen Wesensform als Überwindung der zweideutigen Existenzform.

3. Wunder und Gesetz

§ 130. Das Wunder steht nicht im Widerspruch zum Wesen und seiner Form, sondern zur Existenz und ihrer Deformierung des Wesens. Die supranaturalistische Auffassung des Wunders als Aufhebung des Naturgesetzes ist ebenso abzulehnen wie die rationalistische, die es mit dem Geheimnis alles Geschehens gleichsetzt.

4. Wunder und Geschichte

§ 131. Wunder ist Ausdruck der grundsätzlichen Überwindung der Wesenswidrigkeit in der Heilsgeschichte und kann nur im Zusammenhang mit der religiösen Geschichtserkenntnis verstanden werden.

II. Das Seins-Jenseits als Träger des Seienden in der Zweideutigkeit: Die Weisheit Gottes

1. Die Weisheit als Symbol für das Seins-Jenseits

§ 132. Von dem Bewußtsein um die Sinnerfüllung in der Sinnwidrigkeit aus wird das Seins-Jenseits angeschaut unter dem Symbol der Weisheit.

2. Die Güte als Symbol des Seins-Jenseits

§ 133. Von dem Bewußtsein um die Erhaltung des Seienden in der Selbstzerstörung des Seienden aus wird das Seins-Jenseits angeschaut unter dem Symbol der Güte.

3. Die Gerechtigkeit als Symbol für das Seins-Jenseits

§ 134. Von dem Bewußtsein um die moralische Weltordnung aus wird das Seins-Jenseits angeschaut unter dem Symbol der Gerechtigkeit.

Zweiter Teil: Das Seiende als Geschichtliches in der vollkommenen Erscheinung des Seins-Jenseits: Von der Erlösung − Theologische Geschichtserkenntnis

A. Die Geschichte als Vorbereitung der vollkommenen Erscheinung des Seins-Jenseits: Die Religion

I. Die Geschichte als Kampf gegen das Dämonische: Forderung und Verheißung

a. Die Geschichte unter der Herrschaft des Sakramentalen: „Das Heidentum"

1. Das Sakramentale als Ausdruck der Uroffenbarung

§ 135. Der Ausgangspunkt der religiösen Geschichtserkenntnis ist die Herrschaft des Sakramentalen oder die Auffassung der unmittelbaren Gegenwärtigkeit des Heiligen in einem Gegenstand oder Vorgang. In der sakramentalen Situation kommt die bleibende Gebundenheit des Bewußtseins an das Seins-Jenseits auch in der Sphäre der Zweideutigkeit zum Ausdruck.

2. Das Sakramentale als Dämonisierung der Offenbarung

§ 136. Sofern die sakramentale Anschauung des Seins-Jenseits in gleicher Weise in formschaffenden wie in formzerstörenden Vorgängen anschaut, bewirkt es eine Dämonisierung des religiösen Bewußtseins.

3. Der Kampf gegen das Dämonische auf dem Boden des Sakramentalen

§ 137. Sofern auf dem Boden des Sakramentalen ein Kampf gegen das Dämonische sich vollzieht, (im monarchischen Monotheismus, in den Mysterien, in der Mystik, im Dualismus) hat es den Charakter einer Vorbereitung der vollkommenen Erscheinung des Seins-Jenseits.

b. Die Geschichte unter der Herrschaft des Profanen: „Griechentum"

1. Das Profane als Protest gegen das Dämonische

§ 138. Als Erhebung der reinen rationalen Form im Logischen und Ethischen bedeutet Profanität Kampf gegen dämonische Heiligung und Fixierung des Formwidrigen.

2. Profanisierung und Entgöttlichung

§ 139. Mit der rationalen Überwindung des Dämonischen ist verbunden eine rationale Entgöttlichung des Seienden. Der tragende Grund wird verdeckt durch die reine rationale Form.

3. Die Tragik der Profanität

§ 140. Mit der Losreißung vom Seins-Jenseits durch die autonome in sich ruhende Form gerät die Profanität in eine wachsende Entleerung, deren tragischer Ausklang die praktische und theoretische Skepsis ist und die notwendig zu einer Wiederkehr des in den Hintergrund gedrängten Dämonischen führt.

c. Die Offenbarungsgeschichte unter der Herrschaft des Gesetzes: „Judentum"

1. Das Gesetz als grundsätzlicher Widerspruch gegen das Dämonische

§ 141. Zu einem grundsätzlichen Widerspruch gegen das Dämonische kommt es allein auf dem Boden des Gesetzes oder der Erfassung des Seins-Jenseits als Ort der unbedingten Forderung. Damit ist notwendig verbunden der exklusive Monotheismus.

2. Das Gesetz als Vorbereitung und Widerspruch der vollkommenen Erscheinung des Seins-Jenseits

§ 142. Als Überwindung des Dämonischen ist das Gesetz Bedingung, als ausschließliche Erfassung der unbedingten Forderung ist es Widerspruch zur vollkommenen Erscheinung des Seins-Jenseits.

3. Die Überwindung des Gesetzes auf dem Boden des Gesetzes

§ 143. Sofern neben die unbedingte Forderung die Aussicht auf die unbedingte Erfüllung gestellt wird, findet eine Überwindung des Gesetzes auf dem Boden des Gesetzes statt. Darin kann die vollkommene Erscheinung des Seins-Jenseits sich selbst wiederfinden.

II. Das Sein[s]-Jenseits als Träger der Geschichte: Gott der Vater

1. Die Liebe als Symbol für das Seins-Jenseits

§ 144. Von dem Kampf gegen das Dämonische aus wird das Seins-Jenseits angeschaut unter dem Symbol der Liebe. Auf dem Boden der reinen

Kreatürlichkeit kann das Symbol der Liebe nicht erfaßt werden, obwohl die Mächtigkeit nie ohne die Liebe gedacht werden darf.

2. Das allgemeine Vatersymbol

§ 145. Das Seins-Jenseits als Träger der Geschichte wird angeschaut unter dem Symbol des Vaters. Der Sinn des Vatersymbols ist abhängig von der Auffassung des Vater-Kindverhältnisses in jeder Geisteslage. Demgemäß kann in bestimmten Situationen die Anwendung dieses Symbols fragwürdig sein.

3. Das spezielle Vatersymbol und der trinitarische Gedanke

§ 146. Eine besondere Verwendung findet das Vatersymbol in der Auffassung des Verhältnisses der religiös erkannten Geschichte zum Seins-Jenseits. Das Seins-Jenseits entfaltet sich als Vater, Sohn und Geist. Der Sinn und die Fragwürdigkeit dieser trinitarischen Verwendung des Vater- und Sohn-Symbols kann erst am Ende der religiösen Geschichtserkenntnis dargestellt werden.

B. Die Geschichte als Durchbruch der vollkommenen Erscheinung des Seins-Jenseits: Der Christus

I. Die Geschichte als Überwindung des Dämonischen: Die Gnade

a. Der Durchbruch der vollkommenen Erscheinung als geschichtlicher Augenblick

1. Der spezielle Begriff des Kairos

§ 147. Die vollkommene Erscheinung des Seins-Jenseits ist abhängig von der Vollendung der vorbereiteten Geschichte. Der Augenblick dieser Vollendung wird durch den Begriff des Kairos oder der Zeitenfülle bezeichnet.

2. Der allgemeine Begriff des Kairos

§ 148. Sowohl die Begriffe Heidentum, Griechentum, Judentum, als auch der Kairos-Begriff verbinden mit ihrem historisch Einmaligen einen typisch allgemeinen Sinn. Dadurch bekommen die Begriffe der vorbereitenden Offenbarungsgeschichte aktuelle Bedeutung für jeden Moment der Geschichte.

b. Der Durchbruch der vollkommenen Erscheinung des Seins-Jenseits als persönliche Tat: Jesus Christus

DAS GRUNDLEGENDE URTEIL ÜBER JESUS ALS DEN CHRISTUS

1. Der Inhalt des Urteils

§ 149. Alle Verkündigung von der vollkommenen Erscheinung des Seins-Jenseits ruht auf dem Satz, daß Jesus der Christus ist.

2. Der historische Charakter des Urteils

§ 150. Über den historischen Hintergrund und die historischen Folgen dieses Satzes urteilt die empirische Geschichtswissenschaft.

3. Der religiöse Charakter des Urteils

§ 151. Der religiöse Sinn des Urteils ist unabhängig von jedem Ergebnis der historischen Arbeit. Er kann nur durch innerreligiöse Dämonisierung oder Profanisierung erschüttert werden.

4. Die theologische Verteidigung des Urteils oder die Christologie

§ 152. Die wesensmäßige und jederzeit notwendige Aufgabe der Christologie ist es, den grundlegenden Satz über Jesus als den Christus unter Abwehr jeder Dämonisierung und Profanisierung zur Darstellung zu bringen.

DAS URTEIL ÜBER DAS SEIN JESU ALS DAS SEIN DES CHRISTUS

1. Die Grundlagen des Urteils

§ 153. Das Urteil über den Charakter Jesu als des Christus kann weder der historisch erkennbaren Wirklichkeit Jesu von Nazareth noch dem historisch erkennbaren mythischen Bewußtsein der Gemeinde entnommen werden, sondern nur dem, was durch die Wechselwirkung beider relativ unbekannter Faktoren geschaffen ist, dem neutestamentlichen Realbild Jesus Christus.

2. Der Inhalt des Urteils und die biblische Geschichte

§ 154. Die mythisch = legendären Aussagen, die mit der ursprünglichen Verkündigung von Jesus Christus verbunden sind, können benutzt werden, wenn sie sein Realbild verdeutlichen. Sie müssen ausgeschieden werden, sofern sie die Anschauung seines Realbildes hemmen. Ein

Urteil über Dinge wie das Berufungsbewußtsein oder „den numinosen Charakter" Jesu kommt nicht der systematischen Selbstbesinnung der religiösen Erkenntnis sondern der historischen Wissenschaft zu.

3. Das neue Sein und sein Verhältnis zur Zweideutigkeit des Seienden

§ 155. In dem Realbild Jesu Christi haben wir die Anschauung eines Kreatürlichen, das in seiner Selbstmächtigkeit gebunden bleibt an das unbedingt Mächtige. Es finden sich, ohne daß die menschliche Wahrheit zerstört wird, in seinem Bilde keine Spuren einer Dämonisierung seines religiösen Bewußtseins und darum keine Züge von isolierender Selbstliebe. Die Deutung dieses Tatbestandes als Sündlosigkeit ist unzulänglich, insofern sie negativ ist, und irreführend, insofern sie den falschen Anschein einer feststellbaren historischen Behauptung erweckt.

4. Die Anerkennung und Aufhebung des Zusammenhanges der Zweideutigkeit in dem neuen Sein

§ 156. Das in dem Realbild Jesu Christi angeschaute neue Sein hebt den empirischen Zusammenhang der Zweideutigkeit nicht auf. Der Träger des neuen Seins geht in die Zweideutigkeit ein und erfährt ihre Wirkung bis zu den letzten Konsequenzen der Seinszerstörung. Der symbolische Ausdruck dafür ist das Kreuz. Zugleich erfährt er sie nicht als Gericht. Der symbolische Ausdruck dafür ist die Auferstehung oder die Überwindung des vom Leben isolierten Todes.

5. Das Verhältnis des neuen Seins zu sakramentaler, profaner und gesetzlicher Haltung

§ 157. Das in Jesus Christus angeschaute neue Sein ist zugleich Aufhebung und Bestätigung der sakramentalen, der gesetzlichen und der profanen Haltung.

DAS URTEIL ÜBER DIE WIRKUNG JESU ALS DIE WIRKUNG DES CHRISTUS

1. Die Wirkung Jesu als Wirkung des in ihm angeschauten neuen Seins

§ 158. Die Wirkung Jesu als des Christus ist die Wirkung des in ihm angeschauten neuen Seins, nämlich seiner unbedingten Verbundenheit mit dem Seins-Jenseits.

2. Die Vermittlung seines Seins durch seine Worte

§ 159. Der unmittelbare Ausdruck des in ihm angeschauten neuen Seins sind zuerst seine Worte. Nur durch sie hindurch kann sein Sein wirksam werden. Unbedingt abzulehnen ist dagegen jede Auffassung, die die Worte und ihren Sinngehalt von dem Sein, das sie ausdrücken, isolieren will.

3. Die Vermittlung seines Seins durch seine Geschichte

§ 160. Der unmittelbare Ausdruck des in ihm angeschauten neuen Seins ist zweitens seine Geschichte. Nur durch sie hindurch kann sein Sein wirksam werden. Unbedingt abzulehnen ist dagegen jede Auffassung, die die Geschichte isolieren will gegen das Sein, das in ihr zum Ausdruck kommt und dem bloßen Vollzug der Geschichte die Wirkungen Jesu als des Christus zuschreibt.

4. Die Wirkung Jesu als die Mitteilung seines Seins

§ 161. Die Wirkung Jesu als des Christus ist die Mitteilung seines Seins an die bewußt oder unbewußt in der Geschichte mit ihm Verbundenen.

DER CHARAKTER DER WIRKUNG JESU ALS DES CHRISTUS

1. Die Überwindung des Mißtrauens oder der Sonderung des Seienden vom Seins-Jenseits

§ 162. Das in Jesus Christus angeschaute neue Sein zerbricht die dämonische Verhüllung des Seins-Jenseits und überwindet die von ihm ausgehende Abstoßung des Seienden. (Satz der Sündenvergebung)

2. Die Überwindung der Selbstliebe oder die prinzipielle Aufhebung der Wesenswidrigkeit

§ 163. Das in Jesus Christus angeschaute neue Sein durchbricht den übergreifenden Zusammenhang der Wesenswidrigkeit und überwindet grundsätzlich die Selbstliebe. (Satz der Wiedergeburt)

3. Das Verhältnis beider zueinander

§ 164. Obgleich beide Wirkungen eins sind, und untrennbar zusammen gehören, gründet sich die Gewißheit der Überwindung des Dämonischen ausschließlich auf die erste Seite.

Appendix 2: Die Gestalt der religiösen Erkenntnis (1927–1928)

4. Die Unbedingtheit und Voraussetzungslosigkeit der Wirkung Jesu als des Christus

§ 165. Die in Jesus Christus angeschaute Überwindung des Dämonischen ist allein durch sich selbst bedingt. Ihre Wirkung ist unabhängig von jeder durch den Menschen geschaffenen Voraussetzung, sowohl vor wie nach der Erscheinung des neuen Seins.

5. Die Fragwürdigkeit der Theorien Jesu über die Wirkung Jesu als des Christus

§ 166. Das in Jesus Christus angeschaute neue Sein ist Erscheinung des Seins-Jenseits im Sein. Es ist in keiner Weise bedingt durch seinen Träger. Darum sind alle Theorien abzulehnen, in denen eine Wirkung des Trägers der vollkommenen Erscheinung des Seins-Jenseits auf dieses angenommen wird.

c. Der Durchbruch der vollkommenen Erscheinung des Seins-Jenseits als übergeschichtliche Wirkung: Glaube und Geschichte

1. Der Begriff des Übergeschichtlichen[7]

2. Die Einheit von Geschichtlichem und Übergeschichtlichem in der vollkommenen Erscheinung des Seins-Jenseits

§ 168. Das in Jesus Christus angeschaute neue Sein ist zugleich innergeschichtlich – in die Geschichte eingehend und übergeschichtlich – die Geschichte tragend. Auf der ersten Aussage beruht die konkrete geschichtsgestaltende Kraft der vollkommenen Offenbarung auf der zweiten Aussage beruht ihre allgemeine Geschichte ermöglichende Kraft.

3. Die Hinwendung zum Übergeschichtlichen als Hinwendung zum Geschichtlichen

§ 169. Die religiöse Hinwendung zu der übergeschichtlichen Erfüllung vollzieht sich notwendig als Hinwendung zu dem in der Geschichte erschienenen neuen Sein.

4. Die Hinwendung zum Geschichtlichen und die empirische Historie

§ 170. Die Verbindung des Geschichtlichen mit dem Übergeschichtlichen befreit die religiöse Hinwendung zu ihm von Belastungen mit historisch-empirischen Urteilen.

---

[7] A gap of several lines is left in Tillich's typescript following the cipher '§ 167'.

II. Das Seins-Jenseits in die Geschichte eingehend: Gott der Sohn[8]
   a. Das christologische Problem
      1. Die Bedeutung der altkirchlichen Christologie
      2. Protestantismus und altkirchliche Christologie
      3. Die Abwendung von der altkirchlichen Christologie
      4. Das christologische Problem in der gegenwärtigen Lage

   b. Die christologische Aussage
      1. Der christologische Satz
      2. Der Sohn als Symbol für das Seins-Jenseits
      3. Das Sohnessymbol und der trinitarische Gedanke[9]

---

[8] No propositions exist beyond this point.
[9] Typescript ends. Below this is written by hand, 'Bis zu diesem Punkt ging die Vorlesung'.

BIBLIOGRAPHY

Containing over five hundred entries, the chronologically arranged list of material in GW. XIV. 139−219 has established itself as the standard bibliography of Tillich's published works. For full details about the particulars of sources cited in the present volume, the reader should consult the bibliography in GW. XIV. In addition to published sources, I have made extensive use of certain unpublished material. Unless otherwise stated in the text or footnotes, all such material is in the Paul-Tillich-Archiv, Göttingen/Marburg. See GW. XIV. 283−6. I am very grateful to Frau Gertraut Stöber for her assistence with archival material.

SELECTED MATERIAL ABOUT TILLICH

Adams, J. L. 'Paul Tillich on Luther', *Interpreters of Luther: Essays in Honor of Wilhelm Pauck*. Philadelphia, 1968, pp. 304−34.
−. *Paul Tillich's Philosophy of Culture, Science and Religion*. New York, 1965.
Adorno, T. W., et al. *Werk und Wirken Paul Tillichs: Ein Gedenkbuch*. Stuttgart, 1967.
Alston, W. P. 'Tillich on Idolatry', *JRel*, XXXVIII (1958), 263−7.
Amelung, E. 'Die Funktion des Religionsbegriffes für die christliche Botschaft in der Gegenwart: Einige Bemerkungen zum Religionsbegriff Paul Tillichs', in *Glaube-Geist-Geschichte: Festschrift für Ernst Benz zum 60. Geburtstag*, ed. G. Müller and W. Zeller. Leiden, 1967, pp. 144−59.
−. *Die Gestalt der Liebe: Paul Tillichs Theologie der Kultur*. Gütersloh, 1972.
−. *Religious Socialism as an Ideology: A Study of the 'Kairos-Circle' in Germany between 1919 and 1933*. Th. D. diss., Harvard University, 1962.
Armbruster, C. J. *The Vision of Paul Tillich*. New York, 1967.
Bastian, H. D. *Theologie der Frage: Ideen zur Grundlegung einer theologischen Didaktik und zur Kommunikation der Kirchen der Gegenwart*. Munich, 1969.
Benktson, B.-E. *Christus und die Religion: Der Religionsbegriff bei Barth, Bonhoeffer und Tillich*. Stuttgart, 1967.
Bowker, J. W. 'Can Differences Make a Difference? A Comment on Tillich's Proposals for Dialogue between Religions', *JThST*, XXIV (April, 1973), 158−88.

Breipohl, R. *Religiöser Sozialismus und bürgerliches Geschichtsbewußtsein zur Zeit der Weimarer Republik*. Zürich, 1971.

Brinkschmidt, E. *Paul Tillich und die pädagogische Normproblematik*. Bielefeld, 1977.

Brügmann, V. *Die Durchführung der Methode der Korrelation in den religiösen Reden Paul Tillichs*. Hamburg, 1969.

Buchter, J. *Die Kriterien der Theologie im Werke Paul Tillichs*. Bonn, 1975.

Büchsel, F. 'Die Stellung der Theologie im System der Wissenschaften: Eine Auseinandersetzung mit Paul Tillichs *System der Wissenschaften*', *ZSysTh*, I (1924), 399–411.

Clayton, J. P. 'Dialektik und Apologetik in der theologischen Entwicklung Paul Tillichs', *ZThKirche*, LXXV (1978), 213–32.

—. 'Is Jesus Necessary for Christology?: An Antinmomy in Tillich's Theological Method', in *Christ, Faith and History: Cambridge Studies in Christology*. Eds. S. W. Sykes and J. P. Clayton. Cambridge, 1972, pp. 147–63.

—. 'Questioning, Answering and Tillich's Concept of Correlation', in *Kairos and Logos*. Ed. J. J. Carey. Cambridge, 1978, pp. 135–57.

—. 'Was heißt „Korrelation" bei Paul Tillich?', *NeueZSysTh*, XX (1978), 175–191.

—. 'Was ist falsch in der Korrelationstheologie?', *NeueZSysTh*, XVI (1974), 93–111.

Cobb, J. B. *Living Options in Protestant Theology: A Survey of Methods*. Philadelphia, 1962.

Crary, S. *Idealistic Elements in Tillich's Thought*. Ph.D. diss., Yale, 1955.

de Deugd, C. 'De methode van correlatie tussen theologie en filosofie in Paul Tillichs filosofische theologie', *NTTij*, XVII (1963), 161–80.

Dell, A. 'Der Charakter der Theologie in Tillichs System der Wissenschaften', *Theologische Blätter*, II (1923), 235–45.

Demos, R. 'Tillich's Philosophical Theology', *PhilPhenomenolRes*, XIX (1958), 74–85.

Dixon, J. 'Is Tragedy Essential to Knowing? A Critique of Dr. Tillich's Aesthetic', *JRel*, XLIII (1963), 271–84.

Doerne, M. „Die Idee des Protestantismus bei Tillich", *ZThKirche*, XI (1930), 206–25.

Dowey, E. A. 'Tillich, Barth and the Criteria of Theology', *ThToday* XV (1958), 43–58.

Eberhardt, H. *Der Reich-Gottes-Begriff im Denken Paul Tillichs*. Hamburg, 1969.

Edwards, P. 'Professor Tillich's Confusions', *MIND*, LXXIV (1965), 192–214.

Emmet, D. M. 'Ground of Being', *JThSt*, XV (1964), 288–92.

—. Review of *Systematic Theology*, volume I, by Paul Tillich in *JThSt*, IV (1953), 294–8.

Ferré, N. F. S. et al. *Paul Tillich: Retrospect and Future*. New York, 1966.

Ferrell, D. R. *The Relationship of Philosophy and Theology in the Thought of Paul Tillich.* Ph.D. diss., Graduate Theological Union, 1974.

Ford, L. S. *The Ontological Foundation of Paul Tillich's Theory of Religious Symbol.* Ph. D. diss., Yale University, 1963.

—. 'The Three Strands of Tillich's Theory of Religious Symbols', *JRel*, XLVI (1966), 104—30.

Förster, H. *Die Kritik Paul Tillichs an der Theologie Karl Barths.* Göttingen, 1964.

Fuchs, E. 'Gesellschaftliche Befangenheit im Werke Paul Tillichs', *WissZdKarl-Marx-Univ-Leipzig*, XIII (1964), 83-9.

Gerhards, H.-J. *Utopie als innergeschichtlicher Aspekt der Eschatologie.* Gütersloh, 1973.

Gill, J. H. 'Paul Tillich's Religious Epistemology', *RelSt*, III (1968), 477—98.

Good, G. S. *The Christian Message in the Theology of Paul Tillich.* Ph. D. diss., University of Iowa, 1967.

Green, W. B. *The Concept of Culture in the Thought of Paul Tillich.* Ph. D. diss., University of Edinburgh, 1955.

Groves, R. E. *The Concept of Religion in the Writings of Dietrich Bonhoeffer and Paul Tillich.* Ph. D. diss., Baylor University, 1974.

Hamilton, K. M. '*Homo Religiosus* and Historical Faith', *Journal of Bible and Religion*, XXXIII (1965), 213—22.

—. 'Tillich's Method of Correlation', *CanJTh*, V (1959), 87—95.

—. *The System and the Gospel.* London, 1963.

Hammond, G. B. 'Examination of Tillich's Method of Correlation', *Journal of Bible and Religion*, XXXII (1964), 248—51.

—. *Man in Estrangement.* Nashville, 1965.

Hartmann, W. H. 'Heilsgeschichtliche Utopie: Über Paul Tillichs Begriff des Utopischen', *Monatsschrift für Pastoraltheologie*, L (1961), 409—16.

—. *Die Methode der Korrelation von philosophischen Fragen und theologischen Antworten bei Paul Tillich.* Göttingen, 1954.

—. 'Paul Tillich', *Tendenzen der Theologie im 20. Jahrhundert: Eine Geschichte in Porträts.* Ed. H. J. Schultz. Stuttgart, 1966, pp. 270—6.

Henel, I. C. *Religion des konkreten Geistes.* Stuttgart, 1968.

Hennig, K. ed. *Des Spannungsboden: Festgabe für Paul Tillich zum 75. Geburtstag.* Stuttgart, 1961.

Herberger, K. 'Historismus und Kairos: Die Überwindung des Historismus bei Ernst Troeltsch und Paul Tillich', *Theologische Blätter*, XIV (1935), 129—41, 161—75.

Hiltner, S. 'Tillich the Person: A Review Article', *ThToday*, XXX (1974), 382—8.

Hinrichs, J. 'Der Ort der Metaphysik im System der Wissenschaften bei Paul Tillich', *ZKathTh*, XCII (1970), 249—86.

Hirsch, E. *Christliche Freiheit und politische Bindung.* Hamburg, 1934.
—. Review of 'Religionsphilosophie' by Paul Tillich in *ThLit.* LI (1926), 97–103.
Holmer, P. L. 'Paul Tillich and the Language about God', *JRelTh*, XXII (1965), 35–50.
—. 'Paul Tillich: Language and Meaning', *JRelTh*, XXII (1965), 85–106.
Hook, J. M. v. *Paul Tillich's Conception of the Relation between Philosophy and Theology.* Ph. D. diss., Columbia University, 1966.
Hook, S. ed. *Religious Experience and Truth.* London, 1962.
Hopper, D. H. *Paul Tillich: A Theological Portrait.* Philadelphia, 1968.
—. *Presuppositions of the Method of Correlation: A Study of the Theological Method of Paul Tillich.* Th. D. diss., Princeton Theological Seminary, 1959.
Johnson, W. G. *Martin Luther's Law-Gospel Distinction and Paul Tillich's Method of Correlation: A Study of Parallels.* Ph. D. diss., University of Iowa, 1966.
Kaufman, G. D. 'Can a Man Serve Two Masters?', *ThToday*, XV (1958), 59–77.
Kegley, C. W. 'Paul Tillich on the Philosophy of Art', *JAesArtCrit*, XIX (1960–1), 175–84.
—. and R. W. Bretall, eds. *The Theology of Paul Tillich.* New York, 1952.
Kelsey, D. H. *The Fabric of Paul Tillich's Theology.* New Haven, 1967.
Kriegstein, M. von. *Die Methode der Korrelation und der Symbolbegriff Paul Tillichs.* Hamburg, 1972.
Kuhlman, G. *Brunstäd und Tillich: zum Problem einer Theonomie der Kultur.* Tübingen, 1928.
Langford, T. A. *A Critical Analysis of Paul Tillich's Method of Correlation.* Ph. D. diss., Duke University, 1958.
Leese, K. „Die Geschichtsphilosophie des religiösen Sozialismus", *Christliche Welt*, XXXVII (1923), cols. 370–85.
—. Review of *Das System der Wissenschaften* by Paul Tillich in *Christliche Welt*, XL (1926), 317–25, 371–75.
Leibrecht, W., ed. *Religion and Culture: Essays in Honor of Paul Tillich.* London, 1958.
Lewis, D. 'The Conceptual Structure of Tillich's Method of Correlation', *Encount*, XXVIII (1967), 263–74.
Lindner, R. *Grundlegung einer Theologie der Gesellschaft, dargestellt an der Theologie Paul Tillichs.* Hamburg, 1960.
Loomer, B. M. 'Tillich's Theology of Correlation', *JRel*, XXXVI (1956), 150–6.
Lyons, J. R., ed. *The Intellectual Legacy of Paul Tillich.* Detroit, 1969.
Macleod, A. M. *Tillich: An Essay on the Role of Ontology in his Philosophical Theology.* London, 1973.
Mahan, W. W. *Dislocations in the System and Method of Paul Tillich's Systematic Theology.* Ph. D. diss., University of Texas, 1967.
Mahlmann, T. 'Eschatologie und Utopie im geschichtsphilosophischen Denken Paul Tillichs', *NeueZSysTh*, VII (1965), 339–70.

Martin, B. *Paul Tillich's Doctrine of Man*. London, 1966.
May, R. *Paulus: A Personal Portrait of Paul Tillich*. New York, 1973.
McKelway, A. J. *The Systematic Theology of Paul Tillich*. Richmond, 1964.
Mews, S. P. 'Paul Tillich and the Religious Situation of American Intellectuals', *Religion*, II (1972), 122–40.
Michel, M. *De Schleiermacher a Tillich*. Diss. Strasbourg, 1975.
Mokrosch, R. *Theologische Freiheitsphilosophie*. Frankfurt, 1976.
Moritz, H. 'Karl Barths und Paul Tillichs „unterirdische Arbeitsgemeinschaft" und Gegensatz während der Zeit der Weimarer Republik', in *Ruf und Antwort: Festgabe für Emil Fuchs zum 90. Geburtstag*. Leipzig, 1964, pp. 90–9.
—. ‚Macht und politische Romantik: Die religionssoziologische Analyse Paul Tillichs im Jahre 1931/32', *WissZd Karl-Marx-Univ Leipzig*, XII (1963), 595–8.
Niebuhr, R. 'The Contribution of Paul Tillich', *Religion in Life*, VI (1937), 574–81.
Noack, H. ‚Der Ort der Kunst im Denken Paul Tillichs', *Zeitwende*, XXXIII (1962), 598–611.
Nörenberg, K.-D. *Analogia Imaginis: Der Symbolbegriff in der Theologie Paul Tillichs*. Gütersloh, 1966.
O'Meara, T. A., and C. D. Weisser, eds. *Paul Tillich in Catholic Thought*. London, 1965.
Osborne, K. B. *New Being*, The Hague, 1969.
Pannenberg, W. *Basic Questions of Theology*. vol. 2. London, 1971, pp. 201–33.
Pauck, W. and M. *Paul Tillich: Life and Thought*, vol. I. New York, 1976.
Perkins, R. W. *The Christologies of Friedrich Schleiermacher and Paul Tillich*. Ph. D. diss., Boston University, 1968.
Petit, J.-C. *La philosophie de la religion de Paul Tillich*. Montréal, 1974.
—. ‚Tillichs Religionsphilosophie und der Anspruch der neuen Politischen Theologie', *NeueZSysTh*, XIX (1978), 150–71.
Pfeiffer, A., ed. *Religiöse Sozialisten*. Olten and Freiburg, 1976.
Rathburn, J. W., and F. Burwick, 'Paul Tillich and the Philosophy of Schelling', *IntPhilQuart*, IV (1964), 373–93.
Ratschow, C. H., ed. *Evangelische Theologie in den Fraglichkeiten der modernen Welt*. Stuttgart, 1968.
Reetz, U. *Das Sakramentale in der Theologie Paul Tillichs*. Stuttgart, 1974.
Reisner, E. ‚Die Frage der Philosophie und die Antwort der Theologie', *ZThKirche*, LIII (1956), 251–63.
Rhein, C. *Paul Tillich, Philosoph und Theologe: Eine Einführung in Sein Denken*. Stuttgart, 1957.
Robinson, J. A. T. *Honest to God*. London, 1963.
Rößler, A. *Die Predigttheorie Paul Tillichs*. Tübingen, 1971.
Rowe, W. L. *Religious Symbols and God: A Philosophical Study of Tillich's Theology*. Chicago, 1968.

Rückert, H. ‚Echte Probleme und falsche Probleme: zur Auseinandersetzung zwischen Hirsch und Tillich', *Deutsche Theologie*, II (1935), 36–45.
Satrom, M. *Der Begriff der Religion im Werk Paul Tillichs*. Marburg, 1973.
Scharlemann, R. P. ‚Der Begriff der Systematik bei Paul Tillich', *NeueZSysTh*. VIII (1966), 242–54.
—. *Reflection and Doubt in the Thought of Paul Tillich*. New Haven, 1969.
—. 'The Scope of Systematics: An Analysis of Tillich's Two Systems', *JRel*, XLVIII (1968), 136–49.
—. ‚Seinsstruktur und Seinstiefe in der Tillichschen Methode der Korrelation', *KerDo*, XI (1965), 245–55.
—. 'Tillich's Method of Correlation: Two Proposed Revisions', *JRel*, XLVI (1966), 92–103.
Schedler, K. *Natur und Gnade: Das sakramentale Denken in der frühen Theologie Paul Tillichs (1919–1935)*. Stuttgart, 1970.
Schmidt, E. ‚Gedanken zu Paul Tillichs philosophischer Theologie: eine Apologie', *NeueZSysTh*, V (1963), 97–118.
—. Review of *Systematische Theologie*, volume I, by Paul Tillich in *ThLit*, LXXXII (1957), 622–4.
Schmitz, J. *Die apologetische Theologie Paul Tillichs*. Mainz, 1966.
Schneider-Flume, G. ‚Kritische Theologie contra theologisch-politischen Offenbarungsglauben: Eine vergleichende Strukturanalyse der politischen Theologie Paul Tillichs, Emanuel Hirschs und Richard Shaulls', *EvangTh*, XXXIII (1973), 114–37.
Schrader, R. W. *The Nature of Theological Argument*. 'Harvard Dissertations in Religion'. Missoula, 1975.
Schwanz, P. ‚Das für Tillichs „Methode der Korrelation" grundlegende Problem der Vermittlung', *NeueZSysTh*, XV (1973), 254–71.
Schwerdtfeger, E. *Die politische Theorie in der Theologie Paul Tillichs*. Marburg, 1969.
Smart, R. N. 'Being and the Bible', *RevMetaph*, IX (1956), 589–607.
—. 'The Intellectual Crisis of British Christianity', *Th*, LXVIII (1965), 31–8.
Smith, D. M. 'The Historical Jesus in Paul Tillich's Christology', *JRel*, XLVI (1966), 131–48.
Soden, H. von. 'Kirchentheologie und Kulturtheologie', *ZThKirche*, II (1921), 468–77.
Sommer, G. F. *The Significance of the Late Philosophy of Schelling for the Formation and Interpretation of the Thought of Paul Tillich*. Ph. D. diss., Duke University, 1961.
Sprague, E. 'On Professor Tillich's Ontological Question', *IntPhilQuart*, II (1962), 81–7.
Streiker, L. D. *The Mystical A Priori: Paul Tillich's Critical Phenomenology of Religion*. Ph. D. diss., Princeton University, 1968.

Stumme, J. R. *Socialism in Theological Perspective*. 'AAR Dissertation Series'. Missoula, 1978.
Taubes, J. 'On the Nature of the Theological Method: Some Reflections on the Methodological Principles of Tillich's Theology', *JRel*, XXXIV (1954), 12—25.
Tavard, G. H. Review of *Systematic Theology*, volume III, by Paul Tillich in *Commonweal* (7 February, 1964) and reprinted in *JRel*, XLVI (1966), 223—6.
—. *Paul Tillich and the Christian Message*. New York, 1962.
Theek, B. ‚Ein kurzer Gang von Paul Tillich zu Emil Fuchs', in *Ruf und Antwort: Festgabe für Emil Fuchs zum 90. Geburtstag*. Leipzig, 1964, pp. 90—9.
Thomas, J. H. 'Correlation of Philosophy and Theology in Tillich's System', *LonQuartHolR*, CLXXXIV (1959), 47—54.
—. *Paul Tillich*. London, 1965.
—. *Paul Tillich: An Appraisal*. London, 1963.
—. 'The Problem of Defining a Theology of Culture with Reference to the Theology of Paul Tillich', in *Creation, Christ and Culture*. Edited by R. W. A. McKinney. Edinburgh, 1976, pp. 272—87.
Tillich, H. *From Time to Time*, New York, 1973; London, 1974.
Track, J. *Der theologische Ansatz Paul Tillichs*. Göttingen, 1975.
Trillhaas, W. ‚Die Grenze und das Ganze: Zum Gedenken an Paul Tillich', *ThLit*, XCI (1966), 562—7.
Ulrich, T. *Ontologie, Theologie, Gesellschaftliche Praxis: Studium zum religiösen Sozialismus Paul Tillichs und Carl Mennickes*. Zürich, 1971.
Valen-Sendstad, A. 'Ontologiske Implikasjoner I Paul Tillichs Korrelasjonsmethode', *NTTid*, LXXI (1970), 30—61.
Veatch, H. 'Tillich's Distinction Between Metaphysics and Theology', *RevMetaph*, X (1957), 529—33.
Wagner, F. ‚Absolute Positivität: Das Grundthema der Theologie Paul Tillichs', *NeueZSysTh*, XV (1973), 172—91.
Wainwright, W. J. 'Paul Tillich and Arguments for the Existence of God', *JAmARel*, XXXIX (1971), 171—85.
Wardlow, H. R. *The Problem of Theological Method: A Study of Kierkegaard and Tillich*. Ph. D. diss., University of Glasgow, 1963.
Welch, C. 'Paul Tillich and Theology of Correlation', *Religion*, Ed. Paul Ramsey, Englewood Cliffs, New Jersey, 1965, pp. 249—59.
Wendland, H.-D. ‚Was bedeuten Tillichs Thesen über den Protestantismus?', *NeueZSysTh*, V (1963), 192—213.
Wernsdörfer, T. *Die Entfremdete Welt: Eine Untersuchung zur Theologie Paul Tillichs*. Zürich, 1968.
White, F. T. *Systematic Theological Principles of Friedrich Schleiermacher and Paul Tillich*. Ph. D. diss., Columbia University, 1966.
Williamson, C. M. 'Tillich's Two Types of Philosophy of Religion', *JRel*, LII (1972), 205—22.

Winter, G. *Zur Geschichtsauffassung Paul Tillichs*. Berlin, 1967.
Wittschier, S. *Paul Tillich: Seine Pneuma-Theologie*. Nuremberg, 1975.
Wrzecionko, P. 'Die Grundlegung der Theologie Paul Tillichs', *ThLit*, LXXXV (1960), cols. 875—8.
Zabala, A. J. *Myth and Symbol: An Analysis of Myth and Symbol in Paul Tillich*. Ph. D. diss., Institut Catholique de Paris, 1959.
Zahrnt, H. *Die Sache mit Gott*. Munich, 1966, pp. 382—467.

SELECTED RELATED MATERIAL

Aaron, R. I. *Theory of Universals*. 2nd. ed.; Oxford, 1967.
[Adelung, J. C.] *Versuch einer Geschichte der Kultur des Menschlichen*. Leipzig, 1782.
Alston, W. *Philosophy of Language*. Englewood Cliffs, New Jersey, 1964.
Altmann, A. ‚Hermann Cohens Begriff der Korrelation', *In Zwei Welten: Siegfried Moses zum 75. Geburtstag*. Edited by H. Tramer. Tel-Aviv, 1962, pp. 377—99.
Antoni, C. *From History to Sociology: The Transition in German Historical Thinking*. London, 1962.
Austin, J.-L. *Philosophical Papers*. Oxford, 1961.
Ayer, A. J. *The Problem of Knowledge*. 2nd ed.; Harmondsworth, 1967.
Baillie, J., ed. *Natural Theology*. Trans. P. Fraenkel. London, 1946.
Bambrough, J. R. *Reason, Truth and God*. London, 1969.
—. 'Universals and Family Resemblances', *ProcArisSoc*, LXI (1960—1), 207—22.
Banton, M., ed. *The Relevance of Models for Social Anthropology*. London, 1965.
Barth, K. *Church Dogmatics*. Eds. G. W. Bromiley and T. F. Torrance; trans. G. T. Thomson *et al*. Edinburgh, 1936—72.
—. *The Epistle to the Romans*. Trans. E. C. Hoskins. Oxford, 1933.
—. *The Humanity of God*. Richmond, 1960.
—. ‚Nein!: Antwort an Emil Brunner', *Theologische Existenz Heute*, nr. 14 (1934).
—. *Protestant Theology in the Nineteenth Century*. London, 1972.
—. *Römerbrief*. Bern, 1919; 2nd. ed., repr. Zürich, 1971.
—. *Theological Existence Today: A Plea for Theological Freedom*. Trans. R. B. Hoyle. London, 1933.
—. *Theology and Church*. Trans. L. P. Smith. New York, 1962.
—. *The Word of God and the Word of Man*. New York, 1957.
—. and E. Thurneysen. *Briefwechsel*, vol. II. Zürich, 1974.
Bell, R. H. 'Wittengstein and Descriptive Theology', *RelSt*, V (1969), 1—18.
Birkner, H.-J. ‚Liberale Theologie' in *Kirchen und Liberalismus im 19. Jahrhundert*. Eds. M. Schmidt and G. Schwaiger. Göttingen, 1976.
—. *Schleiermachers christliche Sittenlehre*. Berlin, 1964.
Black, M. *Models and Metaphors*. Ithaca, 1962.

Böbel, F. ‚Allgemein menschliche und christliche Gotteserkenntnis bei Emanuel Hirsch', *NeueZSysTh*, V (1963), 296–335.
Bodenstein, W. *Neige des Historismus*. Gütersloh, 1959.
Bonhoeffer, D. *Widerstand und Ergebung*. Ed. E. Bethge. 13th ed.; Munich, 1966 [1951].
Bosse, H. *Marx, Weber, Troeltsch: Religionssoziologie und marxistische Ideologiekritik*. 2nd ed.; Munich, 1971.
Braithwaite, R. B. *Scientific Explanation*. Cambridge, 1953.
Brandt, R. B. *The Philosophy of Schleiermacher: The Development of His Theory of Scientific and Religious Knowledge*. New York, 1941.
Brown, W. A. *The Essence of Christianity: A Study in History of Definition*. London, 1904.
Bruford, W. H. *The German Tradition of Self-Cultivation*. Cambridge, 1975.
Bultmann, R. *Glauben und Verstehen*. 4 vols. Tübingen, 1933–65.
Burckhardt, J. *Die Kultur der Renaissance in Italien*. Basel, 1860.
Cassirer, E. *The Philosophy of the Enlightenment*. Translated by C. A. Koelin and J. P. Pettegrove. Boston, 1955
Clayton, J. P., ed. *Ernst Troeltsch and the Future of Theology: The Lancaster Symposium*. Cambridge, 1976.
–. ‚Sprache, Sinn und Verifizierungsverfahren: Aspekte moderner Religionsphilosophie in Großbritannien', *PhilJahr*, LXXXV (1978), 144–62.
Cochrane, A. C. *The Church's Confession Under Hitler*. Philadelphia, 1962.
Cohen, H. *Ethik des reinen Willens*. Berlin, 1907.
Conway, J. S. *The Nazi Persecution of the Churches 1933–1945*. London, 1968.
Cornford, F. M. *Plato's Theory of Knowledge*. London, 1960.
Douglas, M. Review of *The Interpretation of Cultures* by C. Geertz in *Times Literary Supplement* (8. August 1975), pp. 886–7.
Durrant, M. *The Logical Status of "God" and the Function of Theological Sentences*. London, 1973.
Dyson, A. O. *History in the Philosophy and Theology of Ernst Troeltsch*. D. Phil. diss., Oxford University, 1968.
Ebel, W. *Catalogus Professorum Gottingensium, 1734–1962*. Göttingen, 1962.
Ebeling, G. ‚Die Bedeutung der historisch-kritischen Methode für die protestantische Theologie und Kirche', *ZThKirche*, XLVII (1950), 1–46.
–. *Theology and Proclamation*. London, 1966.
–. *Word and Faith*. Philadelphia, 1963.
Elert, W. *Der Kampf um das Christentum*. Munich, 1921.
Emmet, D. M. *Rules, Roles and Relations*. London, 1966.
Engel, S. M. *Wittgenstein's Doctrine of the Tyranny of Language*. The Hague, 1971.
Eyck, E. A. *History of the Weimar Republic*. 2 vols. New York, 1970.
Fichte, J. G. *Sämmtliche Werke*. Ed. J. H. Fichte. Berlin, 1845–1846.
Flew, A. G. N. (ed.) *Logic and Language*. 2nd series; London, 1953.

Flückiger, F. *Philosophie und Theologie bei Schleiermacher*. Zollikon – Zürich, 1947.
Frey, C. *Reflexion und Zeit*. Gütersloh, 1973.
Fürst, W., ed. *„Dialektische Theologie" in Scheidung und Bewährung, 1933–1936*. Munich, 1966.
Gadamer, H. G. ‚Martin Heidegger und die Marburger Theologie', *Zeit und Geschichte: Dankesgabe an Rudolf Bultmann zum 80. Geburtstag*. Ed. by E. Dinkler. Tübingen, 1964, pp. 479–90.
Galling, K., ed. *Religion in Geschichte und Gegenwart*. 6 vols.; 3rd ed.; Tübingen, 1957–62.
Gay, P. *The Enlightenment: An Interpretation*. 2 vols. New York, 1966, 1969.
–. *Weimar Culture: The Outsider as Insider*. London, 1968.
Geertz, C. *The Interpretation of Cultures*. London, 1975.
Gerrish, B. A. 'Jesus, Myth and History: Troeltsch's Stand in the "Christ-Myth" Debate', *JRel*, LV (1975), 13–35.
Gestrich, C. *Neuzeitliches Denken und die Spaltung der dialektischen Theologie*. Tübingen, 1977.
Gierke, O. *Natural Law and the Theory of Society*. Cambridge, 1923.
Gogarten, F. 'Historismus', *Zwischen den Zeiten*, VIII (1924), 7–25.
Gombrich, E. H. *In Search of Cultural History*. Oxford, 1968.
Graf, F. W. ‚Ursprüngliches Gefühl unmittelbarer Koinzidenz des Differenten', *ZThKirche*, LXXV (1978), 147–86.
Gray, R. *The German Tradition in Literature, 1871–1945*. Cambridge, 1965.
Groll, W. *Ernst Troeltsch und Karl Barth – Kontinuität im Widerspruch*. Munich, 1976.
Härle, W. ‚Der Aufruf der 93 Intellektuellen und Karl Barths Bruch mit der liberalen Theologie', *ZThKirche*, LXXII (1975), 207–24.
Haftmann, W. *Painting in the Twentieth Century*. 2 vols. 2nd ed.; London, 1965.
Harnack, A. v. *Das Wesen des Christentums*. Munich and Hamburg, 1964.
Harris, M. *The Rise of Anthropological Theory: A History of Theories of Culture*. London, 1968.
Hartlaub, G. F. *Kunst und Religion: Ein Versuch über die Möglichkeit neuer religiöser Kunst*. Leipzig, 1919.
Harvey, V. A. *The Historian and the Believer*. London, 1967.
Hegel, G. W. F. *Werke in 20 Bänden*. Frankfurt, 1969–71.
Heidegger, M. *Einführung in die Metaphysik*. Tübingen, 1953.
–. *Die Frage nach der Wahrheit*. Frankfurt, 1976.
–. *Kant und das Problem der Metaphysik*. Bonn, 1929.
–. *Sein und Zeit*. 2nd. ed.; Halle, 1929.
Herder, J. G. *Ideen zur Philosophie der Geschichte der Menschheit*. 1784–91; repr. Darmstadt, 1966.
Herms, E. ‚Die Ethik des Wissens beim späten Schleiermacher', *ZThKirche*, LXXIII (1976), 471–523.

—. *Herkunft, Entfaltung und erste Gestalt des Systems der Wissenschaften bei Schleiermacher*. Gütersloh, 1974.
Hesse, M. B. *Models and Analogies in Science*. 2nd ed.; Notre Dame, 1966.
Hester, D. E. *Schleiermacher in Tübingen: A Study in Reaction*. Ph. D. diss., Columbia University, 1970.
Hick, J., ed. *The Myth of God Incarnate*. London, 1977.
Hilderbrandt, H. *Die Kunst des 19. und 20. Jahrhundert*. Potsdam, 1924.
Hirsch, E. *Deutschlands Schicksal*. 3rd ed. Göttingen, 1925.
—. *Die Gegenwärtige, Geistige Lage*. Göttingen, 1934.
—. *Geschichte der neueren evangelischen Theologie*. vols. 4 and 5. Gütersloh, 1949—1968⁴.
—. ‚Meine theologischen Anfänge', *Freies Christentum*, nr. 10 (1951).
—. ‚Meine Wendejahre', *Freies Christentum*, nr. 12 (1951).
—. *Die Reich-Gottes-Begriffe des neueren europäischen Denkens*. Göttingen, 1922.
—. *Der Weg der Theologie*. Stuttgart, 1937.
—. *Zweifel und Glaube*. Frankfurt, 1937.
Hiż, H., ed. *Questions*. Dordrecht, 1977.
Hodges, M. 'Wittgenstein on Universals', *PhilSt*, XXIV (1973), 22—30.
Horney, K. *Our Inner Conflicts*. New York. 1945.
Hospers, J. *An Introduction to Philosophical Analysis*. 2nd ed.; London, 1967.
Iggers, G. *The German Conception of History*. Middletown, Conn., 1968.
Ihmels, L. *Theonomie und Autonomie*. Leipzig, 1903.
Jay, M. *The Dialectical Imagination*. London, 1973.
Johnson, W. A. *On Religion: A Study on Theological Method in Schleiermacher and Nygren*. Leiden, 1964.
Jørgensen, P. H. *Die Ethik Schleiermachers*. Munich, 1959.
Kähler, M. *Geschichte der protestantischen Dogmatik im 19. Jahrhundert*. Edited by Ernst Kähler. Munich, 1962.
—. *The So-called Historical Jesus and the Historic Biblical Christ*. Trans. and edited by C. E. Braaten. Philadelphia, 1964.
—. *Die Wissenschaft der christlichen Lehre von dem evangelischen Grundartikel aus im Abriß dargestellt*. 3rd ed.; Leipzig, 1905.
Kaftan, J. ‚Erwiederung', *ZThKirche*, VIII (1898), 70—96.
—. ‚Die Selbständigkeit des Christentums', *ZThKirche*, VI (1896), 373—94.
Kandinsky, W. *Über das geistige in der Kunst*. Munich, 1912.
Kant, I. *Gesammelte Schriften*. Berlin, 1910ff.
Kasch, W. *Die Sozialphilosophie von Ernst Troeltsch*. Tübingen, 1963.
Kattenbusch, F. *Die Deutsche Evangelische Theologie seit Schleiermacher*. 2 vols. Gießen, I (1924⁴), II (1934).
Katz, S. T., ed. *Mysticism and Philosophical Analysis*. London and New York, 1978.
Kierkegaard, S. *Concluding Unscientific Postscript*. Trans. D. F. Swenson. Princeton, 1968.

—. *Philosophical Fragments*. Trans. D. Swenson. Princeton, 1967.
—. *The Point of View for my Work as an Author: A Report to History*. Trans. Walter Lowrie. New York, 1962.
Klee, P. *Über moderne Kunst*. 1924; repr., Bern, 1949.
Klemm, G. *Allgemeine Kulturgeschichte der Menschheit*. Leipzig, 1843.
—. *Allgemeine Kulturwissenschaft*. Leipzig, 1854.
Knox, J. *The Church and the Reality of Christ*. London, 1963.
—. *Limits of Unbelief*. London, 1970.
Kroeber, A. L. *An Anthropologist Looks at History*. Berkeley, 1963.
—. *Style and Civilization*. Ithaca, New York, 1957.
—. and C. Kluckhohn. *Culture: A Critical Review of Concepts and Definitions*. New York, 1952.
—. and T. Parsons. 'The Concepts of Culture and of Social System', *American Sociological Review*, XXIII (1958), 582–3.
Kroner, R. *Culture and Faith*. Chicago, 1951.
—. *Von Kant bis Hegel*. 2 vols in 1. 2nd ed.; Tübingen, 1961.
Laqueur, W. *Weimar: A Cultural History, 1918–33*. London, 1974.
Leipold, H. *Offenbarung und Geschichte als Problem des Verstehens: Eine Untersuchung zur Theologie Martin Kählers*. Gütersloh, 1962.
Lessing, E. *Die Geschichtsphilosophie Ernst Troeltschs*. Hamburg, 1965.
Leuze, R. *Die außerchristlichen Religionen bei Hegel*. Göttingen, 1975.
Lewin, K. *Field Theory in Social Science*. New York, 1951.
Lichtenstein, E. *Zur Entwicklung des Bildungsbegriffs von Meister Eckhardt bis Hegel*. Heidelberg, 1966.
Liebing, H. ‚F. C. Baurs Kritik an Schleiermacher', *ZThKirche*, LIV (1957), 225–43.
Link, H.-G. *Geschichte Jesu und Bild Christi*. Neukirchen, 1975.
Lütgert, W. *Natur und Geist Gottes: Vorträge zur Ethik*. Leipzig, 1910.
MacKinnon, D. M. *The Problem of Metaphysics*. Cambridge, 1974.
Mandelbaum, M. 'Family Resemblances and Generalizations Concerning the Arts', *AmerPhilQuart*, II (1965), 219–28.
Mann, G. *The History of Germany since 1789*. Harmondsworth, 1974.
Mannheim, K. *Essays on the Sociology of Knowledge*. London, 1952.
—. *Ideology and Utopia: An Introduction to the Sociology of Knowledge*. London, 1960.
Manser, A. R. 'Games and Family Resemblances', *Phil*, XLII (1967), 210–25.
Marx, K. H. *Critique of Hegel's "Philosophy of Right"*. Ed. J. O'Malley. Cambridge, 1970.
—. and F. Engels. *The German Ideology*. Ed. C. J. Arthur. London, 1970.
Marx: Early Writings. Ed. Lucio Colletti. London, 1975.
Marx – Engels: Selected Works. Moscow and London, 1970.
Meier, K. *Die Deutschen Christen*. 3rd ed.; Göttingen and Halle, 1967.
Moltmann, J., ed. *Anfänge der dialektischen Theologie*. 2 vols. Munich, 1962–3.

Mowat, C. L., ed. *The Shifting Balance of World Forces, 1898–1945*. Vol. XII of *The New Cambridge Modern History*. 2nd ed.; C. U. P., 1968.
Myers, B. *Expressionism: A Generation in Revolt*. London, 1963.
Nadel, S. F. *The Foundations of Social Anthropology*. London, 1951.
Nagel, O. *Käthe Kollwitz*. London, 1971.
Neuenschwander, *Denker des Glaubens*, vol. II. Gütersloh, 1974.
Niebergall, F. ‚Über die Absolutheit des Christentums', *Theologische Arbeiten aus dem Rheinischen wissenschaftlichen Predigerverein*, IV (1900), 46–86.
Niebuhr, H. R. *Christ and Culture*. New York, 1959.
—. *Ernst Troeltsch's Philosophy of Religion*. Ph. D. diss., Yale University, 1924.
—. *The Social Sources of Denominationalism*. Cleveland, 1957.
Niebuhr, R. R. *Schleiermacher on Christ and Religion: A New Introduction*. New York, 1964.
Nielsen, K. 'Wittgensteinian Fideism', *Phil*, XLII (1967), 191–209.
Nietzsche, F. *Werke*. Ed. K. Schlechta. 3 vols. Darmstadt, 1966.
Ogden, S. M. *Christ without Myth*. New York, 1961.
O'Shaugnessy, R. J. 'On Having Something in Common', *Mind*, LXXIX (1970), 436–40.
Otto, R. *The Idea of the Holy*. Trans. J. W. Harvey. Oxford, 1958.
Overbeck, F. *Christentum und Kultur*. 1919; repr. Darmstadt, 1963.
Pannenberg, W. *Wissenschaftstheorie und Theologie*. Frankfurt, 1973.
Pfeiffer, A. *Franz Overbecks Kritik des Christentums*. Göttingen, 1975.
Piper, O. *Recent Developments in German Protestantism*. London, 1934.
Pitcher, G., ed. *Wittgenstein: The Philosophical Investigations*. London, 1968.
Pretzel, U. ‚Ernst Troeltschs Berufung an die Berliner Universität', *Studium Berolinense*. Berlin, 1960, pp. 507–14.
Prolingheuer, H. *Der Fall Karl Barth, 1934–1935*. Neukirchen, 1977.
Quapp, E. H. U. *Christus im Leben Schleiermachers: Vom Herrnhuter zum Spinozisten*. Göttingen, 1972.
Quine, W. *From a Logical Point of View*. 2nd. ed.; New York, 1963.
Radcliffe-Brown, A. R. *A Natural Science of Culture*. Glencoe, Ill., 1957.
—. *Structure and Function in Primitive Society*. London, 1952.
Raphael, D. D. 'Universals, Resemblances, and Identity', *ProcArisSoc*, LV (1954–5), 109–32.
Rauhut, F. ‚Die Herkunft der Worte und Begriffe „Kultur", „Civilisation" und „Bildung"', *Germanisch-Romanische Monatsschrift*, n. s. III (1953), 81–91.
Reardon, B. M. G. *Hegel's Philosophy of Religion*. London, 1977.
Richmond, J. *Faith and Philosophy*. London, 1966.
—. *Theology and Metaphysics*. London, 1971.
Rickert, H. *Allgemeine Grundlegung der Philosophie*. Tübingen, 1921.
Ringer, F. K. *The Decline of the German Mandarins: The German Academic Community, 1890–1933*. Cambridge, Mass., 1969.

Ritter, J., and K. Gründer, eds. *Historisches Wörterbuch der Philosophie*. Darmstadt, 1971 ff.
Robinson, J. M., ed. *The Beginnings of Dialectic Theology*. Trans. by K. R. Crim and L. De Grazia. Richmond, 1968.
—. *A New Quest of the Historical Jesus*. London, 1959.
Rupp, G. *Culture Protestantism: German Liberal Theology at the Turn of the Twentieth Century*. Missoula, 1977.
Rust, E. C. *Towards a Theological Understanding of History*. Oxford, 1963.
Ryder, A. J. *The German Revolution of 1918*. Cambridge, 1967.
Ryle, G. *The Concept of Mind*. New York, 1949.
Samuel, R., and R. H. Thomas. *Expressionism in German Life, Literature and the Theatre (1910–1924)*. Cambridge, 1939.
Sapir, E. 'Culture, Genuine and Spurious', *The American Journal of Sociology*, XXIX (1924), 401–29.
Schaper, E. 'The Concept of Style: The Sociologist's Key to Art?', *British Journal of Aesthetics*, IX (1969), 246–57.
Schelling, F. W. J. *Sämtliche Werke*. Ed. K. F. A. Schelling. 14 vols. Stuttgart, 1856–61.
Schleiermacher-Auswahl. Ed. H. Bolli. Munich and Hamburg, 1968.
Schleiermacher, F. D. E. *Der Christliche Glaube*. 2 vols. 7th ed.; Berlin, 1960.
—. *Grundriß der philosophischen Ethik*. Ed. A. Tweston. Berlin, 1841.
—. *Kleine Schriften und Predigten*, vol. I. Eds. H. Gerdes and E. Hirsch. Berlin, 1970.
—. *On Religion: Speeches to Its Cultured Despisers*. Trans. J. Oman. New York, 1958.
—. *Über die Religion*. Ed. R. Otto. Göttingen, 1967^6.
Schlippe, G. von. *Die Absolutheit des Christentums bei Ernst Troeltsch auf dem Hintergrund der Denkfelder des 19. Jahrhunderts*. Neustadt, 1966.
Schmidt, E. *Hegels System der Theologie*. Berlin, 1974.
Schmithals, W. *An Introduction to the Theology of Rudolf Bultmann*. London, 1968.
Schneider-Flume, G. *Die politische Theologie Emanuel Hirschs, 1918–1933*. Bern and Frankfurt, 1971.
Scholder, K. *Die Kirchen und das Dritte Reich*, vol. I. Frankfurt, 1977.
Schweitzer, A. *Geschichte der Leben-Jesu-Forschung*. 2 vols. Munich and Hamburg, 1966.
—. *The Philosophy of Civilization*. 2 vols. London: 1932^2, 1929.
Seligman, E. R. A., and A. Johnson, eds. *Encyclopedia of the Social Sciences*. New York, 1931.
Sherry, P. J. 'Is Religion a "Form of Life"?', *AmerPhilQuart*, IX (1972), 159–67.
—. *Religion, Truth and Language Games*. London, 1977.
—. 'Truth and the "Religious Language Game"', *Phil*, XLVII (1972), 18–37.
Siegfried, T. *Das Wort und die Existenz: Eine Auseinandersetzung mit der dialektischen Theologie*, vol. I: *Die Theologie des Worts bei Karl Barth*. Gotha, 1930.

Smart, J. D., ed. *Revolutionary Theology in The Making: Barth-Thurneysen Correspondence, 1914–1925.* London, 1964.
Smart, R. N. *The Phenomenon of Religion.* New York, 1973.
—. *Reasons and Faiths: An Investigation of Religious Discourse, Christian and Non-Christian.* London, 1958.
—. *The Religious Experience of Mankind.* 2nd. ed.; New York, 1976.
Sölle, D. *Politische Theologie.* Stuttgart and Berlin, 1971.
Sokel, W. H. *The Writer in Extremis: Expressionism in Twentieth-Century German Literature.* Stanford, 1959.
Spengler, O. *The Decline of the West.* Trans. C. F. Atkinson. 2 vols. as 1. London, 1932.
Spiegel, Y. *Theologie der bürgerlichen Gesellschaft: Sozialphilosophie und Glaubenslehre bei Friedrich Schleiermacher.* Munich, 1968.
Spiegler, G. *The Eternal Covenant: Schleiermacher's Experiment in Cultural Theology.* New York, 1967.
Spranger, E. *Wilhelm von Humboldt und die Humanitätsidee.* Berlin, 1909.
—. *Wilhelm von Humboldt und die Reform des Bildungswesens.* Berlin, 1910.
Stahl, E. L. *Die religiöse und die humanitätsphilosophische Bildungsidee.* Bern, 1934.
Streck, K. G. 'Der Einfluß Karl Barths in der Bekennenden Kirche Deutschlands seit 1935', *EvTheol*, XXXVIII (1978), 252–68.
Stephan, H. and M. Schmidt. *Geschichte der evangelischen Theologie in Deutschland seit dem Idealismus.* 3rd. ed.; Berlin, 1973.
Strauss, D. F. *Die christliche Glaubenslehre.* 2 vols. Darmstadt, 1973.
—. *The Old Faith and the New.* Trans. M. Blind. 2nd ed.; London, 1873.
Sykes, S. W. ‚Deutschland und England: Ein Versuch in theologischer Diplomatie', *ZThKirche*, LXIX (1972), 439–65.
—. 'The Essence of Christianity', *RelSt*, VII (1971), 291–305.
Tate, R. F., and H. Hotelling. 'Multivariate Analysis: Correlation', *International Encyclopedia of the Social Sciences.* Ed. D. L. Sills. New York, 1968, Vol. X, pp. 537–53.
Taylor, C. *Hegel.* Cambridge, 1975.
Teichmann, J. 'Universals and Common Properties', *Analysis*, XXIX (1969), 162–5.
Thielicke, H. *Der Evangelische Glaube: Grundzüge der Dogmatik.* Vol. I Tübingen, 1968.
Trillhaas, W. *Dogmatik.* Berlin, 1962.
—. *Perspektiven und Gestalten des Neuzeitlichen Christentums.* Göttingen, 1976.
Troeltsch, E. *Die Absolutheit des Christentums und die Religionsgeschichte.* Ed. T. Rendtorff. Munich and Hamburg, 1969.
—. *Die Bedeutung des Protestantismus für die Entstehung der modernen Welt.* Munich and Berlin, 1928.
—. *Christian Thought: Its History and Application.* Ed. F. v. Hügel. London, 1923.
—. *Deutscher Geist und Westeuropa.* Ed. H. Baron. Tübingen, 1925.

—. *Gesammelte Schriften*. 4 vols. Tübingen, 1912–25.
—. ‚Geschichte und Metaphysik', *ZThKirche*, VIII (1898), 1–69.
—. *Glaubenslehre*. Ed. G. v. l. Fort. Leipzig, 1925.
—. *Das historische in Kants Religionsphilosophie*. Berlin, 1904.
—. *Der Historismus und seine Überwindung*. Ed. F. v. Hügel. Berlin, 1924.
—. ‚Protestantisches Christentum und Kirche in der Neuzeit', *Die Kultur der Gegenwart*, vol. I/IV. Ed. P. Hinneberg. Leipzig and Berlin, 1906.
—. *Protestantism and Progress: A Historical Study of the Relation of Protestantism to the Modern World*. Trans. W. Montgomery. Boston, 1958.
—. ‚Die Selbständigkeit der Religion', *ZThKirche*, V (1895), 361–436; VI (1896), 71–110, 167–218.
—. *Vernunft und Offenbarung bei Johann und Melanchthon*. Göttingen, 1891.
—. *Die Wissenschaftliche Lage und ihre Anforderungen an die Theologie*. Tübingen, 1900.
Tylor, E. B. *Primitive Culture*. 1871; repr. New York, 1924.
Urban, W. M. *Language and Reality*. London, 1939.
Waismann, F. *The Principles of Linguistic Philosophy*. Ed. R. Harré. London, 1965.
Watson, J. *The Double Helix*. Harmondsworth, 1968.
Watt, R. M. *The Kings Depart*. London, 1969.
Weber, M. *The Protestant Ethic and the Spirit of Capitalism*. London, 1930.
Welch, C. *Protestant Thought in the Nineteenth Century*. Vol. I: 1799–1870. New Haven, 1972.
Whitford, F. *Expressionism*. London, 1970.
Williams, R. *Culture and Society, 1780–1950*. Harmondsworth, 1963.
—. *Keywords: A Vocabulary of Culture and Society*. London, 1976.
Wirsching, J. *Christologische Texte aus der Vermittlungstheologie des 19. Jahrhunderts*. Gütersloh, 1968.
Wisdom, J. *Philosophy and Psychoanalysis*. London, 1953.
Wittgenstein, L. *The Blue and Brown Books*. 2nd ed.; Oxford, 1969.
—. *Philosophical Investigations*. Trans. G. E. M. Anscombe. 2nd ed.; Oxford, 1958.
Wright, J. R. C. *"Above Parties": The Political Attitudes of the German Protestant Church Leadership, 1918–1933*. Oxford, 1974.
Wundt, W. *Völkerpsychologie*, Vol. X: *Kultur und Geschichte*, Leipzig, 1920.

INDEX OF NAMES

Aaron, R. I. 238
Adams. J. L. 88f, 92, 118, 192, 196, 203f
Adelung, J. C. 124
Adorno, T. W. 135
Albers, J. 200
Alston, W. P. 237
Amelung, E. 37, 118, 129, 204, 208, 226
Armbruster, C. J. 116, 118
Augustine of Hippo 90
Austin, J. L. 122
Ayer, A. J. 238

Bambrough, R. 13, 236f, 238, 239–41, 242
Banton, M. 45
Barbu, Z. 120
Baron, H. 55
Barth, K. 3, 4, 7, 9, 31, 35f, 46, 62, 63–6, 69, 87f, 113, 126, 160–4, 167f, 176, 184, 190, 209, 210, 211f, 215
Bastian, H. D. 15
Baur, F. C. 44
Beckmann, M. 200
Benktson, B.-E. 90
Benson, J. 42
Birkner, H.-J. 47, 51
Black, M. 18, 156–9, 224f
Bodenstein, W. 54
Bolli, H. 39
Bosse, H. 50, 53
Bowker, J. 117
Bradley, F. H. 187

Braithwaite, R. B. 156
Brandt, H. 166
Braque, G. 219
Breipohl, R. 37
Brinkschmidt, E. 15
Brügmann, V. 15
Bruford, W. H. 124f
Brunner, E. 9, 64, 178
Buchter, J. 8, 68, 97, 184
Büchsel, F. 196
Bultmann, R. 3, 27, 104
Burckhardt, J. 118, 143f

Camus, A. 13
Carnley, P. 52
Carroll, Lewis [C. L. Dodgson] 72
Cézanne, P. 195
Cicero 123
Cohen, H. 37
Cornford, F. M. 166
Crary, S. T. 92

Dehn, G. 208
Dell, A. 196
Dessoir, M. 172, 174
Dilthey, W. 118
Dinkler, E. 169
Dix, O. 200
Douglas, M. 120
Downie, R. S. 42
Drescher, H.-G. 53
Drews, A. 230
Durrant, M. 243

Ebel, W. 162
Ebeling, G. 8f, 97
Elert, W. 34
Emmet, D. 45
Ezekiel, M. 71

Fichte, J. G. 121, 124, 126, 194, 209
Fichte, J. H. 121, 194
Flatt, J. F. 39
Flatt, K. C. 39
Flew, A. 238
Flückiger, F. 46
Förster, E. 27, 160, 184
Francis of Assisi 90
Frey, C. 93
Fritz, A. 162
Fuchs, Emil 208
Fuchs, Ernst 65

Gadamer, H.-G. 169
Gay, P. 35
Geertz, C. 120, 122, 140, 151
Gerdes, H. 39
Gerrish, B. A. 46, 50
Gestrich, C. 64
Gierke, O. 58
Gogarten, F. 35, 163, 164
Gogh, V. van 195, 219
Gombrich, E. H. 117, 122, 140
Graf, F. W. 102
Green, W. B. 118
Groll, W. 63
Grosz, G. 200
Groves, R. E. 90
Gründer, K. 35

Härle, W. 64
Hamilton, K. 15, 110, 115, 182
Hammond, G. B. 25, 177
Harnack, A. v. 50, 55f, 163, 236, 245, 247f

Harris, M. 118
Hartlaub, G. F. 199, 200f
Hartmann, H. 208
Harvey, V. A. 52
Heald, S. S. 117
Heelas, P. L. F. 117
Heidegger, M. 13, 22, 27, 121–2, 152, 169–75
Hegel, G. W. F. 6, 7, 21, 41, 66, 68, 92–5, 103, 107, 109, 124, 131–5, 137f, 148, 164, 194, 198, 229f
Henel, I. 5
Herder, J. G. 121, 130–1, 132, 133, 148
Herms, E. 40, 47
Hervé 194
Hesse, M. 18, 156, 158, 178f
Hester, C. E. 44
Hick, J. 243
Hilderbrandt, H. 194
Hinneberg, P. 55
Hirsch, E. 8, 31, 39, 60–3, 64–6, 69, 100, 162, 164, 175f, 205, 206, 209–18
Hirsch, M. 210
Hiż, H. 186
Hodges, M. 238
Hook, J. M. van 193
Hook, S. 71, 143
Hopper, D. 26, 27, 210
Horney, K. 44
Hospers, J. 244
Hügel, F. v. 49, 55
Humboldt, W. v. 124
Hume, D. 238
Husserl, E. 169

Iggers, G. 133
Ihmels, L. 196

Jacobi, F. H. 40f
Jaspers, K. 13
Jay, M. 135

Index of Names

Jørgensen, P. H. 47
Johnson, A. 71

Kähler, M. 8, 26, 46, 108, 194, 196, 232f
Kaftan, J. 53, 54
Kandinsky, W. 199, 200
Kant, I. 34−7, 78, 87, 90, 100, 103, 104, 107, 116, 123, 126, 163, 170, 173, 196, 273
Kasch, W. F. 47
Kattenbusch, F. 7, 46
Katz, S. T. 91
Kaufman, G. D. 193
Kelsey, D. H. 116, 192, 228, 234
Kennedy, J. F. 4
Keyserling, H. A. v. 200
Kierkegaard, S. 6f, 22, 54, 171, 215, 230, 245
Kirchner, E. L. 194, 195
Klee, P. 200
Klemm, G. 141
Kluckhohn, C. 48, 118, 121
Knox, J. 231
Koehler, W. 162
Kollwitz, K. 200
Kriegstein, M. v. 15, 16, 116
Kroeber, A. L. 48, 118, 120, 121, 140, 141, 146, 151f
Kroner, R. 118
Kuhlmann, G. 215

Lamprecht, K. 118
Laqueur, W. 152
Le Fort, G. v. 46
Leipold, H. 4, 232
Lesse, K. 196
Lessing, E. 49, 53
Leuze, R. 93
Lewin, K. 158
Lewis, D. 114f, 184ff
Lichtenstein, E. 120

Liebing, H. 44
Link, H.-G. 232
Loew, W. 208
Lücke, F. 8, 39f, 41, 43, 45
Lüthgert, W. 126
Luther, M. 4

McKelway, A. J. 184
MacKinnon, D. M. 14
Macleod, A. M. 24, 180f
Mahlmann, T. 207, 208
Manser, A. R. 239
Marc, F. 199
Martin, B. 182
Marx, K. 21, 50, 135−9, 148, 168f, 174
Matisse, H. 195
May, R. 20
Mayer, O. 162
Meier, K. 60
Mennicke, C. 208
Mews, S. P. 4, 117
Michalson, C. 220
Michel, M. 5
Mokrosch, R. 93
Moltmann, J. 160
Montgomery, W. 48
Moore, G. E. 10, 12
Morgan, R. 65
Munch, E. 199, 219
Myers, B. 195

Nagel, O. 200
Neuenschwander, U. 61, 62
Niebergall, F. 53, 54
Niebuhr, H. R. 34
Niebuhr, R. R. 7, 102, 108
Nielsen, K. 238
Nietzsche, F. W. 6, 143f, 171
Nitzsch, C. I. 8
Nixon, R. M. 70, 75
Nörenberg, K.-D. 232

Ogden, S. M. 5
O'Shaugnessy, R. J. 239
Otto, R. 49, 108, 110
Overbeck, F. 63

Pannenberg, W. 49
Parsons, T. 120
Pauck, W. and M. 3, 4, 6, 27, 28, 166, 169, 253
Pears, D. F. 238
Pechstein, M. 195
Petit, J.-C. 3, 100
Pfeiffer, A. 37, 63
Picasso, P. 219
Pitcher, G. 238
Pius X, Pope 245
Plato 72, 166, 170, 253
Pohlmann, R. 35, 42
Pretzel, U. 63
Prolingheuer, H. 64
Pye, E. M. 52

Quapp, E. H. U. 40
Quine, W. W. 72

Radbruch, G. 87
Radcliffe-Brown, A. R. 120
Rade, M. 161f
Ragaz, L. 161f
Raphael, D. D. 241
Ratschow, C. H. 14
Rauhut, F. 125
Reardon, B. M. G. 93
Reetz, U. 98
Reinhold, K. L. 40
Rendtorff, T. 47, 50, 51, 59
Richmond, J. 13f
Rickert, H. 37, 118
Ritschl, A. 65, 66
Ritter, J. 35
Robinson, James M. 65
Robinson, John A. T. 3

Rößler, A. 15, 27
Rothe, R. 8, 65, 66
Rouault, G. 195
Rowe, W. L. 71, 238
Rupp, G. 60
Russell, B. 10
Ryle, G. 103

Sahlins, M. D. 45
Samuel, R. 200
Sapir, E. 149
Sartre, J. P. 13
Satrom, M. 90, 166
Schäfer-Kretzler, K. 3
Schaper, E. 143
Scharlemann, R. 7, 15, 16, 30, 159
Schedler, K. 26, 98, 161
Schelling, F. W. J. 27, 92, 108, 171, 194, 198, 209
Schlechte, K. 144
Schleiermacher, F. D. E. 4f, 7f, 9, 25, 31, 39–46, 47, 48–50, 51, 54f, 60, 61f, 63, 65f, 69, 82, 101–4, 106–12, 113, 125–7, 134, 152, 222, 249
Schlesinger, A. J. 4
Schlippe, G. v. 52
Schmidt, E. 93
Schmidt, M. 7, 51
Schmithals, W. 27
Schmitz, J. 15
Schneider-Flume, G. 61f, 210
Scholder, K. 61f, 210
Schrader, R. W. 77, 97
Schröter, M. 194
Schütte, H.-W. 209
Schwaiger, G. 51
Schwanz, P. 8
Schweitzer, A. 52, 118, 230
Schwerdtfeger, E. 3, 217f
Schwöbel, C. 162
Seeberg, R. 50
Seligman, E. R. A. 71

Index of Names

Sherman, Gen. W. T. 247
Sherry, P. J. 238
Siegfried, T. 164
Simmel, G. 253
Smart, R. N. 49, 96
Smith, D. M. 231
Soden, H. v. 88
Sölle, D. 3
Sokel, W. H. 199
Sommer, G. F. 92, 108, 194
Spengler, O. 124, 143–6, 148f
Spiegel, Y. 126
Spiegler, G. 39f, 46
Spranger, E. 125
Stahl, E. L. 125
Stapel, W. 61
Steck, K. G. 64
Steudel, J. C. F. 39, 44
Stevenson, C. L. 118
Storr, G. C. 39, 44
Streiker, L. D. 91
Stumme, J. R. 37
Süskind, F. G. 39
Sykes, S. W. 14, 52, 54, 68, 232, 244

Tavard, G. H. 5, 181f
Taylor, C. 93
Teichmann, J. 239, 240
Telfer, E. 42
Thatcher, A. 24
Thomas Aquinas, 57ff
Thomas, J. H. 10, 12, 173, 237f
Thomas, R. H. 200
Thurneysen, E. 161, 162, 163, 164

Tillich, H. 28, 88, 169
Track, J. 15
Trillhaas, W. 162
Troeltsch, E. 9, 31, 33, 34, 35, 39, 44, 45, 46–60, 61, 62, 63–6, 74, 82, 90, 94, 103, 113, 133, 134, 134, 138, 163, 201, 206, 230, 247
Tweston, A. 47
Tylor, E. B. 119, 141

Ullmann, K. 8
Ulrich, T. 37

Wagner, F. 89
Waismann, F. 186–90
Warnock, G. J. 13
Watson, J. 157f
Weber, A. 118
Weber, M. 53, 136–7, 138
Wegener, C. R. 167, 253ff
Welch, C. 7, 102, 108
White, F. T. 5
Whitford, F. 195, 201
Wilamowitz-Moellendorff, U. v. 253
Williams, R. 117, 119
Wimsatt, W. K. 234
Wirsching, J. 8, 61
Wisdom, J. 238
Wittgenstein, L. 186, 236–49
Wittschier, S. 81
Wundt, W. 118

Zabala, A. 183f
Zahrnt, H. 3, 4

Walter de Gruyter
Berlin · New York

Theologische Bibliothek Töpelmann

Wilfried Härle
Sein und Gnade
Die Ontologie in Karl Barths kirchlicher Dogmatik
Oktav. X, 428 Seiten. 1975. Ganzleinen DM 92,–
ISBN 3 11 005706 9 (Band 27)

Wolfgang Trillhaas
Schleiermachers Predigt
2., um ein Vorwort ergänzte Auflage
Oktav. X, 225 Seiten. 1975. Ganzleinen DM 42,–
ISBN 3 11 005739 5 (Band 28)

Ursula Schnell
Das Verhältnis von Amt und Gemeinde im neueren Katholizismus
Oktav. VIII, 330 Seiten. 1977. Ganzleinen DM 98,–
ISBN 3 11 004929 5 (Band 29)

Kotaro Okayama
Zur Grundlegung christlicher Ethik
Theologische Konzeptionen der Gegenwart im Lichte des Analogie-Problems
Mit einem Vorwort von Helmut Thielicke
Oktav. X, 268 Seiten. 1977. Ganzleinen DM 52,–
ISBN 3 11 005812 X (Band 30)

Joachim Ringleben
Hegels Theorie der Sünde
Die subjektivitäts-logische Konstruktion eines theologischen Begriffs
Oktav. 300 Seiten. 1977. Ganzleinen DM 76,–
ISBN 3 11 006650 5 (Band 31)

Preisänderungen vorbehalten

Walter de Gruyter
Berlin · New York

Theologische Bibliothek Töpelmann

Uwe Böschemeyer	**Die Sinnfrage in Psychotherapie und Theologie** Die Existenzanalyse und Logotherapie Viktor E. Frankls aus theologischer Sicht Oktav. X, 164 Seiten. 1977. Ganzleinen DM 48,– ISBN 3 11 006727 7 (Band 32)
Friedrich Heiler	**Die Frau in den Religionen der Menschheit** Oktav. VI, 194 Seiten. 1977. Kartoniert DM 38,– ISBN 3 11 006583 5 (Band 33)
Peter Henke	**Gewißheit vor dem Nichts** Eine Antithese zu den theologischen Entwürfen Wolfhart Pannenbergs und Jürgen Moltmanns Oktav. XIV, 175 Seiten. 1978. Ganzleinen DM 64,– ISBN 3 11 007524 8 (Band 34)
Rainer Flasche	**Die Religionswissenschaft Joachim Wachs** Oktav. XII, 321 Seiten. 1978. Ganzleinen DM 88,– ISBN 3 11 007238 6 (Band 35)
Herbert Neie	**The Doctrine of the Atonement in the Theology of Wolfhart Pannenberg** Octavo. X, 237 pages. 1978. Cloth DM 64,– ISBN 3 11 007506 7 (Band 36)

Preisänderungen vorbehalten